THE LATIN LOVE POETS

THE LATIN
LOVE POETS

From Catullus to Horace

by
R.O.A.M. LYNE

CLARENDON PRESS · OXFORD
1980

Oxford University Press, Walton Street, Oxford OX2 6DP

OXFORD LONDON GLASGOW
NEW YORK TORONTO MELBOURNE WELLINGTON
KUALA LUMPUR SINGAPORE HONG KONG TOKYO
DELHI BOMBAY CALCUTTA MADRAS KARACHI
NAIROBI DAR ES SALAAM CAPE TOWN

Published in the United States by Oxford University Press,
New York

British Library Cataloguing in Publication Data
Lyne, R O A M
    The Latin love poets from Catullus to Horace.
    1. Love poetry, Latin — History and criticism
    I. Title
    871'.09354   PA6029.L6   80-41356
    ISBN 0-19-814453-9
    ISBN 0-19-814454-7 Pbk

Printed in Great Britain
at The University Press, Oxford
by Eric Buckley
Printer to the University

FOR LINDA

Preface

This book is aimed in the first place at sixth form and under-graduate students of Latin literature. More advanced scholars may find it not entirely negligible. I also want students in comparative literature and literature in translation courses and other non-specialists (the 'general reader'?) to be able to use and enjoy it. I offer a fresh treatment and, I hope, new insight to those who know these poets already; and to those who have not had adequate access to a body of remarkable literature I hope I provide it.

For the benefit of this latter category of reader I have quoted extensively when I discuss texts, and translated all, my main quotations. When these translations are my own, they aim to be as literal as is consonant with readability. In so far as is possible I should like them to be used as keys to the original text. If I write them out in lines approximating to the original verse lines it is not because I think I am writing verse but to facilitate their use as keys.

To translate quotations is, I think, in view of the aims of the book, absolutely necessary. I should also have liked to include much basic information, for example on mythology. Space forbade; and anyway the availability of Classical and mythological dictionaries and handy commentaries on each of the poets I discuss makes it less necessary.

I have placed strong emphasis on practical literary criticism. It is, I think, the only way to come to a full comprehension and appreciation of a Latin as any other poet's work; and it is open, when suitable translations are provided, to readers whose Latin is imperfect or even non-existent.

The book combines literary criticism with literary history. Where possible I have used evaluative criticism to assist in explaining literary history. If we can observe the merits and demerits of one poet's work, or the advantages of this or that formal approach, then so probably could his immediate successor: he could learn from mistakes and benefit from happy inspirations. And this occurred, as can be demonstrated. The formal development of Latin Love Poetry can be much illuminated by such practical study.

To see *how* each individual poet writes is vital. But we must not become too preoccupied with form, slaves to the 'New Criticism'. Poets produce fine verbal artefacts. They may also have things to say. It will reward us to attend to what they say. Because it is said in poetry it will be more suggestive than any statement of prose or speech. A personal poet suggests things about himself. Part of the function of personal poetry is to reveal a poet's ideas, feelings—and personality.

Some will dislike this term. It is not devoid of controversy. They will prefer us to talk of *persona*. This rather dated relic of fashionable criticism strikes me as making sometimes a quibbling distinction, sometimes an insensitive one. Much of what needs to be said on the topic was said brilliantly by one of *persona*'s devoted users, Oscar Wilde.[1] Besides, when poets adopt and change roles—elegantly, evasively, but not un-noticed—as for example Tibullus and Horace do, then the term is demonstrably unhelpful and clumsy. Poets like people play with different faces.

Discovery of personality is one of the rewards of studying poetry. When we have savoured this reward we may, also, better understand the evolution of a genre. The idiosyncrasies of practitioners have some effect on the course of literature. This must be particularly true of love poetry. Love is after all a very personal and individual as well as universal experience, and love poetry is usually (among other things) the expression of an individual who is or has been in love—how often Classical scholars obscure *that* fact!

But social and political circumstances also vitally influence literature, including love poetry. This book has therefore tried to keep Roman society and the relation of poet and society in view.

With a subject as potentially large as 'The Latin Love Poets' I have had to be strict in the limitations I set myself. This was easier than might have been expected. A distinct period *and* genre seem to me to be discernible, starting with Catullus and his Lesbia poetry, proceeding through his more or less like-minded successors, but provoking and finally culminating in reaction (cf. p. 21). I have confined myself not only to the poets of this genre but also to that part of their work that is characteristic of it. Thus I have considered only the Lesbia poetry in Catullus' total *oeuvre* and observed comparable restrictions in the amount of the other poets' work considered.

A special word is perhaps necessary on my lack of attention to the Greek origins of Latin Love Poetry. Since the seminal work of Jacoby nothing has happened to change his conclusion that personal Latin Love Elegy was not anticipated by a comparable Hellenistic Elegy.[2] I have mentioned the influence of Greek poetry where it seemed appropriate. A fuller investigation of Greek sources is available in Luck, Day, or Jacoby himself. But the truth remains that Latin Love Poetry's most important impulse comes from Catullus; and it is then self-sufficient to a remarkable degree.

Finally I offer some definitions of certain key phrases that I use. The definitions are crude and meant to be no more than signposts: I am talking about extensive concepts that everyone intuitively understands and I simply want to indicate which concept is referred to by which phrase. By 'passionate love' I mean love whose primary motivation is sexual attraction. By 'whole love' I mean love that is founded on sexual attraction and profound affection—and the rest: a combination of the first three of Lewis's 'four loves', we might say.[3] By 'romantic love' (J. P. Sullivan in *Two Problems* has reminded us that the ancients could be romantic) I mean love probably in the nature of things 'passionate' for which the lover is prepared to make sacrifices incomprehensible to sober, sensible burghers: see further p. 13. When I use 'romantic' or 'romanticism' generally, I shall have in mind an attitude, character, or decision which reveals a willingness for irrational (irrational, that is, in conventional eyes) sacrifice in exchange for some individual, visionary goal; at any rate my uses will at least be conditioned by memory of this stricter definition.

Acknowledgements

I am grateful to Mr A. G. Lee for permission to quote from his translations of Tibullus and Ovid. Peter Brown, Don Fowler and Jasper Griffin all kindly read and criticised this book in typescript. Their suggestions improved it in many places; I wish I had consulted them more at earlier stages. Richard Bett checked references for me, and exceeded his brief with tact and acuteness. Penny Bulloch devoted scholarly skill to the arduous task of proof-reading — in which task I was also assisted by the patience of Linda and Raphael Lyne. My sincere thanks to all; the mistakes that remain are the result of my own negligence or stubbornness.

Contents

Bibliography

Works which may be referred to simply by the author's name or name and abbreviated title. Other items will be cited at relevant points in the text or notes. Abbreviations of periodical titles generally follow the normal conventions of *L'Année philologique*.

Allen, A. W., 'Sunt qui Propertium malint', in: *Critical Essays on Roman Literature*, ed. J. P. Sullivan (London, 1962), 107–48.
Balsdon, J. P. V. D., *Roman Women* (London, 1962).
Barsby, J. A., *Ovid Amores Book I* (Oxford, 1973).
—— *Ovid* (*Greece and Rome* New Surveys in the Classics, No. 12, Oxford, 1978).
Boucher, J.-P., *Études sur Properce* (Paris, 1965).
Brandt, P., *P. Ovidi Nasonis Amorum Libri Tres* (Leipzig, 1911).
Bright, D. F., *HAEC MIHI FINGEBAM: Tibullus in his World* (Leiden, 1978).
Burck, E., 'Römische Wesenszüge in der augusteischen Liebeselegie', *Hermes* 80 (1952), 163–200.
Cairns, F., *Tibullus: A Hellenistic Poet at Rome* (Cambridge, 1979). Note: this work appeared after my own book was completed.
Camps, W. A., *Propertius Elegies Book I, II, III, IV* (Cambridge, 1961, 1967, 1966, 1965).
Commager, S., *The Odes of Horace* (Yale University Press, 1962).
Copley, F. O., *EXCLUSUS AMATOR: A Study in Latin Love Poetry*, Monograph of the American Philological Association, No. XVII (1956).
Day, A. A., *The Origins of Latin Love-Elegy* (Oxford, 1938).
Dissen, L., *Albii Tibulli Carmina* (Göttingen, 1835).
Du Quesnay, I. M. Le M., 'The *Amores*', in: *Ovid*, ed. J. W. Binns (London, 1973).
Elder, J. P., 'Tibullus: *tersus atque elegans*', in: [see Allen above], 65–105.
Enk, P. J., *Sex. Propertii Elegiarum Liber I (Monobiblos)* (Leiden, 1946), *Liber Secundus* (Leiden, 1962).
Fordyce, C. J., *Catullus, A Commentary* (Oxford, 1961).
Fraenkel, E., *Horace* (Oxford, 1957).
Geiger, H., *Interpretationen zur Gestalt Amors bei Tibull* (Zürich, 1978).
Gotoff, H. C., 'Tibullus: *nunc levis est tractanda Venus*', *HSCP* 78 (1974), 231–51.
Griffin, J., 'Augustan poetry and the life of luxury', *JRS* 66 (1976), 87–105.
Grimal, P., *L'Amour à Rome* (Paris, 1963).
Herter, H., 'Die Soziologie der antiken Prostitution im Lichte des

heidnischen und christlichen Schriftums', *Jb.Ant. Chr.* 3 (1960), 80-111.

Hubbard, M., *Propertius* (London, 1974).

Jacoby, F., 'Zur Entstehung der römischen Elegie', *RhM* 60 (1905), 38-105.

Keyssner, K., 'Die bildende Kunst bei Properz', *Würzburger Studien* 13 (1938), 169-89 = *Properz*, ed. W. Eisenhut (Darmstadt, 1975) 264-86; page references are to the latter.

Kiessling, A., and Heinze, R., *Q. Horatius Flaccus, Oden und Epoden* (8th edn. Berlin, 1955).

Kroll, W., *C. Valerius Catullus* (2nd edn., Leipzig and Berlin, 1929).

— *Die Kultur der ciceronischen Zeit*, vol. ii (Leipzig, 1933).

Lee, A. G., *Ovid's Amores* (London, 1968).

— 'Otium cum indignitate: Tibullus 1. 1', in: *Quality and Pleasure in Latin Poetry*, ed. T. Woodman and D. West (Cambridge, 1974), 94-114.

— *Tibullus: Elegies* (Cambridge, 1975): a text with introduction, translation, and notes.

Lilja, S., *The Roman Elegists' Attitude to Women* (Helsinki, 1965).

Luck, G., *The Latin Love Elegy* (2nd edn., London, 1969).

Maiuri, A., *Roman Painting* (Lausanne, 1953).

Morgan, K., *Ovid's Art of Imitation: Propertius in the Amores* (Leiden, 1977).

Nisbet, R. G. M. and Hubbard, M., *A Commentary on Horace: Odes Book I* and *Odes Book II* (Oxford, 1970 and 1978).

Pomeroy, S. B., *Goddesses, Whores, Wives, and Slaves: Women in Classical Antiquity* (London, 1976).

Quinn, K., *The Catullan Revolution* (Melbourne, 1959).

—, *Catullus, The Poems* (2nd edn., London, 1973).

Reitzenstein, E., 'Das neue Kunstwollen in den Amores Ovids', *RhM* 84 (1935), 62-86 = *Ovid*, ed. M. v. Albrecht and E. Zinn (Darmstadt, 1968), 206-32; page references are to the latter.

Reitzenstein, R., 'Zur Sprache der lateinischen Erotik', *Sitzungsb. der Heidelberger Akad. d. Wissenschaften*, Abh. 12 (1912), 1-36.

Ross, D. O., Jr., *Style and Tradition in Catullus* (Cambridge, Mass., 1969).

— *Backgrounds to Augustan Poetry: Gallus Elegy and Rome* (Cambridge, 1975).

Rothstein, M., *Propertius Sextus Elegien* (2nd edn., Berlin, 1920).

Shackleton Bailey, D. R., *Propertiana* (Cambridge, 1956).

Smith, K. F., *The Elegies of Albius Tibullus* (New York, 1913).

Stroh, W., *Die römische Liebeselegie als werbende Dichtung* (Amsterdam, 1971).

— 'Ovids Liebeskunst und die Ehegesetze des Augustus', *Gymnasium* 86 (1979), 323-52.

Sullivan, J. P., 'Two Problems in Roman Love Elegy', *TAPA* 92 (1961), 522–36.

— *Propertius. A Critical Introduction* (Cambridge, 1976).

Syme, R., *History in Ovid* (Oxford, 1978).

Syndikus, H. P., *Die Lyrik des Horaz* (vol. i, Darmstadt, 1972; vol. ii, 1973).

Vischer, R., *Das einfache Leben* (Göttingen, 1965).

West, D., *Reading Horace* (Edinburgh, 1967).

Wickham, E. C., *Quinti Horatii Flacci Opera Omnia. Vol. I. The Odes, Carmen Seculare, and Epodes* (Oxford, 1877).

Wilkinson, L. P., *Ovid Recalled* (Cambridge, 1955): abridged as *Ovid Surveyed* (Cambridge, 1962).

Williams, G., *Tradition and Originality in Roman Poetry* (Oxford, 1968).

— *The Third Book of Horace's Odes* (Oxford, 1969).

— *Horace* (*Greece and Rome* New Surveys in the Classics, No. 6, Oxford, 1972).

The Latin texts which I cite are based on Mynors's Oxford Classical Text of Catullus (1958), Camps's editions of Propertius, Lee's Tibullus and Ovid, and the Wickham–Garrod Oxford Classical Text of Horace (1901). I permit myself to select different readings where I think it is appropriate.

The most convenient commentaries in English are Fordyce and Quinn, *Catullus, The Poems* (Catullus), Camps (Propertius), Smith (Tibullus), Nisbet and Hubbard, Wickham, and Williams *The Third Book* (Horace), Barsby, *Ovid Amores Book I* (on Ovid *Am.* 1: there is nothing convenient in English on *Am.* 2 and 3; Brandt's German commentary is still very useful).

I

Traditional Attitudes to Love, the Moral and Social Background

1. Preview

An astute slave in one of Plautus' comedies is standing with his young well-to-do master outside a pimp's residence. He utters some lines intended to convey good advice. 'From this place,' he says, 'no one bars you; no one stops you buying (if you've got money) what is openly for sale. The public highway is forbidden to none. . . . Provided that you keep off married women, widows, young ladies, young men and boys of free birth, make love at will!'[1] His instruction to the young man, in short, is to indulge his sexual feelings with professionals, slaves, and the like; women (and men) from his own class are untouchable. Here is advice which few Roman gentlemen would in practice have quarrelled with through the centuries.

Traditional Roman upper-class attitudes to pre-marital love combined reverence for ladies of that class with a down-to-earth pragmatism. The latter went naturally with the former. It was of course only young *men*'s sexual needs that rated comment; a lady's sexuality was hardly considered.

Take Marcus Cato, the famous moralist of the second century BC. We are told that 'when he had seen a young man of good family coming out of a brothel, he praised him, thinking that lust (*libido*) had to be curbed without crime (*crimen*).'[2] It was traditionally regarded as *crimen*, more particularly *stuprum* or *adulterium*, to consort sexually with respectable freeborn girls, freeborn boys, other people's wives, and widows.[3] The famous moralist's views are essentially the same as those of Plautus' astute slave.

Or take Cicero (a century or so later) in relaxed mood:

Everybody agrees in allowing youth a little fun [*ludus*: a difficult word to translate, referring in context to extravagance, indulgence, but particularly erotic indulgence] ; nature itself develops a young man's desires. If these desires break out in such a way that they shatter no one's life and upturn no one's home, they are generally regarded as unproblematic: we tolerate them.[4]

Later on in the same speech:

Let some fun (*ludus*) be granted to youth; this time of life should be freer. Let not everything be denied to pleasure, nor let true and forthright principle always prevail. Desire and pleasure should sometimes conquer principle—provided that the following rule and limitation is observed in such matters. A young man must forbear to damage his own virtue (*pudicitia*), and do no violence to that of others; he must not squander his patrimony, be crippled with debt, or assail the house and family of another; he must not bring vileness upon the pure, a stain upon the virtuous, disgrace upon those of standing. . . . Finally when he has hearkened to pleasures, when he has granted a portion of time to the fun (*ludus*) that suits his age, to these frivolous desires of youth, let him at last recall himself to attend to his household business, to the business of the forum, to the business of state . . .'[5]

Again we hear insistence combined with indulgence. Reputable families must be respected and certain other obvious proprieties observed. Otherwise a young man (and Cicero sees love as properly the province only of the young) should be allowed his fling; with the 'non-pure' and the 'non-virtuous'. Most obviously these would be professionals or slave-girls. But Cicero also has in mind and elsewhere in the speech suggests an additional, significant interpretation: they may include erstwhile respectable ladies, ladies who have excluded themselves by their conduct from decent society.[6] It suits his tactical purpose in the speech to make this point, but it was obviously one that could find support.

So, respectable women of good family, whether married or not, were strictly not potential erotic company for a young unmarried man. That was provided by the many grades of professional women, by slave-girls, by the *déclassées*, or the unfortunate.

In these circumstances it is unsurprising to learn that Roman upper-class marriage was not typically begun in whole or even passionate love. Often indeed the possibility was pre-empted: marriages were regularly arranged by parents—and for children who were still very young. Significantly, it is the special achievement of stage comedy to come up with love marriages. In that pleasant world coincidence can deal with the unwelcome facts of society. A young man falls in love in the plausible and possible way: with a professional or at least a definite social inferior; then, surprise, surprise!—she turns out to be well born after all, so love can end in marriage.[7]

Other considerations hindered the growth of whole love within marriage. The degree of modesty expected in a lady, and the modesty of conduct expected of a husband towards her, prohibited much chance of the necessary passion. Plutarch here as often offers interesting insight when he discusses why Roman husbands made their first approach to their brides in total darkness;[8] and when he reports how the elder Cato proudly announced that he never embraced his wife unless it thundered loudly.[9] From Lucretius we learn that ladies 'don't move'.[10]

Continual attempts by censors to push upper-class men into marriage show that it was always considered something of a duty, and not an institution of loving happiness. Metellus Macedonicus, censor in 131 BC, exhorts with dry humour:[11] 'if, citizens, we could manage without wives, we should all avoid that bother. But since nature's legacy is that we cannot live *with* them comfortably but *without* them cannot live at all, we must consider our long-term well-being rather than our short-term pleasure (*uoluptas*).' Pleasure, at least sexual pleasure, was something that a wife—a lady—did not provide. And if a husband was irked by frustration, then an affair with a slave-girl or a professional was a more or less acceptable indulgence: Roman pragmatism asserted itself in the case of married men as well as youths. The great Scipio Africanus, for example, had a long-standing liaison with a favourite slave-girl and his wife was nobly tolerant.[12]

In short, Roman upper-class men (unlike the luckier heroes of comedy) had traditionally to compartmentalize the totality of love.[13] Women of their own standing might, as their wives, be expected to provide friendship, support, affection, children. But passion was rather to be indulged with professionals, *déclassées* or chattels; and, acceptable before marriage, such indulgence was far from unacceptable afterwards. Meanwhile respectable unmarried girls of good family had no love life at all; and married ladies, *matronae*, led the sort of circumscribed existence we have adumbrated.

There are points in this synopsis which need elaboration or qualification. And time changed many things, as we shall see. We should first look a little more closely at Roman marriage.

2. Marriage: theory[14]

In theory Roman marriage seems remarkably enlightened. It began—in theory—as the free wish of both bride and bridegroom, and it assumed a large measure of equality between the two in their life together. The wedding ceremony itself was essentially secular—and not even legally necessary. The families gathered in the fiancée's house and auspices might be taken, as before any important event. But then both bride and bridegroom simply declared their consent before witnesses and a kind of matron of honour (the *pronuba*) solemnly joined their right hands (*dextrarum coniunctio*). There might then follow sacrifices and prayers to the gods for protection. But the heart of the matter was the consent of bride and groom and their declaration of it. When the bride was finally conducted from her old house to her husband's, she was to become the revered *materfamilias domina*, the mother and lady of the house, partner to the *dominus paterfamilias* in the new *domus*. If she owned property, she continued to own it; and it was no part of Roman marriage that a woman should take her husband's name.

The details of Roman marriage and Roman weddings could be complex and colourful. But the essence—in theory—did not vary fundamentally. To a remarkable degree therefore Roman marriage was, *potentially*, the basis for a mature and complete relationship between a man and a woman. And the ease of divorce which obtained was also essentially or potentially enlightened. Since marriage was grounded in consent it was natural that both parties should be able, in agreement or unilaterally, simply to declare the marriage ended; for if the will had gone, the whole basis of the marriage had also disappeared. Now the practice of Roman marriage, and divorce, did rather belie all this theory. But its rich potential, the basic principles behind it, are important to remember—not least for a proper understanding of features in Latin love poetry.[15]

3. Marriage: practice

Practice was indeed different from theory. The fact that the sexuality of the Roman lady was regarded as it was, the fact that an upper-class Roman youth had little opportunity to form a relationship with a girl of equal status, rather hampered the chances of a felicitous union. There was another, practical point. From early times marriage among the upper classes was seen as an instrument to secure or strengthen the position of great or advancing families: socially, politically, and financially. Marriage was too important to be entrusted to youth and its strange predilections; love or passion, if it did contrive to arise, was the worst and silliest of motives. Fathers betrothed sons and daughters as advantageously as they could, often when they were still very young. Declarations of consent were therefore in this society, in such circumstances, a matter of custom and obedience, rather than the result of rational and willing commitment.

'Dynastic marriage' (so to call it) is the norm in the upper classes by the first century BC, and considerably before. The political history of the time might be written in terms of who married whom. Indeed in the hands of certain historians it virtually is. And the alliances thus made could be formed and then easily re-formed because of the ease of divorce. Rome's enlightened attitude to the conclusion of unwanted marriages was in fact vastly useful in cynically practical manœuverings.

Some examples. Cicero betrothed his daughter Tullia while she was still a child—but to the noble C. Piso Frugi, an advantageous alliance for a 'new man'.[16] Cicero himself when well in his sixties married a very young second wife. Plutarch's account of this[17] affords interesting insight into Roman practical attitudes. Cicero's first wife Terentia alleged that his motive was passion: he married the girl 'out of love for her beauty'. This was not meant to be flattering. Cicero's freedman gave the true explanation, or at least an explanation that was respectable and comprehensible. The girl was rich, Cicero was already her trustee and in charge of her property; by marrying her he would be able to use her money to discharge his many creditors. Antony marries the sister of Octavian to seal the Peace of Brundisium—a marriage which dissolves with the dissolving alliance.[18] Octavian married Scribonia to secure, very deviously, a degree of political hold on Sextus Pompeius.[19] And so on.[20]

A story from the second century BC is less flagrant, but attractively illuminates how the upper classes viewed marriage.[21] Appius Claudius met the noble and talented Tiberius Gracchus—considered a great catch—at a feast of the augurs. He suggested Tiberius should marry his daughter Claudia. Tiberius accepted on the spot; the Claudii were after all one of the great families, and Appius himself had been consul and censor. Appius was so excited by this acceptance that when he went home he shouted out to his wife before he had even got through the front door: 'Antistia, I've betrothed our Claudia to a husband!' His wife replied: 'Why the eagerness? What's the rush? Now if you had caught Tiberius Gracchus for her . . .' Both husband and wife thought in the same way about the future of their daughter, indeed were in fact of the same mind as to the most eligible bachelor; Appius' wife simply did not trust Appius' judgement or efficiency. As for the protagonists, Claudia's part was clearly passive: she would have to follow the wisdom of her parents and the ways of society; and Tiberius Gracchus, though his decision was his own, was scarcely being guided by an ideal of whole love.

These examples give us some idea of how marriage was in practice entered into among the upper classes. And as far as the bride was concerned, free execution of her will tended to be just as illusory in subsequent married life. The reverence that was afforded to her was protective, but negative and hampering in its effect. By tradition, the *domina* of the household was in practice secluded and subordinate. Laudatory tombstones of wives are significant in what they select to praise. The obedience (*obsequium*) of a deceased wife is

very commonly hailed.[22] The famous sepulchral motto
domum seruauit, lanam fecit[23] encapsulates a vision of the
married woman that was deep and persistent: spinning or
weaving (*lanificium*) was typically cited as the proper occupa-
tion of the *matrona* and that says a lot about male attitudes.
These attitudes were emphatically not confined to the lower
classes. Augustus for example saw to it that his daughter and
granddaughters wove clothes at home and he himself preferred
(or took care to appear to prefer) wearing garments produced
by them or by his sister and wife.[24] In a famous inscription a
lady called Turia who is lauded by her husband for extra-
ordinary enterprise and bravery during the period of the
Triumviral proscriptions is also lauded by him for (among
many other traditionally modest virtues) her *obsequium* and
studium lanificii.[25]

Such attitudes towards the *matrona* have their reflection in
stories that range from the laughable to the alarming. In 166
BC, C. Sulpicius Gallus is reported to have divorced his wife
because she appeared out of doors with her head uncovered;
'the law prescribed my eyes alone as the ones to prove your
beauty by . . .' Valerius Maximus writing in the reign of
Tiberius describes this as *horridum maritale supercilium*
('rough, husbandly haughtiness'), but regards Sulpicius'
explanation as, albeit abrupt, 'defended by a certain ration-
ality' (*aliqua ratione munita*).[26] Such is the form reverence
for a *matrona* could take—or its effect. The *matrona* had to
conform to a pattern that Roman gentlemen were prepared
to revere.

Slaves would escort a lady if she left the house,[27] a thing
she was not expected to do often;[28] Cicero makes capital out
of the fact that Verres has forced ladies to appear in court
and hence publicly in the company of men: 'Why do you
compel such select and chaste ladies, unwilling and unaccus-
tomed as they are, to enter so great a concourse of men?'[29]
The elder Cato among others thought that wine-drinking by
wives was a punishable offence.[30] Valerius Maximus, slightly
more tolerant, reckons that 'any woman who seeks the use of
wine immoderately closes the door on all virtues and opens it

to all crimes.'[31] And Cato on adultery demonstrates rather devastatingly his and many people's real feelings on married equality: 'if you have caught your wife in adultery, you could kill her without trial, with impunity. If you were committing adultery, she would not dare to lay a finger on you, nor is it right that she should.'[32]

4. The development of the demi-monde.
Part 1: the (semi-) professionals ·

As we have said, Roman society tolerated men having affairs with professionals, indeed in some circumstances encouraged it. It is time to consider the professionals. The relevant area for our study is not the basic, home-grown Roman one, the brothel (*lupanar*) and common prostitute, but a Greek import, the *demi-monde*: the world of the elegant and accomplished courtesan (more suitably termed a semi-professional) who offered Roman men passionate and glamorous company, not necessarily on a too temporary basis.

When did this society develop in Rome? The institution of the sometimes very well-off courtesan was already native to the Hellenistic cities of the fourth and third centuries BC.[33] Such women play important parts in the Greek comedy of that period ('Middle' and 'New Comedy'). Plautus adapted some of these plays for Roman audiences at the end of the third and the beginning of the second centuries. Now, interestingly, the way he adapts them shows that the courtesan society was unfamiliar to him: when he deals with courtesan scenes, he tends automatically to think of the Roman institutions, prostitutes and *lupanaria*, and his version is at crucial points wittingly or unwittingly coloured accordingly.[34] Clearly in the Rome of Plautus' time a Greek-style *demi-monde* did not properly or widely exist.

But things were perhaps already changing. Cn. Manlius Volso, who celebrated a triumph in 187 BC, was culpable in many people's eyes for the new luxurious habits that his troops brought back from the Greek East. Among other things we are told that now the entertainment of *psaltriae* and *sambucistriae* (types of female harpist who might supply sex as well as music) and other symposiastic amusements began to be part of the Roman dinner-party scene.[35] Glamorous women and Greek pleasures were arriving. Further wars in Greece were to clinch this moral disaster. Polybius catches an important moment for us in the 160s BC: with the exemplary behaviour of Scipio Aemilianus he compares the increasing dissoluteness of the noble youth of the day: 'some', he says, 'had given themselves up to fancy-boys (*eromenoi*), some to courtesans; many to musical displays (*acroamata*) and drinking parties (*potoi*) and extravagance in these things; in the war with Perseus they had swiftly caught the Greek proclivity for these pursuits.'[36] So here are courtesans, *symposia*, and the rest: Greek ways of pleasure are establishing themselves at Rome, together with a *demi-monde* to cater for them.

The war with Perseus ended in 168 BC, so Polybius' account refers to exactly those years in which Terence was producing his versions of New Comedy.[37] Terence gives us vivid pictures of a Greek-style *demi-monde* and we can now assume, because of Polybius' corroborating evidence and because there are no signs of the sort of adaptation we find in Plautus, that they bear some resemblance to contemporary Roman life. For us it is particularly interesting to note the range of Terence's women of pleasure. In one class there is the *cithara* player whom Phaedria falls in love with in the *Phormio*. She is accomplished as well as pretty; indeed she is actually sent to school by a *leno* (pimp) to learn her graces. But she is under the control of a *leno*, and her type was hired to provide entertainment for a party and company for a single night.[38] In another class are the independent courtesans prepared to form long-term liaisons—the mercenary Bacchis of the *Heauton* or the tender and generous-souled Bacchis of the *Hecyra*.

Around the middle of the second century BC, therefore, Greek ways of pleasure and a Greek-styled *demi-monde* take root in Rome. *Scortum* and *meretrix* may now sometimes denote not or not only the common prostitute, but the entertainer of an at least superficially sophisticated evening (*scortum*) and the courtesan (*meretrix*); and the courtesan at least would be a free woman or rather a freedwoman.[39] Consideration of 'entertainers' is more relevant to Horace's poetry and illustration of them may wait for a while. I turn my attention to the society of courtesans ('semi-professionals') which, from the mid-second century on, grew rapidly.

The names of notable upper-class Romans begin increasingly to be coupled with courtesans. A curule aedile of the mid-second century BC, A. Hostilius Mancinus, went to law with a high-class courtesan called Manilia, into whose house he had tried to force an entry in the middle of the night.[40] The upper-class satirist Lucilius, who flourished in the latter part of the second century and was famed for the candour and autobiographical nature of his poetry, wrote about his relationship with one Hymnis who was it seems heavy in her financial demands but enthralling in her singing; and a whole book of his verse took its title from his *amica* Collyra.[41] Sulla the dictator who was (like Volso) notorious for the way he had allowed his troops to indulge themselves in Asia, was also notorious for the way he consorted with members of the *demi-monde*: actors, actresses, and female guitarists (*mimae, citharistriae*) and the like. He was also famous for his lasting love of the female-impersonator actor Metrobius.[42] More to our point is his relationship with the courtesan Nicopolis. As a young man Sulla fell in love with her; and she, Plutarch tells us, because of his youthful charm and grace came to love him and made him her heir—which was not to be sneezed at, since she was 'wealthy' (*euporos*).[43] That tells us something about the sort of money a high-class woman of pleasure could now command, as well as the kind of lasting relationship that might be formed with her.

A courtesan could wield alarming influence too. Cicero alleged that Chelidon was the real power during Verres' praetorship and graphically describes business being conducted in her house.[44] During Verres' governorship of Sicily Tertia stepped into Chelidon's shoes and her authority was, according to Cicero, almost as efficacious as Chelidon's had been. Tertia was the daughter of a mime actor called Isidorus and Verres had allegedly taken her away, by guile or force (Cicero's account varies), from a Rhodian clarinetist (*tibicen*).[45]

The great Pompey, not perhaps a man whom one immediately thinks of as a romantic, was linked with the courtesan Flora—a famous beauty—who enjoyed telling in her later years how she never left a session with Pompey without bearing the marks of his teeth. Incidentally, this affair ended rather curiously. Flora's attentions were solicited by a friend of Pompey's. She refused because of him. The friend talked it over man to man with Pompey, who acquiesced. But he himself never again had anything to do with Flora 'although', as Plutarch says, 'he seemed to love her'. A curious mixture of Roman male comradeship and a romantically 'monogamous' sensitivity.[46]

Antony *is* of course a man whom we think of as a romantic. Before his liaison with Cleopatra, he had developed notoriety for his associations with male and female *artistes*, and had been the lover in particular of the actress and courtesan Cytheris; Cicero refers to Antony as *Cytherius* in a letter of the time.[47] (Cicero once found himself at the same dinner table with Cytheris and reports the occasion in a letter to Paetus with a certain coy *frisson*.)[48] Cytheris is of rather special interest to us. As well as being Antony's mistress she was also at one time most probably the mistress of the poet and soldier Cornelius Gallus—it is likely that Gallus and Antony were rivals for her affections.[49] The case of Cytheris, the plaintively lamented 'Lycoris' of Gallus as well as the well-documented mistress of Antony, offers an attractive window on to the world behind love elegy.

We see therefore that over a wide range of upper-class society Roman men became accustomed to forming attachments with women of the *demi-monde*. Here they found the sex and glamour that women of their own class traditionally did not offer. Sometimes the relationships formed were quite lasting.

What was the reaction of urbane society to all this? In principle, of course, an association with a courtesan should provoke no more censure (anyway in the case of an unmarried man) than that elicited from the elder Cato when he saw the young man emerging from a brothel.[50] In fact there was now something to cause concern. The traditional order of sexual things was being shaken—in a way that must be clarified. Not only were the relationships formed sometimes lasting. Our sources on occasion clearly suggest romance.

There is an important sequel to the Cato anecdote. 'Afterwards', the story goes on, 'when Cato had noticed the young man coming more frequently out of the same brothel, he said "young man, I praised you because you came here from time to time, not because you lived here."' This expresses in Cato's rather blunt way a basic Roman anxiety. *Amor* should never assume a disproportionate role. Not only was it to be indulged (if it had to be indulged) with women who were appropriately *déclassées*; such indulgence belonged very firmly to the amusing margins of life. *ludus* ('play') is Cicero's revealing term for love-affairs (above, pp. 1–2); to a sensible father in Terence *amo* ('to love') and *scortor* ('to whore') are synonymous,[51] which, if pondered, is equally revealing. Cicero in fact is prepared to grant that love may conceivably preoccupy a youth without permanent damage to him;[52] but his feeling that it is properly a casual diversion, and that too of youth, is clearly evident, indeed stated, in the passage quoted (above, p. 2). Love is amusement, an amusement tolerated in youth; a suitable occupation of youthful *otium*, emphatically not *negotium*. Here in fact was the essential point in Cicero's attack upon Verres in the matter of Chelidon and Tertia: both women preoccupied him, even controlled him, to the point where he neglected his *negotium*, and indeed surrendered it to them.

In short, therefore, society required that a gentleman indulge his amorous feelings with discretion and dispatch, not compromising his social equals, nor his own proper duties; and such conduct was really the prerogative of youth. So if affairs with the new type of courtesan could be conducted with a suitable sense of proportion, all would be fine.

The trouble with courtesans however was exactly that they could make 'keeping a sense of proportion' very difficult. It was in their power to inspire romantic love. That is the impression we get from the sources of the effect of (for instance) Cytheris on Antony, who flouted public feeling by carrying her around Italy with him in a litter. And such love *is* at times precisely capable of making a man lose his sense of proportion, confuse *otium* with *negotium*, disregard good name and duty, even consider life itself as unimportant beside love and the beloved. This is, I suppose, a fair definition of what we mean by 'romantic love'. To the Roman it was insanity—*insanus* is the stock epithet of such a lover.[53] So society had grounds indeed to object to an affair with a courtesan. Not because it meant mixing with the professional classes. That was tolerable and regular enough. But because the courtesan with her sophistication, glamour, and liberation offered real opportunities for 'insanity'—for romantic love— and therefore threatened the nicely ordered conventions of Roman sexual morality. Roman gentlemen were losing their heads, behaving like boys! Roman gentlemen were falling in love. This was the threat of the courtesan. It is identified and satirized by two first-century poets (Lucretius and Horace) who, unorthodox in many respects, are basically orthodox in their view of love.[54]

5. Part 2: the amateurs

By the first century it was not only the glamorous courtesans who posed a threat to traditional moral order. In a variety of ways and for a variety of reasons Roman *ladies* had begun to assert rights that they had always theoretically had, and to trespass happily where they had traditionally had no rights at all. This 'emancipation' of women shows itself in various ways; politically, socially, and sexually. It is the last that concerns us. As the Hellenizing life of pleasure grew and prospered, some ladies started to want their cut. They put their minds to it diligently. If on many occasions courtesans had begun to command the constancy of attention notionally due to a wife,[55] wives now began to command among an admiring public the passionate attention due to courtesans. They behaved like courtesans and are indeed at times indistinguishable from courtesans. They thus added spice to their own lives and flaunted before their baffled lovers a compelling mixture of scarlet eroticism and blue blood. Now, therefore, the professional lady of pleasure is joined by an amateur partner or rival. The amateur phenomenon was doubly objectionable in the eyes of society: gentlemen were losing their heads in love *and* violating other people's marriages. But one gets the strong impression that—anyway until Augustus' legislation—the former point was at least as serious as the latter. That is what Horace fastens on when he derides adulterers in his second *Satire*.

The successions of adulteries that we hear of in upper-class first-century society are symptomatic of the rival appeals now offered by amateurs. Julius Caesar for example is reported to have had adulterous relationships with many luminous *matronae* including the wives of M. Crassus and Pompey.[56]

Some ladies we know of worked hard at being alluring—for example the Sempronia immortalized by Sallust. Sempronia was a member of the famous noble family of the Gracchi and in 77 BC the wife of a consul; subsequently she became associated with the Catilinarian conspiracy. Sallust tells us that she was cultivated and accomplished: she was well up in Greek and Latin literature; could compose verses, be witty, and converse well to suit a variety of occasions. 'She was in short', says Sallust, 'possessed of much charm and elegance' (*facetiae* and *lepos*). He also tells us that she was able to play the guitar (*psallere*) and dance 'more elegantly than was necessary for a virtuous woman', and had many other accomplishments which cater to pleasure (*quae instrumenta luxuriae sunt*). The accomplishments are significant: she sounds exactly like a high-class courtesan. That was probably precisely her intention—she wanted nothing more than to outshine the glamorous *demi-mondaines*. Her sexual behaviour suited the role too—or rather it overstepped it. Sallust tells us that her lust was such that she more often solicited men herself than was solicited. Few genuine courtesans would commit that blunder.[57]

Matronae, we know, should reveal nothing but their faces in public; the long *stola* they wore extended to the feet. But one first-century lady, Catia, was so proud of her beautiful legs that she shamelessly wore a high hem-line to show them off. Her alluring ploy obviously worked at least once: she is reported to have committed adultery with the tribune of the people, Valerius Acisculus, in the temple of Venus in Pompey's theatre. Horace alludes to this lady in his second *Satire* and the details, scandalous, but not altogether unconvincing, are supplied by his scholiast Porphyrio.[58]

It is a shock when one recalls the vision of the *matrona* implied in *domum seruauit, lanam fecit* (which still of course held true in most or many cases) to find Cicero claiming that jurors were bribed at Clodius' trial in 61 BC with 'nights with certain women and introductions [for homosexual purposes] to young noblemen'. The women he had in mind were *matronae*, as is clear from other references to the occasion.[59] Even if the claim was false, it is significant that Cicero could believe it or at least seriously mention it in private correspondence. It is hardly anyway unparalleled in its outrageousness. In 52 BC a party was reputedly arranged for the delectation of the consul Metellus Scipio and a tribune of the people at which two aristocratic ladies and a noble youth were prostituted.[60] The gap between amateur and professional might indeed be small.

I conclude my selected examples of courtesans' amateur rivals with a glance at Clodia, the sister of the tribune P. Clodius and wife of the nobleman Q. Metellus Celer, consul in the year 60 BC—whom Clodia was suspected of poisoning when he died in 59. Her political influence was remarkable.[61] Her social and sexual success was outstanding. We are lucky enough to possess a vivid evocation of her life-style in the speech which Cicero wrote in defence of one of her ex-lovers M. Caelius Rufus (in 56 BC). Cicero avidly recounts *libidines, amores, adulteria, Baias, actas, conuiuia, comissationes, cantus, symphoniacas, nauigia*: orgies, love-affairs, adulteries, jaunts to Baiae (a resort of scandalous reputation), beach-parties, dinner-parties, revels, musical entertainments, and boating picnics; he makes satirical play with her *horti ad Tiberim*, her river-side gardens, a fashionable place for young men to swim and for Clodia to pick up young men. And so on.[62] All this is presumably a reasonably true if one-sided picture of Clodia's existence. Here is the Greek life of pleasure, first-century aristocratic Roman style—it is interesting to compare the above passage of the *Pro Caelio* with Polybius' account of the Greek invasion of the 160s.

Clodia's world is like a *demi-monde*, and in it she plays the part of a courtesan. According to one source she was keen on dancing 'more extravagantly and immoderately than befitted a *matrona*';[63] her promiscuity was proverbial (see below; though in a tantalizingly obscure *mot* Caelius seems to imply that her eventual willingness or performance belied her promise).[64] She sounds very like Sempronia. Caelius and Cicero could and of course did use all this in evidence against her. Caelius called her the 'penny Clytemnestra'[65] alluding both to her role as husband-killer and to the story that one of her lovers had sent her small coins, as to a prostitute.[66] Cicero takes up the jibe, working in a reference to 'the usual penny deal';[67] he also maliciously refers to her as *amica omnium* ('everybody's girl-friend')[68] and savages the *meretricius mos* ('the prostitute's, or courtesan's, manner') of her life-style.[69] Labels like these crudely uttered and tied to a noble Roman widow of close on 40 (as Clodia was at the time of Caelius' trial) were of course insulting. But that was to put on the hat of the moralist. To other sorts of minds in other sorts of contexts a lady who combined luxury, blue blood, and beauty (Clodia's brilliant eyes were famous)[70] with a capricious promiscuity which might or might not favour oneself at any given moment—a lady like this might seem irresistibly if painfully compelling.

Clodia is of course of especial interest to us because she is almost certainly the 'Lesbia' of Catullus' poetry; it is possible, too, that Catullus contended for her affections with the same Caelius Rufus whom Cicero defends.[71] The case of Cytheris above offered us an interesting glimpse of the real world behind the laments of Elegy. When we come to the first great

Latin love poet whose work survives, we are fascinatingly informed on the background of his poetry. We know not only something of Catullus' social and erotic ambience but even (most probably) the identity and something of the nature of the woman he loved. We can have a distinct sense of the life behind the poems. The wonder for us is to observe how comprehensible events and feelings are then transmuted into, at moments, very great literature.

6. Conclusion

It is now possible to sum up the state of upper-class love, marriage, and society in the first century BC, when Catullus writes.

We must firmly remember the remarkable theoretical potential of Roman marriage: in theory it might be the expression of a whole and satisfying love. In practice the rule was different. Fascinating exceptions to this rule can be adduced, and in the lower classes love marriages would be much commoner;[72] but, in the upper classes, the rule basically holds good. By tradition, upper-class marriage was at best an institution in which a man and woman could enjoy friendship, mutual respect and affection, and be partners in the maintenance of the *domus* and the propagation of the family. At worst its forms were a mockery, it might keep a woman in effective subservience, and it was often simply a cynical manœuvre for money, power, or position. In no case was it likely to be, nor was it traditionally expected to be, an institution of love in all love's aspects combining reciprocated passion and affection, and the rest. It is worth recalling the case of Turia (see above p. 7) whose long laudatory funeral inscription we are lucky enough to possess. In this *laudatio* which celebrates and laments an extraordinarily devoted wife and which claims for the marriage an extraordinary felicity, any actual mention of *love* is conspicuously lacking.[73]

The fact was that traditional Roman society made it socially and psychologically difficult (to the point of impossibility) for gentlemen to find whole love with someone of equal status and circumstances. It prescribed that men (and not exclusively the unmarried) should, if necessary, indulge passion with *déclassées*; but (and this was obligatory) keep a due and proper sense of proportion in such unimportant business. For ladies tradition prescribed knitting. The wholeness of love was not expected; love was traditionally compartmentalized.

But exciting new horizons had opened up, complicating the picture. The advent of the *demi-monde* and the development of an amateur *demi-monde* meant that opportunities for a completer love were now more real for Roman gentlemen—and for that matter for Roman ladies. It was now more possible for mature people to find affection, tenderness, mutual interest, *and* passion together.

Yet to what extent could such relationships, once formed, last? Here there was a difficulty. A love-affair with a *demi-mondaine* or a lady *faisant fonction de demi-mondaine* was always at risk. Fashion and economics with the one, fashion and social pressures with the other—not to mention human nature in both cases—would always make for problems and encourage an early dissolution. Love in such circumstances would always have a chasm to bridge; it would, in the final count, be romantic rather than whole.

The situation must indeed have seemed tantalizing. On the one hand, outside the conventional erotic scheme, people might now—for a time—find completer love, something approaching 'whole love'. But all the pressures in this 'society' would work for instability; certainly no forms and little precedent or encouragement existed for solemnizing such affairs. Meanwhile within the conventional order there was, in theory, an institution that encouraged and laid down the principles of a permanent and reciprocal relationship. But in practice it had little to do with love or, indeed, with permanence and reciprocity. We can see that a lover of a certain sensibility must have longed to combine the best of both societies: to formalize and make permanent 'whole love', or something approaching it. It was a problem and a challenge.

II

Catullus

1. Introduction

Catullus was born *circa* 84 BC and died about thirty years later. He came from a well-to-do family in provincial Verona but soon moved to Rome, which he henceforth regarded as his home (poem 68.34–5).[1]

I shall now assume that the Lesbia concerned in his finest love poetry is Clodia, wife of Metellus, described in the last chapter. Catullus therefore loved a lady who acted the courtesan. And Catullus longed to meet the challenge described at the end of the last chapter. He wished (he says so: e.g. poem 109) to solemnize and perpetuate a kind of 'whole love'; he wanted to commit himself, and he wanted his beloved to commit herself, to their love in the way that conventional Roman society committed itself—in theory—to marriage. A problematic aspiration. Catullus' love and life must have been fraught with tension. Out of it came his love poetry: life transmuted into art.

The more sympathetic we are at the outset to the problems intrinsic in Catullus' love, the more receptive we may be to his poetry. A few more moments of preliminary thought are in order. The personality and impact of Clodia should be pondered. Caelius' and Cicero's fairly vicious picture of her is hardly the whole truth. But it is some of the truth and Catullus often enough shows himself aware of it. On the other hand Clodia can be the 'fair goddess', the light upon which the sweetness of life depends.[2] She must have had qualities to inspire such devotion: we are not simply witnessing the discrepancy between the face the world sees and the hallucinated vision of a sentimental fool. Clodia must have had elements of both the sublime and the abysmal, baffling to her lover. And promiscuity in a lover is a curious thing. It is a strange but psychologically explicable fact (observed by Marcel Proust among others) that the very availability of available and widely attractive women can be just the thing to excite or exacerbate dreams of unique possession among romantic but unfortunate lovers.

Tension is inherent in Catullus' life and love, his aspirations are made up of probably incompatible elements. Here are the sources, or rather the matter, of much of his love poetry. We could say in fact that Catullus' Lesbia love poetry boils down to being *either* an attempt to express his conception of love and his aspirations in it; *or* to an attempt to communicate the wonderfully significant trivia of an affair going well or only marginally badly; *or* to an attempt to express feelings consequent upon a knowledge of failed ideals. But that of course is vastly to over-simplify. And one doesn't boil down poetry. We must shift our mode of approach.

It is vital (and this is why I have opened the chapter in this way) for us to respond to the fact that Catullus' love poetry springs from his life; it is vital to remember that poetry for Catullus was a medium of communication. But we must not become too focused on what is communicated—on content rather than form, in so far as these two are separable. Certainly we must not fall a prey simply to abstracting and eulogizing Catullan ideas, ideals, and feelings. Unconventional and remarkable as these may have been, they will hardly have been unique or unrivalled. Other people before Catullus loved and hated simultaneously—and indeed virtually said as much.[3] If we want to find out what is truly great and unique about Catullus, we must study the *process whereby* Catullan life, his thoughts and feelings, are transmuted into art. We must study his different methods of fixing the chameleon nature of feelings, the intangible quality of moments, the indefinable essence of an ideal, in the enduring substance of literature.

2. The importance of Lesbia

There is one general feature of Catullus' Lesbia love poetry that we must notice. It is a strikingly original feature which stands out but which is insufficiently remarked. Whereas Catullus the lover of Clodia is special but not of momentous importance, Catullus the poet–lover of Lesbia is unique in his time and incalculably important. Catullus is, so far as we can judge, the first poet in Greek or Latin who decided to write about a particular love-affair in depth in a related collection of poems. Compare and contrast two influential predecessors, the archaic Greek poetess Sappho and the Alexandrian epigrammatist Meleager. The former of course said startling and original things about love in startling and original ways; it is likely enough too that she addressed numbers of poems to favourites like Anactoria and Atthis. Meleager writes numerous epigrams to Zenophila—and Heliodora, and the boy Myiscus. But a profound, systematic, and continuing exploration of a single relationship through poems which relate to and illuminate each other this is not in these lover-poets' manner or nature. It is not in any ancient poet's manner or nature before Catullus. There is no precedent in ancient literature for Catullus and Lesbia.

And 'Lesbia' we might say (to look ahead for a moment) is Catullus' single most important bequest to Latin (and subsequent) literature. For after Catullus numerous lover-poets found that they too were irresistibly committed to loving a figure like Lesbia and unavoidably compelled to write related cycles of poems about her. Some indeed had to enhance or perhaps invent all-engulfing love-affairs about which then perforce to write. Such can be the influence of art on art and art on life. Such was the influence of Catullus' Lesbia poetry; and a study of the great Latin love poets properly starts with him. Catullus' poems relating the ecstasy, suffering, and ambivalences of a romantic commitment to one dominating mistress set the fashion for other such poetry. And all this, together with the love poetry of anti-romantic reaction, forms a coherent genre of literature: Latin Love Poetry.

3. The Lesbia Epigrams

It is clear that Catullus experimented with different methods of communicating the feelings of love. Interestingly, his most original work is (I think) not his best. I start by looking at his most original work, the Lesbia epigrams. (For convenience's sake I refer to poems 69–116, which are all in elegiac metre, as the 'epigrams', and to poems 1–60, which are in a variety of lyric metres, as the 'polymetrics'.)

Catullus had remarkable ideals in love; he was profoundly interested in the strange and conflicting emotions of love. It is natural that he should want to analyse these ideals and feelings in his poetry. It is also natural, incidentally, that this desire to analyse should become more acute when reality began more obviously to fall short of ideals. That is simple psychology. It is when ideals are might-have-beens that one is impelled to analyse them; it is the feelings consequent upon failure that one scrutinizes, morbidly and obsessively. In the optimism of a present happiness ideals are an irrelevant abstraction and feelings too natural for analysis.

Catullus attempts to analyse ideals and feelings in the epigrams. The desire to analyse (usually morbidly) fuels a succession of poems in this part of his work. Such poems make up most of the Lesbia epigrams. And it is *only* in the epigrams that we find such analyses. The typical Lesbia epigram is therefore *analytical*, endeavouring to isolate what it was that was in the lovers' grasp, what it was that went wrong, what were the feelings that were then in consequence generated.

Catullus' methods in these poems are startlingly original. He takes over but transforms the traditional erotic epigram. In the hands of the Greek epigrammatists like Callimachus or their Roman imitators like Q. Lutatius Catulus this had been a vehicle of wit, pathos, or sentiment. Typically it enacted or suggested some often stock little scene or drama which was brought to a neat and pointed end. Epigram's structure lent itself naturally to antithesis (hexameter alternates with pentameter, couplet with couplet, and so on) and this was regularly used to enhance the pointed pathos, sentiment, or wit. Note for instance the following piece (*A.P.* 5. 107) by Philodemus, a contemporary of Cicero:

> 'I know, graceful girl, how to kiss when I am kissed,
> and again I know how to bite when I am bitten.
> Don't pain me too much—someone who loves you.

Don't wish to provoke the grievous anger of the Muses
   against you.'
So I continually cried and forewarned
but you were as deaf to my words as is the Ionian sea.
So now *you* wail and weep mightily.
I sit in Naias' lap.

Philodemus uses the antithetical pattern of pentameter and
hexameter in the first couplet to emphasize the range of his
potential amorous response: reciprocation or retaliation as
the occasion demands. And he organizes antithesis in the
structure as a whole. At the exact turning-point in the poem
we are greeted with the surprise that the first four lines were
in fact quoted speech from a *past* occasion, a warning that,
in the event, has been unheeded (the ancient reader or hearer
of course did not get the clue provided by modern quotation
marks). Past time is contrasted neatly with present time. The
final couplet provides a typically epigrammatic conclusion.
Philodemus' present happy state is sketched, and the first
girl's folly dramatically (in the literal sense of the word)
demonstrated. Again antithesis of hexameter and pentameter
accentuates the effect.

    This is the form that Catullus chooses for his analytical
poetry. But his handling of it transforms it. He almost entirely
expels all the dramatic element. The suggestions of situation
(as in Philodemus' poem) or other little enacted scenes (like
for example the typical 'excluded lover': below, p. 247)
which typified the genre—these are all jettisoned. Catullus
in fact leaves himself with just the bare bones of the epigram
form. His motives are comprehensible and recoverable. The
epigram thus laid bare offered him opportunities not only for
succinct analytical statement; he could also exploit the anti-
thetical structure for his own ends. By (for example) balancing
his own ideas against a common view of mankind he could
point and emphasize his own originality—just as Philodemus
accentuates his own felicity by putting it in the balance with
the misery of the heedless girl.

    However, having evolved himself a clever and promising
form, what *language* was Catullus to use? Given that the kind

of whole love that he aspired to was hardly a familiar pheno-
menon, its analytical expression naturally presented problems.
He had to evolve his own vocabulary. One method that he hit
upon I have already hinted at. Since Roman marriage was
founded in theory upon principles of mutual consent and
commitment, principles which were basic to Catullus' concep-
tion of love, marriage might provide him with some of his
needs; and (as we shall see) it did.

But only rather special occasions could be served in this
way. Catullus needed a more general vocabulary of commit-
ment. Now if Rome lacked a vocabulary for profound com-
mitment in love, it did have a highly developed code, and
therefore language, of *social* commitment. And here Catullus
found more of what he was looking for.

Rome was in essence an aristocratic society and possessed
an elaborately developed code of social conduct, a code
determining the mode and standards of relations and obliga-
tions among its upper classes. All aristocratic societies evolve
such codes: norms of morality and responsibility upon whose
general acceptance (in the relevant classes) they depend for
their cohesion, indeed existence. These norms are of course
ultimately founded only upon convention; but they are so
socially vital that they gather an aura of untouchability,
even sacrosanctity. And a virtually technical terminology
grows up, a terminology of 'proper behaviour': a vocabulary
of highly and particularly charged words, capturing the
obligations of aristocracy.

The Roman social code was deeply felt and, as a rule,
elaborately practised. Virtually every page of the correspond-
ence of Cicero (to name one obvious source) attests both
code and terminology. I mention here simply the essential
elements. *Fides* ('fidelity', 'integrity') was, or should be, the
foundation of all actions and relationships; one conducted
oneself in accordance with *pietas* ('sense of loyalty', 'con-·
scientiousness'). One had a profound sense of *officium*
('service', 'dutifulness'); one was pleased, indeed compelled,
to find and to display *gratia* ('favour'). Embracing and apply-
ing all these and other ideas was the extensive, sometimes

very formal relationship connoted by *amicitia*: a complex and profound 'friendship' implying at best mutual obligation, mutual affection, and mutual pleasure. *Amicitia* was, among the Roman aristocracy, the essence of any proper relationship, private or public, business or pleasure. So: *fides*, *pietas*, *officium*, *gratia*, *amicitia*: these and other such ideas arc the bases of Roman aristocratic conduct and the pillars of its society. (The English glosses are of course woefully inadequate. The nuances of a vocabulary of correct social conduct are very hard to recover and even harder to translate succinctly, once the society in question has vanished or changed.)[4]

It is this language, the highly-charged language of Roman aristocratic fellowship, that Catullus tried to adapt to the purpose of communicating what he saw as important aspects of love. It was an unconventional tactic, but in a way, in the circumstances, natural enough. Lovers had not yet worked out a language of mutual commitment; society had, so Catullus used it. (In an analogous way, English love poets have availed themselves of the language of Christian devotion and commitment.)[5] It is worth stressing, I think, that there is not really any question here of *metaphor*. Catullus did actually conceive of love or part of love as a form of *amicitia*; he did actually think that love ought to involve the sort of ideals and standards that were inherent or theoretically inherent in the aristocratic code; and therefore he used that language. The procedure was rather *faute de mieux* and liable perhaps to incongruity as well as vagueness: there must always have been a danger of prosaicness, of heaviness, in using words like *officium* and *pietas* of love. But because the aristocratic code involved ideas and terms which matched or closely approximated to Catullus' own feelings about love, it was a logical step to talk in the same way—without any thought of metaphor.

I ought to take this opportunity to refute explicitly one highly misleading statement—that in the Lesbia epigrams Catullus uses the 'Vocabulary of Political Alliance', 'the (almost technical) terminology of the workings of party politics and political alliances at Rome', 'the metaphor . . . of a political alliance'.[6] The origin of this seemingly incredible claim (what could induce a romantic lover-poet to picture his relationship metaphorically in terms of the workings of party politics?) is easy to uncover—and to explain. And it has its interest. True, the language of Catullus' Lesbia epigrams does closely resemble the language used by Roman politicians. But that is for a simple reason. Men in political life *also* used the language of aristocratic commitment and obligation;[7] and they did this very naturally. In Roman society government was almost exclusively in the hands of a technically amateur aristocracy; there was no professional machinery of political parties as we know them; there was no profession of politics in the sense that we would mean it. Nobles formed alliances and understandings with each other (which might indeed have the *effect* of parties) following the normal procedures of their society and class, and in theory respecting the usual obligations and standards; and when 'new men' like Cicero came along they fell into the pattern of their betters. Political life in Rome was, in origin and essence, an extension of the normal life of aristocratic society or rather just one department of it. And naturally therefore it followed, or purported to follow, the traditional code of behaviour; and naturally it used the customary terminology: *amicitia*, *officium*, etc. Political life and Catullus simply had a common source for their terminology. But while politics, being an increasingly cynical business, tended to debase it, Catullus tried to protect and exalt it.

So: to express some of his unconventional ideas about love Catullus sought to adapt the still emotive language of aristocratic obligation; and he deployed it in a stripped-down epigram form. I begin with a convenient but not the most obvious example: poem 75.

> huc est mens deducta tua mea Lesbia culpa
>   atque ita se officio perdidit ipsa suo,
> ut iam nec bene uelle queat tibi, si optima fias,
>   nec desistere amare, omnia si facias.

> Lesbia, by your wrongdoing my mind has been
>   forced so far

and by its own dutifulness so destroyed itself,
that now, should you become a paragon, it could have no affection
    for you;
and whatever you should do, it could not but go on loving you.

In this poem Catullus confronts and attempts to analyse despairing, ambivalent feelings. He reports the confusion of his present mental state, seeking to identify the components of that confusion; and he reports the source of the confusion. We may compare the famous and lauded analysis of ambivalence, poem 85:

> odi et amo. quare id faciam, fortasse requiris?
>   nescio, sed fieri sentio et excrucior.

> I hate *and* love. Perhaps you ask why I do this?
> I do not know; but I feel it happen and am in torment.

But 75 is a more probing analysis of a more complex ambivalence.

In the second couplet of 75, Catullus informs us that even if Lesbia should become a paragon, he could not now feel 'affection' for her; but nothing she might do could stop him 'loving' her. The source of this ambivalence is stated in the first couplet; the second couplet is all in consequence of (*ut*) the first.

In part the ambivalence is due to the effect on Catullus' mental state of Lesbia's 'wrongdoing', *culpa* (*culpa* embraces the notions of blame, offence, and more particularly sexual infidelity); and in part it is due to the effect of his own 'dutifulness'. It should be stressed that both of these items have contributed to both aspects of the ambivalence; that is the implication of the syntax. Only if we appreciate this shall we appreciate the full message of the poem.

Thus the consequence of Lesbia's 'wrongdoing' (line 1) is to be seen in the fact that Catullus is incapable of 'affection' *and* in the fact that he remains irrevocably passionate about her (we infer that 'loving' means in particular *'passionately* loving': see below). The second part of this is striking, though comprehensible. Other people besides Catullus have found that a lover's faithlessness far from diminishes passion, indeed leads to it. More striking perhaps are the implications of line 2. Why should Catullus' own 'dutifulness' lead to his ceasing to feel 'affection' for Lesbia but his continued 'loving'? That seems not so clear. We need a better understanding of terms like *belle uelle* and *officium*. Does Catullus guide us towards such an understanding?

We should first note how the antithetical potential of the epigram form is being exploited to point meaning. *bene uelle* is formally contrasted with *amare*; the terms are presumably semantically contrasted. *bene uelle* seems to cover emphatically unsexual affection; so we may assume *amare* covers strongly sexual love: passion. Antithesis in short helps to confine the general and vague term *amare* to a specific function.

But we need more help, with *bene uelle* and *officium*. We need in fact the knowledge that a contemporary reader would have had instinctively and which Catullus presupposes. Both *bene uelle* and *officium* are emotive and charged terms within the language of aristocratic obligation. *officium* covers the duty, the service that one undertakes for *amici*—that one delights to undertake for them; and it covers one's *sense* of that duty. It also carries with it a clear implication of reciprocity: *officium* by definition deserves, and within sincere *amicitia* duly obtains, *officium* in return.[8] Not so clearly in Catullus' relationship with Lesbia. And *bene uelle* is one of the characteristic terms to express the generous feelings that underlie the relationship of *amicus* to *amicus*. It is one of the definitions and one of the splendours of *amicitia* that one *bene uult*, one feels a disinterested warmth for an *amicus*.

The technical terms show the framework in which Catullus is thinking: *amicitia*; the terms were so particular and resonant for a Roman that this patent fact did not have to be stated. Once upon a time, we gather, Catullus had believed that a very special bond of fellowship existed between himself and Lesbia—their own *amicitia*. Because of that belief he assiduously displayed his 'dutifulness'. Evidently, however, Lesbia failed to reciprocate in the manner demanded by such a relationship. The belief in the existence of the relationship had therefore to be abandoned. That meant inevitably that the special generosity of feeling (*beneuolentia*) that he had felt or thought to feel for Lesbia had also to go; for it can only exist in such a relationship. But passion of course could persist, being independent of *amicitia*; and human nature being human nature, no doubt it would. The logic of the poem becomes clearer.

So Lesbia's failure to reciprocate *officium*—and her *culpa*—led to Catullus' abandonment of belief in *amicitia* and to the results consequent upon that, chronicled in the second couplet. But Catullus phrases himself more distinctively, and pathetically, than our summary implies: 'My mind has so destroyed *itself*, by *its own* dutifulness.' Catullus acknowledges that the idea of *amicitia* had been his, that he had behaved with regard to Lesbia according to the exalted standards of a relationship of his creation, of his imagination. His unilateral observance of this ideal led to the demonstration that such an ideal was unfounded; Catullus set himself up for his cruel disappointment and in part therefore caused it. All this he admits, in the powerful and pathetic second line.

I turn now to the famous poem 76. Again we find a poem riven with ambivalence: a man loathing a relationship has to pray to the gods to help him break it. There is (on more than one account) an interesting comparison to be made between 76 and 8 (see below, pp. 47 ff.). In poem 8 Catullus tries to come to terms with Lesbia's loss of interest in him; in 76 he tries to effect a conclusion to the affair himself and come to terms with that. The situation of 76 is more tragic than that of 8; its utterance is far more bitter suiting its strange and unkind birth.

> siqua recordanti benefacta priora uoluptas
>   est homini, cum se cogitat esse pium,
> nec sanctam uiolasse fidem, nec foedere in ullo
>   diuum ad fallendos numine abusum homines,
> multa parata manent in longa aetate, Catulle,
>   ex hoc ingrato gaudia amore tibi.
> nam quaecumque homines bene cuiquam aut dicere possunt

aut facere, haec a te dictaque factaque sunt.
omnia quae ingratae perierunt credita menti.
    quare iam te cur amplius excrucies?
quin tu animo offirmas atque istinc teque reducis,
    et dis inuitis desinis esse miser?
difficile est longum subito deponere amorem,
    difficile est, uerum hoc qua lubet efficias:
una salus haec est, hoc est tibi peruincendum,
    hoc facias, siue id non pote siue pote.
o di, si uestrum est misereri, aut si quibus umquam
    extremam iam ipsa in morte tulistis opem,
me miserum aspicite et, si uitam puriter egi,
    eripite hanc pestem perniciemque mihi,
quae mihi subrepens imos ut torpor in artus
    expulit ex omni pectore laetitias.
non iam illud quaero, contra me ut diligat illa,
    aut, quod non potis est, esse pudica uelit:
ipse ualere opto et taetrum hunc deponere morbum.
    o di, reddite mi hoc pro pietate mea.

If there is any pleasure for a man in recollecting his former
        kindnesses—
when he reflects on his conscientiousness,
that he has not outraged sacred fidelity, nor in any pact
misused the gods' authority in order to deceive his fellow men—
then there are many pleasures laid up in store for you Catullus,
        in the long life ahead of you,
resulting from this love of yours that has received no thanks.
For whatever men can do in the way of kindness of word or deed
        for anyone
this you have done, kindnesses of word and deed.
But it's all been thrown away, an investment in a thankless heart.
Wherefore, why will you now torture yourself further?
Why do you not stiffen your resolve, bring yourself back
and cease to be wretched in despite of heaven?
It is hard suddenly to set aside a long love.
It is hard. But achieve it in any way you can.
This is your one deliverance, it must be completely won.
Do this—whether it is possible or not.
Gods, if it is your wont to pity, if ever
you have brought help at the last to people even in the hour of
        death,
look at me in my wretchedness and if I have lived an unstained
        life
tear out from me this disastrous disease
which creeping to the extremities of my limbs like a numbness

has driven all joy from my heart.
I do not now ask that she should return my love,
or want to be what she cannot be, decent.
I pray that *I* may be healthy, and set aside this foul disease.
Gods, grant me this, for my conscientiousness.

Our first reaction to the beginning of this poem may be one of incredulity. Catullus may seem to be associating himself with people who are *in general* charitable, conscientious, faithful, and scrupulous; if (he seems to be saying) there is pleasure for such saintly folk in mulling over their goodness, there is pleasure in store for him. The suggestion of possible pleasure is of course ironical. But that does not affect the pretentiousness of the apparent claim.

Things are not as bad as they seem. In the sixth line Catullus limits the range of his own virtue to his love-affair: 'there are many pleasures . . . for you . . . resulting from this love of yours'; and it is in fact a very particular company of virtuous people with whom he is associating himself in the first five lines: those who have been virtuous *in the particular relationship of* 'amicitia'. For virtually all the key words in 1–6 (*benefacta, pius, sancta fides*, and indeed *ingratus*; cf. *gratia*) are part of the semi-technical terminology of aristocratic obligation and therefore evoke that particular situation. *benefacta* (cf. *beneficia, benefacere, benigne facere*) is the only term yet to be fixed as semi-technical: *benefacta* are the 'kindnesses' that earn one *amici*, that keep *amici*, that are naturally and without solicitation exchanged between 'friends' in formal and informal ways.[9]

Catullus means therefore in the opening lines of 76 that if anyone can have pleasure from pondering conscientious behaviour *in amicitia*, he can; he, if anyone, has displayed that kind of *pietas*. This he does mean to claim: for he has indeed faithfully observed a very special *amicitia*, one he himself conceived, a relationship of affection and loyalty with a lover. And what is more, he persisted for a long time in the face of lack of proper reciprocity, a lack of due *gratia*: *ex ingrato amore*. Here is the same sort of statement as in 75 and the same plaint; and Catullus adapts the same type of language to communicate it, only here more extensively.

But now he wishes to end the ill-starred affair. The rest of the poem shows Catullus trying to accomplish and come to terms with such an end, describing the feelings and thoughts involved. So it is a dynamic rather than a static analysis of feeling—and more besides. The poem *enacts* Catullus declaring and trying to impose his will upon intense and ambivalent *shifts* of feeling. We seem to witness this actually happening. Note particularly the questions at lines 10–12 and the prayer at 17, all revealing wavering of purpose. In a sense therefore the poem is, as well as dynamic, dramatic (in the literal sense of the word)—and very immediately so. It almost seems to be itself a drama, an emotional event actually happening, rather than an artistically composed re-enaction.

It is this immediacy that is the cause of certain poetical faults. Catullus is not distanced from feeling in the way that an artist should be, and emotion runs away with language producing laxity of expression, incoherence, and confusing hyperbole.

Our account of lines 1–6 was certainly right. But an initial misunderstanding was forgivable. Catullus leans very heavily on an instinctive appreciation of the scope of his *amicitia* vocabulary. We eventually grasp what he means but the poem's composition in those lines scarcely compels a proper understanding. At line 7 expression is even more lax and more liable to mislead: *nam quaecumque homines . . .*, 'whatever men can do . . .' Catullus actually says here (whatever he meant) that any good in word or deed that men can perform for anyone (*cuiquam*), this he has done. The range of the couplet is in fact strictly (whatever the intention) unlimited. Note too for example *si uitam puriter egi* (19). In what sense has Catullus led a spotless life? Presumably (or perhaps) he means: in regard to Lesbia. But he does not say so. Nor is there any technical *amicitia* nuance to *puriter* which might help to define and confine it. The effect of such language is to imply an outrageous and implausible self-righteousness. And there is much else at the end of the poem that is clearly emotional and unmeant hyperbole—but I do not think I need to labour examples.

A study of poem 76 once more shows us Catullus attempting to analyse feelings; and once more it shows us him adapting the language of *amicitia* to that end. Interestingly, too, it is dramatic: the analysis and description of feeling occur within an action. But it is a poetic failure. It is itself more of a dramatic event, an emotional and fairly direct description of feeling, than an artistically created drama (examples of which we shall see below). The latter is, the former obviously is not, promising poetry. Because it is an event rather than art we find laxity of expression incompatible with art. We see here, I think, one obvious danger of 'analytical poetry'. A poet who deals with emotions so directly risks letting emotion run away with expression.

In the course of poem 76 Catullus uses the word *foedus* ('treaty' or 'pact'). This is a vital word in Catullan love poetry, but unfortunately its implications are disputed. We must identify them. The study will lead us into a general and important topic.

Foedus is used in contexts of *amicitia*, but it is reserved for occasions when an exceptionally strong or formal degree of commitment is at issue. Just as international treaties, *foedera*, were 'ratified by solemn oaths and to break them was perjury',[10] so the same sanctity applied or should apply to pacts of social obligation. For this reason it is much rarer than other *amicitia*-terminology, indeed hardly classes as one of the usual technical terms.

A good place in which to observe its special force as a term of aristocratic obligation is Cicero's letter to Crassus making his peace with the 'triumvirs'. Here Cicero demonstrably intends an especial solemnity, indeed has the full sense 'treaty' in mind:[11] 'I want you to consider that what I write here is going to have the force of a treaty (*foedus*) not of a letter; and what I promise you and take upon myself, I shall observe most sacredly (*sanctissime*) and pursue most diligently.' We can note too the pained passion with which the exiled Ovid reproaches a friend who scorned the 'sacred and venerable name of *amicitia*' while others sympathized with him who had *'not* been joined by any *foedus'*.[12] It suits Ovid, who has an axe to grind, to propound a very elevated view of friendship, and *foedus* in these circumstances is a useful term. And Catullus, in poem 76 (line 3), clearly thinks that when a *foedus* exists between *amici* it is literally sacred, protected by the authority of the gods. He himself (he implies) has honoured his relationship with Lesbia as though it were not only *amicitia* but special and sanctified *amicitia*: a *foedus*.

But *foedus* has another and very particular function in Catullus. He uses it directly or indirectly of marriage. His two certain examples of this occur in his mythological poem on the marriage of Peleus and Thetis, poem 64. Line 335: *nullus amor tali coniunxit foedere amantes,/ qualis adest Thetidi, qualis concordia Peleo* ('no love ever joined lovers in such a *foedus'*—as Peleus' and Thetis' love did); and line 373: *accipiat coniunx felici foedere diuam,/ dedatur cupido iam dudum nupta marito* ('let the husband receive the goddess [i.e. his bride] in happy *foedus* . . .'). Now this is a use which is well paralleled after Catullus;[13] but as far as I can judge it is unparalleled before him. It seems therefore that the idea of referring to a marriage as a *foedus* is Catullus' invention—and that later poets are following his precedent. This is plausible enough. *Foedus* is a particularly happy choice for the marriage of Peleus and Thetis and so may well have been made specially for it: the connotations of *foedus* suitably stress the unparalleled degree of reciprocity and sanctity that this romantic, mythical marriage (in Catullus' version) apparently possessed.

Foedus therefore can refer in Catullus to an —ideal—'pact' of marriage. Let us put this fact on one side for a moment, and consider another fact. At times Catullus talks of his own relationship with Lesbia in terms of marriage; marriage, like *amicitia*, afforded him vocabulary to express things in love which were difficult to express in normal erotic terminology. I mentioned this above (p. 24), and we shall shortly observe a striking and extended example in poem 68 (pp. 56ff.). But note too poem 70:

nulli se dicit mulier mea nubere malle
    quam mihi, non si se Iuppiter ipse petat.
dicit: sed mulier cupido quod dicit amanti,
    in uento et rapida scribere oportet aqua.

My woman says that she prefers to marry no one
rather than me, not if Jupiter himself should court her.
That's what she says: but what a woman says to her
        passionate lover
ought to be written on the wind and on rushing water.

One does not imagine that Lesbia meant her stated preference
to marry Catullus too seriously, or that she thought very
deeply about it. It will have been a casual, romantic indul-
gence. Why does Catullus react so bitterly, so scornfully?
Because, presumably, he did take the idea seriously; he did
have a belief that his life with Lesbia might be, or have been,
in very true senses, in the best senses, if not in literal senses,
marriage. (Notice incidentally how epigram's antithetical
structure is again exploited: the second couplet is formally
opposed to the first, and the contrast between protestation
and reality thereby highlighted.)

So we now have two facts. (1) Catullus idiosyncratically
and originally refers to an apparently ideal, mythical marriage
as a *foedus*. (2) He is inclined to imagine his own love-affair
as an—ideal—marriage. We must therefore interpret a poem in
which he talks of his own affair as a *foedus* with care.

Poem 109:

iucundum, mea uita, mihi proponis amorem
    hunc nostrum inter nos perpetuumque fore.
di magni, facite ut uere promittere possit,
    atque id sincere dicat et ex animo,
ut liceat nobis tota perducere uita
    aeternum hoc sanctae foedus amicitiae.

You declare, my life, that this our love
    will be between us 'delightful' and 'eternal'.
You gods, make it that she be capable of promising truly,
    and that she say this candidly and from the heart.
Then we may be able throughout life to carry through
    this eternal pact of inviolable friendship.

Here Catullus is (as in 70) echoing a declaration of Lesbia's: 'this love between us will be delightful, eternal.' He seems to be repeating her actual words: *iucundus* ('delightful') was probably an *à la mode* word at the time for pleasant things or experiences, the sort of word Lesbia would use.[14] Catullus clearly regards this rather glib declaration with scepticism. However, if she *should* mean what she says, and mean it fully—and Catullus prays to that end fervently—then it would be possible for them to live out the Catullan ideal of a reciprocal relationship. And as he makes this point Catullus attempts an analytical description of that ideal:[15] *tota . . . uita/aeternum hoc sanctae foedus amicitiae.*

A key concept is 'eternity' and the basis of the definition seems, as was to be expected, to be the complex of ideas contained in *amicitia* (mutual pleasure, trust, obligation, etc.). However *amicitia* is here *exalted* by the epithet *sanctae* —so that it is now something *explicitly* beyond the range of normal *amicitia*; and it also seems in some way to be transformed by *foedus*. Now it is possible that Catullus simply means to emphasize the sanctity and commitment of this special *amicitia* by using a word allied to the terminology that was reserved for exceptional cases. But considering that he is here effectively defining his ideal, considering that ideas of marriage seem to have been very close to his ideal, and considering that he elsewhere uses *foedus* of the pact of an ideal marriage—then I think that that is likely to be the intended significance here. Catullus is talking therefore of a '*marriage*-pact of friendship', a lively phrase which connotes (among much else) a reciprocal relationship possessing the solemnity of marriage but founded on true affection.

If my interpretation is right, which all the pointers suggest it is, then we have an important observation to make. Catullus is, I think, directly confronting the problem facing the Roman lover which I mentioned at the end of the last chapter (above, p. 18), and going some way towards defining a solution. I remarked how some Roman lovers must have been tantalized to see that on the one hand an institution existed (marriage) which was suited to the solemnizing of whole love—but it was abused; meanwhile, on the other hand, relatively whole love was confined to precarious, unformalized circumstances (the *demi-monde*). The 'marriage-pact of friendship', the *foedus amicitiae*, seems to me to be proffered as an at least partial resolution of this paradox. Achieving this a lover would achieve a fair synthesis: a relationship that was permanent, reciprocal, solemnized, and loving[16] and sincere. And it is Catullus' belief, or at least it is his prayer, that it can be achieved.

Before we leave this poem let us note how Catullus, who obviously questions Lesbia's ability to live up to such an ideal, adumbrates his own capability and commitment. The *foedus* is to be maintained *tota uita*; if Catullus calls Lesbia *mea uita* in that context, it is a simple but eloquent statement of where he stands.

It is probable that when *foedus* occurs in other Lesbia epigrams it is meant to suggest not just the pact of a special *amicitia* but the pact of ideal marriage. This may be true of poem 76 but if so the ambiguity (for that is what it would have to be) is hardly perspicuous. More significant is poem 87.

> nulla potest mulier tantum se dicere amatam
>   uere, quantum a me Lesbia amata mea est.
> nulla fides ullo fuit umquam foedere tanta,
>   quanta in amore tuo ex parte reperta mea est.
>
> No woman can say that she has been so truly loved
>   as my Lesbia has been loved by me.
> There has never ever been such great fidelity in any pact
>   as has been discovered on my part in my love for you.

Catullus is again looking back, analysing the degree and kind of his past devotion. In the first couplet he expresses himself in simple terms, in terms that others might use (*uere amare*). But this is insufficient or liable to be misunderstood: the words are too common. So he defines what he means by *uere amare* in the second couplet.

Two features throw emphasis on this definition. First, antithesis. The conventional language of the first couplet, set in the balance with the very different language of the second, highlights the unconventional and particularly Catullan nature of that second couplet. Antithesis invites us to probe its implications. The second feature is an easy-to-miss apostrophe. As Catullus turns to clarify his special love for Lesbia, he (very suitably) switches from third-person description to a second-person address, to Lesbia. The message becomes personal and particular.

Two formal devices therefore call attention to the individuality of the definition in lines 3–4. Given this I feel sure that the particularly Catullan sense of *foedus* is operative. The language is of course essentially that of 'aristocratic obligation' and one can translate simply in those terms. Thus: 'No fidelity was ever in any pact (of *amicitia*) so great as that discovered in my love for you.' But that must also imply: 'No fidelity was ever in any pact so great as that discovered in *the pact of* my love for you.' Catullus implies a love-*foedus*, that is, *his* conception of a *foedus*; he alludes by a neat and sweet ambiguity to his vision of love as an ideal marriage.

To sum up so far. Catullus has been trying to describe complex ideas and feelings: a special degree and nature of love; feelings of injury consequent upon bitter disappointment, including (very characteristically) ambivalence. To communicate some of his ideals he has used the language of aristocratic obligation. I stress that 'metaphor' is not here the word to apply. Catullus actually means that he feels or felt for Lesbia a kind of *amicitia*. Of course his was an exalted *amicitia* to which the values and therefore the basic, unqualified terms of the more conventional variety might only approximate. But it was *amicitia* none the less. He has also found it relevant to suggest that his relationship was in some senses 'marriage'. And it is perhaps wrong, or an over-simplification, to call this metaphor. Catullus *means* that his relationship had, or might have had, the best essence of marriage. His vision *was* marriage —albeit again in an exalted form.

So, two unexpected areas of life are providing language to analyse Catullan erotic ideals. Catullus also made a very interesting attempt to use a third area of life—this time metaphorically: the family.[17] Poem 72:

dicebas quondam solum te nosse Catullum,
    Lesbia, nec prae me uelle tenere Iouem.
dilexi tum te non tantum ut uulgus amicam,
    sed pater ut gnatos diligit et generos.
nunc te cognoui: quare etsi impensius uror,
    multo mi tamen es uilior et leuior.
qui potis est, inquis? quod amantem iniuria talis
    cogit amare magis, sed bene uelle minus.

Once upon a time Lesbia you used to say that Catullus was
        the only lover you knew,
that you did not wish to possess Jupiter before me.
I loved you then not just as ordinary people love their girl-
        friends,
but as a father loves his sons and sons-in-law.
Now I know you. Wherefore, although I burn more fiercely,
you are much cheaper, more paltry in my estimation.
'How can that be?', you say. Because such injustice
compels a lover to love more, to feel the warmth of true
        affection less.

The similarities of this poem to 70 and particularly to 75 are
obvious. They are interesting too: for at crucial points
Catullus says not only more but rather different things, and
in different ways.

The structure of 72 again offers an antithesis, 'then' (1-4)
against 'now' (5-8); and the one sets in relief the other in the
usual way. I look at the second half first. It contains a
striking use of *amicitia* language.

Nunc te cognoui . . . Now Catullus knows the true nature
of Lesbia. In consequence his physical feelings are *more*
intense (that is interesting, somewhat unexpected, but one
instinctively understands it; cf. 75, above, pp. 27 f., but the
greater intensity here is to be noted); his respect for her
character much less (a more natural reaction). The final
couplet purports to explain this ambivalence (*qui potis est*).
Here we switch to *amicitia* language. Unlike poem 75, this
poem lays the final blame for loss of generous warmth of
feeling (*bene uelle*) fairly and squarely on Lesbia: on actions
of hers, or rather the spirit informing her actions (*iniuria*,
'injustice'). *Iniuria* is a crucial term: it is precisely what, in
the language of aristocratic relations, will destroy *amicitia*,

implying severe things about the intent of the offender.[18]
Catullus means that Lesbia has not just committed wrongs
against him (i.e. acts of infidelity), she has committed them
with such wilful and inimical intent that the wholeness of
Catullan love (exalted *amicitia*) is now impossible. So warmth
of feeling is gone; but passion persists—indeed increases.

The last couplet therefore adds the *cause* of Catullus'
paradoxical dilemma. But we might note that it does not
explain how or why it takes the form it does, which is
rather what *qui potis est* leads us to expect. That is a pity.
I should like to have seen Catullus' explanation of why
infidelity and offence excite *greater* sexual passion in the
lover. However, having added the cause, all Catullus really
does is restate his ambivalent dilemma in a tauter, more
intimate, though perhaps not fully successful paradox (see
below, p. 41).

To turn to the first half of the poem—to 'once upon a
time'. Lesbia was then all specious protestations of devotion
(cf. 70). Catullus echoes her words in the first couplet to set
in relief an analysis of his own sincere feelings at the same
time. 3–4: 'I loved you then not just as ordinary people love
their girl-friends, but as a father loves his sons and sons-in-law'
—perhaps one of the most famous lines in Catullus. It is
unique and it is brilliant and it does not quite come off.

What Catullus is trying to do is to communicate an indefin-
able feeling of unequivocal, committed love. He resorts to
simile to illustrate it. And, clearly, an unequivocal, committed
love is what a father feels, often enough, for his sons and
sons-in-law. (The presence of *generos*, 'sons-in-law', should
not trouble us; as Fordyce ad loc. says, their inclusion 'reflects
a traditional attitude which puts the sons-in-law within the
head of the family's protective concern'.)[19] But the equation
cannot be quite true. Paternal love embraces all sorts of other
things, all sorts of motivations and feelings, that a lover could
not and would not want to have. Catullus really means that
some of his love resembled some of a father's; he did not
actually love Lesbia as a father loves his sons and sons-in-law.
We must interpret the simile selectively, eliminating much of

our natural response. It is hardly completely informative, and hardly a complete poetical success. But it is a fascinatingly original attempt by Catullus to express things arguably quite out of his time.[20]

Catullus' work in the Lesbia epigrams was brilliantly original. But it is not his best poetry. There are criticisms to be made which have literary-historical as well as aesthetic relevance. First a relatively minor point.

Analysis like this in epigram, while benefiting from the pointed antithetical form, runs the risk (because of the extreme compression) of inexactness. Analysis is the job of prose and scientists. Catullus tries to be careful about his use of words but he falls into traps. For example his use of *amor* and cognates is careless (and confusion over this word is in the circumstances if most understandable also most undesirable). In poem 87 he uses it (I take it) of whole love; in 75 of one part of love, passion. In poem 72 in the space of two lines he actually uses it in *both* these senses and produces a flawed *sententia* in the process.[21] Or take the lauded *odi et amo* (85): is the sense of *amo* clear there? And what is the force of *excrucior*?[22] Again, is not some of the special Catullan terminology, in particular *foedus*, very liable to be misunderstood? Yes, demonstrably: people have misunderstood it repeatedly.

Description of feelings also runs another risk, that of too immediate involvement, leading not just to inexact but to incoherent expression (poem 76).

These one might say are minor quibbles considering the magnitude of Catullus' originality. My next point is more serious. I think that Catullus' venture in the epigrams was bound to fail *as poetry* more or less by definition. If that seems a bold statement, it is one that the practice of later love poets tacitly supports.

Analysis and poetry are essentially conflicting occupations. To define the constituent elements of ideas and feelings can hardly be the proper function of poetry. For if one succeeds in doing it, one will *also* have succeeded in confining words to a particular sense in a tight and static syntax. And that is the character of scientific or philosophical prose, whose job therefore analysis properly is. My remark above ('analysis is the job of prose and scientists') has more profound implications. The poetic art is to stimulate the imagination, to *suggest* not define. All great poetry is a dynamic not a static texture in which words can (as it were) *move*, combining and recombining to yield shifting aspects of meaning. Unlike a successful analysis a great poem is not the same thing each time one picks it up. Nuances have realigned to suggest new aspects and new colours.

The relevance and truth of these comments will be confirmed as we proceed. I conclude my remarks on the Lesbia epigrams by recalling one which was, in one discreet respect, different and arguably more interesting: poem 87. This is an epigram which I think starts to come alive, to become real poetry. The point to appreciate is the sudden apostrophe in the second couplet. For his very individual description of devotion Catullus suddenly switches from third to second person, and addresses Lesbia. The effect of this unexpected apostrophe is to startle the reader into thinking about the apostrophized person, into thinking about Lesbia. It brings Lesbia's personality suddenly into the reckoning; into indeed the poem. The words are now, suddenly, in an emotive *context*: we cannot call them merely analytical; they are in the literal sense dramatic. They exist in an implicit, artistically created drama —words of idealism addressed to the woman who shatters that idealism. Pathos haunts their utterance, other resonances and adumbrations—and suddenly an epigram is poetry.[23]

4. The Lesbia Polymetrics

Adapting the epigram form for analysis Catullus had by and large ejected the dramatic element that had typified the genre. He had attempted to analyse thought and feeling, exploiting the antithetical structure that the form offered. In his Lesbia polymetrics his practice is completely different, and from one point of view conventional. The poems remain dramatic: each one enacts, suggests, or reacts to some specific 'drama'. It should be stressed that these poems are artistically composed re-enactions, and not veritable events like poem 76. Now we may in fact—I think we demonstrably do—learn as much or more about Catullus' love and feelings, but we learn it indirectly: through the interaction of personality with personality or personality with event within a dramatic context. The kind of phenomenon we observed fleetingly in poem 87 is the rule in the Lesbia polymetrics.

What we are observing then is that Catullus decided upon two radically different strategies of love poetry, basically practising one in the polymetrics and the other in the epigrams. (This is a slight over-simplification, but true in essence.) He therefore drew a sharp distinction between polymetric and elegiac short poems that had hardly existed before. There is a reason why he divided his work in this way. The metres that he favoured in the Lesbia polymetrics (hendecasyllables and scazons) offer less opportunity for pointed antithesis,[24] but they are relatively close to the natural rhythms of Latin speech. They therefore suit dramatic poems, poems that artistically enact life.

Now the approach of the polymetrics is as I say basically more conventional. The feelings informing them tend, too, to be less agonized than those analysed in the epigrams. But less agonized feelings are not necessarily less profound or complex; and (of course) a more conventional poetical strategy does not inevitably mean inferior poems. And in fact Catullus transmogrifies his inherited form.

I start by looking at poem 7.

> quaeris, quot mihi basiationes
> tuae, Lesbia, sint satis superque?
> quam magnus numerus Libyssae harenae
> lasarpiciferis iacet Cyrenis
> oraclum Iouis inter aestuosi
> et Batti ueteris sacrum sepulcrum;
> aut quam sidera multa, cum tacet nox,
> furtiuos hominum uident amores:
> tam te basia multa basiare
> uesano satis et super Catullo est,
> quae nec pernumerare curiosi
> possint nec mala fascinare lingua.

> You ask me, how many kisses
> are enough for me, Lesbia, enough and to spare?
> As many as is the number of grains of Libyan sand
> that lie in Silphium-bearing Cyrene
> between the oracle of sweltering Jupiter
> and the sacred tomb of Battus of old.
> Or as many as the stars that, when night is silent,
> witness people's love-affairs.
> To kiss you so many kisses
> is enough and to spare for mad Catullus,
> kisses which busybodies would not be able to reckon up
> nor an evil tongue bewitch.

The poem is addressed to Lesbia, answering a question from her. It is phrased as a piece of persuasion, aimed at Lesbia in a specific context. Its expression should therefore (we might expect) be tailored to suit her personality and mood. The poem exists in a carefully adumbrated dramatic situation, and Lesbia is part of the drama and therefore part of the poem as she was in a much more rudimentary way a part of poem 87. The whole poem is *living* in the way that the final couplet of 87 was.

Let us follow the drama—the persuasion—through. We must note that although the piece is an artistic creation, an artifice, it is absolutely vital to respond to it as it is designed: as a drama.

The opening two lines suggest Lesbia's original question, the occasion of the drama. Lesbia has apparently found her lover's lavish attentions (cf. poem 5) a mite too much of a good thing. 'Just how many kisses *do* you want?' she has asked with an edge of impatience. This is the basic, assumed fact governing the shape of the poem. The task of Catullus' persuasion is to win a slightly wearied woman back into good humour and compliance.

His basic tactic in response is candour. To the impatient 'How many kisses?' he answers 'An infinity'. In other words, to a question 'Are you insatiable?' he answers 'Yes'. There is obvious potential appeal in such candour. And the way it is deployed and amplified makes it, we must suppose, quite disarming.

Catullus starts the poem lightly. It is kisses (*basia*) which seem to have got on Lesbia's nerves, so he immediately clowns with the word and with her irritable question. He humorously travesties the question she presumably asked, namely *quot basia . . .?*, producing the comically pompous version *quot basiationes . . .?* (*basium* is the colloquial word for 'kiss'; *basiatio* is a coinage on the analogy of *osculatio*, a word of high diction; it is therefore a colloquial word got up in overformal clothes). In this way he removes any edge to the question, already making Lesbia smile at her own objection.

The subsequent lines express the idea of 'infinity', an infinity of kisses, in two images. Both images are in essence obvious and well-paralleled illustrations of innumerability. But the first, the image of the grains of sand (3–6), has been extraordinarily embellished with learned elaboration. The second, the picture of the stars (7–8), contrasts by virtue of its warm simplicity. Why two so very differently handled images to illustrate one basic idea? Because (and this is vital to appreciate) Catullus is shaping and amplifying his reply to suit Lesbia's personality. He is candidly saying 'infinity', i.e. 'I am insatiable', but phrasing it in ways that will particularly appeal to her. Since the poem is as it were trying to win a case with a particular and individual person that is the obvious explanation for such particular and individual phrasing.

In fact the allusive details of 3–6 are so thick-laid as to border on caricature. Catullus embroiders the simple notion 'desert sand' with extravagant vigour. He is striking a pose, to flatter and amuse Lesbia. *She*, it is assumed, has the *doctrina* to see and understand all the allusions provided by the *doctus poeta*; she also has the wit to see through them. She can appreciate the learned coinage *lasarpiciferis*, and the wit and learning in *Iouis aestuosi*; she can detect the allusion to Callimachus in *Batti* and admire the artfully contrived alliteration of *s*'s in the description of the desert (hearing the sound of winds in sand).[25] She also knows the limits to plausible embellishment. Catullus is writing to her presupposing, and adapting to, her cultivation, her aesthetic sensibility, and her sense of humour.

He also presupposes and adapts to a certain warmth and sentimentality. In 7-8 he switches to a tactic of 'appealing to the heart', dressing the idea of infinity in the tender image of the stars. We should note that it is Catullus who has made the image tender, and tender in a particularly relevant way. These are stars which 'witness the love-affairs of mankind when night is silent (and therefore conducive to *furtiuus amor*)'.[26] The lines are attractively redolent of stolen love— love like Catullus' and Lesbia's. Catullus is, while saying 'an infinity', while saying in effect 'my love for you is insatiable', rcminding Lesbia of the warm moments of their love-affair—tactfully and pertinently.

In 7-8, I suppose, is the centre of the poem's persuasion and the centre of the poem. But clearly one does not dally long over sentimentality with a woman like Lesbia. In line 9 Catullus returns swiftly to his note of clowning, concluding with a humorous reaffirmation of his insatiability. So many good things (the *basia*) might seem to be inviting nemesis in the shape of the malevolent spells of jealous ill-wishers. But the kisses will simply be too many to count and hence beyond such malevolence.

Such then are the tactics of Catullus' persuasion—a carefully packaged candour. First he casts the whole issue humorously (1); then cuts a dash (3 ff.); then he introduces tones of personal warmth (7-8), but finally returns swiftly to humour and clowning. We have watched these tactics in action; we have seemed to eavesdrop on a drama of persuasion. The poem offers us a living event transmuted into and immortalized by art.

And there is much to be learnt about the personality and psychology of the lovers from it: that should be clear. We have seen what Catullus regards as the right routes to Lesbia's good humour; and so the ingredients of the poem (humour, urbanity, extravagence, warmth, and a touch of sentimentality), and the proportion and ordering of those ingredients, must allow invaluable insight into the personalities of both Catullus and Lesbia and into how the two interact. In fact, if duly pondered, the poem tells us—indirectly—more about two people and their relations with one another than could ever be conveyed adequately by paraphrase. Or for that matter by analytical epigram.

Here is a point that we should identify clearly: the different potential as well as method of the dramatic poem compared with the analytical epigram. The poetical enactment of scene or situation can tell us things about feeling and personality that defy direct analysis. True, we are not given succinct and clear statement but things are adumbrated to us which statement could never encompass. We watch characters in a context and infer our knowledge. And language is expressive, not confined. The dramatic poem by giving its diction a living context encourages a subtle and suggestive verbal texture. That is richer than statement. One very simple example: *amores* in poem 7 occurring in a living exchange between Catullus and Lesbia and hinting persuasively at their stolen love is more suggestive, more emotive, more *meaningful* (in the literal sense of that word) than any use of *amor* in any of the analytical epigrams.

Another fine and very interesting example of a dramatic poem is poem 8:

> miser Catulle, desinas ineptire,
> et quod uides perisse perditum ducas.
> fulsere quondam candidi tibi soles,
> cum uentitabas quo puella ducebat
> amata nobis quantum amabitur nulla.
> ibi illa multa cum iocosa fiebant
> quae tu uolebas nec puella nolebat,
> fulsere uere candidi tibi soles.
> nunc iam illa non uolt: tu quoque impotens noli,
> nec quae fugit sectare, nec miser uiue,
> sed obstinata mente perfer, obdura.
> uale, puella. iam Catullus obdurat,
> nec te requiret nec rogabit inuitam.
> at tu dolebis, cum rogaberis nulla.
> scelesta, uae te, quae tibi manet uita?
> quis nunc te adibit? cui uideberis bella?
> quem nunc amabis? cuius esse diceris?
> quem basiabis? cui labella mordebis?
> at tu, Catulle, destinatus obdura.

My poor Catullus, do stop being foolish,
and what you see is gone, well realize it's lost.
Once upon a time the sun shone bright for you,
when you used to follow where she led
(a girl beloved by me as no girl will ever be).
Then, when there were those many playful intimacies,
which you so wanted and she was not averse to,
truly the sun shone bright for you.
Now she is disinclined. So you also, undisciplined fellow,
don't chase a fugitive, don't live in misery.
Bear up, apply your mind resolutely, be firm.
Goodbye, girl. Now Catullus is being firm.
He won't seek you back nor ask favours from you thus
    unwilling.
But you'll be sorry when no one asks your favours.
Wretched girl, pity on you! What life awaits you?
Who will now approach you? Who will think you pretty?
Whom will you love now? Whose will you be said to be?
Whom will you kiss? bite whose lips?
But Catullus!—be fixed, be firm!

The poem suggests its dramatic background: Lesbia is finished
with Catullus. One should not I think get the impression that
Catullus regards this as the end to end all ends—the poem is
very much tinged with humour which rather precludes such
an interpretation. Nevertheless, Catullus must face the worst;
and the poem conveys his consequent feelings and reactions.
They are of course ambivalent. Catullus wants to be proud
and firm in the separation; but he wistfully longs for a return
to the old days.

The poem conveys these feelings (and all the subtle ramifi-
cations which I shall not try to paraphrase) by, precisely,
dramatizing them. It is of course difficult to dramatize one
man's ambivalence. But Catullus has found a way. His basic
tactic is the self-address. A strong Catullus addresses a weak
Catullus and the interaction of the two produces a lively and
suggestive *event*. So again we have a drama (as in poem 7),
albeit ingeniously contrived; again we witness a piece of
action, transmuted into art, from which we intuit our
knowledge of feeling.

Strong Catullus bids Weak Catullus be sensible and realistic.

He admits that once upon a time things were marvellous; he even evokes those days rather patronizingly (3 ff.): *fulsere quondam candidi tibi soles . . .*; and he manages to insinuate that the happiness of the time was not only at the expense of some Catullan dignity but regarded with less than total enthusiasm by Lesbia ('when you used to follow where she led'; 'intimacies which you so wanted and she was not averse to', 4 and 7). So Strong Catullus admits that things were once upon a time marvellous. . . . And the memory has been too much for him. Strong Catullus has become lost, at one with Weak Catullus in romantic nostalgia. He repeats his evocation of the time of bliss but now emphatically without the patronizing tone: '*truly* the sun shone bright for you (8)'. Ambivalence, and how its emphases shift, is being clearly—dramatically— conveyed to us. It is worth noting that there was an earlier sign that Strong Catullus' strength was not all it might be. He was addressing Weak Catullus in the separated second person singular in these lines; but he could not dissociate himself from the affecting *cri*, line 5, 'beloved by me as no girl will ever be'. (*nobis* there may in fact be a true plural, 'beloved by *us*': Strong Catullus associates himself momentarily and as it were unwittingly with Weak Catullus in his adoration.)

However, Strong Catullus reasserts himself and utters a sterner admonition to be firm: *nunc iam illa non uult*, etc. (9–12). After this Catullus seems united in obduracy: *uale puella . . .* He turns and dispassionately—or perhaps, we should rather say, *vindictively*—evokes for Lesbia the implications of a mateless future, a future without Catullus. *at tu dolebis, cum rogaberis nulla./ scelesta, uae te, quae tibi manet uita? . . .* (14 f.). But again sentiment—the Weak Catullus—soon intrudes. The first and glaring equivocation is in fact already there in 13, 'nor ask favours from you *thus unwilling* (*inuitam*)'. That is after all a formidable qualification of the bald *uale puella*. And we soon feel Catullus palpably slipping into sentiment. It becomes more and more plain that Catullus fears the answer to the repeated questions (*quis nunc te adibit? . . .*) is *not* going to be 'no one', and more and more plain that he wishes it might be himself.

Another stern admonition is then required from Strong Catullus: *at tu, Catulle, destinatus obdura*—the end of the poem. Not, we should imagine, of the conflict. How the conflict then progressed is and is meant to be anybody's guess. We have witnessed an intentionally inconclusive event, moments of Catullus' inner life externally dramatized: ambivalence in action.

And that I maintain is a better way to be apprised of the nature and complexity of ambivalence than to read an attempted analysis of it (even the spontaneously dramatic analysis that 76 offers; 76 is very interesting to compare with poem 8). Of course the famous epigrams of ambivalence deal with a different degree—perhaps even kind—of ambivalence; but to an extent they are tackling the same subject and they do it, I maintain, demonstrably less successfully, certainly less poetically than poem 8. Here in poem 8 Catullus again composes an event for us, characters in a context. The event has to be contrived with more artifice than in poem 7: this time it is not Catullus and another character on stage, but Catullus and himself, Catullus in two capacities. He has in fact taken great trouble to contrive drama, so we can see what store he set on the poetic medium of drama. And it works. We respond to the interaction of personality with personality, and personality with event, within a context, analogously to poem 7. And we *infer* the necessary messages rather than listen to someone trying to state them. Again language is not confined but encouraged to expressiveness by a living context. *fulsere . . . candidi soles* for example (note that *candidus* has connotations of good fortune as well as brightness, whiteness, and beauty) evokes past happiness better than a thousand paraphrases or epigrams could analyse. It is at once actual and symbolic; it feeds the imagination. Or test the power of *uere* here and in poem 87. Our present context gives it implications of deep wistfulness and in turn (in retrospect) irony. It is, literally, more meaningful here than in poem 87— than it would be in any use outside a living context. And *amata . . . amabitur*, an emotional utterance of total love, with, in context, repercussions of irony and pathos; where can you find such a resonant and therefore meaningful use of *amo* in the epigrams? We note incidentally that the connotations are quite different from those of *amores* in poem 7—because the context is quite different. In both poems Catullus has, by constructing or adumbrating a drama, provided the basis and stimulus for a rich verbal texture—a poetic texture. That is something that an analytical epigram with its lack of context and its pursuit of precision cannot (by definition) do.

These are I think Catullus' best dramatic poems. But other polymetrics could have been selected to illustrate the technique. For instance poem 2, one of Catullus' most famous pieces:

> passer, deliciae meae puellae,
> quicum ludere, quem in sinu tenere,
> cui primum digitum dare appetenti
> et acris solet incitare morsus,
> cum desiderio meo nitenti
> carum nescio quid lubet iocari,
> et solaciolum sui doloris,
> credo, ut tum grauis acquiescat ardor:
> tecum ludere sicut ipsa possem
> et tristis animi leuare curas!

> Oh sparrow, my girl's darling!—
> whom she is wont to play with, to hold in her bosom,
> to whom she is wont to give her fingertip (you seek it)
> and provoke eager pecks:
> a favourite game for her
> when her eyes shine with longing for me,[27]
> and a little solace for her anguish
> to make her *grievous* passion abate—
> Would that I could play with you as she does—
> and alleviate the sad cares of my spirit.

(There is irony in *doloris* and *grauis . . . ardor*, and perhaps *desiderio meo nitenti*. I have emphasized 'grievous' in the translation in an attempt to bring out the tone.) Catullus and Lesbia are it seems perforce separated from one another; Lesbia is taking the separation better than Catullus. Through a witty address to Lesbia's pet bird Catullus manages to convey his current feelings: his pain at the separation which is considerably greater than Lesbia's, his rueful awareness of that fact that it is greater than Lesbia's; his jealousy of the fact that she can so easily divert herself in what should be her time of suffering; his jealousy of the way Lesbia casually disposes her affections; and so on. All this is wittily and tactfully communicated to Lesbia herself, and to us, via the dramatized address to Lesbia's pet.

Or take poem 11 (*Furi et Aureli, comites Catulli*). Here Catullus dramatizes a farewell to Lesbia that combines the bitterest of sarcastic repudiations with (I think) an appeal to ignore that repudiation.[28] The feelings that inform such a poem and come across to us are of course highly complex. One could endeavour to spell it all out; but paraphrase would hardly encompass it all. That is one reason why Catullus composed in this dramatic way. A dramatic poem can embody extraordinary complexity, subtlety, or delicacy. It offers us *life*, transmuted into art: deftly selected scenes or moments artfully presented so as to stimulate an imaginative response. We share experience with the poet and thereby come to an intuitive appreciation of often inexpressible things. And that is a richer adventure than being told the expressible.

5. Aspects of Poem 68

On one splendid occasion Catullus makes extensive use of myth in his love poetry. Poem 68 is probably the most extraordinary poem in Latin. It is clearly experimental in many respects and its quality highly uneven, laboured artificiality vying with sublimity. Not a small part of its extraordinariness lies in the disparate facets of Catullus' experience it covers: his relationship with Lesbia, the death of his brother. But I must confine my attentions to its function as a Lesbia love poem and in particular to the role played by the elaborate comparison with Laodamia and Protesilaus. And even here I must comment selectively. I quote some important passages.

> is clausum lato patefecit limite campum,   (lines 67–86)
>   isque domum nobis isque dedit dominae
> ad quam communes exerceremus amores.

quo mea se molli candida diua pede
intulit et trito fulgentem in limine plantam
    innixa arguta constituit solea,
coniugis ut quondam flagrans aduenit amore
    Protesilaeam Laudamia domum
inceptam frustra, nondum cum sanguine sacro
    hostia caelestis pacificasset eros.
nil mihi tam ualde placeat, Ramnusia uirgo,
    quod temere inuitis suscipiatur eris.
quam ieiuna pium desideret ara cruorem,
    docta est amisso Laudamia uiro,
coniugis ante coacta noui dimittere collum,
    quam ueniens una atque altera rursus hiems
noctibus in longis auidum saturasset amorem,
    posset ut abrupto uiuere coniugio,
quod scibant Parcae non longo tempore abesse,
    si miles muros isset ad Iliacos.

aut nihil aut paulo cui tum concedere digna   (lines 131–41)
    lux mea se nostrum contulit in gremium,
quam circumcursans hinc illinc saepe Cupido
    fulgebat crocina candidus in tunica.
quae tamen etsi uno non est contenta Catullo,
    rara uerecundae furta feremus erae,
ne nimium simus stultorum more molesti.
    saepe etiam Iuno, maxima caelicolum,
coniugis in culpa flagrantem concoquit iram,
    noscens omniuoli plurima furta Iouis.
atqui nec diuis homines componier aequum est—

nec tamen illa mihi dextra deducta paterna   (lines 143–8)
    fragrantem Assyrio uenit odore domum,
sed furtiua dedit mira munuscula nocte,
    ipsius ex ipso dempta uiri gremio.
quare illud satis est, si nobis is datur unis
    quem lapide illa diem candidiorc notat.

He opened up a fenced field with a broad path,   (67–86)
and he gave a house to me, and gave a house to a mistress,
a house where we might pursue the love we shared.
And my fair goddess betook herself there with gentle step;
she set her shining foot on the worn threshold,

halting, her sandal sounding—
Just as once upon a time burning with love
came Laodamia to the house of Protesilaus—
a house that was begun vainly, for not yet with holy blood
had a victim appeased the lords of heaven.
May nothing, maid of Ramnus [i.e. Nemesis], so mightily
    appeal to me
that it be undertaken rashly with our lords unwilling!
And how hungrily the altar desires the pious blood
Laodamia learnt, losing her husband:
compelled to loose her bridegroom from her arms
before the coming of a first and a second winter
had satisfied their eager love in length of nights
so that, her marriage sundered, she might bear to live.
And *that* the Fates knew was close at hand
if once Protesilaus went to fight at Troy . . .

Hardly, or not at all worthy to give place to her   (131–41)
she who is my light brought herself to my bosom.
Cupid, darting round on either side of her,
gleamed brightly in a saffron cloak.
And though she is not happy with Catullus alone,
I shall bear with the affairs of my mistress, for they are rare
    and she is circumspect,
lest I should be too tedious, in the manner of boors.
Often even Juno, greatest of the heaven-dwellers
swallows burning anger due to her husband's infidelity,
knowing all-loving Jupiter's plenteous affairs.
And yet to compare men with gods is not right. . .

But she did not, conducted by her father's hand,   (143–8)
come to a house fragrant with Assyrian scent,
but granted me stolen favours in a night of wonder,
favours taken from her very husband's bosom.
And so it is enough if to me and only me is given
the day which she marks out with the whiter stone of luck.

Catullus is thanking a friend (Allius) for a service rendered. The service sounds relatively small; Allius put at his and Lesbia's disposal a house to make love in. But clearly what it meant to Catullus, the quality of the moments passed there (I shall come back to this), made the service in effect inestimable.

I start by looking at lines 70-2, *quo mea se molli candida diua* . . . These are in fact a fine example of Catullus' exploitation of dramatic situation, the technique of the Lesbia polymetrics; though here Catullus re-creates the drama in a report rather than an enactment. Lesbia is approaching the house lent by Allius; Catullus is already waiting within. We witness Catullus waiting. But the Lesbia he waits for seems positively numinous, a creature of dreams ('and my fair goddess betook herself there with gentle step. She set her shining foot on the worn threshold . . .'). We must ask, *why*? Why does she seem so numinous? The simple answer to that is: because that is how she seemed to Catullus at the time; because, to put it another way, of the special quality and effect of those particular moments. And Catullus now re-creates those moments for us, to impart understanding of them to us. Dramatic re-creation will give us an understanding of things hard to analyse.

The particularity of these moments is their condition of heightened expectancy. Catullus is in fact touching on a phenomenon which is probably familiar to all. It is by way of being a truth that expectation creates excitement, and excitement can magnify even mythicize the object of excited expectancy. Perhaps no beloved is ever quite so beautiful, so divine, as in the moments just before she arrives. That is a rather sombre but frequent fact of life that lovers with impressionable sensibilities have to face. That is anyway what Catullus is talking about. Lines 70-2 re-create his own romanticizing of Lesbia in the moments of expectation just before she arrived at the *domus*. And by re-creating the moments and the romanticizing, Catullus communicates to us an abundance of knowable but hardly expressible things: the power of romantic expectancy to magnify.

These lines in fact take us to a climactic and pivotal moment: the sound of Lesbia's shoe on the threshold. It is indeed a climactic moment, and it is pivotal. It is the high point of romance; but in seconds Lesbia will enter the house and then she will *change*. She must change. She will be a creature of flesh. However wonderful, she can hardly remain the *candida diua*. That was the creation of expectancy.

What Catullus now does (73 ff.) is remarkable. He holds the pivotal, climactic moment—through 58 lines. Lesbia's foot is frozen on the threshold while a massive simile (plus sundry diversions) develops: Laodamia. Why this huge simile? What does it represent?

For one thing it means (I suppose) that Catullus in his re-experiencing of the events of the *domus* clings very tenaciously to the last seconds of the period of expectancy. That must make us have our doubts or fears about how reality matched romantic expectations. It certainly creates suspense. More importantly it means that Catullus has not yet conveyed all he wants to convey about those final moments. He has dramatically evoked the scene and communicated understanding that way, but still there are things he wants to say which he senses are unsaid. Therefore he enlists the assistance of comparison and myth.

Why particularly Laodamia? The basic answer to that lies in Catullus' vision of his relationship with Lesbia as *marriage* (above, p. 34). His sense of expectation while waiting not only elevated Lesbia into a goddess; it also set a marriage dream into motion. Therein in fact had lain much of the magic of Allius' service: it had enabled the actualization, for a while, of that dream. Line 68 is crucial. In Catullus' eyes Allius had given them not simply a place for a clandestine meeting but: *isque domum nobis isque dedit dominae*, 'he gave a house to me and to a (or *its* or *my*) mistress.' *domus* connotes 'home', the home of man and wife; and though the interpretation of *dominae* is problematic I think it is certain that it refers to Lesbia and that it means 'mistress'. And it means 'mistress' not in the sense of 'mistress of a slave' but 'mistress of a house', 'the lady': in combination with *domus*, *domina* can hardly mean anything else.[29] Allius' kindness therefore had allowed the Catullan fancy of marriage to take shape: Catullus was the *dominus* awaiting the arrival of a beloved *domina*. He was a romantic husband waiting for a divine wife. A wife, who was, too, like Laodamia.

In a way Laodamia selected herself. Traditionally she was the loving, passionate wife *par excellence*, the beautiful, faithful wife *par excellence*, devoted to her husband to the extent that life was insupportable without him. In fact without him she was literally unable to live: note 106 *ereptum est uita dulcius atque anima/coniugium*, 'marriage snatched away that was sweeter than life, sweeter than her soul'; note too line 84. Laodamia is one of the most touching and appealing figures from the resonant world of mythology, certainly the most appealing wife. She connoted more to someone familiar with mythology than could ever have been stated. That is why Catullus used myth at this point—and Laodamia in particular. Since he was trying to illuminate and to maintain the vision he had possessed of Lesbia as a romantic devoted wife, Laodamia did rather suggest herself.

But the myth obviously had other and discordant implications and Catullus has other and profounder purposes in using it. He in fact selected the story of Laodamia because it could serve *two* broad functions. It could illuminate and maintain a romantic vision, as I have just described. It could also simultaneously adumbrate darker things. At this point it is vital to stress that the use of myth here is not allegory: there is no 'one for one' correspondence between what illuminates and what is illuminated. Rather, the myth generates many implications on various levels. That is its great value. I can of course only hope to point to a few of them here.[30]

And to focus some of them, it will be useful to look ahead: to the point where Lesbia actually crosses the threshold. In a last burst of fancy Catullus describes her entry (131–4). And then in lines that are still tender and loving he confronts the truth (135–48). The magic of expectancy has (as we anticipated) dissipated and Lesbia is no longer—she no longer could be—the creature of dreams. She is not a goddess, not a mythical faithful wife, not a wife or *domina* at all (emphatically not), and not even faithful in her adultery to Catullus. All this is explicitly stated. But Catullus will not make a fuss or be tediously insistent. He loves her and it is enough. Indeed Lesbia, Lesbia the creature of flesh, is dearer to him than life itself. That is the sense of the very last lines of the poem: *mihi quae me carior ipso est/lux mea qua uiua uiuere dulce mihi est*, 'she who is dearer to me than myself, my light of life; while she is alive, life is sweet for me.'

What we witness here in fact (from 131 on) is the step-by-step collapse of the romantic vision started in 70-2, then maintained and amplified in the myth of Laodamia. All the wonderful things that Laodamia was, Lesbia is not after all and is said not to be. Nevertheless, Catullus loves her—a moving declaration. Let us note in particular the final pathetic irony that the poem delivers. In those last two lines of the poem Catullus affirms precisely the transcending fidelity and devotion that he had attributed to Laodamia and, therefore, wishfully to Lesbia. Compare those lines with lines 84 and 106 mentioned above. It almost sounds as if Catullus chose and narrated the Laodamia myth with the very intention of setting up his own romanticizing for a cruel fall. And that I think is in a way exactly what he did do.

I think simply that Catullus' choice and manner of telling Laodamia's story not only issues from a desire to maintain and amplify a romantic vision of Lesbia; it also evidences a simultaneous awareness in the romancer that the vision is fantasy and bound to collapse. The implications of the myth are too unerringly at odds with truth in crucial respects for Catullus not to have had some sense of the discrepancy from the beginning. The emotional sources of the myth are therefore quite literally ambiguous: romanticizing and insight. Its purpose is to communicate a romanticism compromised by a sense of more sombre reality. And Catullus means us (I think) to have some awareness of the ambiguity in his mythical comparison virtually from the start. As his praises of Laodamia mount, so our awareness of the incongruity of the comparison should mount; and so should our sympathy for Catullus who is also aware of the incongruity but trying to cling to a romantic vision.

Further thought supports this line of interpretation; and both the romanticizing and the pathetic self-knowledge implicit in the myth are more pronounced than I have perhaps so far suggested. In the moments of expectancy of 70–2 and the immediately ensuing myth, Catullus is not just generally assimilating Lesbia to a wife. He sees these moments more precisely as the culmination of a *wedding* and views the future of their whole relationship as a romantic mythical marriage stretching before them. The text is in this respect quite explicit. The myth opens with Laodamia's arrival at Protesilaus' house as a *bride*; and that (the arrival at a *domus*) is the immediate point of contact between the situation of the myth and the situation of Catullus and Lesbia. And the implication that Catullus imagined specifically a wedding is confirmed by the sequel. When the romantic vision of the myth is demolished, the idea of a wedding is specifically rebutted: note lines 143 ff.: *nec tamen illa mihi dextra deducta paterna/fragrantem Assyrio uenit odore domum,/sed furtiua dedit mira munuscula nocte.*[31] (The *mira nox* refers I think to the night in the *domus* of Allius, and Catullus is here emphatically admitting that Lesbia was not then his bride.) So: the expectancy of 70–2 caused Catullus not just to compare Lesbia to a wife (and to a goddess, etc.) but to imagine those moments as the climax of a wedding, and the future of their relationship stretching before them as a whole romantic mythical marriage.

Or rather as a marriage like Protesilaus' and Laodamia's. The comparison is of course disastrously equivocal, as becomes clear when we view it in this more exact way. The marriage of Protesilaus to Laodamia was indeed one of the most romantic and tender in mythology. It was also uniquely tragic, doomed from its inception. And Catullus emphasizes that fact by inventing or highlighting a detail: the *pax deorum*, the agreement of the gods to the marriage, had not been obtained by sacrifice at the outset (75–6); hence inevitably the tragic end followed. So Catullus' choice of myth supports his romantic vision; but it also radiates disaster. A *domus* that was *incepta frustra* (74–5) is an unhappy illustration for someone imagining a romantic *domus* for himself and his beloved. Catullus wishes and tries to believe in his 'marriage' to Lesbia; *and* he knows it is doomed. His choice of so ambiguous a myth implies and communicates just that. There was in fact a presentiment of the fantasy marriage's doom already in the dramatic scene of 70–2. Lesbia's foot knocking on the threshold is, whatever else, an unlucky omen for a bride.

Catullus therefore both in his initial dramatic re-creation and in his myth dreams and sees through his dreaming. Re-created drama allows us to intuit more than could ever be encompassed by statement. And so does myth: this is something we have not met before. Like drama myth allows us to infer the inexpressible; it suggests, adumbrates (it does *not* dictate), stimulating and drawing upon our imaginative response. Like drama, too, myth provides a living context for diction, encouraging a rich verbal texture; I shall not even begin to try to paraphrase the implications and repercussions in context of (for example) *coniugis, amore,* and *domum* in lines 73–4. The use of myth to assist in the illumination of personal feelings is one of the original *and* great accomplishments of this poem.

6. Conclusion

I shall now try to summarize the achievements of Catullus as a love poet. The first must be, in a word, 'Lesbia'. Catullus is the first ancient poet to treat a love-affair with one commanding lover in depth, in a related collection of mutually deepening poems. This had simply not happened before. But it will now be the fashion. Art will imitate art and life will imitate art and we shall observe how Propertius finds himself compelled to write about Cynthia, Tibullus about Delia, and Ovid about Corinna. And before them we know that Varro of Atax wrote about a Leucadia and Cornelius Gallus wrote about Lycoris (Cytheris); but their works are unfortunately lost. In this respect alone Catullus' influence was enormous.

He experimented with different methods of love poetry, some more successful than others; and that meant that lessons were available to be learnt by the next generation. His analytical epigrams, in spite of their originality of form and language, were not successful poetry. But they did pithily advertise his remarkable aspirations and feelings in love. The social implications of these aspirations I shall touch on in chapter four. But let us here note that the epigrams brought into the conscious awareness of succeeding poets something they might only have been unconsciously aware of: a sense of the great ambivalences that love can engender. And (I now make explicit a point so far only implicit) they promulgated the principles of a new erotic romanticism. Formulating a relationship of profound equality (*amicitia*, *foedus*–marriage) Catullus was in fact making a definably romantic statement. He was sacrificing in exchange for his ideal of love the pride of place that the male in a heterosexual affair might at that time reasonably have expected. It was not just that the object of an upper-class man's passionate love was traditionally his social inferior. She was his psychological inferior too (the constant Greek distinction between *eron* and *eromenos* or *eromene* is implicit in Roman thinking).[32]

Catullus also richly developed the potential of the traditional dramatic poem. And perhaps there is his most consistently good poetry. The success of these poems and how it was achieved must have much impressed his followers. Finally in one poem, poem 68, he treated aspects of his relationship with Lesbia at great length in the elegiac metre; and he exploited not only dramatic re-creation but mythical narrative. The Alexandrian Greek poets had perfected the art of allusive, subjectively told myths in elegiacs. None, however, had used it systematically and explicitly like this to illuminate their own current feelings. This was another example of Catullus' that was to have most important and direct influence.

III

Propertius and Tibullus: Preliminaries

Propertius was born not earlier than 57 BC and probably in the early 40s, at Assisi in Umbria (he was thus about thirty-five years younger than Catullus). His family was equestrian and suffered in land confiscations—presumably those of 41/40.[1] After the success of his first book, the *monobiblos* (which he addresses to a friend, Tullus; it was published in the early twenties BC: see below), Propertius was admitted to the imperial circle of poets under the patronage of Maecenas. Something of Propertius' personality will emerge from the poems I discuss; readers of the complete works will find fuller revelation.

Cynthia, the mistress who (so Propertius says) inspired his poetry, must delay us a moment. I think the poems do offer us a coherent, and vivid picture.[2] We find a woman of fine artistic accomplishments who is also fond of the lower sympotic pleasures; superstitious, imperious, wilful, fearsome in temper—but plaintive if she chooses, or feels threatened; pleasurably passionate—again if she chooses.[3] I could go on: Propertius provides a lot of detail, direct and circumstantial. But the point I simply want to make is that the figure who emerges is rounded and credible: a compelling 'courtesan', amateur or professional; her exact social status is impossible for us to pin down, in spite of a poem (2. 7) which must have spoken clearly to Propertius' contemporaries.[4]

I ought to clarify one assumption that I am making here and shall make in my chapter on Propertius' poetry. When Propertius writes a poem that concerns a beloved but does not actually name her, I assume that she is Cynthia unless there is good reason to believe otherwise. This seems to me reasonable, indeed the only sensible course. Repeatedly and throughout his work Propertius tells us, Cynthia, and anyone who will listen, that he is the lover of one girl, Cynthia; he has only been the lover (the true lover) of this one girl; and she will in the future be his only girl: see for example 1. 12. 19–20,

2. 13. 35-6, 2. 15. 31 ff., 2. 20. 17 ff., 2. 25. 1, 2. 30B, 3. 15. 1-10. If that is what he says throughout his poems, then it seems perverse to deny that a girl who, in these poems, is talked of in captivated, loving terms, is Cynthia. Note too that Propertius explicitly refuses at times of love-troubles what was the conventional advice on those occasions:[5] get another girl (1. 12. 17 ff., 2. 9. 45 f., 2. 17. 17 f. (cf. 1. 19. 13 ff.)). And when he does suddenly adopt a promiscuous attitude, it startles one by its difference (2. 22A); Propertius explicitly announces that it is a radical turn-about (2. 23) and (I think) explains it as due to Cynthia's non-compliance (2. 24A);[6] and the mood does not last long: 2. 24C, 2. 25, etc.

Tibullus was born between 55 and 48 BC. He died in 19 BC. An anonymous *Life* offers us the interesting information that he was good-looking (confirmed by Horace, *Epist.* 1. 4. 6)— and something of a macaroni (*insignis forma cultuque corporis obseruabilis,* 'remarkably handsome and punctilious in his attention to dress'); also that he was of equestrian rank.[7]

From Horace (*Epist.* 1. 4. 2) we gather that Tibullus had a country estate at Pedum, between Tibur and Praeneste. A family estate figures prominently in his poetry. He tells us that it has been much diminished (1. 1. 19 f., 41 f.), presumably in confiscations to provide settlements for soldiers (cf. Propertius). He makes a big thing of his consequent straitened circumstances. That was not quite how Horace saw it (*Epist.* 1. 4. 7, 'the gods have given you wealth'); but poverty is always relative.

A most interesting fact is that he was never attracted or never admitted to the imperial circle of writers. His patron was the soldier, statesman, and orator, M. Valerius Messalla Corvinus, who gathered quite a number of poets around him. (And Tibullus was not just a poet in Messalla's entourage; he served on *militia* with him (p. 74).) Messalla was deeply conservative, indeed republican in spirit; but not so much or in such a way that he could not well complement Augustus.[8] We may infer a rival circle of poets around him, but not, I think, an anti-imperial one.

Tibullus writes love poems of comparable intensity to or about *three* lovers—a fact of some interest, which we shall have to evaluate: Delia and the boy Marathus in Book I, Nemesis in Book 2. I shall comment on the identity or character of the lovers at appropriate moments. None stands out with the individuality of Propertius' Cynthia.

Ovid lists Tibullus before Propertius (*Trist.* 4. 10. 51-3) but they were approximate contemporaries. Tibullus' first book appeared after Propertius' *monobiblos* but before the completion of Propertius' second book.[9] The two poets do not mention each other—but each influenced the other (pp. 132-3, 179 ff.); and the Elegist of the imperial circle indulges in at least one swipe at his counterpart among Messalla's poets: 2. 5.[10]

Poem 5 of Tibullus' Book 2 refers to an event that could not have long antedated his death and this short book may be a posthumous collection.[11]

IV

The Life of Love

1. Introductory

When Propertius' *monobiblos* appeared in the early twenties the civil wars had brought an end to the republic and the door was open for regular imperial government. It had been a time of revolutionary political activity, fervour, and change.

Changes in moral and sexual attitudes were of a different kind; in a way they did not really change. Attitudes simply became more entrenched, the separating lines more clear-cut. And the manner of making one's views felt changed. Conservative traditionalism acquired a formidable advocate. Already in the 30s, it seems, Octavian (the future Augustus) was turning his thoughts to moral regeneration. And he was prepared to lend traditional veneration for family, *patria*, and honour the muscle of an autocrat: where the *maiores* had for the most part observed, exhorted, praised, or deplored, Octavian was prepared to punish and compel. He *organized* morality as everything else and brought it into the scope of public law.[1]

Opponents shifted their emphasis. Rather than simply defy accusations of immorality, they argued their case as an alternative morality; what was implicit became explicit. The generation of Catullus became the generation of the Elegists. The 'life of love' was codified.[2]

2. The life of love (1): eternity

It had been Catullus' aspiration that love should be for life (see p. 37). Note too the implications of poem 5, *uiuamus, mea Lesbia, atque amemus*. The attitude assumed here (simple though it may seem) is important. If we recall the conventional view that love was properly a *ludus*, a *ludus* belonging to youth (responsible men had more important things to do, see pp. 1–2), we shall realize that Catullus' position has a provocativeness (moral, philosophical, and social) that is easy to miss.

The early Elegists adopt the Catullan view and broadcast it. Neither fickle time nor even the onset of age (but see below) will change their love. It is hoped with greater or lesser confidence that the beloved will be similarly devoted. Cf. e.g. Prop. 1. 12. 19 f.:

> mi neque amare aliam neque ab hac desistere
> fas est
> Cynthia prima fuit, Cynthia finis erit.

> For me it is not right to love another or stop
> loving her.
> Cynthia was the first, Cynthia will be the end.

Cf. too 1. 15. 29 ff., 2. 6. 41 f., 7. 19, 21. 19–20. Lines 2. 1. 65 f. phrase the idea differently; as often (cf. below) Propertius adopts the condemnatory terms that society might use:

> hoc si quis uitium poterit mihi demere, solus
> Tantaleae poterit tradere poma manu.

> If anyone could remove this vice from me,
> he could put fruit in Tantalus' hand.

That is, it is impossible. 2. 15. 36 is characteristic in another way:

> huius ero uiuus, mortuus huius ero.

> I shall be hers in life and hers in death.

Love until *death* is a favoured Propertian emphasis: see p. 141. He can consider love after death too: pp. 100–102.

One fact to notice (it is psychologically very plausible and therefore revealing) is that although Propertius is committed to love's surviving for life, he does not as a rule face the full implications of that commitment. His own and Cynthia's *ageing* is usually ignored. Exceptions to this are few and interesting.[3] One sees Propertius' point. Horace confronted the fact of ageing and came to a very different view of life and love (pp. 204–15). Romantic aspiration needs the indulgence of a blind eye.

Unless (apparently) you are Tibullus: Tibullan commitment

to lifelong love can, it seems, more easily accommodate the problem of age. Cf. 1. 6. 85–6:

> nos, Delia, amoris
> exemplum cana simus uterque coma.

> Delia, you & I
> must be Love's paradigm when we are both
> white-haired.
>
> (Lee)

And 1. 1. 59–62

> te spectem suprema mihi cum uenerit hora;
>   te teneam moriens deficiente manu.
> flebis et arsuro positum me, Delia, lecto,
>   tristibus et lacrimis oscula mixta dabis.

> O let me gaze at you, when my last hour comes—
> hold you, as I die, in my failing grasp!
> Delia, you will weep for me laid on the bed of
>   burning
> and you will give me kisses mixed with bitter tears.
>
> (Lee)

is followed in 69 ff. by these 'Horatian' lines:

> interea, dum fata sinunt, iungamus amores:
>   iam ueniet tenebris Mors adoperta caput;
> iam subrepet iners aetas, neque amare decebit,
>   dicere nec cano blanditias capite.

> Meanwhile, with Fate's permission, let us unite and
>   love.
> Tomorrow Death will come, head hooded—in the dark,
> or useless Age creep up, and it will not be seemly
> to make white-headed love or pretty speeches.
>
> (Lee)

But perhaps 1. 1. 59 ff. and 69 ff. are inconsistent. There is a point worth attention here.[4]

3. The life of love (2): the lover and society (militia amoris)

Attitudes to life implicit in Catullus' poetry (including 'love is forever') amounted, we could say, to a virtual alternative social creed; his romanticism had public as well as private (above, p. 61) implications.

Catullus served a spell in the entourage of the governor of Bithynia.[5] This (*militia*, 'military service') was as we shall see exactly the sort of thing a young man of Catullus' class should do if he had a proper, conventional career in mind. For Catullus it was clearly no more than a distasteful brush with convention.[6] His priorities and values were different. He was profoundly and provocatively devoted to occupations of leisure (*otium*), to poetry, and (in particular) to love. Years of effort lavished on a poem is a matter for praise;[7] solemn protestations of deeply Roman obligation are uttered to a girl-friend; the girl-friend is called his 'life', and the implications of that term are accepted. Catullus ignores the normal rewards and honour that a man of his class could expect in *negotium*, to court the rewards of *otium*. Love is not only to last for life, it is the most serious occupation of life; love and poetry are his *negotium*, for which he sacrifices virtually all else. Here was a set of values—romantic values—to enrage conventional opinion; we should remember (for example) Cicero's careful qualification of the role of love in life (above, pp. 1-2). And we have evidence that the Catullan phenomenon did actually enrage Cicero: in his oration *Pro Sestio* (56 BC) Cicero vilifies an idle society of pleasure in terms that sound very like a jaundiced and malevolent misrepresentation of the world we see reflected in Catullus' poems.[8]

By the time we get to the first books of the early Elegists we find a renunciation of conventional life explicitly and formally declared. An alternative social creed finds and emblazons itself.

Interestingly the two Elegists put it (at this stage) in rather different ways, or at least moods. Tibullus, whose first book is published a little after Propertius' *monobiblos* (above, p. 64), makes the more unequivocal statement. His first poem is virtually programmatic. In the opening lines he expresses hopes for a *uita iners*, a life without *negotium*, in the country (a typically Tibullan emphasis) and derides the wealth that *labor* in military service brings. In 45–52 wealth, which demands effort, is judged inferior to love and serenity in comparative idleness. In 53–8 Tibullus directly expresses his preference for a life of love with Delia to a life of honourable military action. He starts politely (because he is contrasting himself with his patron, the great Messalla) but nevertheless firmly:

> te bellare decet terra, Messalla, marique
> ut domus hostiles praeferat exuuias.
> me retinent uinctum formosae uincla puellae . . .
>
> It befits you Messalla, to make war by land and sea
> so that your house may display spoils taken from the enemy.
> But the bonds of a lovely girl hold me, a prisoner . . .

He concludes with an enthusiastic statement of his own commitment to love and unmanly *otium*:

> non ego laudari curo, mea Delia; tecum
> dum modo sim, quaeso segnis inersque uocer.
>
> I don't care about esteem, Delia.
> Provided that I am with you, I court the name idle, inactive.

And the life of love with Delia is also (it is hoped) to be in truth lifelong, as we saw above (lines 59–60).

Many more such passages could be cited from this and other poems. But the message is clear and for the moment adequately illustrated. Tibullus is explicitly advocating inactivity, *otium*, and love in contrast to conventionally proper and honourable pursuits: military service, the pursuit of esteem and wealth. And he provocatively accepts for himself society's pejorative terms, positively emblazoning what Cicero, for example, had derided (this had *not* been a Catullan habit).[9] The Elegist's declaration is designed as a deliberate affront. Catullan attitudes have been codified into a flagrantly provocative creed.

Propertius argues for the life of love in his first book as explicitly as Tibullus. But he acknowledges more complexity; and (a fact not unconnected with this: see below) he doesn't talk in generalities but considers a specific case, that of himself and his friend Tullus.

In poem 6 he rejects an invitation from Tullus, nephew of the proconsul of Asia in 30–29 BC, to accompany him as a member of his uncle's staff, and in the course of the poem contrasts his own life of love with Tullus' approaching life of military action. He commits himself, like Tibullus, to his life of love, which he avows to be disreputable, and rejects Tullus' honourable course. But his espousal of the dishonourable is less enthusiastic than Tibullus' (25 f.):

> me sine quem semper uoluit fortuna iacere
> hanc animam extremae reddere nequitiae

> Allow me, whom fortune always wished to be low,
> to surrender this life to utter depravity.

Cf. too 29 f.:

> non ego sum laudi, non natus idoneus armis
> hanc me militiam fata subire uolunt.

> I was not born for esteem and arms.
> The fates want me to undergo *this* soldiering (i.e.
> love).

Meanwhile there is no derision at, nor even overt criticism of, Tullus' life of military action—rather indeed the contrary (21-4). Like Tibullus, Propertius is committed to the life of love for life: cf. 26 above; also 27 f.:

> multi longinquo periere in amore libenter,
> in quorum numero me quoque terra tegat.

> Many have willingly died in a long love.
> Among this number may earth also cover me.

And see above, p. 66. But unlike Tibullus, as these lines show (and cf. 2. 1. 65 f.), he does not seem too overjoyed about it.

We find the same general pattern in poem 14 where Propertius contrasts love with wealth, an obvious achievement of a conventionally successful life. Again it is discussed in the specific situation—Propertius' love and Tullus' wealth; and again there is no obvious criticism of Tullus' portion and far from unequivocal praise of love. So in these two poems

Propertius emerges, like Tibullus, explicitly committed to the life of love; and he takes upon himself society's condemnatory terms—he does so more strikingly in 1. 1 (also addressed to Tullus) where he represents himself as subject to degradation, disease, folly, and madness.[10] But he suggests that his way is more of a painful necessity than a happy and clear-cut choice; his acceptance of condemnatory terms seems to be much less cheerful.

Propertius will in later books argue the superiority of the life of love with more confidence and vigour; and Tibullus will admit to more pain, problems, and compulsion in his choice.[11] In their first books in fact we catch an interesting moment. Propertius is perhaps the earliest poet so explicitly to argue so unorthodox a life. For him the issue is very topical and still *specific*; he is not yet interested in—he perhaps has not yet thought of—generalizing. That is one reason why his decision is difficult and his attitude more complex. A friend's career and achievements are not to be simply dismissed or decried; his own love which he admits to that same friend is painful and humiliating cannot be glibly preferred without some acknowledgement of the objections to such a preference. Tibullus writes in the wake of these Propertian beginnings; he formulates the life of love more generally; and while generalizing he can desire it more unequivocally. And perhaps his love-life was easier.

Militia amoris (the soldiering of love)

The Elegists found one distinct and telling method of projecting their creed which we should notice: *militia amoris*. (And approaching the figure from this, the proper direction, we shall be able to give a truer account of it than exists in the standard books.)[12]

Military imagery of love had been sparingly used in Greek (Hellenistic) poetry. Its growth and development was particularly Roman. We find it mainly in Roman Comedy—and then in the Elegists (it is not for example Catullan). Literary historians might have scrutinized this peculiar distribution with profit.

The general attraction of such imagery for Romans is comprehensible. Military life and customs were very close to ordinary Roman citizens—closer than to Hellenistic readers of Hellenistic literature.[13] Soldiering therefore offered lively and immediate illustrations that might be wittily discordant or unexpectedly and amusingly appropriate—love is both violent and supremely non-violent. These considerations account for the popularity of the image in the very Roman comedian Plautus.

They account partially for the popularity of the image with Propertius and Tibullus. But a comedian making fictional characters speak of the soldiering of love (when soldiers were often on stage) is something rather different from, rather more obvious than, personal love poets speaking of themselves in those terms. We remember that Catullus, the great progenitor of the Elegy, did not; and among the Alexandrian erotic epigrammatists it was a fairly insignificant conceit. Yet with the Augustan Elegists it suddenly becomes (it seems) fashionable. There must be particular reasons for this new interest. There are. They lie in the reality of *militia*, in what real 'soldiering' stood for at the time when the Elegists wrote and what its implications for them were.

In the first place *militia*, service under a provincial governor or general on campaign was, as has often been said above, a standard stage in the career of an ambitious young man. Whether or not he intended his ultimate *negotium* to be military in emphasis, *militia* was a wise course for him—for a time—to follow: it offered valuable experience, financial benefits, and a chance to secure the friendship and support of important people. This could be demonstrated countless times over. An interesting and amusing illustration is offered by letters of Cicero to a protégé, the jurist Trebatius Testa (known to us also from Horace, *Satires*, II. 1). Cicero had secured a position for Trebatius on the staff of Julius Caesar in Gaul. But Trebatius was none too thrilled with his golden opportunity, either before or during it, having a strong taste for the town; and Cicero had to write to him repeatedly, strengthening his resolve and pointing out the advantages.

(When Trebatius was finally reconciled to his *militia*, Cicero wrote to him again, with some humour, praising him for his fortitude: 'your letter showed that you are now bearing *militia* with firmness of purpose and that you are a brave and stout fellow (*esse fortem uirum et constantem*).')[14]

Here, in the fact that *militia* was a standard stage in a conventional career, lies one important reason for the popularity of the *militia amoris* figure with the Elegists. They were organizing and proclaiming the life of love as an alternative to conventional life; *militia* was symptomatic of conventional life; by professing their own *militia* the Elegists might neatly declare their dissociation. With bland insolence or subtler irony the figure could demonstrate that the life of love was *by definition* incompatible with, an aggressive alternative to, the life decreed by society.

Let us recall Tibullus' programmatic poem (1. 1), where Tibullus dissociates himself (at first very tactfully) from Messalla's military life of action:

> te bellare decet terra, Messalla, marique . . .   (53)
>
> It befits you, Messalla, to make war by land and sea . . .

Some lines later (75–7) he writes:

> hic ego dux milesque bonus: uos signa tubaeque,
>   ite procul, cupidis uulnera ferte uiris,
> ferte et opes.
>
> Here [i.e. amidst the boisterous brawls of love] I am general
>   and stout soldier. You standards and trumpets [of real
>   *militia*]
> hence far away! Take your wounds to greedy men,
> take wealth too!

Tibullus' attitude to a life of military action ultimately becomes clear and less tactful. He strikes a neatly provocative stance by transferring its esteemed terms to his own dishonourable but cherished life.

Tibullus we should note had an especial stimulus to use this particular method of provocatively stating his creed. At some time around this period he *did* himself do the standard thing and perform real *militia*: he was present on Messalla's Aquitanian campaign, and started with Messalla for other campaigns in the East but was prevented by sickness.[15] For Tibullus therefore, the one-time or occasional and no doubt pretty unwilling *miles*, the *militia amoris* must have been a particularly enjoyable, certainly a very relevant, way to present an unorthodox philosophy of comparative idleness.[16]

Propertius has only one manifest example of the image in the *monobiblos* but it is very prominent (since Propertius was never a *miles* himself, the image might not have suggested itself so immediately to him as to Tibullus). It occurs in the sixth poem, the poem to Tullus opting for the life of love rather than conventional life in the form of, precisely, *militia*. To Tullus he says

> tu patrui meritas conare anteire securis   (19)
>
> Do you make ready to march before your uncle's well-earned
> *fasces*.

As for himself (29–30):

> non ego sum laudi, non natus idoneus armis
>   hanc me militiam fata subire uolunt.
>
> I was not born suited for esteem and arms.
> The fates want me to undergo this *militia* [i.e. love] .

His use of *militia amoris* allows him *in a word* to show that the life of love is a rival to, completely incompatible with, a conventional and honourable life. It is itself *militia*.

At this interim point we may notice an incidental but interesting difference in Propertius' and Tibullus' understanding of the *militia amoris*. For Tibullus the stuff of erotic soldiering is, typically, the often physical quarrels lovers may have with their beloveds; he seems in fact to have found these unusually spicy. Propertius has in mind the act of love or the strategy leading to love as well as quarrels.

There was another aspect of real *militia* and another plank in the platform of the life of love which made the *militia* figure magnetic. *Militia* broadly considered might mean violence, savagery, and death; but the life of love proclaimed a virtual pacifism—something quite different incidentally from orthodox Augustan eulogies of Augustus' peace. The Elegists used *militia amoris* to declare their dissociation from war. The conventional world made wars and wars were frightful; 'war' existed in the life of love but was something other, and more or less delightful. Offering their own kind and definition of war the Elegists neatly demonstrated the incompatibility of real war with the life of love.

In 1. 3 Tibullus praises the Golden Age and castigates present times thus (47–50):

> non acies, non ira fuit, non bella, nec ensem
>   immiti saeuus duxerat arte faber.
> nunc Ioue sub domino caedes et uulnera semper,
>   nunc mare, nunc leti mille repente uiae.

> Anger and armies and war were not yet known:
> no blacksmith's cruel craft had forged the sword.
> But now, in Jove's dominion, it is always wounds & slaughter;
> now there is the sea and sudden Death's one thousand roads.
>
>   (Lee)

Soon after he is describing Elysium, where lovers live their afterlife in bliss. He includes these two lines (63 f.):

> ac iuuenum series teneris immixta puellis
>   ludit, et assidue proelia miscet Amor.

> Young men and tender girls make sport, lined up together,
> continually engaging in the battles of Love.
>
>   (Lee)

Love, the implication is, offers its own battles, harmless indeed pleasurable battles, alternative and obviously preferable battles to those of the real *militia* earlier evoked.

Tibullus opposes *bella Veneris* more directly to real war, carefully defining them and distinguishing them from military violence, in 1. 10. First note lines 1–4:

> quis fuit horrendos primus qui protulit enses?
>   quam ferus, et uere ferreus, ille fuit!

tum caedes hominum generi, tum proelia nata;
    tum breuior dirae mortis aperta uia est.

Tell me, who invented the terrifying sword?
Hard he must have been and truly iron-hearted.
War that day & slaughter were born to humanity;
that day there was opened a short cut to grim death.

(Lee)

Then 51 ff. (the aftermath of a country festival):

rusticus e lucoque uehit, male sobrius ipse,
    uxorem plaustro progeniemque domum.
sed Veneris tunc bella calent, scissosque capillos
    femina perfractas conqueriturque fores.
flet teneras subtusa genas, sed uictor et ipse
    flet sibi dementes tam ualuisse manus.
at lasciuus Amor rixae mala uerba ministrat,
    inter et iratum lentus utrumque sedet.
a lapis est ferrumque, suam quicumque puellam
    uerberat: e caelo deripit ille deos.
sit satis e membris tenuem rescindere uestem,
    sit satis ornatus dissoluisse comae,
sit lacrimas mouisse satis. quater ille beatus
    cui tenera irato flere puella potest.
sed manibus qui saeuus erit, scutumque sudemque
    is gerat et miti sit procul a Venere.

Home from the sacred grove the farmer far from sober
drives wife and children in the wagon.
Then Venus' war flares up. The woman then bewailing
torn hair and broken door
weeps for soft cheeks bruised, & the winner also weeps
for the mad strength in his hands.
But Love, the mischief-maker, feeds the brawling with abuse
& sits there obstinate between the angry pair.
Ah stone is he & steel who strikes his girl:
he drags down Gods from heaven.
It is enough to rip off the thin dress,
enough to disarrange the well-set hair,
enough to draw her tears. O four times happy he
whose anger makes a tender woman weep!
But the cruel-handed should carry shield & stake
& soldier far away from gentle Venus.

(Lee)

Love's 'war' is placed by Tibullus both implicitly and explicitly in complete opposition to real war; the life of love is totally (therefore) incompatible with it.

Propertius uses *militia amoris* to pacifist effect (for Propertius' pacifism see the splendid lines 2. 15. 41 ff.)[17] more boldly than Tibullus (though not in the *monobiblos*); his use also tends to be more general and inclusive, combining an effectively pacifist dissociation from war with a dissident dissociation from current patriotic posturing. E.g. 3. 5. 1-2:

> pacis Amor deus est, pacem ueneramur amantes:
> stant mihi cum domina proelia dura mea.

> Love is a god of peace, we lovers revere peace:
> my hard battles are with my mistress.

That is not only effectively pacifist, it is bravely pacifist: it alludes to and passes mute comment on Propertius' previous poem, ostensibly a jubilant reaction to Augustus' military preparations (3. 4. 1):

> arma deus Caesar dites meditatur ad Indos.

> Divine Caesar plans arms against the rich East.

pacis Amor deus est picks up and thus undermines the sincerity of *arma deus Caesar*. Note too 2. 14. 21-4:

> pulsabant alii frustra dominamque uocabant:
> mecum habuit positum lenta puella caput.
> haec mihi deuictis potior uictoria Parthis,
> haec spolia, haec reges, haec mihi currus erunt.

> Others knocked on the door in vain and called her 'mistress';
> relaxed, my girl rested her head by mine.
> This victory for me will be more potent than the conquering
> of Parthians,
> this will be my spoils, this my [captive] kings, this my
> triumphal chariot.

That implies a triumphant rejection of war (as a career as well as generally) and decries contemporary military aspirations. Finally let us look at 2. 7. 13-18:

> unde mihi patriis natos praebere triumphis?
> nullus de nostro sanguine miles erit.

> quod si uera meae comitarem castra puellae,
>   non mihi sat magnus Castoris iret equus.
> hinc etenim tantum meruit mea gloria nomen,
>   gloria ad hibernos lata Borysthenidas.

> How should I furnish sons for our country's triumphs?
> No one of my blood will be a soldier.
> But if the soldiering for me to do was the true kind, soldiering
>   under my mistress,[18]
> Castor's horse would not be big enough for me.
> From love-soldiering my glory has earned its great renown,
> glory that has been carried to the wintry inhabitants of
>   Borysthenis [on the Dnieper].

These brave lines also combine dissociation from current patriotic causes with a general rejection of war. They do it with splendid and brave insolence (*true* war is love-making . . .). And, as in the passages above, the *militia amoris* figure implies that the views uttered are part and parcel of the life of love. The life of love being war rules out cruder conceptions of war by definition.

4. The life of love (3): the lover and his beloved (seruitium amoris)

We have seen that Catullus' poetry embodied a romantic attitude towards society, and that the early Elegists then organized and emblazoned it. Catullus' attitude towards his beloved was also in a defined sense romantic (above p. 61). This the Elegists took up, but they also intensified it, and emblazoned their intensified form.

We remember that Catullus introduced three main areas of non-erotic life to illuminate his feelings for, and attitudes towards, his beloved: marriage, family relations, and *amicitia*. Two of these provided Propertius with notable assistance. First, the family. 1. 11. 21:

> an mihi nunc maior carae custodia matris?

> Would I guard more anxiously my own dear mother?

This implies a disinterested, protective concern analogous to that expressed in Catullus 72 (*sed pater ut gnatos diligit et generos*, above, p. 40). Two lines later in the same poem we find a more general expression of devotion that uses family imagery:

> tu mihi sola domus, tu, Cynthia, sola parentes.
>
> You only, Cynthia, are my home, you only my parents.

We might notice that *tu sola parentes* implies devoted *dependence* rather than protectiveness, almost in fact the opposite emphasis to line 21 and Catullus 72.

Propertius is fond of marriage terminology, particularly in his second book. I quote two examples, one obvious, one not so. At the end of 2. 6 (which throughout views Cynthia rather as a wife)[19] he protests devotion in these unambiguous terms:

> nos uxor numquam, numquam seducet amica.
>   semper amica mihi, semper et uxor eris.
>
> Never will a wife, never will a girl-friend separate me from
>   you.
> You will always be my girl-friend and always my wife.

The lines not only of course illuminate Propertius' feelings for Cynthia; they are also socially and politically provocative, against a background of legislation to enforce marriage: cf. 2. 7 and above, p. 65 (with note). In poem 13 he prophesies Cynthia's devotion to himself after his death (lines 51–2; some wishful or rhetorical thinking here):

> tu tamen amisso non numquam flebis amico.
>   fas est praeteritos semper amare uiros.
>
> Sometimes you will weep for your lost lover.
> It is right to love departed men/husbands for always.

Discreetly Propertius claims to be no more than a friend. But in his heart he feels that he is, or he wants to be, Cynthia's *husband*. Though *uir* is an ambiguous term ('man' or 'husband', like German *Mann*), it was 'right' (*fas*, that is, right and proper according to divine or natural law) for a woman to continue love for a deceased husband, not lover: that way she remained honourably *uniuira*. In fact Propertius seems here to slip into marriage *thinking* rather than adopt marriage terminology. It is often his way: this Catullan mode of devotion was most congenial and natural to him, and is frequently discernible.[20] We can discern it (but not family imagery) in Tibullus too: it shapes (possibly) the way Tibullus imagines Delia waiting for him in 1. 3 (lines 83 ff.); it shapes his vision of Delia officiating at the beloved country estate (1. 5. 21 ff.).

Catullus' third area of non-erotic language, *amicitia*, was in some ways his most revealing. It expressed his romanticism most definably: Catullus offered the full and resonant equality of *amicitia* to a lover. The language of *amicitia* does not play a very significant role in Propertius and Tibullus; to be more precise, they are *not* customarily disposed to represent their relationships fully, systematically as *amicitiae*.[21] On the contrary. Their romanticism now took a different direction—a direction incompatible in fact with their marriage dreams, but we should not look for consistency in romantics.

Conventional folk had derided or vilified abject lovers as sick, insane, and debased. The early Elegists, provocative spokesmen of an alternative morality, admitted as their inescapable (and, as we soon infer, elected) portion sickness or madness,[22]—and, too, debasement. And here, in debasement, was the material of a new romanticism, a possible trump. Catullus had offered the sacrifice of traditional superiority; Propertius and Tibullus would surrender equality. The altered emphasis that we observed in Propertius' use of family imagery was significant; but the Elegists found a more striking, a shocking way to play their trump.

The surrender of equality was emblazoned. Just as a telling method of projecting the lover's attitude towards society had been developed (*militia amoris*), so a way was evolved of concretely proclaiming the flagrantly provocative relation of the lover to his mistress—the personal condition of the life of love. Catullus had aspired to be the 'friend' of Lesbia; Propertius and Tibullus, debased and subject beyond such dreams, were their lovers' professed *slaves*. The *seruitium amoris*, 'slavery of love', takes shape.[23]

The emphases of the two poets in their use of the 'figure'

(so to call it)[24] are again different, and characteristic. In his first book Propertius professes his slavery as something that he bears unwillingly; and he concentrates on servile loss of free speech. He would even, he says (in a neat paradox, conveyed by ambiguity)[25], submit to servile punishments, provided that he gained the opportunity to speak what his anger prompted—to speak as a free man (1. 1. 27-8). In fact he only finds such liberty when he is alone in a forest and far from Cynthia (1. 18). Note too his comments on love and its servile effects in poems to Ponticus (1. 9) and Gallus (1. 10). Tibullus concentrates on servile physical humiliations—which he embraces almost masochistically. The two poets' difference in emphasis is neatly demonstrated by Tibull. 1. 5, where Tibullus *repents* of an outburst of brave, free words and *invites* servile punishments to prevent another such occurrence (lines 5-6):

> ure ferum et torque, libeat ne dicere quicquam
>   magnificum posthac: horrida uerba doma.

> Brand me for my wildness, rack me lest it please me to speak anything
> grandiloquent again. Tame my rough words.

We see therefore (among other things) a by now familiar variation in the degree to which the poets acquiesce in their state. But slavery as the state of both of them is sure and admitted. It is their most characteristic personal posture, proclaimed with increasing explicitness and generality.[26] It was, I think, Propertius and Tibullus who popularized, who gave effective shape to the *seruitium amoris* 'figure' as we know it. In it they found a concrete and provocative way of declaring the lover's avowed abjectness, the personal condition of the life of love, the new romanticism. The lover a self-confessed slave! Here was a focus for the appalled attentions of conventional sensibilities and a delightfully awful programme for the unconventional to rally to.

V

Propertius

1. Propertius and myth

At the end of my section on Catullus I discussed his use of
the Protesilaus and Laodamia myth in poem 68; and I said
that this use of mythical narrative to illustrate personal feel-
ing was both original and influential. I shall start my discus-
sion of Propertius' poetry with the topic of myth. Propertius
was one of those who were, directly or indirectly, much
influenced by Catullus; his invocation of myths is one of the
more striking features of his love poetry. He compresses the
long, circuitous Catullan story into compact *exempla*[1]—but
uses the technique pervasively.

With Propertius it is necessary to give some general intro-
duction on myth. We need to know what the position of
Greek mythology, more particularly the kind of Greek mytho-
logy that Propertius favours (erotic, sentimental, emotional,
bizarre), was in Propertius' time. How did he and his readers
view it?

We must pay attention to sources. How did Propertius
acquire his knowledge of the myths he uses? More impor-
tantly, what sort of familiarity did his readers have with this
type of myth, and how did they acquire it? Consideration of
sources is not simply an academic exercise. Sources affect the
knowledge they supply. The way we acquire knowledge
affects our reaction to that knowledge. The way in which
Propertius and his readers acquired their knowledge of myth
shaped their basic attitude to that myth. We need to know
something of that attitude; and therefore we must understand
something about their sources. We are trying to identify what
the world of myth *meant* to Romans of Propertius' time; for
without some such general understanding we can hardly
begin to appreciate the more particular contextual effects of
mythical *exempla* within a poem.

Possible sources are basically threefold: (1) poetry, (2)
mythological handbooks, (3) visual arts.

(1) It was the difficult Alexandrian rather than the Classical Greek poets who were attracted to the kind of myth Propertius tends to favour. They would therefore be his readiest poetical source. I have strong doubts whether Propertius read them very much, for any purpose, during his earlier career (the period of Books 1 and 2; cf. too below, pp. 147 f.). There is, simply, an absence of evidence; and he had little motive. He certainly had little motive to use them as source books.

(2) We are lucky enough to possess one of the many mythological handbooks that were produced. It refers to other handbooks; and it itself is a very interesting example: Parthenius' *Erotica Pathemata*, 'Tales of Tribulation in Love'. The book is written in simple, succinct Greek prose and contains summaries of many Alexandrian poems, including some by the proverbially obscure Euphorion. It is dedicated to the great Elegist and predecessor of Propertius, Cornelius Gallus, and marked down for his use. Parthenius stresses the simplicity of his summaries compared with the difficulty of the poetical sources and believes that Gallus will be able 'to draw from it what is suitable for him, whether for epic or elegiac verse'. We may infer from this that Cornelius Gallus, whom subsequent generations (and even it seems his contemporary Vergil)[2] regarded as an emulator of Euphorion, was in fact (at times anyway) content to get his Euphorion and other such poets in a conveniently simplified form; and I must say it doesn't surprise me. I have strong suspicions that Propertius availed himself of the same sort of source. Probability as well as the negative fact mentioned above suggests so. Where is a young man writing love Elegy most likely to hunt out mythical details? In the devious complexities of Callimachean and Euphorionic verse, or in the plain, handy summaries provided precisely for that purpose?

But here I am talking more of Propertius than his readers; the craftsman has more technical and detailed needs than his market. The third source was probably the most important for Propertius' readers and indeed (viewing the question widely) for Propertius: the visual arts, in particular wall-painting. This was the source that most significantly shaped writer's and reader's *general* attitude to the world of myth; for not only did it constantly offer familiarity with that world, it pressed it upon them. (The influence of the visual arts on Propertius is of course quite compatible with his use of handbooks which would be for *details*.)

By the second half of the first century BC mythological wall-painting filled the houses and therefore pervaded the lives of well-to-do Romans. 'The Roman house . . . becomes a kind of art gallery', as Strong puts it.[3] The documentary evidence for this is abundant (and interesting);[4] and invaluable examples of such art dating from a period at most only a little later than Propertius survive from Pompeii, Herculaneum, and Stabiae: vivid testimony to its nature and prevalence. Campania's disaster is our good fortune. The types of myth favoured by the mythological wall-painters are frequently erotic and sentimental; and there are parallels between particular subjects popular with the painters and Propertian mythical *exempla*.[5] The probability of my contention is therefore clear; and Propertius' specific indebtedness to visual art can sometimes be plausibly argued.[6] Let me here simply point to one interesting phenomenon, at 1. 3. 1-6: a famous opening trio of myths: Ariadne, Andromeda, and—a Bacchante. The third subject is in fact scarcely a myth, not a myth anyway like the story of Ariadne or Andromeda. The three *exempla* do not seem of a sort. But they are. The sleeping Bacchante was a favourite subject of the visual arts. So was the scene of Ariadne's abandonment; and so was Andromeda. Propertius shows his hand. He is thinking in terms of *pictures*, pictures of (quasi) myths, rather than of *mythology*.[7]

Given the paramount importance of painting as a medium of myth, we shall have to gain some idea of what that painting was like: for people's attitude to myth will have been conditioned by their response to and therefore the nature of that painting. And we can gain a vivid impression of it by going to Pompeii and the other towns and relevant museums, by looking at the various books of reproductions—or even a popular general book like Maiuri's *Roman Painting*.

Some comments of Maiuri will have to suffice here.

<The> fabulous world of heroes and amorous adventures was a godsend for our painters (i.e. the mythological painters at Pompeii), and we find an aura of romanticism clinging to all their pictures, whose basic theme was love's ineluctable dominion over the hearts of men and gods. Thus Hercules is not merely the benevolent hero, slayer of monsters; he is also love's victim and its henchman. . . . Theseus' famous victory over the Minotaur (Basilica of Herculaneum) had an inglorious sequel in his desertion of Ariadne (House of the Tragic Poet) and this theme of the lovely, hapless victim marooned on the desert island . . . was very popular with Campanian painters.[8]

On the landscape of mythological paintings he writes:

From the Second Style (i.e. the second part of the 1st century B.C.) onwards, landscape bulked large in the paintings with mythological or epic subjects. It took a poetic, idealized form . . . the painter did not set out to paint the 'likeness' of any real place, he built up an imaginary world . . . the colour is subdued, romantic, and there is a poetic glamour . . .[9]

The general style of painting begins to be evident: 'romantic' is a word that recurs. And it is not only in 'romantic' stories that we find a 'romantic' style and aura. For example, this is Maiuri's comment on a picture of Diana the Huntress at Stabiae: 'Diana wears a chiton and a flowing mantle reaching to the ankles . . . she looks more like a *citharoedus* than like the Goddess of the hunt.'[10]

Now if we digest these and other descriptions by critics of art, if we look at the paintings ourselves bearing in mind not only that mythology is popular in wall-painting but that wall-painting is in the real world its most prevalent medium ('the Roman house . . . becomes a kind of art gallery'): this is the way we shall come to the most genuine understanding of what the myths in practice, in actual life, meant to Romans of Propertius' time. They did not represent a grander stage of history as the Classical myths had done to the Classical Greeks—whose own quasi-historical traditions those myths were. They did not offer a 'means of expressing universal and absolute truth',[11] as some scholars think and as (arguably) the Classical myths had done to Pindar and Aeschylus. What myth could and typically did provide for Romans was a world of fable and glamour. We must never forget that it was the sort of thing that the well-to-do used to decorate their houses. It was *untruth*[12] rather than absolute truth: attractive fiction to brighten the tedious truth of house walls and everyday lives. The myths opened on to a fabulous world: a world of *fabulae*, where beings more beautiful, attractive, or terrible than real beings lived lives out of this world; a *romantic* world, in a defined sense. The world of these myths which diverted the prudent might command the credence of the romantic. A romantic, but only a romantic (prepared to suspend disbelief, to forego the certainties and securities of sensible citizens), might believe that this world could exist.

And if a 'romantic world' is what these myths basically suggested to the average well-to-do Roman of Propertius' time, it is probably what they basically suggested to Propertius. It was certainly I think the foundation upon which he worked; it was the response in his readership that he presupposed. But it was only a foundation. He then proceeded to build on that foundation, to develop his particularly Propertian use. I shall now describe in outline what this use was, and then illustrate it in practice.

A lover—a romantic lover—often dreams of reaching and sometimes feels he does reach splendid heights; he thinks he is in touch with a fabulous ecstasy. Or he may believe he is subject to fabulous suffering. At other times he may have a sense of disillusionment, of prosaic reality: such heightened states are mere fable. At one moment life and the beloved seem to him beautiful and wonderful (or appalling) beyond belief; at another time it may seem beyond belief that he could ever dream up such fiction. And there are many times when he must feel uncertain: what *is* real? His experience swings like a pendulum; and his sense of reality is unstable.

This anyway was Propertius' lot, as he represents it in his poetry. Fabulous peaks and fabulous troughs are characteristic of him, and so is an uncertain attitude towards his own fabulous feelings. And to express these characteristic moods myth was a favoured and most useful medium. It could illustrate his elation, his despair, his uncertainty—and disillusionment. It had just the right ambiguities. Since it evoked a romantic world it could (*function 1*) suggest the heightened existence that he as a romantic often believed he experienced —ecstasy or suffering. On the other hand since it evoked a romantic world, it could (*function 2*) suggest the fictional status that a sober mind might attribute to all such experience. And because it could suggest both these, it could also be useful in communicating (*function 3*) Propertius' uncertain attitude towards his own fabulous existence. Since Propertius does not often view himself and the world in total sobriety, (*3*) is more usual than (*2*).

So the romantic nature of myth made it a superb tool for the romantic poet. It has (*4*) a further function, or rather refinement in function. Propertius writes as a self-conscious romantic lover, a lover-poet. He writes in greater self-knowledge than a romantic lover would speak in. When therefore he cites myths suggesting a belief in romantic ecstasy, we should be on the look-out for hints of disbelief. This happens: sometimes but not always. I mean here something different from the quite neat ambiguity of mood communicated by myth in *function 3* above. I mean a credulously ecstatic mood that recognizes but suppresses intrusive reality and thus remains, for a time, dominant. The intricacy and detail of myth allowed Propertius to communicate this complex state of mind. Into a myth that projects belief in a heightened, splendid existence, the poet insinuates details that hint at but only hint at a different awareness. The myth shows the poet believing—but aware of facts which will destroy that belief. We should of course now think back to Catullus 68. The myth of Protesilaus and Laodamia showed Catullus dreaming—and seeing through his dreaming. Catullus used aspects of a myth to undermine its initial, apparent import. His procedure was more conspicuous than Propertius', and he was communicating a mood more clearly ambiguous than Propertius does with myth in *function 4*—a mood nearer in fact to those Propertius communicates with myth in *function 3*; but his method is close to the method of this last Propertian category.

Thus the summary: now some illustrations. The headings

in my summary will be revealed as too mechanical; but they are helpful starting-points. (I hope incidentally that the above paragraphs will further illuminate Catullus 68; I hope too that we now further appreciate the literary–historical importance of that poem.)

(1) *Myth believed*

2. 14. 1–10 provide a splendid example of Propertius' use of myth to illustrate a mood of accredited ecstasy:

> non ita Dardanio gauisus Atrida triumpho est,   ·
>   cum caderent magnae Laomedontis opes;
> nec sic errore exacto laetatus Ulixes,   .
>   cum tetigit carae litora Dulichiae;
> nec sic Electra, saluum cum aspexit Oresten,
>   cuius falsa tenens fleuerat ossa soror;
> nec sic incolumem Minois Thesea uidit,
>   Daedalium lino cum duce rexit iter;
> quanta ego praeterita collegi gaudia nocte:
>   immortalis ero, si altera talis erit.

> Not thus did Agamemnon rejoice in his triumph over Troy,
> when the great riches of Laomedon fell;
> not so happy was Ulysses when, his wandering completed,
> he touched the shores of his beloved Ithaca;
> not so happy was Electra when she saw Orestes safe,
> whose pretended bones she, his sister, had held and wept over;
> nor with as great joy did Ariadne see Theseus safe
> when he had governed his path through Daedalus' maze with
>   guiding thread:
> none had such joys as I gathered in the night gone by:
> I shall be immortal if there will be a second such as that!

Grand examples of happiness are cited from the world of myth to illustrate Propertius' feelings after a good night. Here he believes in the possibility, indeed the realization, of fabulous bliss, and the mythical *exempla* vividly expound that belief (but there is perhaps one discordant note: see p. 100). They evoke *romantic* happiness and that is what Propertius at the moment believes he has achieved. He believes he is on a par with these romantic figures. Or rather, he claims to believe he is actually superior: *non . . . nec . . . nec . . . nec.* The hyperbole is characteristic of Propertian elation—and has its humorous aspect (cf. the fabulous women whose beauty Cynthia surpasses at 1. 4. 5-8). And the choice of such heroically happy figures as Agamemnon and Odysseus is obviously made in the same spirit of *humorous* elation—and Agamemnon prepares the way for the polemical use of military imagery in lines 23-4 (see above, p. 77).

Myth representing a heightened existence in which the lover believes can be used less statically. At 2. 15. 11-16 Propertius puts a case to Cynthia and cites mythical *exempla* as evidence. Again we sense his humour as well as his romantic belief:

> non iuuat in caeco Venerem corrumpere motu:
>   si nescis, oculi sunt in amore duces.
> ipse Paris nuda fertur periisse Lacaena,
>   cum Menelaeo surgeret e thalamo:
> nudus et Endymion Phoebi cepisse sororem
>   dicitur et nudae concubuisse deae.

> Loving debased to blind motions holds no joy;
> The eyes, you must surely know, show love the way.
> Paris was lost, they say, as soon as he saw
> Helen rise naked from Menelaus' bed;
> And Endymion too in his nakedness took captive
> Apollo's sister and so he lay
> With the naked Goddess.
>   (translated by Ronald Musker)

Propertius is arguing that Cynthia should wear nothing in bed. The powerfully persuasive nakedness of Helen and Endymion is cited in support of his contention. Since Propertius and Cynthia live or may live on the plane of fabled lovers, they should act to type: so the witty reasoning goes.

Myth illustrating a heightened existence in which the lover believes can be used in argument with poignance and pathos. 2. 32. 29-40:

> sin autem longo nox una aut altera lusu
>   consumpta est, non me crimina parua mouent.
> Tyndaris externo patriam mutauit amore,
>   et sine decreto uiua reducta domum est.
> ipsa Venus fertur corrupta libidine Martis;
>   nec minus in caelo semper honesta fuit.

quamuis Ida Parim pastorem dicat amasse
   atque inter pecudes accubuissse deam,
hoc et Hamadryadum spectauit turba sororum
   Silenique senes et pater ipse chori;
cum quibus Idaeo legisti poma sub antro,
   supposita excipiens, Nai, caduca manu.

But if a night or two has been spent in lengthy indulgence,
   petty crimes do not affect me.
Helen exchanged her country for a foreigner's love,
   and was brought back home alive uncondemned.
Venus herself is said to have been corrupted by lust for Mars;
   but was not less honoured in heaven always.
Although Mount Ida tells how a goddess (Oenone) loved
      Paris, a shepherd,
   and lay with him among his flocks,
yet this her band of sister Hamadryads (nymphs) regarded
      with tolerance,
   and the old Sileni and the father of the company himself;
with them, o Naiad (Oenone), you gathered fruits in the
      glens of Ida,
   catching the falling fruits with upstretched hand.

Propertius tries to convince himself (in the mood of Catullus 68, a poem which is much in his mind here) that 'indiscretions' on Cynthia's part are tolerable. The examples of Helen, Venus, and Oenone are adduced. Since Propertius and Cynthia live or may live on the plane of such beings, he must remember its customs. The reasoning here is, or attempts to be, like that in the previous example; the world of myth illustrates the heightened existence of romantic lovers. But the effect is now most pathetic. Circumstances have compelled Propertius to entertain the belief that infidelity in the loved one is not incompatible with such heightened existence; and he seeks his *exempla* accordingly. Eloquently he makes the best of a bad job.

   We find Propertius using myth to communicate a heightened suffering that he believes he feels at 2. 13. 43–50:

atque utinam primis animam me ponere cunis
   iussisset quaeuis de Tribus una Soror.
nam quo tam dubiae seruetur spiritus horae?
   Nestoris est uisus post tria saecla cinis:

cui si longaeuae minuisset fata senectae
  barbarus Iliacis miles in aggeribus,
non ille Antilochi uidisset corpus humari,
  diceret aut 'O mors, cur mihi sera uenis?'

And oh that one of the three Sisters (the Fates)
had commanded that I should die in my cradle.
For to what purpose is life of such uncertain term
preserved? Nestor's ashes were seen only after three
generations. But if some foreign soldier on Troy's
ramparts had lessened his doom of long-drawn old
age, he would not have seen the body of (his son)
Antilochus being buried, or cried 'Oh death, why
do you come so late for me?'

What is the point of living? asks Propertius, after wishing that
he had died at birth. He then shifts to the story of Nestor,
illustrating the sadness that life can bring: Nestor lived to a
vast old age and witnessed the death of his own son. The
logical sequence hereabouts is hardly impeccable, but the aim
of the lines is not to display logic. The point got across is that
Propertius' despair is despair of fabled proportions: he passes
immediately from his own to the romantic world, effectively
equating the two, and thereby illustrates the fabulous,
romantic extent (as he sees it) of his own personal suffering.

Propertius uses myth to communicate heightened suffering
again at 2. 8. 29–40 (beautiful lines that we shall return to):

ille etiam abrepta desertus coniuge Achilles
  cessare in tectis pertulit arma sua.
uiderat ille fuga stratos in litore Achiuos,
  feruere et Hectorea Dorica castra face;
uiderat informem multa Patroclon harena
  porrectum et sparsas caede iacere comas,
omnia formosam propter Briseida passus:
  tantus in erepto saeuit amore dolor.
at postquam sera captiua est reddita poena,
  fortem illum Haemoniis Hectora traxit equis.
inferior multo cum sim uel matre uel armis,
  mirum, si de me iure triumphat Amor?

Even the great Achilles, when left forlorn, his mistress
    snatched away,
endured that his arms should lie unused in his tent.
He had seen the Greeks scattered in flight on the shore

and the Dorian (Greek) camp glowing from the torch of Hector.
He had seen Patroclus lying stretched out hideously over an
    expanse of sand
his hair spattered with blood.
All this Achilles suffered for the sake of lovely Briseis:
such is the force and savagery of grief when love is snatched
    away.
But after the captive girl (Briseis) was given back in
    tardy retribution,
then he dragged that mighty Hector at the heels of his
    Thessalian horses.
Since I am far inferior to him in mother and arms,
what wonder if Love rightfully triumphs over me?

Here the myth is used more dynamically, in an argument
again. Propertius cites Achilles' vast and destructive grief at
the loss of Briseis to justify his own grief at losing Cynthia.
One, the most immediate, aspect of the argument is based on
a professed *dissimilarity* to the mythical *exemplum*: if it is
right and unsurprising that mighty Achilles grieved, is it
wrong and surprising for feeble me? But the lines presuppose
a belief in the romantic world, in romantic suffering, and
imply the *affinity* of suffering of that vast extent with his
own: Propertius believes in grief like Achilles' and the text
suggests, inevitably, that Achilles' grief is, more or less, his.
(The statement of inferiority has in fact, from one point of
view, the effect of a rhetorical device—like the claim to
superiority in 2. 14. The latter emphasized Propertius' huge
elation, the former enlarges our sense of Propertian depres-
sion; but in both the underlying suggestion is of the identity
of his own and the mythical states.)

At 2. 17. 5-10 myth is used to make a more general
statement about the suffering of the lover (though the state-
ment is clearly meant to reflect Propertian experience). Here
the particular choices of myth are very relevant: they inform
about the nature of the suffering as well as suggest its fabulous
proportions:

> uel tu Tantalea moueare ad flumina sorte,
>   ut liquor arenti fallat ab ore sitim;
> uel tu Sisyphios licet admirere labores,
>   difficile ut toto monte uolutet onus;

durius in terris nihil est quod uiuat amante,
 nec, modo si sapias, quod minus esse uelis.

You may be moved by the lot of Tantalus at the river,
 how the water deceives his thirst, moving away from his
   parched mouth;
 you may marvel at the labours of Sisyphus,
 how the intractable weight of the stone rolls down the whole
   hill;[13]
 but in all the earth there is nothing that lives a harder
   life than a lover,
 nothing, if only you are wise, that you would less want to be.

This tells us not only that (according to Propertius' belief) the lover lives in romantic torment; it suggests detail about that torment. The lover is fabulously tantalized (*sitis*, 'thirst', is nicely suggestive, since it is used metaphorically of sexual frustration),[14] and subject to endless, futile (Sisyphian) labour.

(2) *Myth disbelieved*

The opening poem of Book 1 is programmatic, describing the nature of Propertius' love. He admits the sort of accusations that the sober were accustomed to level at romantic lovers—and uses their pejorative labels; and he invokes their and other remedies in despair of their efficacy. Unwillingly, it seems—in a very negative way—he declares his romantic heterodoxy (cf. above, pp. 69 ff.; the poem partners 1. 6 and 14).

Now let us follow the argument in the beginning of the poem. First Propertius tells his friend Tullus how his love started, how it threw him into his abject indignity and irresponsibility (1–6). Then he tells how he has been mad for a year; but Cynthia's reciprocation clearly leaves almost everything to be desired (7–8). Then he launches into the myth of Milanion, a lover who in great hardship constantly wooed his girl (Atalanta), constantly served his girl—and eventually got his girl. In Elegiac terms, the myth demonstrates *obsequium* rewarded:

Milanion nullos fugiendo, Tulle, labores
 saeuitiam durae contudit Iasidos.

nam modo Partheniis amens errabat in antris,
  < *there may well be a lacuna of two lines here* > [15]
ibat et hirsutas ille uidere feras;
ille etiam Hylaei percussus uulnere rami
  saucius Arcadiis rupibus ingemuit.
ergo uelocem potuit domuisse puellam:
  tantum in amore preces et bene facta ualent.

Milanion, Tullus, by fleeing no labours
quelled the cruelty of harsh Atalanta.
For sometimes he wandered distraught in Parthenian glens
< and uttered lamenting prayers amid the trees;
sometimes he carried hunting-nets in her service> [15]
and went to look upon shaggy wild beasts;
again, he was dealt a blow by Hylaeus' club
and, wounded, groaned on the crags of Arcadia.
So he was able to tame the swift-footed girl;
such is the power of prayers and services in love.

Now how will Propertius' reader react (reading the first
poem of this new book) at this point? He has been told (in
stark terms) that Propertius suffers madness, folly, debase-
ment, and frustration in the service of his beloved: he is a
romantic. A myth then follows which seems to paint Proper-
tius' type of suffering in more positive, or at least more
attractive, *romantic* terms (this version of Milanion is, though
rare, the sort of story that might colourfully adorn a wall): a
mythical lover suffers on mountains in the service of his wild
and uncomplaisant girl. And he wins her.

The Roman reader's expectations must now be assured.
The romantic lover has cited his romantic *exemplum*; we wait
for the equation. Even as Milanion, so Propertius. All is not
as stark as it seemed. Propertius' suffering *is* appalling, but
the moral tones of society do not reveal its real colour. It is
out of society's ken, out of this world, fabulous. And it will
be crowned with success, also out of this world. Even as
Milanion, so Propertius.

Not so, however. Propertius plays on these expectations
and surprises us. Milanion's success is *not* his: *in me tardus
Amor non ullas cogitat artes*, 'in my case Love is slow and
contrives no arts.' And he then reverts (19 ff.) to negative

terms again, to society's censorious terms, to evoke his suffering. He has cited Milanion only to dissociate himself from Milanion, from the world of romance. He cites the romantic world in *disbelief*: it is, as far as he is concerned, at this time, *mere* romance.

This is indeed a heterodox romantic. He opens his collection of poems admitting to the disgrace and folly of romantic life, but denies experience of, and suggests disbelief in, any compensatory ecstasy. And he even seems to find conventional society's terms of condemnation better suited to describing his suffering than the attractive hyperbole of myth. In a way this is doubly provocative. Propertius lives a life of folly and degradation but claims no compensatory factor and exploits no romantic camouflage. He sees himself in his opening poem *totally* (it seems) with sober, moral eyes—and yet does not do, or rather cannot do, anything about it.

But since Propertius launched into the myth leading us to expect equation, and since the contrast comes against our expectations, perhaps the myth suggests Propertius' *equivocal* rather than disbelieving attitude towards fabulous existence. When he started the myth perhaps he believed in it or half-believed; when he exits perhaps he still half-believes or wants to believe. Perhaps so. After all there is still time for his *obsequium* to be rewarded—fabulously. But all that negative, censorious, despairing terminology in 1–8 and 19 ff. confirms our impression of someone who at this point believes that myth (romance) is fiction. A strange and striking programmatic poem for a romantic poet—particularly stimulating, probably, for those who knew their Cornelius Gallus.[16]

(3) *Equivocal myth*

An uncertain attitude towards fable, towards romantic reality, seems to me clear in 1. 15. 9 ff.:

> at non sic Ithaci digressu mota Calypso
> desertis olim fleuerat aequoribus:
> multos illa dies incomptis maesta capillis
> sederat, iniusto multa locuta salo,

et quamuis numquam post haec uisura, dolebat
    illa tamen, longae conscia laetitiae . . .   (14)

quarum nulla tuos potuit conuertere mores,   (23)
    tu quoque uti fieres nobilis historia.

But not thus Calypso: moved by Ulysses' departure
she (once upon a time) wept by the deserted ocean.
For many days she sat in sorrow, her hair undressed,
complaining to the unfair sea.
And although she was never going to see him again, she
    continued to grieve,
aware of their long happiness . . .   (14)

Of these none could change your ways   (23)
so that you also might become glorious story.

Here again myth is used in argument. Propertius remonstrates
bitterly with Cynthia about her lack of fidelity in his time of
danger (illness). He cites a list of examples the first of which
is Calypso, expressively devoted to Odysseus even when he
left her. The implication is that Calypso is a fitting standard
for Cynthia. Do not he and she as romantic lovers live on the
same plane? Propertius believes in that kind of reality. Perhaps
he and she do not live on that plane; perhaps he does not
believe. Citing the *exemplum* makes Propertius face a certain
discrepancy. Lines 23-4 confess the inefficacy of Calypso's
(and others') example—and perhaps suggest its irrelevance.
But Propertius who soon proceeds to an eloquent declaration
of romantic devotion is not here *stating* the unreality or
impossibility of romantic experience. His attitude to myth is
simply uncertain, ambiguous. (The situation is very similar in
2. 9. 1-20, and indeed the whole movement of that poem is
interestingly comparable.)
    An uncertain attitude is also revealed in 2. 2:

liber eram et uacuo meditabar uiuere lecto;
    at me composita pace fefellit Amor.
cur haec in terris facies humana moratur?
    Iuppiter, ignosco pristina furta tua.

fulua coma est longaeque manus, et maxima toto
    corpore, et incedit uel Ioue digna soror,
aut cum Dulichias Pallas spatiatur ad aras,
    Gorgonis anguiferae pectus operta comis;
qualis et Ischomache Lapithae genus heroine,
    Centauris medio grata rapina mero;
Mercurio aut qualis fertur Boebeidos undis
    uirgineum Brimo composuisse latus.
cedite iam, diuae, quas pastor uiderat olim
    Idaeis tunicas ponere uerticibus.
hanc utinam faciem nolit mutare senectus,
    etsi Cumaeae saecula uatis aget.

I was free, I meant to live and sleep alone;
but Love deceived me when peace was made.
Why lingers on earth a mortal form like hers?
Jupiter, I pardon your stolen pleasures in olden times!
Auburn hair; long hands; a majestic stature;
a bearing worthy of Juno, sister of Jove,
or of Pallas Athene when she strides to Ithacan altars,
shielding her breast with the Gorgon's head that has
    snakes for hair.
She is like Ischomache, heroine child of the Lapiths,
a fitting spoil for the Centaurs amid the wine;
or like Brimo who, so it is said, by the waves of Boebeis,
laid her virgin side by Mercury.
Now yield, you goddesses whom of old the shepherd saw
set aside your clothes on the peaks of Ida!
Oh that old age may be unwilling to change this beauty,
although she will live for the ages of the Sibyl of Cumae!
    (This translation lifts much from Musker)

Propertius celebrates the extraordinary beauty and power of Cynthia. She is as mysterious, beautiful, and divine as the figures cited in comparison. Propertius believes in the romantic world in which he places his beloved. At least he believes until the end. At the end he admits (by implication) one doubt. If Cynthia is really divine (cf. Juno, Athene), she is immortal; but Propertius has enough sense of her mortality to wish away the effects of mortality from her. What he is doing is, at the last, tacitly modifying his romantic belief in one respect, responding to his own doubt. The divine myths which were believed now seem not entirely believed. They are real or not real, depending upon one's vantage point in the poem. (Note that the admission of doubt is in its turn compromised: the *etsi* clause maintains the possibility of a romantically long life. Incidentally, it is striking that Propertius should confront this most unwelcome of topics —Cynthia's mortality—at all (cf. above, p. 66). The extravagance of the claim implicit in his own *exemplum* more or less forces him.)

(4) *Myth believed—precariously*

1. 3. 1–8

> qualis Thesea iacuit cedente carina
>   languida desertis Cnosia litoribus;
> qualis et accubuit primo Cepheia somno
>   libera iam duris cotibus Andromede;
> nec minus assiduis Edonis fessa choreis
>   qualis in herboso concidit Apidano:
> talis uisa mihi mollem spirare quietem
>   Cynthia non certis nixa caput manibus . . .

Just as Ariadne lay, swooning on the deserted beach as Theseus' bark departed; just as Andromeda reclined in her first sleep free now from the harsh rocks; just as the Bacchante, no less wearied <than Andromeda> by her continuous dances, fell in sleep by the grassy Apidanus; so Cynthia seemed to me to breathe gentle rest, her head supported on uncertain hands . . .

Propertius reports and, as he does so, re-creates the atmosphere of a past, emotive episode (I have further discussion on the technique and effect of this poem, below, pp. 114 ff.). He returned home late one night from a party, tight. He found Cynthia asleep. The quoted myths (or rather 'myths': see above, p. 84) expound his attitude to and feelings for Cynthia on seeing her. She seemed like . . . the deserted Ariadne, the liberated Andromeda, a sleeping Bacchante. Two and probably three of these were familiar subjects from the visual arts (above, p. 84); all would radiate an immediate glamour to Propertius' readership, communicating the romantic aura in which he saw her. The basic power of the myths is enhanced by exotic language: the allusive Greek antonomasia, the elevated diction, the ornate phrasing, all increase the sense of romance. The details of the myths make further contributions. The deserted and faint Ariadne suggests a pathetic loneliness in Cynthia; the relaxation of Andromeda implies trials gone through; the Bacchante's weariness suggests a mighty exhaustion. These are the rapturous images of a lover believing in the romantic wonderfulness of his beloved; they are the sentimentally rapturous images of a lover believing in her romantic pathos. Notice however that it is a *comfortable* pathos. Cynthia has an air of weariness and loneliness deriving from the mythical world, but she is also sleeping the sleep of one who in the mythical world is freed from care. Her pathos demands no action. She rests secure in her world of statuesque romance.

So Propertius starts the poem believing in romance. He is credulously ecstatic. But he won't end the poem that way (see pp. 118 f.). Nor is his ecstatic mood at the beginning totally unshadowed. The myths contain details that hint at a different awareness. The myths show the poet believing—but with an uneasy, underlying appreciation of facts that will destroy that belief.

For he chooses myths that beg certain questions. There is, we might say, tension in them. If Cynthia seemed deserted and lonely like Ariadne, well, she was in a way. She had been deserted by Propertius who had been out at a late party; and Ariadne would have had harsh things to say to her Theseus. If Cynthia had worries from which, like Andromeda, she was released, these worries might be construed as Propertius' fault. It was certainly not he who released her; he was no rescuing Perseus. We sense behind the myths—they point that way—intrusive voices from the real world. We sense the sort of questions Cynthia is going to raise (when she wakes), questions which must put an end to Propertius' romanticizing. Propertius senses them too. His choice of such vulnerable myths reveals exactly that. And what of Cynthia the sleeping Bacchante? Bacchantes wake, and they may wake to rave. Behind his belief in Cynthia's romantic, beautiful exhaustion we detect his memory of her fearsome and well-documented

temper (above, p. 62). He duly gets a taste of it—and the
questions are asked, inevitably, and much more of the real
Cynthia is displayed in a romance-shattering way when,
inevitably, she wakes.

In 1. 3 belief in romance is forced to yield to an awareness
of prosaic reality. The sequence is clearly demonstrated.
Propertius is able to demonstrate it clearly because of the
role he has assigned to sleep. At the opening Cynthia was
asleep and compared to sleeping mythical figures. Already
that really begged a fundamental question. What happens
when she wakes? It is easy to build cosy fantasies round a
sleeping figure. Romance, though aided and abetted by wine,
is dependent upon Cynthia's sleep. Asleep Cynthia's person-
ality cannot much affect her lover's creative credulity. But
awake . . . Cynthia's sleep is the effective and clear condition
of Propertius' romanticizing, and her waking marks the
onset of reality. Sleep gives the poem clarity of plot and
sequence.

This clear sequence resolves the tension inherent in the
initial myths. Tracing such a sequence (from romantic to more
prosaic belief) is a distinct Propertian interest, though he
chooses not to match the clarity of 1. 3; he prosecutes this
interest via myth in *functions (3)* and *(4)*: cf. 2. 2 discussed
above. And myth in *function (4)* allows Propertius to illus-
trate underlying hesitations about romantic belief that are
often present at the outset. There is hesitation I think even in
the ecstacy of 2. 14 (above p. 88). Propertius puts his joy in
comparison with Ariadne's on seeing Theseus; but Theseus
was soon to leave his lover. In this way Propertius suggests his
fears about intrusive reality. Whether the poem then confirms
these fears or even takes them up again depends on one's
understanding of the text and its integrity.[17]

My last example shows hesitations in the myth which are
then resolved; romance gives way to cooler belief: 1. 19. In
this poem (which I look at again, pp. 140–146) the myth of
Protesilaus expounds Propertius' romantic belief (strange and
individual though it is, it is still belief) in the power of love to
transcend death. Lines 7–10:

illic Phylacides iucundae coniugis heros
   non potuit caecis immemor esse locis,
sed cupidus falsis attingere gaudia palmis
   Thessalus antiquam uenerat umbra domum.

There, in the regions of darkness, the hero Protesilaus
could not be unmindful of his sweet wife, but desirous
to reach his joy with illusory hands the Thessalian
came to his ancient home a shade.

But the myth hedges. By tradition Protesilaus returned to
Laodamia in full, satisfying form.[18] But Propertius talks of
his *falsis* . . . *palmis* (*falsus* 'false', 'pretended', 'illusory' could
also, significantly, mean 'cheated', 'deceived') and terms him
at the last only *umbra*, a word which ranges in implication
from shade and ghost to shadow and semblance. The myth
projects belief in a romantic truth (love transcending death)
—and yet adumbrates dubiety.

   This is confirmed at the end of the poem. Propertius con-
cludes:

quare, dum licet, inter nos laetemur amantes:
   non satis est ullo tempore longus amor.

Wherefore, while it is possible, let us love and be glad
   together:
love is not long enough in any extent of time.

What is the connection in thought? Why *wherefore*? One may
suppose that Propertius' injunction to love 'while it is possible'
issues from the doubts he has just previously expressed (19–
24) about the living Cynthia's likely fidelity to his dead self.
But it does not satisfactorily follow. Note particularly *dum
licet*: 'while it is possible', not 'while you love me', or 'before
you despise my tomb', or anything particular like that. The
obvious impulse for this sort of general injunction (as Catullus
confirms: poem 5) is the thought of *death*: 'since we cannot
rejoice as lovers *when dead*, let us do so *while it is possible*.'[19]
The conclusion tacitly admits what in fact has become increas-
ingly evident in the poem: Propertius' disbelief in the ability
of love *effectively*, *satisfactorily* to transcend death (below,
pp. 141–3). Propertian romanticism has had to cede to a

different and cooler view of love and death, resolving a tension implicit in the earlier part of the poem (in the myth). Again Propertius has shown himself forced to confront prosaic reality; again he has shown how suppressed doubts beset him at the outset; again we have a fine use of myth in *function* (*4*).

2. Propertian technique and structure
A. *The 'monobiblos'*

In his Lesbia epigrams Catullus tried to analyse the emotions, ideas, and ideals of love. The attempt I thought was a poetic failure, but a memorable one. As such it was important: true feelings about love that had hitherto largely been confined to implicit understanding or utterance were now advertised. Subsequent love poets could not but be influenced. In his polymetrics Catullus built upon more traditional modes of love· poetry, composing poems which enacted a little drama. In these and through these he *implied* the subtleties of emotion, idea—and personality. Some of them were a marked success. In poem 68 he combined this latter technique with a spectacular use of myth, and cast the whole in elegiacs, which, unlike the elegiacs of the epigrams, exploited that metre's potential for complex, formal artistry. Of all this Propertius (and presumably Cornelius Gallus before him) took careful note.

The metre of the epigrams and poem 68 was exclusively preferred. There are I think two, not entirely separable, reasons for this. The Elegists were clearly very much interested in formal artistry, and the elegiac metre provided them with a scope and flexibility that was unavailable in, say, hendecasyllables or scazons: although Propertius opted initially for the dramatic poem (see below), he was prepared to sacrifice the dramatic verisimilitude offered by these lyric metres (above, p. 43) for the *ars* of elegiacs. Secondly, it is clear that Gallus and Propertius consistently cared about their literary rank and role in a way that Catullus did not.[20] Propertius was keen to establish himself in a society where epic poetry stood in more or less undisputed prominence as *the* genre; and it was elegiac poetry that had been epic's continual and particular rival—so anyway it would appear from Propertius' vantage point. Elegiacs had a status and a particular kind of status which the little lyrics had not, and it appealed to him.

Propertius and no doubt Gallus were also influenced by the content of the epigrams. But the technique Propertius adopts in the *monobiblos* is fundamentally that of the Lesbia polymetrics. Virtually every Cynthia poem in the book enacts or reacts to a definite and single dramatic situation; it seems itself to *be* (or it reports) a drama—and it implies its content of feeling and personality. And virtually every poem makes a use of myth indebted to the splendours of Catullus' Protesilaus and Laodamia. The best of Catullus' Lesbia poetry has been abstracted, condensed, ordered.

1. 4. 1-4:

> quid mihi tam multas laudando, Basse, puellas
> mutatum domina cogis abire mea?
> quid me non pateris uitae quodcumque sequetur
> hoc magis assueto ducere seruitio?

> Why, Bassus, by praising so many girls
> do you compel me to change and leave my mistress?
> Why do you not allow me to lead whatever of life remains
> in this accustomed slavery?

Bassus has suggested to Propertius that he try other girls, easy girls (line 9). Propertius reacts: we have our poem.

Propertius suggests Bassus is *compelling* him (*cogo* is a word whose significance we should not underestimate),[21] that he will not *allow* him to stay as he is. How so? Obviously Bassus does not and cannot really *constrain* him. The impulse to change must ultimately be Propertius'. Bassus merely calls attention to an option whose compelling force Propertius has to recognize. Love with Cynthia is after all slavery to a slave-mistress (2 and 4) and the prospect of lauded and less demanding girls must be attractive. He wants to leave (and what Roman would not want to leave slavery?). But by a

very comprehensible psychological process he shifts responsi-
bility for that problematic impulse (to leave a lover) on to
another. He wants to leave. He doesn't want to leave: 'allow
me to *continue*', he says. An impulse to stay in slavery to
Cynthia contends with an impulse to leave—and for the
moment dominates. Lines 1-4 express the paradoxes and
ambivalences of Propertius' love. Or rather, they *enact* them.
Responding dramatically to Bassus, Propertius acts something
of the ambivalence that Catullus had sought to analyse; and
possibly we learn more. It is certainly more vivid. The ensuing
medley of explanation, admonition, and statement—all still
dramatically declared to Bassus within the given situation—
then adumbrates something of what it is about this woman
that engenders such powerful and confused feelings. And (I
think) it adumbrates more, or more vividly, than a descrip-
tion would tell. Poem 4 is not a particularly fine poem but it
is a convenient and straightforward example of *monobiblos*
dramatic poetry.

In poem 2 Propertius addresses Cynthia directly. Why does
she flaunt herself in cosmetics and finery? Her beauty is
dazzling on its own, only marred by adornment. Lines 1-8:

> quid iuuat ornato procedere, uita, capillo
>   et tenuis Coa ueste mouere sinus,
> aut quid Orontea crinis perfundere murra,
>   teque peregrinis uendere muneribus
> naturaeque decus mercato perdere cultu,
>   nec sinere in propriis membra nitere bonis?
> crede mihi, non ulla tuae est medicina figurae;
>   nudus Amor formae non amat artificem.

> What is the point, my love, of going forth with elaborately
>   arranged hair,
> of swaying the fine-textured folds in a Coan dress?
> What is the point of drenching your hair in myrrh of Orontes,
> and setting yourself off with gifts from abroad,
> of spoiling the grace of nature with purchased adornment
> and not allowing your limbs to shine in their own glory?
> Believe me, doctoring of your appearance is worthless;
> naked Love does not love a craftsman of beauty.

Propertius seems to be delivering tactful advice against tasteless and unnecessary display, wrapping it up in a pretty compliment—and in humour. *medicina*, 'doctoring', adds a touch of lively and unexpected metaphor which the more normal words for cosmetics (*medicamen, medicamentum*) would not (and possibly it brings out a significance 'doctor' in *artificem*);[22] and the argument in 8 that Cupid anyway disapproves of dressing-up because he is naked is a witty inference from his conventional depiction in the visual arts (note too the momentary paradox *Amor . . . non amat*).[23]

The address to Cynthia proceeds. Limpid *exempla* from Nature are marshalled to illustrate the beauty of naturalness (9-14):

> aspice quos summittat humus formosa colores,
>   ut ueniant hederae sponte sua melius,
> surgat et in solis formosius arbutus antris,
>   et sciat indocilis currere lympha uias.
> litora natiuis persuadent picta lapillis,
>   et uolucres nulla dulcius arte canunt.

> See what colours the beautiful earth sends up,
> how ivy grows better of its own accord,
> and the arbutus springs more beautifully in lonely glens
> and water knows how to run <more beautifully> down ways
>   untaught.
> The shores beguile decorated with their natural gems,
> and birds sing more sweetly from their lack of art.

Resonating myths then hold up the example of heroines who were extremely magnetic but who did *not* resort to cosmetics and finery: great mythical *femmes fatales* who attracted men and gods, and indeed caused considerable havoc in the process, but by their natural beauty (15-22):

> non sic Leucippis succendit Castora Phoebe,
>   Pollucem cultu non Hilaira soror;
> non, Idae et cupido quondam discordia Phoebo,
>   Eueni patriis filia litoribus;
> nec Phrygium falso traxit candore maritum
>   auecta externis Hippodamia rotis:
> sed facies aderat nullis obnoxia gemmis,
>   qualis Apelleis est color in tabulis.

> Not thus did Phoebe daughter of Leucippus inflame Castor,
> not by adornment did Hilaira her sister inflame Pollux;
> not thus <Marpessa> , an object of strife to Idas and desirous
>   Apollo,
> the daughter of Euenus, by her father's banks;
> nor did Hippodamia draw her husband with a fake complexion,
> she who was carried away by alien wheels.
> Their beauty was beholden to no jewels
> being in colour like the colours in pictures by Apelles.

(Note how this last line picks up a paradoxical conceit of the Nature section: naturalness has its own 'art'.)[24]

Now sooner or later—surely by the time these ramifying and complex myths get under way—we start to ask: why so much ink and fuss over adornment, *cultus*? The point soon emerges. Propertius' deduction from the myths is that (23-4):

> non illis studium uulgo conquirere amantis:
>   illis ampla satis forma pudicitia.

> They had no eagerness publicly to procure lovers.
> Modesty was sufficiently ample beauty for them.

The exemplary mythical heroines were in short no tarts. The implication of *that* must be that someone—Cynthia—is: Cynthia *is* trying publicly to procure lovers.

The implication was always there: for example *uendere* in 4 means not just 'set off' but '*sell* yourself'; and the images from nature even suggested it: the strange and striking *persuadent* ('beguile') reflects Cynthia's motives.[25] But why, in this case, the concentration on *cultus*? Why doesn't Propertius come straight out with his criticism of Cynthia's meretricious aims if that was always his real point?

Because he must be diplomatic. The poem is dramatic; it is addressed *to Cynthia*. Let us recapitulate.

Propertius addresses Cynthia on a touchy topic. He wants to *persuade* her; the poem is the persuasion. Propertius wants to persuade Cynthia to stop behaving promiscuously. He must proceed tactfully. To say 'stop being a whore' might be satisfying, but with certain temperaments counter-productive. So he *packages* the message. He concentrates his criticism on her *cultus*. As Propertius sees it, that is the visible manifestation of her promiscuity, but it provides an indirect and therefore more tactful way of tackling the topic. Indeed it allows him for a time to cloak his real criticism in flattery and humour; it allows him to write limpid lines extolling natural beauty and by implication Cynthia's natural beauty. It offers a *discreet* method of introducing the ultimately rather pointed myths.

These myths have much significance (I do not spell it all out here by any means). It is they that begin most openly to show Propertius' awareness and criticism of Cynthia's real motives. On the face of it they are introduced as *exempla* for Cynthia of great women who did not need to set off their natural beauty with *cultus*. But they are also *exempla* of studiously non-meretricious conduct. That is the way the heroines' stories are phrased: Propertius stresses that they did *not* artificially try to procure their lovers. The implications of that are clear. And yet there is still flattery: Propertius still has his eye on tact and persuasion. The *exempla* are *mythical* heroines; that is to say, heroines from a romantic world. Propertius holds up as models for Cynthia's conduct not boring paragons of chaste fidelity but romantic women, indeed romantic *femmes fatales*, who were dangerously successful in their power to attract. And if these are the models he holds up, he is implying that Cynthia is or rather could be such a romantic *femme fatale* herself. This is a rather devious, witty version of the argumentative use of myth that I discussed above (pp. 89 ff.). In his efforts to persuade Cynthia Propertius ends up implying that being chastely faithful is not incompatible with being glamorously *fatale*— unlikely but intriguing.

So: circuitousness, flattery, humour, deviously chosen *exempla*: these are the ingredients of Propertius' complaint and persuasion, his method of tackling the topic of Cynthia's apparently meretricious behaviour. They are, more particularly, the ingredients of his complaint and persuasion *to Cynthia*. His method of tackling the topic must therefore reflect not only his own notions of tactics and his own personality but his view of Cynthia's personality (he must reckon for example that she would like the image of herself as a *femme fatale*). In short, in and through the poem Propertius must be providing all sorts of insights into his and Cynthia's personality and into how the two interact—in the manner of Catullus' poem 7. It is in fact one of the purposes of this longer analysis to point up the similarity of the two poems' techniques: much of what I said in conclusion about Catullus' poem 7 applies to Propertius 1. 2 (above, p. 46).

After the reproving implications of the myths, the even clearer conclusions from them (23-4 quoted above). Then Propertius drops circuitousness for a moment almost completely. But he assumes that Cynthia has by now taken the point—that he recognizes and objects to her meretricious signals to other lovers; and he does not labour it (which would be unnecessarily tactless) by spelling it out—it is, I think, a reflection of how realistically or carefully dramatic the poem is that he does not spell it out for the reader either. He comments instead obliquely, assuming that both of them now know the score. And he comments with considered tactics (25):

> non ego nunc uereor ne sim tibi uilior istis.

> I do not fear lest I be cheaper to you than those.

istis refers dismissively to the prospective other lovers, his knowledge of whose existence is now clear (and with some irony he has adopted Cynthia's supposed mercenary values). To act dismissively and confidently, to belittle the opposition, and to make light of the threat, is probably in the circumstances, for a time, good tactics. Propertius feels confident he can outweigh his rivals. Line 26 then seeks to supply a reason for such confidence: one lover is enough.

> uni si qua placet, culta puella sat est .

> If a girl pleases one man, she has attention enough

(*culta est* must in the first place be understood as the perfect passive of *colo* in the sense of 'cultivate', 'pay court to', a lover.)[26] The reason is far from compelling, indeed it is naïve and vulnerable. But it makes a point Propertius wants to make: one lover is enough for her. And even as he makes it, Propertius is starting to retreat, starting to drop blunt and vulnerable argument. He is packaging his message again. Line 26 has in fact a witty ambiguity. Not only is a girl who pleases one man well enough courted; she is also *culta* enough in the sense of sufficiently *adorned*. Her chastity (which the Elegist would interpret as faithfulness to one man, himself) is her beauty—as the heroines' was: *illis ampla satis forma pudicitia*. Propertius has neatly returned to the familiar and less contentious topic of adornment. He has returned via a persuasive wit. And he then concludes the poem with the most winsome of compliments—the persuasion once more of flattery—making a further play on *culta*. It is especially true that chastity is adornment enough (*culta puella sat est*) if a girl has, as Cynthia has, graceful accomplishments, *cultus* in the sense of 'cultivation' (27 ff.; for his complimentary conclusion Propertius switches back from rather general phrasing to emphatic second person address):

> cum tibi praesertim Phoebus sua carmina donet
>   Aoniamque libens Calliopea lyram,
> unica nec desit iucundis gratia uerbis,
>   omnia quaeque Venus, quaeque Minerua probat.
> his tu semper eris nostrae gratissima uitae,
>   taedia dum miserae sint tibi luxuriae.

> Especially since Apollo gives to you his songs,
> and Calliope willingly her Aonian lyre,
> a singular grace is present in your charming speech,
> and you have all that Venus, all that Minerva, approves.
> Through these things will you be most pleasing to my life,
> —provided that wretched luxuries are wearisome to you.

Cynthia is poetess, lyrist, graceful conversationalist, and so on. Further insight here into Cynthia's nature, or more particularly (since this is persuasion) into Cynthia's cherished idea of her nature. And so (after a last disguised caveat) a fine piece of dramatic persuasion and a fine poem ends.

Virtually every poem in the *monobiblos* reacts to a single

dramatic situation and seems itself to be a little drama. In poem 5 the promiscuous Gallus (not the great poet), who has no knowledge of romantic love, has bidden for Cynthia's favours. The reply to him, which makes up the poem ('what a fool he is to want anything so frightful; though Propertius himself of course wants it . . .') again allows insight into the personality of Cynthia and the strange intensity and ambivalences of Propertius' love. So does poem 18, Propertius' solitary, puzzled, agonized lament amid wild country. Poem 11 appears as a letter from Propertius to Cynthia at Baiae, a resort of notorious morals and therefore full of dangerous distractions for her. Propertius writes winsomely, humorously, pathetically, fearfully—yearning over the miles that separate them: splendid, enacted illumination of loving, morbid, tender jealousy. And so on. Not one poem attempts any systematic analysis of feeling. Each implies its content of feeling through a drama; the poem *is* the drama. Apparent exceptions are hardly so. The splendid nineteenth poem (pp. 100 ff. and 140 ff.) which may seem more loosely reflective (prompted by thoughts of death) is much more dramatic and specifically occasioned than first appears. It is uttered to and, to an extent, conditioned by the immediate Cynthia. It is with her in mind—for her benefit, *because* of her—that Propertius grapples with the problem of love in death. It is because she is in mind that the question of her fidelity to him intrudes into the sequence of the poem (19 ff.).

Poem 10, which issues from an occasion and mood rather different from those so far observed in this section, will bear longer exposition:

> o iucunda quies, primo cum testis amori
>   affueram uestris conscius in lacrimis!
> o noctem meminisse mihi iucunda uoluptas,
>   o quotiens uotis illa uocanda meis,
> cum te complexa morientem, Galle, puella
>   uidimus et longa ducere uerba mora!
> quamuis labentis premeret mihi somnus ocellos
>   et mediis caelo Luna ruberet equis,
> non tamen a uestro potui secedere lusu:
>   tantus in alternis uocibus ardor erat.

sed quoniam non es ueritus concredere nobis,
  accipe commissae munera laetitiae:
non solum uestros didici reticere dolores,
  est quiddam in nobis maius, amice, fide.
possum ego diuersos iterum coniungere amantis,
  et dominae tardas possum aperire fores;
et possum alterius curas sanare recentis,
  nec leuis in uerbis est medicina meis.
Cynthia me docuit semper quaecumque petenda
  quaeque cauenda forent: non nihil egit Amor.
tu caue ne tristi cupias pugnare puellae,
  neue superba loqui, neue tacere diu;
neu, si quid petiit, ingrata fronte negaris,
  neu tibi pro uano uerba benigna cadant.
irritata uenit, quando contemnitur illa,
  nec meminit iustas ponere laesa minas:
at quo sis humilis magis et subiectus amori,
  hoc magis effectu saepe fruare bono.
is poterit felix una remanere puella,
  qui numquam uacuo pectore liber erit.

O pleasant time of rest, when I witnessed first love
and was present, privy to your tears!
O what a keen pleasure it gives me now to remember the night,
O how often it is to be summoned in my prayers!—
when I saw you, Gallus, swooning in your girl's embrace,
and murmuring long-drawn words of love.
Although sleep oppressed my sinking eyes
and the Moon blushed in the sky, her horses in mid-career,
I could not bear to withdraw from your amorous game,
so great was the fire in the words passing between you.
But since you were not afraid to confide in me,
accept a reward for allowing me to witness your happiness.
Not only have I learnt to keep silence as to your pangs:
there is in me something greater than faithfulness.
I can join again sundered lovers,
and I can open a mistress's reluctant doors;
and I can heal another's fresh-smarting pangs;
no trifling remedy is in my words.
Cynthia taught me what should be constantly aimed for,
what avoided; Love was not unefficacious.
Have no desire to fight with a girl out of humour,
no desire for proud utterance or long-drawn silence.
Do not with graceless face deny her requests
or let your generous promises go for nothing.[27]
When the girl is scorned she comes in wrath,

when offended she remembers not to set aside her just threats.
But the humbler you are, the more submissive to love,
the more often are you likely to enjoy a good outcome.
That man will be able to remain happy with one girl
who is never free, never disengaged in heart.

Propertius speaks as Gallus' confidant. He was a witness of
Gallus' 'first love' (1–2); he saw him with a girl, weeping with
pleasure, swooning in her embrace, talking passionately (3 ff.);
and (I think we are to infer) he saw much more. *laetitia* (12)
naturally suggests love-making in Elegy; and that Propertius
actually saw Gallus in the act is also suggested by 1. 13. 15 ff.
All this Propertius reports to Gallus in what appears to be an
address or letter composed soon after the action described;
he reports it saying what *pleasure* it afforded him: *o, o, o!*
It afforded him enormous pleasure. How kind it was of
Gallus to vouchsafe it to him. In return for this kindness he
gives Gallus the benefit of his wisdom and experience (15 ff.).
There basically is the poem: reactions to a given event, uttered
to a friend who had been one of the protagonists.

The expressions of pleasure are indeed enormous, and
curious. The claims made and advice given in 15 ff. are also
curious. Propertius lays claim to extraordinary power over
love, greater power in fact than a god possesses (cf. 2. 1. 57 ff.,
Tibull. 2. 3. 13). What is his secret? Simply, it seems, the
rules of *seruitium amoris*: that is what he proceeds to enjoin
upon Gallus, the fruit of his knowledge. Curious too is the
protestation of friendship. Gallus is not a person we expect
to be addressed by Propertius in terms of fulsome affection.
In poem 5, as I mentioned, he appeared as a promiscuous
philanderer, lover of easy girls, ignorant of true love—and yet
bidding for Cynthia's affection.

The information of poem 5 is in fact crucial. It casts a
different and very illuminating light on the facts of our
poem, and the oddities I mentioned become swiftly intelligible.
Gallus the casual philanderer has now at last fallen *really* in
love—effectively (Propertius can say) he is in love for the first
time; Gallus the would-be rival for Cynthia's favours now has
his own troubles. There is double cause here for Propertian

joy. The poem records it. What we have here is *Schadenfreude*, malicious glee. The joy is at Gallus' discomfiture; the protestations of friendship, the enthusiastic expressions of pleasure at Gallus' happiness are all an elaborate irony. Abjectly weeping in love is *not* how Gallus would have wanted to be seen, especially by Propertius.

The protestations of friendship are ironic; so of course is Propertius' assumption that Gallus meant him to be privy to the scene. There we have the heart of the malicious humour. Few people—certainly not a Gallus—are fond of spectators when they are uttering and acting an abject infatuation (even the moon blushed: 8). Propertius must have witnessed Gallus' fall by chance; but his absorption in the girl was so total, and his blissful unconsciousness of his surroundings, which included Propertius, was so complete, that Propertius could pretend that his own presence was a designed complicity. From this beginning the poem grew: enthusiastic cries pretending joy at a friend's happiness but in fact celebrating a rival's come-uppance, an anti-romantic's come-uppance. The rival now has his hands occupied, the philanderer has discovered the bittersweetness of romantic love.

Propertius continues his malicious expressions of pleasure and friendship for thirteen lines or so. Then the old hand turns (with further irony) to give the novice the 'kind' benefit of his experience, a quid pro quo for the latter's 'kind' trust. He speaks with comprehensible loftiness (15 ff.), relishing the position of superiority in power and knowledge that he can reasonably claim. But he cannot resist exaggerating it too, at this his moment of triumph. He elevates the power and influence which *qua* lover-poet he may plausibly claim and which he phrases plausibly elsewhere,[28] to a hyperbolic, magical, even divine level (15-18). But then of course it all boils down to knowledge of the laws of *seruitium*. He spells them out for Gallus; and they have a nice and cruel relevance. Gallus who had bidden unsuccessfully for a Cynthia whom he comprehended as little as he did the true God of Love (5, *passim*) receives humiliating advice from those puissant sources; Gallus the cheerfully promiscuous noble (5. 7 and 23-4) is lectured on the need for abject servility to his one girl—a servility which, incidentally, he seems well on the way to displaying already. (We should also remember that in poem 5 Propertius had implied that Gallus would need his advice if ever he won Cynthia, that is, if ever he tasted true love. In the event he is able to demonstrate and answer Gallus' need in analogous but pleasanter circumstances.)

Irony, malice, humour: Propertian weapons at a moment of pleasurable triumph; at a moment when he thinks that an essential truth of love is being demonstrated. Propertius rubs in his pleasure; Propertius lectures. We witness a stage in a drama—and we should note that it is the second stage in a continuing drama: Propertius presupposes knowledge of the first stage, 1. 5.[29] We learn about personality: about how Propertius reacts in certain circumstances and relates to a type of person. And we learn about love. Propertius' lecture is not all hyperbole, far from it; and talking to an unsympathetic rival he says things about love he might not say to a genuine friend or to the beloved herself. Other aspects of personality, other aspects of love are revealed. Propertian dramatic poetry has many faces.

One poem in the *monobiblos* does not actually enact a drama but reports it, re-creating its atmosphere in the manner of Catullus' poem 68: poem 1. 3.[30]

> qualis Thesea iacuit cedente carina
>   languida desertis Cnosia litoribus,
> qualis et accubuit primo Cepheia somno
>   libera iam duris cotibus Andromede,
> nec minus assiduis Edonis fessa choreis
>   qualis in herboso concidit Apidano,
> talis uisa mihi mollem spirare quietem
>   Cynthia non certis nixa caput manibus,
> ebria cum multo traherem uestigia Baccho
>   et quaterent sera nocte facem pueri.
> hanc ego nondum etiam sensus deperditus omnes
>   molliter inpresso conor adire toro.
> et quamuis duplici correptum ardore iuberent
>   hac Amor hac Liber, durus uterque deus,

subiecto leuiter positam temptare lacerto,
  osculaque admota sumere et arma manu,
non tamen ausus eram dominae turbare quietem
  expertae metuens iurgia saeuitiae;
sed sic intentis haerebam fixus ocellis,
  Argus ut ignotis cornibus Inachidos.
et modo soluebam nostra de fronte corollas
  ponebamque tuis, Cynthia, temporibus;
et modo gaudebam lapsos formare capillos;
  nunc furtiua cauis poma dabam manibus;
omniaque ingrato largibar munera somno,
  munera de prono saepe uoluta sinu.
et quotiens raro duxti suspiria motu,
  obstupui uano credulus auspicio,
ne qua tibi insolitos portarent uisa timores,
  neue quis inuitam cogeret esse suam:
donec diuersas praecurrens luna fenestras,
  luna moraturis sedula luminibus,
compositos leuibus radiis patefecit ocellos.
  sic ait in molli fixa toro cubitum:
'tandem te nostro referens iniuria lecto
  alterius clausis expulit e foribus?
namque ubi longa meae consumpsti tempora noctis
  languidus exactis, ei mihi, sideribus?
o utinam tales perducas, improbe, noctes,
  me miseram quales semper habere iubes!
nam modo purpureo fallebam stamine somnum,
  rursus et Orpheae carmine fessa lyrae,
interdum leuiter mecum deserta querebar
  externo longas saepe in amore moras,
dum me iucundis lapsam Sopor inpulit alis.
  illa fuit lacrimis ultima cura meis.'

Just as Ariadne lay, exhausted on the deserted beach
as Theseus' bark departed;
just as Andromeda reclined in her first sleep
free now from the harsh rocks;
just as the Bacchante, no less wearied <than Andromeda>
    by her continuous dances,
fell in sleep by the grassy Apidanus;
so Cynthia seemed to me to breathe gentle rest,
her head supported on uncertain hands,
when I trailed back my drunken steps
and the slave boys shook their torches in the deep of night.
Not yet bereft of all my senses
I try to approach her gently pressing her bed.

And although a twofold fire had hold of me
and on one side Love urged me, on the other side Bacchus, both
    harsh gods,
to put my arm about her and gently assail her where she lay,
caressing her, taking kisses—and taking up arms,
nevertheless I did not dare to disturb my mistress's rest,
fearing the savage abuse which I knew well.
So I stayed fast fixed with eyes intent
just as Argus at the strange horns of Io.
And now I loosened the garlands from my brow,
and placed them, Cynthia, on your temples;
now I delighted to shape your tumbled hair;
now stealthily I bestowed fruits in your cupped hands;
and all my gifts I lavished on ungrateful sleep,
gifts that rolled in profusion from my inclined bosom.
When from time to time you moved and heaved a sigh,
I was amazed (believing it to be an omen, vainly)
in fear that visions were bringing you strange terrors,
or that some phantom was compelling you to be his against
    your will—
until the moon passing by the open window,
the busy moon with beams that would have lingered,
opened with gentle rays her peace-closed eyes.
Propping her elbow on her soft bed she spoke thus:
'At last another's "injustice" has brought you back to our bed,
and thrown you out and bolted the door behind you.
For *where* have you spent the long hours of *my* night?—
exhausted as you are (to my grief) now that the night is over.
O may you, you shameless creature, spend such nights
as you order me in my wretchedness to have always.
At one time I cheated sleep by weaving purple thread,
at another in my weariness with the music of Orphean lyre.
Sometimes forlorn I gently made my lonely plaint
over your frequent long dalliance in another's love,
till Sleep touched me with his pleasant wings as I was already
    slipping.
That was my final anxious thought amid my tears.'

Propertius recalls an emotive scene. Recalling it, he re-creates it and suggests to us things about himself, Cynthia, and love that it would be hard completely to analyse or tell.

I have discussed the opening myths above (pp. 98 ff.). Propertius returns home late and drunk from a party. These rapturous comparisons expound the belief that he immediately conceived in Cynthia's romantic beauty and romantic pathos. But hesitations underlie the myths, written into the myths. It is also pretty clear to the reader that Cynthia's mythical status has much to do with the fact that she is safely asleep, as well as with Propertius' vinous condition. We wait for her to wake.

While we wait Propertius progresses through a delightful sequence of scenes. They project a variety of sentimental moods, all dependent on Cynthia's romantic (her mythic) status—and her sleep. It is true that he experiences a momentary, worldly temptation in connection with Cynthia (the responsibility for which he shifts on to third parties, Love and Bacchus; 13-16); but he rapidly restores his respect for her statuesque, romantic *quies*, assisted by a momentary and timely memory of her worldly, waking self: note *domina*, 'mistress', the word indicating another, non-mythic romanticism; note too *iurgia saeuitiae*, blasts from a place outside myth.

Cynthia's place in myth is then explicitly restored, (19-20). And Propertius himself becomes a romantic figure. The Io myth restates his belief in Cynthia's wondrousness and pathos (Io was wronged, persecuted, and, in her transformed state, incredibly strange); and his own equation is significantly chosen. Delightfully and humorously over-reacting to the role of worldly rapist, Propertius saw himself as the mythical, disinterested *guardian*. (We see that these myths do work in dramatic context. But there is much in their choice, I think, which reflects the humour of the narrating poet rather than the re-created actor: see below.)

Next the poem describes a series of loving gestures (21-6). They bespeak tenderness, sentiment, love. They are the sort of gestures happy, romantic lover makes to happy, romantic beloved. Happy Propertius makes them to romanticized Cynthia; happy Propertius makes them to sleeping Cynthia. The equivalence of Cynthia's sleeping state and her romantic status becomes more obvious. It is half-appreciated by Propertius in the scene: *omniaque ingrato largibar munera somno*, 'and I lavished all my gifts on ungrateful sleep.' But he restores his romanticizing mood and at 27–8 is amazed as at a portent when Cynthia sighs. Once more, too (29–30), he is the solicitous, virtuous guardian: echoes of Argus. And there is a pleasant additional touch. He is solicitous on account of the possible importunities of phantom lovers in her dreams. His own real impulse (15 f.) has become neatly transposed. Reality is dream and dream reality. Romance is patently dominant.

It is maintained through the transitional passage which brings Cynthia to wakefulness (31–3). The conception of the moon's beams (or eyes: *luminibus* is ambiguous) being fain to linger over Cynthia's beautiful form is the product of a mind still romancing. It gives the moon her personified, mythical nature and half-suggests the specific myth of Endymion. The tender thought and beautiful language are also the product of a romanticizing mind. It is sweetly ironic of course (and indicative of his state of mind) that Propertius so lovingly describes (recalling his mood at the time) the very action that must dispel his romance.

And it is dispelled with arresting sharpness. Cynthia wakes and utters an outburst that must drive away all dreams. She employs furious sarcasm (35 ff.); 'so at last the *injustice* of some girl (unjust to you, *poor* Propertius) has brought you back.' She employs gratuitous and unfounded accusation (38); she suggests Propertius has not only been with some girl, but is sexually exhausted (*languidus* can have that implication); whereas in fact he seems to have been drinking at a *symposion* and come duly to Cynthia for his love (as a *comissator*: note the garlands). She employs tenuous, feminine logic, not unviciously: *namque* (37). The thought process underlying that is: 'you must have been sleeping with another girl for where *else* could you have been'; note too the splendidly proprietary *meae*: that implies a flat claim to own Propertius' nights. She displays vindictiveness and self-pity (39–40)—and exaggeration (*semper*). She employs, with another change of tactics, whining reproach (41 ff.). She casts herself in a role of traditional pathetic virtue, the woman at home weaving;[31] she probably intends to bring specifically to mind the pathetically patient, devoted, and weaving Penelope. She then describes herself in another pathetic occupation, whiling away the time on a lyre in hope of her lover's return—tinged with the tragedy of Orpheus. And in this vein her speech continues to the end: in unjustified, inappropriate, calculated self-pitying pathos. The whole is a burst of reality, every part of it destructively incompatible with any of the imagined, romantic Cynthias.

Another point. Cynthia seems here to claim the rights and to cast herself in the role of a *wife* (note '*meae* noctis', and the weaving scene and the implicit comparison with Penelope). She certainly acts like an only too real wife: complaining, suspicious, illogical, proprietorial. That destroys another romance that Propertius frequently believes in (but does not explicitly introduce here), the Catullan vision of the beloved as an ideal romantic wife.[32] So Cynthia wakes and shatters Propertius' initial mythical beliefs and concomitant sentimentality (all of which exploited her sleep), and another myth for good measure. And to crown it all she manages to repeat key words and phrases from Propertius' romancing at the beginning of the poem and turn them to her own romance-shattering ends.[33] She even turns romantic myth to her ends too (Orpheus, Penelope). The irony is clear.

Propertius reports an episode that demonstrates a truth. It illustrates the processes and consequences of idealizing in love; it traces a sequence from romance to reality, a forced shift from fond belief to wry acknowledgement of that belief's inappropriateness. (The acknowledgement is I think all the more eloquent for being implicit: Propertius lets events speak for themselves.)[34] We have read a drama; and because the report re-created the atmosphere of the time of the drama (only once did we detect the narrator Propertius overriding the 'point of view' of that time) we seem to have *witnessed* the drama in action. It is a much more striking drama than usual: a veritable little play, wry, tender, pathetic, and humorous, with a superbly calculated end. From it we *infer* our content of personality, psychology, and feeling in the usual way. We could say indeed that there is more of such content than usual: the poem displays personality in more rounded clarity, it illustrates a larger truth of human character than we find elsewhere. But this poem is perhaps a case where the 'play is the thing'. The processes of witnessing and inference are hardly separable, but if someone were to maintain that the strength of this poem was in the brilliant way it re-creates action, that the interest for the reader was particularly in witnessing the drama, it would be difficult to argue. This can be said about more than one of Propertius' poems.[35]

Virtually every poem in the *monobiblos* seems itself to be (or it reports) a drama, and implies its content of feeling and personality. Each we could say has *dramaturgical* immediacy —and unity.[36] What happens in later Propertius?

B. *Book 2*

What we possess as Propertius' second book is probably an editorial amalgam of two original books.[37] In the Cynthia poems we can observe the basic technique of the *monobiblos*; and we can observe another technique.

> quid fles abducta grauius Briseide? quid fles
>   anxia captiua tristius Andromacha?
> quidue mea de fraude deos, insana, fatigas?
>   quid quereris nostram sic cecidisse fidem?
>   2. 20. 1–4

> Why do you weep more grievously than Briseis carried off
>   (from Achilles); why weep
> in anxiety more sadly than captive Andromache?
> Why do you weary the gods about my perfidy?
> Why complain that my faithfulness has as you say fallen?

Propertius suggests a dramatic situation. Further information follows later (33): *ne tu supplicibus me sis uenerata tabellis*, 'please do not beseech me with letters of entreaty!' The girl— Cynthia I think we must assume[38] —has suspected Propertius' faithfulness and sent him plaintive letters. *sic* in line 4 refers to them—with authentic economy: 'as you say'. Our poem is Propertius' reply to Cynthia's complaint: it is dramatic, in

the manner of the *monobiblos*. We are on familiar ground;
but it is worth pausing over the poem, a particularly attractive
piece. It has the quality, not as common as all that in Pro-
pertius, of unequivocal gentleness. Gentleness was not often a
feature of the Propertian love story.

The task of the poem is once more persuasion: to convince
Cynthia of his fidelity, to demonstrate that suspicion and
grief on her part are unnecessary—generally to sweeten her.
The poem seeks to get across to her that his devotion unam-
biguously abides.

The opening tone is gently, humorously chiding. The
solemn language *fles grauius* already suggests a grief out of
proportion. Only a tragedy would merit diction of this
gravity [39] The myths (Briseis, Andromache) advance the
point; the use of myth is a very pleasant one. Why does
Cynthia, who is not (as she ought to know) a tragically
suffering mythical heroine, weep like one? (or rather, *more*
than one: cf. above., p. 88). Propertius does not here imply
disbelief in the romantic world, nor for that matter in Cynthia's
romantic status; he simply suggests that romantic *sorrow* is at
this time inappropriate. He then elaborates the picture of
such sorrow in the *exempla* of Philomela and Niobe, empha-
sizing its inappropriateness by the romantic melodrama of
these two stories. And he counters with a romantic declaration
of his own devotion. 5–12:

> non tam nocturna uolucris funesta querela
>   Attica Cecropiis obstrepit in foliis,
> nec tantum Niobe bis sex ad busta superba,
>   sollicito lacrimans defluit a Sipylo.
> mi licet aeratis astringant bracchia nodis,
>   sint tua uel Danaes condita membra domo,
> in te ego et aeratas rumpam, mea uita, catenas,
>   ferratam Danaes transiliamque domum.

> Not so does the mourning bird with night-time plaint,
> the Attic one (Philomela), clamour in the leaves of Cecrops;
> not so does Niobe, whose pride issued in twelve graves,
> weeping, her tears flowing from sad Sipylus.
> Though they bind my arms with brazen knots,
> though you be immured in Danae's tower,

> to get to you I would burst brazen chains, my love,
> and leap over Danae's iron domain.

In fact Propertius plays very deftly with *belief* in myth (above, pp. 88 ff.). Romantic grief exists but Cynthia has no cause for it. Romantic devotion exists and Propertius could and would display it—but there is no need for such display. The touch of humour in the picture of himself as an ardent Jupiter breaking into his Danae's tower suggests his feeling that such histrionics are not now absolutely necessary. All that *is* necessary, is trust and sincerity: she should trust him as he trusts her; for (simply) he loves her. And, now that the myths have broken the ice with their gently chiding, relaxing humour, Propertius can proceed to say so. 13-18, the heart of the poem:

> de te quodcumque, ad surdas mihi dicitur auris:
>   tu modo ne dubita de grauitate mea.
> ossa tibi iuro per matris et ossa parentis
>   (si fallo, cinis heu sit mihi uterque grauis)
> me tibi ad extremas mansurum, uita, tenebras:
>   ambos una fides auferet, una dies.

> Whatever gossip there is about you, is said to my deaf ears:
>   only do you not doubt my steadfastness.
> I swear to you by my mother's and father's bones
>   (if I deceive, oh may the ash of both be burdensome to me)
> that I shall remain yours, my life, till the last darkness:
>   one selfsame day shall bear both of us away in one selfsame
>   love.

He then supports this declaration with a gently humorous, paradoxically tender description of his familiar condition, his *seruitium*:

> quod si nec nomen nec me tua forma teneret,
>   posset seruitium mite tenere tuum.   (19-20)

> But if neither your renown nor your beauty could keep me fast,
> my *gentle* slavery to you could do it!

And he recalls relevant facts, figures, and scenes connected with their affair, the things he has to be grateful for (21-7):

septima iam plenae deducitur orbita lunae,
    cum de me et de te compita nulla tacent:
interea nobis non numquam ianua mollis,
    non numquam lecti copia facta tui.
nec mihi muneribus nox ulla est empta beatis:
    quidquid eram, hoc animi gratia magna tui.
cum te tam multi peterent, tu me una petisti.

The full moon is now drawing out its seventh circuit,
since every street corner has been talking of you and me.[40]
Meanwhile your door has been compliant to me not unoften,[41]
not unoften your bed has been made available to me.
But not one night was purchased with costly gifts.
Whatever I was I owed to your heart.
When many sought you, you sought only me.[42]

In these circumstances how *could* he forget her (28):

possum ego nunc curae non meminisse tuae?

Can I now forget my love for you?[43]

The point has been well made: lines 21-7 express besides
gratitude and flattery a sense of warm complicity which is
surely in itself emotional proof of continuing love: a man
who can talk like this is not one to be unfaithful. So Cynthia
can believe; she is certainly intended to. Persuasive sincerity
(13-18) makes way for persuasive tenderness (19-20) which
makes way for persuasive complicity.

The tactics then change again. The persuader hedges his
bets. Someone so plangently, romantically suffering as Cynthia
has been may appreciate another romantic declaration—which
she can bask in, or perhaps by now (depending on the success
of the previous persuasion) smile at. So Propertius proceeds
to protest vividly, invoking upon himself romantic (mythical)
punishments in the event of his not remembering his love.
29-32:

tum me uel tragicae uexetis Erinyes, et me
    inferno damnes, Aeace, iudicio,
atque inter Tityi uolucris mea poena uagetur,
    tumque ego Sisyphio saxa labore geram.

In that event may you, Furies of Tragedy, hound me,
and may you Aeacus pass on me the judgement of hell;
may my ghost in torment roam among Tityos' vultures
and (in that event) may I bear rocks in labour like Sisyphus.

But at the end Propertius returns to the persuasion of limpid
sincerity (33 ff.):

ne tu supplicibus me sis uenerata tabellis:
    ultima talis erit quae mea prima fides.
hoc mihi perpetuo ius est, quod solus amator
    nec cito desisto nec temere incipio.

Do not entreat me with suppliant letters:
my faithfulness at the last will be as it was at the first.
This is a changeless law for me, that alone of lovers
I neither cease hastily nor begin rashly.

So again we find a drama. The poem is again a piece of
persuasion, composed of various ingredients and changing
tactics. It must reflect the personality of the protesting lover,
and suit the personality of the aggrieved beloved. Again
therefore there is opportunity for insight into the interaction
of the two lovers. We should be reminded of 1. 2 (above,
pp. 104 ff.) or indeed of Catullus 7. Catullus 7 in fact deploys
complicity to persuasive effect in a very similar way to 2. 20
(p. 46). Propertius does therefore on occasion write in Book
2 in the manner of the *monobiblos*. Note too, for example,
the delightful poem 19 which can be interestingly compared
with 1. 11, though it is in a much lighter vein; or 18B and 18C;
and 29B re-creates an event while reporting it in the manner
of 1. 3—though it is a vastly simpler and more jejune poem.

Poem 8 of Book 2 is also a highly dramatic poem. It starts:

eripitur nobis iam pridem cara puella
    et tu me lacrimas fundere, amice, uetas?

The girl who has long been my love is snatched away
and do you, my friend, forbid me to weep?

Propertius then continues his address to his friend, elaborating
and explaining his grief and sense of injury: *nullae sunt inimi-
citiae nisi amoris acerbae* . . . etc. (3–12), 'no feuds are truly

bitter save those concerned with love'. Once more we seem to have a poem like the typical product of the *monobiblos*. But then things change. Propertius proceeds to communicate other, quite different emotions aroused in him by his desertion: a sense of uncomprehending anger and injury, melodramatic almost masochistic despair, murderous hate, the incapacitation of sorrow. I suppose he might have been able to communicate all this within the initial dramatic situation (his reply to his friend). But he chooses another method: he abandons the first situation and directs other utterances (embodying the other emotions) to other people— to people who might most naturally elicit them. The poem is still in a sense dramatic. But its dramaturgical unity, its impression *of being itself a drama*, goes: the people successively addressed could not plausibly be addressed on one occasion, at one time. Propertius offers a sequence of *rhetorical* apostrophes. He exploits an orator's or writer's privilege. He no longer creates the illusion of himself uttering on an occasion outside literature, in life.

It is natural to reveal injury to a friend (*amicus*) and discuss enmity (*inimicitia*) with him; to the girl who wrongs you belong expressions of uncomprehending anger and vengeful hate; soliloquy is the natural place for masochistic despair; and to a friend also belong eloquent and pathetic confessions of incapacitating sorrow. That is how such utterances might most naturally arise, that therefore is how they might most vividly be presented. And that is how Propertius phrases them (the friend, 1-12; Cynthia, 13-16 and 25-8; the soliloquy, 17-24; the friend again, 29-40). We understand what he is doing and why he is doing it. And we observe that he is still in a way exploiting drama: saying *things* to *people*; embodying rather than analysing the underlying feeling. But he is now exploiting a variety of quasi-dramatic addresses, a shifting sequence of rhetorical addresses, in one poem; and though he gains thereby a greater ease to imply a greater variety of feeling, he can no longer achieve the same quality or type of drama as before. Abandoning dramatic unity, he has abandoned the illusion of the poem being in itself a drama in life. He wins on the roundabouts, he loses on the swings. (We should note how he is sensitive to the loss of dramatic unity: architectural symmetry replaces it—and helps the poem's articulation. He has organized a chiastic pattern of lines, 12 + 4 + 8 + 4 + 12, corresponding to a chiastic pattern of addresses: friend, Cynthia, self, Cynthia, friend.)

So this is a rather different type of poem from the typical *monobiblos* product. Yet it is obviously related as well as different (it actually closely resembles the technique of the programmatic 1. 1), and so provides an interesting link between the *monobiblos* type and more advanced structures that Book 2 offers.

Poem 2. 15. 1–10

> o me felicem! nox o mihi candida! et o tu
>   lectule deliciis facte beate meis!
> quam multa apposita narramus uerba lucerna,
>   quantaque sublato lumine rixa fuit!
> nam modo nudatis mecum est luctata papillis,
>   interdum tunica duxit operta moram.
> illa meos somno lapsos patefecit ocellos
>   ore suo et dixit 'sicine lente iaces?'
> quam uario amplexu mutamus bracchia! quantum
>   oscula sunt labris nostra morata tuis!

> O my fortunate lot! O my radiant night! and o you
> my dear bed made blessed by my delight!
> How much we said in the light of the lamp,
> what a struggle there was when the light was put to one side!
> At one moment she grappled with me with bared breast,
> sometimes she teased me covering herself with her tunic.
> When my eyes closed in sleep she opened them
> with a kiss and said 'Hey you, lying sluggish like this!'
> How varied our arms' embraces! How long
> my kisses lingered on your lips!

Propertius recalls a night with Cynthia. In a mixture of perfect and vivid present tenses he evokes the scenes of love and splendour acted out on his bed. Up to this point the poem would almost fit the *monobiblos* type: Propertius reacts dramatically on a definite occasion (the morning after) to a definite event. He addresses primarily us his readers, but

includes exuberant apostrophes, for example to the bed (1–2)
and Cynthia (10). Then:

> non iuuat in caeco Venerem corrumpere motu:
>   si nescis, oculi sunt in amore duces.
> ipse Paris nuda fertur periisse Lacaena,
>   cum Menelaeo surgeret e thalamo:
> nudus et Endymion Phoebi cepisse sororem
>   dicitur et nudae concubuisse deae.
> quod si pertendens animo uestita cubaris,
>   scissa ueste meas experiere manus:
> quin etiam, si me ulterius prouexerit ira,
>   ostendes matri bracchia laesa tuae.
> necdum inclinatae prohibent te ludere mammae:
>   uiderit haec, si quam iam peperisse pudet.   (11–22)

There is no profit in debasing love in blind movement:
you must be aware that the eyes are love's guides.
Paris himself, they say, died of love for Helen naked,
when he saw her rise from Menelaus' bed.
And naked Endymion is said to have taken Apollo's sister captive
and lain with the naked goddess.
But if you persist in going to bed clothed,
I'll rend your dress and you'll feel the force of my hands:
indeed, if my anger carries me on further,
you'll have bruised arms to show your mother.
Not yet do sagging breasts prevent you from love-play.
Leave that worry to one who is ashamed to have given birth.

Propertius urges Cynthia not to wear anything in bed, adding
arguments and threats. There is a stimulus for the line of
thought here in line 6; but nothing can disguise the fact that
the poet does at this point shift very abruptly. As in 2. 8, it
is revealed that we cannot imagine Propertius fixed in a
dramatic time and place (either here, in the opening lines, or
anywhere in the poem): the poet is delivering rhetorical
utterances stimulated by a recalled drama. But here we have a
more radical shift than the shifts between apostrophes in 2. 8:
addressee, direction, tone, and subject-matter, all abruptly
change. Propertius having enthused stops, then lectures
Cynthia on (as it were) a matter arising.[44]

The lecture is, of course, humorous in effect: the incon-
gruity of an earnestly delivered homily, complete with

romantic mythical *exempla* (on which see above, pp. 82 ff.),
prosaic argument, and threats on the rightness of stripping
for love, cannot be missed. Propertius develops the lecture
into an injunction to them both to spend life in love, a
version of Catullus' *uiuamus atque amemus* (above, p.
65) wittily adapted to the lecture's theme (note the introduction
of 'eyes' into the topic):

> dum nos fata sinunt, oculos satiemus amore:
> nox tibi longa uenit, nec reditura dies.

> While the fates allow let us glut our eyes with love:
> the long night comes and the day that will not dawn.

And Propertius then backs this up with an exuberant wish
(which shows him reverting in thought to the event behind
line 9: note *sic*), an *exemplum*, and an assertion. 25-30:

> atque utinam haerentis sic nos uincire catena
>   uelles, ut numquam solueret ulla dies!
> exemplo iunctae tibi sint in amore columbae,
>   masculus et totum femina coniugium.
> errat, qui finem uesani quaerit amoris:
>   uerus amor nullum nouit habere modum.

> And oh that you might wish to bind us, clinging thus,
>   with a chain,
> so that no day might ever loose us!
> Let doves joined in love be your model,
> the male and, a total union, the female.
> He errs who seeks a limit to the madness of love:
> true love knows no measure.

There is a nice wit to lines 25 f.: the content recalls the *punish-
ment* imposed upon Mars and Venus—which Propertius in the
circumstances would gladly settle for. But the lines in total
impact are expressive and moving.

The poem proceeds (31-6):

> terra prius falso partu deludet arantis,
>   et citius nigros Sol agitabit equos,
> fluminaque ad caput incipient reuocare liquores,
>   aridus et sicco gurgite piscis erit,
> quam possim nostros alio transferre dolores:
>   huius ero uiuus, mortuus huius ero.

Sooner will the earth deceive the ploughmen by bearing false
    progeny,
and sooner the Sun-god drive the horses of night,
and rivers begin to recall their waters to their fount,
fish thirst in a dried up ocean,
than I could transfer my love-pain to another:
in life I shall be hers, and hers in death.

A protestation of Propertius' own undying devotion. That
arises naturally enough out of his injunction to spend life in
love (23–30). But again addressee and (as we shall see) mood
have changed. The change of addressee is rather surprising.
Propertius switches back to his readers, and protests his
devotion to this third party. Surely it would have been more
natural to continue addressing Cynthia, assuring the girl upon
whom he has enjoined continuous love of his own undying
devotion? I think we see the point in the next four lines,
37–40:

quod mihi si interdum talis concedere noctes
    illa uelit, uitac longus et annus erit.
si dabit et multas, fiam immortalis in illis:
    nocte una quiuis uel deus esse potest.

But if she should sometimes be willing to grant me nights
    such as this,
a year of life will be long.
If further she gives me many, they will make me immortal:
in one such night anyone can be a god.

This expressive (cf. p. 263) but perhaps rather arch addition,
that given a few nights such as last night a single year of life
would seem an age and given many such nights he would be
immortal, sits oddly indeed amusingly with the preceding.
Paradoxes about the relativity of erotic time ill cohere with,
even undermine, a romantic declaration of eternal devotion.
They are meant to. The juxtaposition is meant to be humor-
ous. Propertius who had been exuberantly, movingly romantic
to Cynthia in 23–30 is now, in 31–40, offering romanticism
accompanied by a wink. That is not pertinently addressed to
Cynthia. It suits us, his knowing readers. And so the section
with this different mood is addressed to us.

41–8:

> qualem si cuncti cuperent decurrere uitam
>   et pressi multo membra iacere mero,
> non ferrum crudele neque esset bellica nauis,
>   nec nostra Actiacum uerteret ossa mare,
> nec totiens propriis circum oppugnata triumphis
>   lassa foret crinis soluere Roma suos.
> haec certe merito poterunt laudare minores:
>   laeserunt nullos pocula nostra deos.

> If all men wished to live like this,
> and lie with their limbs weighed down with ample wine,
> there would be no cruel iron nor ship of war,
> nor would the sea of Actium toss Roman bones
> nor would Rome, beleaguered so often by triumphs of civil war,
> be weary of loosening her hair (in mourning).
> This, certainly, will our descendants be able to praise in us:
> our wine-cups outraged no gods.

Propertius continues to address his readers, but makes another and radical shift. He branches abruptly out to a general topic. He turns to consider the implications of *otium* at their widest, and he is led to his brave, outspoken comment on the life of action and war (cf. above, p. 77). After this he shifts back to apostrophize Cynthia, reviving his injunction to spend life in love—but now with a new urgency, prompted by evil thoughts of war and death, 49 ff.:

> tu modo, dum lucet, fructum ne desere uitae.
>   omnia si dederis oscula, pauca dabis.
> ac ueluti folia arentis liquere corollas,
>   quae passim calathis strata natare uides,
> sic nobis, qui nunc magnum spiramus amantes,
>   forsitan includet crastina fata dies.

> Do you only, while there is light, not forsake the fruit of life.
> If you give me all your kisses, you will still give me few.
> And just as leaves drop from withered garlands,
> and you can see them scattered and floating in the wine-bowls,
> so for us too, who now in love are proud in confidence,
> perhaps tomorrow's day will conclude our life.

Note the choice of *dum lucet*, 'while there is *light*', to express 'while there is life'. It suggests (or confirms) that underlying the earlier, trivial desire to exploit and gratify the eyes (12, 23), that is, to love in the light, was a fear of the greater dark, the night which is death (24; cf. Catull. 5. 6). A thread runs through the sections.

But they are noticeably distinct sections. Propertius exclaims vividly about a night of love; then he addresses a witty lecture arising therefrom to Cynthia, coupled with an appropriately adapted *uiuamus*, which in turn is backed up by other material; next he protests his devotion to Cynthia in an address to the reader, with some humour; and then he branches out to comment on the life of action and war, before returning to apostrophize Cynthia. The poem is best printed in separate paragraphs: 1-10, 11-30, 31-40, 41-8, and 49-54. The shift between paragraphs is distinct and the construction within the paragraphs usually tight; but we might note that thought and structure are allowed to drift quite associatively within 11-30. Notice too that Propertius has again helped the articulation of the poem by numerical means, composing in symmetrical blocks of lines; at the unsymmetrical break at 49 the articulation is clearly marked by syntax.

This is radically different from a typical *monobiblos* poem, more different than 2. 8. An event stimulates a sequence of utterances that embody unexpected shifts of mood, thought, and standpoint. And though again we may miss the vividness of dramaturgical immediacy and unity, the ampler structure and rhetorical nature grant greater possibilities of variety in mood and topic.

We could call this technique 'shifting standpoint'. Many other poems exploit it in Book 2. Convenient and attractive to compare are poems 3, 6, 16, and 25. In some (e.g. 6, I think) the sequence of thought seems more vaguely associative than in others: the poet seems to drift through related topics rather than to construct distinctly shifting sections (cf. lines 11-30 of poem 15).

Poem 5 is both similar and different. We can and do fix Propertius in a dramatic time, in the manner of the *monobiblos*.

He is reacting to hearing scandalous reports of Cynthia. But something happens to the time. During the first eight lines of the poem Propertius reproaches Cynthia and announces his intention of finding another lover. Then he turns and urges himself (in the manner of Catullus, poem 8) to be firm in his resolve while his anger is fresh, or else the opportunity will be lost. Then in the third section (17–30), to quote Camps, 'the opportunity *has* been lost; the poet turns again to Cynthia, addresses her as *uita* (= darling), and only entreats her not to try his patience too far . . .' We must I think assume *a lapse in time*. The shift is too large to be explained as one of Propertius' characteristic changes of mind. As a result we do not have here quite the dramaturgical unity and verisimilitude of a *monobiblos* poem; nor do we have the rhetorical variety of, say, poem 15. What we have is a poem that encompasses a shift in *temporal* standpoint and suggests an embryonic, one-actor mime-script. Distinct shift in *temporal* standpoint is therefore something Propertius is prepared to entertain. If we accept the implications of this simple example, we shall be properly prepared to appreciate M. Hubbard's brilliant inter-pretation of 2. 28,[45] Propertius' most extended exploitation of such 'shifting temporal standpoint' or one-actor mime technique. In this poem which has as its drama an illness of Cynthia, time passes to the extent that at the beginning Cynthia is apparently badly ill, at the end she is recovered. (Editors seeking *monobiblos*-type unities have made any-thing up to four poems out of it.)

There is therefore a significant change in Propertius' second book: Cynthia poems of a quite different structure and technique are attempted. We do not need to posit a stimulus for this, but I think in fact there was one. Tibullus' first book probably appeared between the first and second parts (originally two separate books: above, p. 120) of our Book 2[46] and his poems will anyway probably have been available before publication to a member of the most elevated literary circle in Rome—as Propertius came to be after and because of his *monobiblos*. And Tibullus' characteristic technique is to allow his elegies to admit shifting standpoint, to follow the shifts and drifts of thought. Tibullus' sections are always less dramatic than Propertius' (that is to say, *rhetorically* dramatic: above, p. 125; paradoxically, and perhaps under the influence of the *monobiblos*, he makes half-hearted attempts to site his 'shifting standpoint' poetry in a dramatic time and place); he tends to order his shifts less distinctly; and he does not venture on shifts in *temporal* standpoint (though he evolves his own form of quasi-mime technique). Nevertheless, he seems for a time to have been the spur to his more talented contemporary.[47] (On Tibullus' technique see further below, pp. 175-184.)

C. *Books 3 and 4*

Poem 3. 16:

> nox media, et dominae mihi uenit epistula nostrae:
>   Tibure me missa iussit adesse mora,
> candida qua geminas ostendunt culmina turris,
>   et cadit in patulos nympha Aniena lacus.
> quid faciam? obductis committam mene tenebris,
>   ut timeam audaces in mea membra manus?
> at si distulero haec nostro mandata timore,
>   nocturno fletus saeuior hoste mihi.
> peccaram semel, et totum sum pulsus in annum:
>   in me mansuetas non habet illa manus.
> nec tamen est quisquam, sacros qui laedat amantis:
>   Scironis media sic licet ire uia.
> quisquis amator erit, Scythicis licet ambulet oris,
>   nemo adeo ut noceat barbarus esse uolet.
> luna ministrat iter, demonstrant astra salebras,
>   ipse Amor accensas percutit ante faces,
> saeua canum rabies morsus auertit hiantis:
>   huic generi quouis tempore tuta uia est.
> sanguine tam paruo quis enim spargatur amantis
>   improbus? exclusis fit comes ipsa Venus.
> quod si certa meos sequerentur funera casus,
>   talis mors pretio uel sit emenda mihi.
> afferet haec unguenta mihi sertisque sepulcrum
>   ornabit custos ad mea busta sedens.
> di faciant, mea ne terra locet ossa frequenti,
>   qua facit assiduo tramite uulgus iter!

post mortem tumuli sic infamantur amantum.
   me tegat arborea deuia terra coma,
aut humer ignotae cumulis uallatus harenae:
   non iuuat in media nomen habere uia.

The middle of the night, and a letter has come from my
     mistress
ordering me to present myself at Tibur without delay,
where white hills proffer twin towers[48]
and the water of Anio falls into wide pools below.
What am I to do? Am I to entrust myself to the shrouding
     darkness
and fear in consequence hands bold against my person?
But if I put off the order because of this fear of mine,
I'll find her tears more fierce than any nocturnal enemy.
Once I offended her, and I was banished for a whole year:
she has ungentle hands as regards me.
But there is no one who would injure sacred lovers.
In love one may travel down the middle of Sciron's road.
Whoever loves may walk on Scythian shores:
no one will want to be so barbarous as to injure him.
The moon lights his way, the stars point out the hazards,
Love himself shakes flaming torches before him.[49]
Savage watchdogs turn aside their gaping jaws.
For the race of lovers the road is safe at any time.
Who so lacks shame that he would be splashed with a lover's
     scant blood?
Venus herself becomes companion of the excluded.
But if certain doom were attendant on my dangers,
why, I ought even to pay for such a death!
She will bring unguents for me and adorn my tomb with
     garlands
and sit by my grave and keep watch.
God grant that she does not lay my bones in a busy place,
where the crowd journeys on the busy highway.
Thus after death are lovers' tombs disgraced.
Let some sequestered spot with shading trees cover me,
or may I be buried protected (only) by a mound of nameless
     sand:
I do *not* want to have my name published on the highway.

Propertius receives a midnight summons from Cynthia. She is
at Tibur and wants him there, straight away. 'What am I to
do?' Propertius debates the difficulties; night-time journeys
were hazardous in ancient Italy. The poem seems to be his

soliloquized response, his dramatic reaction, to a definite event: the poem seems to be of the *monobiblos* type.

But Propertius is not here over-occupied with creating a plausible impression of drama: the poem's thought develops in a way which is perhaps not compelled by the dramatic situation. There is something of Tibullan 'shift and drift' about it. A detail reveals Propertius elaborating the thought rhetorically, rather than thinking within a drama as an actor. In line 20 he talks of Venus being the companion of the 'excluded': 'who so lacks shame that he would be splashed with the scant blood of a lover? Venus becomes companion to the excluded.' In an ambience where lovers are typically 'excluded' (*exclusi amatores*) it is a natural variation (indeed a witty *uariatio*) to substitute *exclusi* for *amantes*. But it is natural for a *poet* developing a general *conceit*—not for the actor in a drama where the lover in question (himself) is not in fact excluded.

Clearly Propertius is not very much interested in 'drama' here. Neither is he interested in exploiting 'shifting standpoint'. The poem's associative sequence seems more of a licence than a tactic. What is he interested in?

In lines 11–18 Propertius bolsters his courage in the face of a night-time journey. He cites a belief conventional in love poetry that the lover is inviolable,[50] including the thought that 'nobody will want to be so barbarous as to injure a lover'. The nice witty irony of course is that there is one person readily so barbarous: the beloved herself for whom the lover is meditating hazarding this journey. Cynthia has 'not gentle', that is to say barbarous, hands as regards him (10). Perhaps a purpose of the poem is simply wit.

In most of the section on the lover's inviolability the reason for that inviolability seems to be divine or supernatural favour (11-12, 15-18, 20). But at certain moments, at 14 and especially at 19, this confidence collapses. Quite a different reason is cited why the lover should be inviolable: 'who so lacks shame that he would be splashed with a lover's scant blood?' The argument rests on the lover's *weakness*. It is developed out of his proverbial pallor.[51] Pallor (one could say) means anaemia and anaemia means scanty blood. And someone with scanty blood is surely too pathetic and negligible for anything to attack. With amusing incongruity Propertius maintains that the lover is both too powerful and too weak to touch. We could say that this illuminates the lover's ambivalence, his shifting emotions; or we could say (with more truth I think) that the conjunction of two different and conflicting reasons for the lover's conventional inviolability is simply designed to be humorous. The assumption that the lover is anaemic is amusing in itself: a humorously *literal* inference from his proverbial pallor. This sort of literalism is an Ovidian tactic (pp. 248 ff.). Propertius is, I think, exploiting the situation of the poem for wit.

That Propertius should proceed from thoughts of danger, through thoughts of death, to thoughts of burial is not uncharacteristic (though the occasion hardly compels the progression). But what point is he making when he insists on a certain type of place to be buried in? Or rather, when he insists that he should *not* be buried in a certain type of place —in fact a usual burial place for Romans (by the roadside). Provided he is not buried there he seems prepared to be buried anywhere: for if the 'sequestered spot' reflects some positive choice, a 'mound of nameless sand' does not. That suggests the very minimum requirement of ritual—which Propertius will settle for, if it will prevent his having his 'name published on the highway'. Why does he want anything rather than a public burial (a strange request for a writer)? What's wrong with the highway?

In Book 3 Propertius elaborates his claim to Callimachean pedigree with great detail and (I think) humorous speciousness (see especially poems 1 and 3, and below, pp. 147 f.); what he does is, in effect, equate Callimacheanism with his own sort of love poetry. Now Callimachus' famous *Aetia* preface used vivid imagery to illustrate Callimachean literary exclusivity, originality, esotericism: 'Tread a path which carriages do not trample; do not drive your chariot upon the common tracks of others, nor along a wide road, but on unworn paths though your course be narrow.' Propertius had already adapted some of this to his own purposes. In 3. 1 it assists his grand literary manifesto. In 2. 1 he used it to imply the conceit that the Callimachean poet not only writes according to his principles but lives according to them.[52] What we have in our poem is a further adaptation and a further conceit. The Callimachean poet not only writes and lives according to his principles but must be buried according to them too. Once upon a time (in 2. 13 B) Propertius the morbid lover-poet had dwelt upon his appropriate burial; now as the morbid *Callimachean* poet he dwells humorously on his appropriate *Callimachean* burial. Of course he would dislike the idea of burial by a highway. How could a Callimachean poet be buried by the highway where the crowd journeys? For him the *deuia terra*. We see the logic—delightfully sequential. Propertius constructs a witty conceit out of Callimachean exclusivity and his own morbidity—and again the way he reasons reminds one of Ovid (cf. e.g. p. 248).

It seems to me that in many of the Cynthia poems of Book 3 the emphasis is no longer on what it was. Perhaps the affair was not so interesting or powerful; be that as it may (we are bound to conjecture something of the kind) Propertius seems now to use it as a *vehicle*—for wit or other types of point or display. Exceptions to this are, in particular, poem 10[53] and the last two in the book, which write *finis* to the affair and, it seems, to Cynthia poetry.

Poem 6 reveals a nice paradox: Propertius offering to free his go-between slave if the slave does his job properly, that is, restores Propertius to *his* 'slavery' (that is a paradox that Ovid makes play with).[54] It also displays Propertian technical skill in suggesting *three* characters and their speech, within a drama resembling mime, without infringing the Elegists' law that allows only the Elegist himself to speak (Tibullus does the same thing by different means).[55] This technical achievement and the wit seem to me the main strengths of the poem. Poem 11 proceeds deviously from Propertius' own situation at the beginning to make (among other things) political statements—and innuendo.[56] In the fifteenth poem the opening situation seems little more than a peg on which to hang a short mythical narrative (Dirce).[57] And the aim of poem 17 is surely to amuse. It is cast as a prayer to Bacchus, asking him to bring relief to Propertius in his love-torment ('now o Bacchus I prostrate myself before your altars'). It includes a promise that the poet will serve him as poetical *laudator*—and as vine-grower. This seems to me virtually a burlesque, an absurd inflation, of the more usual entreaty of the lover: to wine to drown his sorrows (cf. e.g. Tibull. 1. 2). That is after all what Propertius really wants. The poem concludes:

> tu modo seruitio uacuum me siste superbo,
> atque hoc sollicitum uince sopore caput.

> Do you only disengage me from haughty imposition of
>   slavery
> and subdue my anguished head with sleep.

That is where Tibullus' poem begins.

It is, we should note, plausible that Propertius should be attempting different things in his Cynthia poems in Book 3. Much of the book is so different from Books 1 and 2 that it is not, even in name, about Cynthia.

The farewell to Cynthia and Cynthia poetry announced in the last poems of Book 3 is not strictly final. Two poems in Book 4 concern her: poem 7, describing an appearance by Cynthia's ghost, and poem 8 on an excursion by the living Cynthia to Lanuvium and Propertius' unsuccessful and interrupted attempt to console himself with two stand-ins. These poems are magnificent reading and do not, I think, require much discussion from me. A sample will lead swiftly to the point I want to make. 4. 8. 47–64:[58]

> cantabant surdo, nudabant pectora caeco:
>   Lanuuii ad portas, ei mihi, totus eram;
> cum subito rauci sonuerunt cardine postes,
>   nec leuia ad primos murmura facta Lares.
> nec mora, cum totas resupinat Cynthia ualuas,
>   non operosa comis, sed furibunda decens.
> pocula mi digitos inter cecidere remissos,
>   pallueruntque ipso labra soluta mero.

fulminat illa oculis et quantum femina saeuit,
  spectaclum capta nec minus urbe fuit.
Phyllidos iratos in uultum conicit unguis:
  territa 'uicini!' Teia clamat 'aquam.'
lumina sopitos turbant elata Quiritis,
  omnis et insana semita nocte sonat.
illas direptisque comis tunicisque solutis
  excipit obscurae prima taberna uiae.
Cynthia gaudet in exuuiis uictrixque recurrit
  et mea peruersa sauciat ora manu . . .

I was deaf to the girls' songs, blind when they bared
    their breasts.
My whole being, alas, was at the gates of Lanuvium.
All of a sudden, the sound of the front door harsh in
    its socket,
tumult at the entrance of the house.
In a second Cynthia flings back the screens
with hair disordered—but lovely in her fury.
My cup fell from my nerveless fingers,
my lips agape with wine went pale.
Lightning flashed from her eyes, she raged with all a
    woman's fury.
It was like a city's sack to look at.
She dashed her angry nails in Phyllis' face;
Teia yelled out 'Help, neighbours, *FIRE*!'
Lamps were brandished; the sleeping burghers awoke.
The whole street rang with the midnight madness.
The girls fled with torn hair and dishevelled dresses
and were taken in by the first tavern in the dingy
    street.
Cynthia rejoicing in her spoils runs back victoriously
and wounds my face with a back-hander . . .

Poems 7 and 8 are both 'reportorial' in technique: they recall
rather than enact events, in the manner of 1. 3 and 2. 29B.
But in both we see the strengthening of a tendency which I
remarked upon above (p. 120): the play is the thing. In the
above quotation Propertius' delight in racy narrative is
manifest; it is hard not to conclude that the narrative exists
for its own sake rather than (if I may be allowed to make a
somewhat artificial dichotomy) to illuminate personality and
feeling. This is generally true of poem 8—and, I think, of
poem 7. It is interesting in this connection that both poem 7

and poem 8 are related in plot to Homeric scenes: poem 7 to the appearance of Patroclus' ghost to Achilles in *Iliad* Book 23, poem 8 to the main plot of the *Odyssey*.[59]

When one looks at Books 3 and 4 as a whole it is clear that Propertius' poetical preoccupation with self, Cynthia, and love is, even in the Cynthia poems, not what it was before. Many readers find this not unwelcome. But it explains why the attention of my book must focus on Books 1 and 2.

3. Conclusion

To prompt some concluding remarks I shall recall one of Propertius' finest poems, 1. 19.

> non ego nunc tristes uereor, mea Cynthia, Manes,
>   nec moror extremo debita fata rogo;
> sed ne forte tuo careat mihi funus amore,
>   hic timor est ipsis durior exsequiis.
> non adeo leuiter nostris puer haesit ocellis,
>   ut meus oblito puluis amore uacet.
> illic Phylacides iucundae coniugis heros
>   non potuit caecis immemor esse locis,
> sed cupidus falsis attingere gaudia palmis
>   Thessalus antiquam uenerat umbra domum.   10
> illic quidquid ero, semper tua dicar imago:
>   traicit et fati litora magnus amor.
> illic formosae ueniant chorus heroinae,
>   quas dedit Argiuis Dardana praeda uiris;
> quarum nulla tua fuerit mihi, Cynthia, forma
>   gratior, et (Tellus hoc ita iusta sinat)
> quamuis te longae remorentur fata senectae,
>   cara tamen lacrimis ossa futura meis.
> quae tu uiua mea possis sentire fauilla!
>   tum mihi non ullo mors sit amara loco.   20
> quam uereor, ne te contempto, Cynthia, busto
>   abstrahat heu nostro puluere iniquus Amor,
> cogat et inuitam lacrimas siccare cadentes!
>   flectitur assiduis certa puella minis.
> quare, dum licet, inter nos laetemur amantes:
>   non satis est ullo tempore longus amor.

> I have no fear now of the gloomy Spirits, Cynthia,
> nor do I mind about the destiny that is owed to the final
>   pyre.

But that perchance my funeral may lack your love—
this fear I find harsher than the rites of death themselves.
Not so lightly has Cupid clung to my eyes
that my dust could be void and forgetful of love.
There in the regions of darkness the hero Protesilaus
could not be unmindful of his sweet wife,
but, desirous to reach his joy with illusory hands,
the Thessalian came to his ancient home a shade.
There, whatever I shall be, I shall always be called *your* image.
Great love crosses even the shores of death.
There, though that band of fabled beauties come,
the heroines which the booty of Troy bestowed on the heroes of
    Greece—
the beauty of none of these will please me more than yours,
    Cynthia.
And (may just Earth allow this to be so)
though the fate of a long old age should delay you,
dear to me, to my tears of welcome, will be your bones.
May you when living have the same feeling for my ashes.
Then death would have no bitterness for me anywhere.
How I fear that, my tomb despised,
unfriendly Love may drag you away from my dust
and compel you against your will to dry your falling tears.
The loyalest of girls is swayed by constant threats.
Wherefore, while it is possible, let us love and be glad together:
love is not long enough in any extent of time.

Throughout his work Propertius exhibits a preoccupation, even an obsession, with death. Thoughts of his own death and burial frequently intrude into unobvious contexts.[60] When he makes romantic statements about 'love until death', these have a striking poignancy and individuality.[61] In 1. 19 Propertius takes that topic a stage further. He tackles the question of love *after* death.

In so doing he reveals another characteristic, which we might label honesty. He faces truth. Indeed the intrusion of prosaic truth upon romance is a process that this romantic poet is concerned to demonstrate. Typically he exploits myth to do so (p. 100). There is a sequence something like this in 1. 19; and such a use of myth. Propertius proceeds from belief in love transcending death to tacit acceptance that this belief is, even if true, irrelevant and unhelpful. I pointed to this above (pp. 100–2). There is more to be said.

The romantic belief itself reflects a stubborn honesty. While we notice this, we may notice a fact of Propertius' style. He means what he says. His vigorous diction is often misrepresented by gratuitous editorial glossing.[62] Propertius sees his existence after death only in terms of bones and ash.[63] His belief in love after death respects this with only temporary deviation; and although the Romans were prepared to associate residual sentience with cremated remains, it is in consequence a macabre, paradoxical, and individual belief. It is his *dust* that will love (6); it is feared that the living Cynthia will not be faithful to his *ash* (19); when he tries to expand his vision of love after death to something more mythically comforting, *ossa*, 'bones' (18) (for that is how Cynthia will be) brings him back to earth. That process is worth noting. Among other things it illustrates another trick of Propertian style.

The myth of Protesilaus contains its intimation of comfortlessness (above, p. 101). But it is still, in the main, a myth positively expounding Propertius' belief (such as it is) in love transcending death. And buoyed up by it, Propertius develops a much more sentimentally comforting picture (11 ff.). There he is, on the other shore, in a mythical Hades untempted by glorious heroines and waiting for Cynthia to come to him. And then he says or seems to say (17 f.): 'although the fate of a long old age delays you <in life>, you will nevertheless be beloved <when you come across> to me, to my tears of welcome.' Naturally, if fleetingly, we take *cara* as feminine singular. Fleetingly we think Propertius has swallowed sentimentality whole. But then comes *ossa* and we see the true function of *cara*. Propertius returns implacably to the only possible version of love transcending death. Cynthia can have no more comforting form of survival than he, and that timely thought cuts his romantic belief ruthlessly back to permissible limits.

Propertius' romantic belief is not therefore rosy. Does it on reflection offer comfort to the lover confronting death? It seems not. The thought of the living Cynthia's inability to remain faithful to his ash, but more importantly I think the realization that the permissible dream even if true lacks comforting substance, leads to the final injunction to love while it is effectively possible, that is to say while they are alive. The poem traces a sequence not exactly from romantic belief to realism, but from a curious, macabre, honest romantic belief to a realistic assessment that that belief is unhelpful, irrelevant, cold. This assessment actually affected the poem before its more explicit acceptance at the end. It explains Propertius' concern for his *funeral* (lines 2-4, 21; the obsession is evident elsewhere).[64] The funeral is perhaps the last time one can meaningfully demonstrate love, the first and last time one can meaningfully demonstrate love in death.

Stylistically *cara . . . ossa* shows what Propertius can achieve by a calculated delay in delivering a word. Transient ambiguity allows him forcefully to surprise us. It allows his poetry more dynamic effect. He demonstrates himself falling prey to one path of thought and bringing himself up sharply. Similarly the myth of Protesilaus itself gains pace and seems to be expounding a larger belief than Propertius essentially holds. Lines 7 f.: the *hero* (with his grand patronymic) was not unmindful in death. The myth concludes *Thessalus antiquam* . . . We expect (I think) a repetition of the pattern of 7, *illic Phylacides . . . heros*. But when the substantive comes for *Thessalus* (*umbra*, 'shade', 'shadow'), it cuts back the import of the myth—and confirms the intimation of *falsis* (see above p. 101). Once again Propertius pulls himself up. Again, we could say, we see Propertian honesty: Propertius demonstrates Propertius' feelings and weaknesses in action.

umbra has its effect on the ensuing sentimental myth. The word used for 'shade' or 'spirit' there is *imago*, the significance of which can extend to the figment of a diseased imagination. *umbra* may help it on its way there. From this angle the grand asseveration *traicit et fati litora magnus amor* (12) may ring less grandly. The force of the words shifts before our eyes, as often in Propertius. Cf. *oculos satiemus amore* in

2. 15. 23 (p. 131): depending on how you view it, that looks back to comedy or on to tragedy.

Poem 19 is complex. Propertius frequently (as we have seen) finds himself beset by more or less conflicting views or feelings, and likes his poems to reproduce psychological uncertainty or vacillation. The ambivalent Propertius produces ambivalent poems; complex Propertius produces complex poems (complex: dense, rich, suggestive. I do not necessarily mean difficult, though sometimes the poems are difficult). Complexity and ambivalence are inherent in his very phraseology. Style matches content. Propertius leans on language as thought and emotion leant on him.

I have translated *lacrimis* in 1. 19. 18 (*cara tamen lacrimis ossa futura meis*) as 'tears of welcome'. That must be a legitimate rendering. But what sort of tears do bones normally evoke? That implication must also be there: indeed the jarring emphasis with which *ossa* affects the reader (and its neighbour *lacrimis*) precipitates it; and it suits one level of the text.

When Propertius thought of Protesilaus' achievement he thought of it as an abstract idea—and he thought of the act which crowned it. He offers us a phrase, *attingere gaudia*, which suggests both: 'to touch his beloved', and 'to attain joy'; the former sense is supported by *palmis*—and undermined by *falsis*. When he requests Cynthia to wear a certain dress on her birthday, he chooses the one in which she 'first caught his eye' (*qua primum oculos cepisti ueste Properti*, 3. 10. 15); but the phrase also means, very significantly in context, 'first made him fall in love with her'.

Such pregnancy of expression is typical of Propertius. It need not be produced by regular semantic or syntactical ambiguity. *lacrimis* was, we might say, ambiguous; but one of its implications was really produced by virtue of its juxtaposition with *ossa*. That juxtaposition contributes meaning: it forces us to associate the two words' resonances and to draw inferences from that association—in the process which Pound would call 'logopoeia', and M. W. Edwards 'intensification of meaning'; and cf. M. S. Silk's 'Interaction outside the grammar'.[65] An inflected language allows considerable freedom in the way one disposes words in a line or sentence, and hence for such effect. It is popular in most Roman poets and ubiquitous in Propertius. Note for example the pathos suggested by the juxtaposition of *umbra* and the resonant *domum* (on which see above, p. 56) in 1. 19. 10; of *ossa* and *rosa* in 1. 17. 22; note how in 2. 20. 17 (p. 122) the protestation implicit in the vocative *uita* (cf. p. 37) is acutely placed next to its only limiting factor *tenebras*; and so on.

'Style matches content', I have said. Let us focus on that now—and on the question of personality. We can draw a contrast between Propertius and Tibullus.

As I shall point out in my discussion of Tibullus (pp. 188–189), the ancient world was very conscious of the reasonable notion that the 'style is the man'. Style reflects character, style projects a personality. In Tibullus we find an odd situation. Tibullus' style is urbane and polished, his content often grovelling and rural. There is a calculated tension between the man of Tibullus' style and the man of his content. To get at Tibullus himself is a teasing process. In Propertius things are different. Propertius generally aims at consonance between style and content; and both reflect his personality, in harmony. This talk of personality may raise hackles (cf. preface). But certainly Propertius' and Tibullus' poetry suggests *a* personality. In Propertius' poetry we deduce a personality that is morbid, honest, ambivalent, complex . . .

Before proceeding I ought to offer further justification of my claim that Propertius aims at consonance between style and content. His diction is far more eclectic, far less *tersus* than Tibullus' and his style as a whole is more flexible and various, suiting his varying subjects and moods. But let us take something specific and perhaps on the face of it problematic. Propertius produces carefully structured lines and neoteric artistries of word-order (notable features of Tibullus' urbane *cultus*)[66] less often than Tibullus. But he does sometimes display them, and prominently. Does he—unlike Tibullus—make them harmonize with content? Basically, yes. Pressure of space forces me to be dogmatic on a very delicate and perhaps subjective topic, but I shall try to illustrate the point with some examples.

In 1. 19. 13 *formosae . . . chorus heroinae*, a phrase frames a noun in apposition to it in an elegant, artificial pattern;[67] its elegance clearly matches the content, the imagined beautiful heroines. Even more obviously the artistic patterning at 2. 31. 8 suits the subject there: the sculptures of an artist; compare too 2. 33. 38, a reference to the charming recitation of poems. And the prettiness of 2. 3. 24, *candidus argutum sternuit omen Amor* (abBA) suits the prettiness of sentiment.

Artistic word-patterning is no less evident in 1. 3. 1–6 (p. 98) and elsewhere in that poem;[68] and the suitability of such style at these points is clear. More challenging is 2. 8. 29–36 quoted on p. 91. Here Propertius distributes nouns and adjectives in abBA and other prominent patterns. On the face of it, stylistic elegance at this point—when Propertius is expounding grief—might seem discordant. This is not, I think, the case. Elegance is not quite the word to use here. Such stylistic exquisiteness suggests *control*; and when we note the sheer *weight* and *length* of the words that are thus *evenly* ordered, we could also say it suggests *dignity*. I find in fact that the style supports the gravity, relentlessness, monumentality of grief that it is the purpose of these lines to expound.

Initially troubling (a penultimate example) may be 2. 9. 9–10:

> nec non exanimem amplectens Briseis Achillem
> candida uesana uerberat ora manu.

> Briseis embracing the dead Achilles strikes
> her fair face with maddened hand.

Line 10 is a pure 'Golden Line' (ab verb AB). Its elegance is surely inconsonant with the thought of the line. Actually (we could say) it is inconsonant with *part* of the line, the ugly mourning act. It *supports* the beauty of Briseis' face. If the line's purpose is to emphasize that a *pretty* face is being lacerated, style suits that purpose. Something similar could

be said about 3. 15. 14, *molliaque immitis fixit in ora manus*
('she fixed her pitiless hands on to (Dirce's) soft face').

Morbid, honest, ambivalent, complex—and of course
suspicious, passionate, romantic . . . epithets of a plausible
personality emerge from the poetry of Propertius. Such is the
poetry. Esoteric too, but mainly functionally so. Propertius
will allude to the other, conventional story of Atalanta (while
giving his own more recondite version) in the epithet *uelocem*
(1. 1. 15), but the epithet has a pleasant point in his own
context. *Amor* who was agile enough even in the case of
swift-footed Atalanta is now, in Propertius' case, *slow* (17).
In his obscurer myths Propertius usually provides enough
basic information for us to know what is going on: for
example, in Brimo, 2. 2. The myth *qua* myth introduces the
general atmosphere of the mythical world (romance) and tells
enough of its own story. The strangeness of the name then
simply lends mystery to the resonance of the comparison.

Talking of esotericism, I think it worth while pointing out
that I do not take Propertius' protestations of Callimachean-
ism in Books 2 and 3 very seriously; nor did he.[69] In Book 1,
before he has entered the imperial circle, it has not occurred
to him that he is in any way a Callimachus. He defends Elegy
(*love* Elegy) against Epic on quite un-Callimachean grounds
(its usefulness)—and invokes not Callimachus but the archaic
Elegist, Mimnermus (poems 7 and 9). It is at the start of
Book 2, when he has been admitted to the grand circle of
Maecenas and finds that a certain pressure goes with the new
position to write up the *res gestae* of the *princeps*, that he
starts making Callimachean noises. Vergil, who was in many
respects a genuinely Callimachean poet, had shown how a
deft re-use of motifs from Callimachus' *Aetia* preface could
enable one to decline such pressure with grace and wit
(*Eclogue* 6. 1 ff.).[70] Propertius observed and learnt. He was
not in any real sense a Callimachean poet but he was prepared
to adopt Callimachus' mantle and invoke his authority for
this purpose. That is what he does (2. 1. 39 ff.). And at this
stage this was his only motive in professing Callimacheanism
(and the only effect of Callimachus on him): he gained access

to a graceful, witty, civilized means of saying no. His poetry is, I think, as yet largely uninfluenced by the theory or practice of his 'master'. In Book 3 Propertius does do new things, but the Callimachean programmatic splendour of poems 1-3 actually boils down (again) to a statement *for* love poetry and *against* epic. The poems are *retrospective*, an 'image' for Propertius the love poet, not a programme for such new poetry as there is in Book 3. It is a self-consciously, intentionally pretentious image, exuberantly and humorously delivered in response to what Propertius saw as the genuinely pretentious Alcaean claims of Horace.[71] I doubt whether Propertius had read very much of Callimachus during the period of composition of Books 1-3. Perhaps in Book 3 he is starting to extend his acquaintance. By Book 4 his flat claim to be *Romanus Callimachus* has some but not a lot of validity.

. . . passionate, romantic—and of course humorous. I have repeatedly pointed to Propertian wit. Propertius uses it functionally within a drama (1. 2); he exercises humour at expense of self (1. 3, etc.), at the expense of others (1. 10). He is a master of irony, hyperbole, bathos, cultivated incongruity, and other devices of wit. And he is unexpected in its deployment. One would not have thought that Propertius who seems so genuinely disturbed by death would construct witty conceits about his own burial (3. 16), a topic of morbid interest elsewhere. Or perhaps one would. One senses again a personality that is individual and real. The psychology is plausible. We may remember Dr. Johnson's huge laughter on the occasion of an acquaintance's making a will—Johnson who had a horror of death.[72]

VI

Tibullus

(For Tibullus' life and the dating of his books relative to Propertius see chapter III)

I preface my discussion of Tibullus' poetry by mentioning an obvious point of contrast between him and Propertius. For Propertius mythology provided an indispensable and frequent vehicle of expression (p. 82). Through mythology he said things otherwise unsaid or unsayable. Tibullus introduces myths very rarely.[1] The comparison of Delia to Thetis (1. 5. 43–6) I shall mention later (p. 263). His other outstanding example is the long myth at 2. 3. 11 ff., an erotic version of Apollo's slavery to Admetus cited in justification and illustration of his own willingness to be a slave to Nemesis. He tells the story with skill, wit, and charm. But one gets the impression that here is much of the real reason why he included the myth: to demonstrate his narrative skill, wit, and charm (cf. further below, pp. 165 and 167). Mythology did not, it seems, offer Tibullus a necessary or attractive medium for communicating ideas and feelings. There are probably various reasons for this, but one thought has, I think, been neglected.

1. Tibullan Romanticism 1: Delia

1. 1. 1–14 and 19–44

> diuitias alius fuluo sibi congerat auro
>   et teneat culti iugera magna soli,
> quem labor assiduus uicino terreat hoste,
>   Martia cui somnos classica pulsa fugent·
> me mea paupertas uitae traducat inerti,   5
>   dum meus assiduo luceat igne focus.
> ipse seram teneras maturo tempore uites
>   rusticus et facili grandia poma manu,
> nec Spes destituat, sed frugum semper aceruos
>   praebeat et pleno pinguia musta lacu: 10
> nam ueneror seu stipes habet desertus in agris
>   seu uetus in triuio florida serta lapis,

et quodcumque mihi pomum nouus educat annus
  libatum agricolae ponitur ante deo.   14

uos quoque, felicis quondam, nunc pauperis agri   19
  custodes, fertis munera uestra, Lares;
tunc uitula innumeros lustrabat caesa iuuencos,
  nunc agna exigui est hostia parua soli:
agna cadet uobis, quam circum rustica pubes
  clamet 'io, messes et bona uina date'.
iam modo, iam possim contentus uiuere paruo   25
  nec semper longae deditus esse uiae,
sed Canis aestiuos ortus uitare sub umbra
  arboris ad riuos praetereuntis aquae.
nec tamen interdum pudeat tenuisse bidentem
  aut stimulo tardos increpuisse boues;   30
non agnamue sinu pigeat fetumue capellae
  desertum oblita matre referre domum.
at uos exiguo pecori, furesque lupique,
  parcite: de magno est praeda petenda grege.
hic² ego pastoremque meum lustrare quotannis   35
  et placidam soleo spargere lacte Palem.
adsitis, diui, neu uos e paupere mensa
  dona nec e puris spernite fictilibus:
fictilia antiquus primum sibi fecit agrestis,
  pocula de facili composuitque luto.   40
non ego diuitias patrum fructusque requiro
  quos tulit antiquo condita messis auo:
parua seges satis est, satis est requiescere lecto
  si licet et solito membra leuare toro.

Wealth let another man gather for himself in yellow gold
and possess great acres of cultivated land—
he whom constant toil in the enemy's vicinity terrifies,
he whose sleep the blare of the trumpet routs.
Let my poorness transfer *me* to a life of inaction,   5
so long as my hearth glows with a constant fire.
Let *me* as a farmer set tender vines early in the season
and tall fruit trees with skilful hand;
nor let Hope fail me but always supply an abundance of crops
and rich new wine in full vats.   10
For I pray at every solitary tree-stump in the fields
or old stone at the cross-roads that is garlanded with flowers,
and the first-fruits that the new year raises for me
are placed in offering to the farmer God, in front of him.   14

You too, guardians of a property once fortunate now poor,　19
you, O Lares, receive your gifts.
In the old days a slaughtered heifer purified countless cattle;
now a ewe-lamb is the sacrificial-offering of my tiny land.
A ewe-lamb will be sacrificed to you, and around her the
　　　country folk
will shout 'Io! [a ritual cry] grant us good wine and harvest.'
Now, if only now, may I be able to live content with little　25
and not be continually handed over to the long road;
but rather avoid the summer rising of the Dog-star in the
　　　shade
of a tree by a stream of water running by.
But I would not be ashamed sometimes to hold a mattock
or reprove slow oxen with a goad;　　　　　　　　　　　30
nor would it irk me to bring home in my arms a lamb or goat's
　　　offspring
deserted by its careless mother.
But do you robbers and wolves spare my tiny livestock:
plunder is to be sought from big flocks.
Here I am accustomed to purify my shepherd annually　　35
and to sprinkle kindly Pales with milk.
Oh gods be present and do not scorn gifts from a poor table
or from spotless earthenware:
a countryman of old first made earthenware,
and shaped cups from pliant clay.　　　　　　　　　　　40
I do not miss the fortune of my father or the profit
that garnered harvest brought my grandfather of old.
A small crop is enough, it is enough if it is possible to rest in a
　　　bed
and lighten the limbs on a familiar couch.

(My translation depends heavily on Guy Lee's. But I have had
to adapt it, and (unfortunately) turn it into prose because I
differ from him, and from most scholars, in my understanding
of the subjunctives in 7–10. In addition a greater literalness is
useful at this point. I have a brief comment to make on the
lines I have omitted in a footnote.)[3]

No mention of girls yet. That is perhaps a surprise—but
Tibullus is rarely purely and simply a love poet in the sense
that Propertius often is. Instead we find here the characteristic
Tibullan emphasis: the desire for a life in the country. This is
the first statement of a repeated wish, and it is important to
understand exactly what Tibullus has in mind. First some

quotations: 'his private idyllic pastoral world', 'a world of mood and not place ... a dreamlike world of escape, located somewhere between Arcadia and the forum'. Many if not most critics would subscribe to this sort of summary and comment.[4] It is actually quite false. Practically every word is misleading. The world and life that Tibullus wishes for is not pastoral in a literary sense and not exclusively pastoral in a literal sense; we must be careful about terms like 'idyllic', eschew terms like 'Arcadia', and even 'dream' is perhaps inappropriate—in the sense that Tibullus' dream was not *merely* a dream, *wholly* unrealized or unrealizable.

The first and vital fact to note is that Tibullus' wishes concern living life *on his own, real country holding*. He makes this quite clear in the lines I have quoted, giving information on its former and its present fortunes. It was once grand but is now much diminished—comparatively poor—a familiar story at the time. Readers would recognize the story; they would probably assume that the estate had been reduced in the notorious confiscations of 42 BC.[5] Note especially lines 19-22. He is addressing the protecting gods (*Lares*) of the estate he wants to live in, and describing their circumstances. The estate clearly exists and is equally clearly his own. This is confirmed and amplified by 35-6 and 41-4. Tibullus' basic aspiration therefore is to live in an *available* rural simplicity. Far from an 'idyllic pastoral world' he seems to want the sort of simplicity that a contemporary country holding reduced in circumstances could offer. This wish is markedly unorthodox and unambitious for someone in Tibullus' position (see further below, pp. 155 ff.) but comprehensible enough—and with some parallel. Even the great Pompey (*si parua licet componere Magnis*) wanted at times, to people's considerable consternation, to opt out of public life and retire to a rural retreat.[6]

Tibullus' basic wish seems therefore realistic—and realizable. So why doesn't he realize it? Perhaps life conspires against him. He certainly tries to reconcile one irreconcilable element with his basic wish. I return to this question shortly.

In the meantime consider 1. 10. 7-12 and 19-24.

diuitis hoc uitium est auri, nec bella fuerunt
    faginus astabat cum scyphus ante dapes.
non arces, non uallus erat, somnumque petebat
    securus uarias dux gregis inter oues.   10
tunc mihi uita foret, Valgi, nec tristia nossem
    arma, nec audissem corde micante tubam.

tunc melius tenuere fidem cum paupere cultu   19
    stabat in exigua ligneus aede deus.   20
hic placatus erat seu quis libauerat uuam
    seu dederat sanctae spicea serta comae;
atque aliquis uoti compos liba ipse ferebat
    postque comes purum filia parua fauum.

Rich gold—the fault lies there. No wars when stoups of
        beechwood
stood at the sacrificial feast,
no citadels, no palisades. The leader led a flock
& sued for sleep in safety among the speckled ewes.
O Valgius, were I living then, never had I known
sad arms or heard the trumpet with a pounding heart.

Men kept better faith in the days when wooden gods
humbly decked & tended stood in tiny shrines,
friendly if one gave them the first of the grapes
or bound their sacred locks with spikes of grain;
& the man whose prayer was answered would bring them
        cakes of meal,
his little daughter following with honey in the comb.
                                                    (Lee)

Here Tibullus *can* be detected yearning for a primal and
idealized (but presumably not totally fictitious) rural simpli-
city. But he knows what he is doing: just yearning. He is
quite clear what is for him the realistic obverse of military
life, which now impends: a life of peace *on his own holding*.[7]
It is to the Lares of his family estate that he commends him-
self; and it is there that he pictures his demonstration of
gratitude if and when he comes through. Note 13–16:

nunc ad bella trahor, et iam quis forsitan hostis
    haesura in nostro tela gerit latere.
sed patrii seruate Lares: aluistis et idem,
    cursarem uestros cum tener ante pedes.

Now I am dragged to war, and some enemy perhaps
already wears the weapon that will pierce my side.
Save me, Lares of my fathers, as you nurtured me
when I ran around in childhood at your feet.

(Lee)

(cf. 1. 1. 19-20); and 25-9:

at nobis aerata, Lares, depellite tela,
    <*lacuna*>
hostiaque e plena rustica porcus hara.
hanc pura cum ueste sequar myrtoque canistra
    uincta geram, myrto uinctus et ipse caput.
sic placeam uobis: alius sit fortis in armis . . .

Then turn aside, O Lares, the bronze missiles from us
    <*there is a gap in the manuscripts at this point*>
& the country offering, a hog from a full sty.
I shall follow, clad in white, bearing a rush basket
bound with myrtle, wearing a myrtle wreath myself.
So may I find your favour. Others can be brave in arms . . .

(Lee)

Poem 1. 10 in fact fills out the picture of the Tibullan farm.[8] And we also see one of the things that prevented him from realizing his basic rural wish: the claims of war (in spite of all he says in 1. 1); more exactly, we may take it, it was loyalty to his patron Messalla.[9] Another factor was love, the claims of Delia. 1. 1. 55 f.:

me retinent uinctum formosae uincla puellae,
    et sedeo duras ianitor ante fores.

But I am held a pris'ner, fettered by a lovely girl,
    and take my post as keeper at her cruel door.

(Lee)

Tibullus actually makes this statement to Messalla, as an implied reason why he cannot go on military campaign; but clearly a man bound to his mistress's door must find it hard to be simultaneously a man of country pursuits on his rural estate. And of course love's and Delia's place in and effect on Tibullus' aspiration is a crucial question.

Before tackling it I shall revert to the basic wish: to Tibullus' desire to live in an available rural simplicity. He means this quite literally. But Tibullus attaches certain implications to it, which need attention. First, he introduces the wish provocatively. He calls the life he seeks a *uita iners*, a life of inaction (a disreputable label), and scorns military and mercantile activity (1. 1. 1 ff. and 49 ff.), i.e. reputable activities for a knight like himself (cf. chapter IV). Secondly, what he chooses to see as a *uita iners*, others might have preferred to view differently. His provocative stance has a nice piquancy.

Tibullus wants to be the undisturbed master of his farm, even (as we shall see) himself to act the *agricola*. Now it was very basic to Roman thinking that a rural life like this was the good life, the original and essentially Roman life. The way of the farmer was indeed easily and naturally a symbol of or a metaphor for *moral* behaviour. This feeling had already been given clear expression by the elder Cato and it is basic to the intention of Vergil's *Georgics*.[10] Therefore to aspire to lead the life of the *rusticus*, the *agricola*, was something potentially emotive; the *agricola* was an emotive figure, the symbol or embodiment of the good, moral life. But here is Tibullus representing rustic life as quite another sort of good life, the life of careless *otium*. Tibullus *contrasts* rustic life with current notions of what were in practice respectable and good occupations for a Roman knight. He is reinterpreting and re-deploying against the Roman establishment's thinking a figure of the establishment's own moral mythology. Tibullus' wish must have made provocative and (initially) puzzling reading. The sturdy *agricola* now represents comparatively peaceful retirement. Tibullus seems to be building insolently on the achievement of the *Georgics* and perhaps we already detect that underestimated quantity, Tibullan humour.

I now look a little more closely at the sequence of thought and implications of 1. 1. 1–44 (they are much misinterpreted by critics; on the four lines I have omitted see note 3).

1–6: Anyone, says Tibullus, is welcome to wealth who is prepared to tolerate *militia*. He himself is suffering from lack of funds (*paupertas*)—the cause of which is subsequently revealed. Now *paupertas* would normally be an added spur to a knight to do the conventional thing, to go on a lucrative *militia*. Tibullus' unexpected and emphatic reaction is to wish that it will be the cause of his retiring (being 'transferred': wittily he uses a term with a military tinge)[11] to simplicity, to inaction, to a way of life that accepts and adapts to lack of funds. . . .

7-8 . . . to, in fact, the life of a farmer. We note that Tibullus emphatically states his wish to participate: *he* will plant. Inaction? It is a slight puzzle. But we soon learn that his idea of country work is very much that of a dilettante, a 'Sonntagslandwirt',[12] a week-end farmer: the circumspect phrasing of 29-32 wittily puts *ipse seram* into perspective (see below). And Tibullus has a *pastor* (35)—and slaves (1. 5). His intention in fact is to dabble—like his friend Horace, on his Sabine farm:

> rident uicini glaebas et saxa mouentem
>
> the neighbours laugh at me moving earth and rocks
> (*Epist*. 1. 14. 39)

He is going to be *rusticus* in a carefully defined sense: the country squire. His aspiration is certainly no vague dream, no idyll, no Arcadia. But neither is it the stern life of the *Georgics*, as he almost suggests.

9-10: Tibullus hopes for success in his real life of rural retreat. And he says (or implies), he deserves it—because of (*nam* . . .) his rural piety. In the country he is accustomed to observe the farmer's religious rites and practices (11-14); and he is duly attentive to the protecting deities of his farm (19-22)—and he assures these deities of his continuing attention (23-4). Note the present indicative tenses in 11-22. The picture clarifies. Tibullus already knows country life, and follows country lore. Indeed he already runs a farm. So the rural life is already real for him; the aspiration of the poem is that it should become full-time (he should be *transferred* to it). He will not allow his *paupertas* to take him off into *militia*; rather he will seize upon it as a motive to retire permanently to the simple life. And his present rural piety should ensure the success of this permanent venture.

19-22 also clarify Tibullus' *paupertas*. It is due to the reduction of his estate—by confiscations, one would assume.

25-32: Spurred by the enticing picture he has himself evoked Tibullus restates his aspiration, again in opposition to a conventional career. Some points should be noticed. First an emphasis. Tibullus says 'Now . . . may I *be able* to live content with little and not be continually *handed over* to the long road' (i.e. go on campaign, *militia*). It is noticeable that he sees himself as the *victim* of events. Tibullan passivity will be remarked elsewhere. Secondly, we should note the caution with which he now phrases his own possible contribution to manual work. *nec tamen interdum pudeat*, 'I would not be ashamed sometimes', suggests a delicacy more urbane than rustic. It offsets the vigorous 7-8 and is surely humorously intended (cf. above, p. 156). And the spotlight is here on ease: '. . . avoid the summer rising of the Dog-star in the shade of a tree by a stream of water running by'. There *will* be a lot of inertia in the *uita iners*. Compare, incidentally, Horace talking (in the very realistic epistle mentioned above, line 35) about the benefits of *his* country farm:

> cena breuis iuuat et prope riuum somnus in herba

> a scant dinner is a pleasure to me, and a sleep in
> the grass by the stream.

Made anxious by one thing and another (consideration of the smallness of his estate; the thought of an abandoned lamb or kid) Tibullus turns to beg predators to leave his exiguous flocks alone and attack larger properties (33-4). Again we sense humour. Lines 35-6 then imply confidence that the predators will not in fact succeed: he is careful to observe the *Palilia*, the shepherd festival. Note again the present indicative tense. This is something Tibullus already does (like the observances mentioned in 11-14 and the offerings made to the Lares (19 f.), it is something in his present conduct that he cites as warranty for the success of his full-time project). The life he aspires to gains further definition.

He then begs the gods generally to be with him (37-43). They are not to spurn poor gifts. He cites reasons why they shouldn't. And poor his offerings will be, owing to the reduced condition of the property. While not impairing the apparent naturalness of his sequence of thought, Tibullus manages yet again to fill in detail and confute his idyllic critics. 'I do not miss the fortune of my father or the profit/that garnered harvest brought my grandfather of old./Enough is a small crop . . .'

In 43-4 Tibullus slips smoothly into a further theme. A small crop is enough. It is enough too 'if it is possible to rest in a bed and lighten the limbs on a familiar couch'. And this then is developed into a familiar sentiment:[13]

> quam iuuat immites uentos audire cubantem

> How pleasant it is lying there to listen to wild winds.

Tibullus presumably has in mind lying in bed *at his farm*; for he has not yet completed his section of rural aspiration: that happens clearly at 49-50 (*hoc mihi contingat* . . . 'let this be my fortune . . .'). So when he continues the theme of peaceful sleep yet further in 46

> et dominam tenero continuisse sinu

> and hold a mistress in tender embrace

that too is presumably sited in the rural context. At last our love poet has hinted at love. And it introduces the first unbelievable note into the long wish sequence. *domina* is the Elegiac lover's word for the domineering, dominating mistress to whom he is slave, *seruus*. Tibullus means his *domina* Delia (57), whose door he is compelled to attend (56). It *is* hard to imagine such an essentially urban and very often highly materialistic figure (so she is presented: see below) happily at home in Tibullus' simple rural existence.[14]

Did Tibullus really have such thoughts? Emphatically (according to his poems) yes. And that, the idea of Delia taking her part in the simple rural life, is the one irreconcilable, impossible, fantastical element in Tibullus' otherwise plausible aspiration. It is only touched on in passing in this first poem; but it is there and will subsequently be amplified. In this respect (but only in this respect) Tibullus the aspiring *rusticus* was spinning dreams of the unrealizable—striving yearningly and pathetically for an impossible goal, a true romantic.

At this point it is convenient briefly to consider Delia.[15] I hope what follows will not be taken as a naïvely biographical approach to a figure in a book of poems. I simply try to interpret a character who is presented to us—in what is after all designed to appear as an autobiographical and consistent collection.

If Apuleius' story that 'Delia' was a pseudonym for Plania is true (and we have no compelling reason to doubt it), then she was a free Roman citizen: only Roman citizens bore gentile names. Poem 1. 5 may suggest she was not married. On the other hand 1. 2 (43 *coniunx tuus*) and in particular 1. 6 clearly imply that she was. But lines 67 f. of 1. 6 equally clearly imply that she was not married in the full and official Roman sense:

> quamuis non uitta ligatos
> impediat crines nec stola longa pedes

> though no band confines her braided hair nor
> long dress her feet

She does not and may not wear the traditional dress of the Roman married lady. The way to reconcile all these points is to assume that she was a freedwoman (*libertina*) rather than freeborn and married in a *de facto* sense to a freeborn Roman 'husband'; to assume, therefore, that when she was 'married', which may not of course have been all the time that Tibullus apparently knew her and wrote about her, she was a *concubina* or equivalent.[16] It would follow a common enough pattern if her 'husband' had been her former master and manumitted her with the partial intention of elevating and stabilizing her status.

A couple more items of circumstantial detail. Delia has a mother, kindly disposed towards Tibullus—whom Tibullus celebrates sentimentally (1. 6. 57 ff.). She may or may not be the same person as the nurse-type figure of 1. 3. 83 ff., who it is hoped is 'guarding Delia's honour with her continual care', while Tibullus is away. There does not seem to have been very profound influence from this quarter. Nor does her husband seem to have been or remained much interested in her faithfulness (1. 6; but I do not discount the wit of the poem: see below, pp. 186 f.).

The details of all this are not too important to us. The general character of Delia is. *libertina* can be synonymous with the professional or semi-professional *demi-mondaine*.[17] That is how Delia appears, promiscuous and tantalizing (1. 6). She is cast as mercenary too (1. 5. 60-8), and open to the influence of a procuress (*lena*): 1. 5. 47 ff. And she is of course an essentially *urban* creature, in soul and location. She is clearly depicted as living in the city (presumably The City: Rome): note for example the 'excluded lover' poem 1. 2, as well as the scenery of 1. 6; and for the beautiful (1. 5. 43-6) *demi-mondaine* with imperial aims in love there can be no other home.

And yet: this is the girl with whom Tibullus wanted to share his rural life. More than that, her presence is really indispensable if the rural life is in fact to be ideal in Tibullus' eyes. He shows his hand suddenly in 1. 2. 73-6. 'Riches are nothing compared with love', he has just (in effect) said; and he continues

> ipse boues—mea si tecum modo Delia—possim
> iungere et in solito pascere monte pecus
> et te dum liceat teneris retinere lacertis,
> mollis et inculta sit mihi somnus humo.

> Myself, if I could only be with you, my Delia,
> I'd yoke the oxen, feed the flock on the familiar hill.
> So long as I could hold you prisoner in tender arms
> my sleep would be soft on the natural ground.

> (Lee)

Tibullus is back to stressing his willingness to do real work in the country—and to undergo discomfort: *but provided that Delia is with him*. That is a crucial qualification of, and a crucial complication for, the way of life aspired to in the bulk of 1. 1. Tibullus' *full* vision requires the love of Delia to supplement rural simplicity. More than that, the faithful love of a Delia transmuted into a chaste wife (1. 5. 21 ff.; see below). The vision is fine and ideal. But it is obviously, in its totality, unrealizable. Roman *equites* may retire to farms but a *libertina* with one living assured (her *coniunx*) and others in the offing is not happily transposed into rustic housewifery.

At this point let us recall Propertius. The romantic Propertius built dreams around Cynthia characteristically using mythology to express them. Sometimes he believed the dreams: he saw in Cynthia the beauty or quality of an Ariadne, or an Andromeda, or a goddess. He didn't always believe the dreams. Even as he uttered them (seeming to believe them) he often realized or half-realized the soberer truth that had to intrude. Their reality was precarious; indeed his romantic utterances were often fraught with tension from the start. Mythology was a useful vehicle for him. It could suggest a variety of romantic beliefs; and it could well suggest their precariousness. They were mythical beliefs (so to speak) and myth can only be true in moments of romantic elation. In addition the details of a myth could insinuate doubt and tension into the apparent import of a myth at the outset (on all this cf. above, pp. 86 f.).

Tibullus built his romantic dream in the Delia poems, a single one. He sited it in the country. To quit Rome and orthodox ambition for a simple rural life was plausible and possible; but Delia's delight and participation in the same simplicity were not. The two combined made an impossible aspiration. But it was exactly and particularly what Tibullus (in the Delia poems) yearned for. It was, we might say, his 'myth'. Now this 'myth' was of course directly uttered and literally meant. But it was as keenly yearned for and as ultimately precarious as the wishes Propertius suggests indirectly through mythology. So Tibullus' 'myth' and Propertian mythology, though the one *is* the dream and the other is the *vehicle* for expressing dreams, are comparable. And perhaps it is partly because Tibullus basically only has the one romantic dream in these poems, and because it can be uttered directly, that he makes so little use of mythology.

And he too realized or came to realize the soberer

truth that pressed upon his dream. Here is its fullest expression:

> rura colam, frugumque aderit mea Delia custos,
>   area dum messes sole calente teret;
> aut mihi seruabit plenis in lintribus uuas
>   pressaque ueloci candida musta pede.
> consuescet numerare pecus; consuescet amantis
>   garrulus in dominae ludere uerna sinu.
> illa deo sciet agricolae pro uitibus uuam,
>   pro segete spicas, pro grege ferre dapem.
> illa regat cunctos, illi sint omnia curae,
>   ac iuuet in tota me nihil esse domo.
> huc ueniet Messalla meus, cui dulcia poma
>   Delia selectis detrahat arboribus,
> et tantum uenerata uirum, hunc sedula curet,
>   huic paret atque epulas ipsa ministra gerat.
>
>   (1. 5. 21-34)

> I'll farm . . . & Delia will be there to guard the grain
> while the sun-baked floor threshes harvest in the heat.
> Or she will watch the grapes for me in the laden troughs
> & the white new wine pressed by trampling feet.
> She will learn to count the sheep. The children of the
>   house-slaves
> will learn to play & prattle on a loving mistress' lap.
> She will offer to the farmer God grapes for the vines,
> ears for the standing corn, a victim for the flock.
> She can rule us all, take charge of everything,
> and I'll enjoy non-entity at home.
> When my Messalla comes to see us, Delia will pick him
> delicious apples from our choicest trees,
> and in the great man's honour attend to all his needs,
> prepare a dinner for him & wait on him herself.
>
>   (Lee)

Delia, his colleague-wife, will help him in the rustic work and religious observances to which he has alluded in poem 1: she will take her materfamilial part in the harvest and the everyday chores; she will learn the rustic pieties. And Delia, the *domina* of Tibullus the lover (the domineering mistress of Tibullus, the slave) is to become the rural *domina*, genial mistress of the family—a telling but unlikely metamorphosis (25-6). She will even wait on Messalla when he takes a trip

out to the Tibullan farm: Delia the solicitous country hostess
(31 ff.). This is, I say, the fullest expression of Tibullus'
dream. It all seems pathetically if not ridiculously implausible.
And at this point that is Tibullus' chief purpose in citing it.
He introduces the vision thus:

> at mihi felicem uitam . . .
>   fingebam demens, et renuente deo: (19–20)

> In my folly I dreamed that the lucky life was mine
> . . . but the God willed otherwise.
>   (Lee)

And he concludes it:

> haec mihi fingebam, quae nunc Eurusque Notusque
>   iactat odoratos uota per Armenios. (35–6)

> These were my dreams of happiness but now East and South
>   winds
> toss them around perfumed Armenia.

He is *quoting* his former dream with bitter irony (lines 21–
34 have to be printed in quotation marks). Tibullus is now
only too well aware that it was an unrealizable myth. The
tension between romantic dream and prosaic reality which
Propertius tends to feel and communicate more or less simul-
taneously Tibullus expounds more schematically. But there is
a sign of tension even within the quoted romanticizing words.
Humility characteristic of Tibullus the urban lover (see
below) obtrudes in the picture of the *felix uita* and that can-
not bode well (29–30, 'She can rule us all . . .'). When Tibullus
starts to include Delia in his dream he cannot totally shed his
typical, and incompatible, urban character.

2. Tibullan Romanticism 2: Nemesis

Nemesis, Tibullus' beloved in Book 2, appears as more rapa-
cious, mercenary, and hard than Delia (see especially poems
3 and 4). She is influenced by a procuress, a *lena* (Phryne:
2. 6. 44 ff.)–though she, like Delia, has a sentimental adjunct
whom Tibullus can sentimentally invoke. In Nemesis' case it

is her dead sister (she fell out of a window, 2. 6. 39-40),
2. 6. 33-5:

> illius ad tumulum fugiam supplexque sedebo
> et mea cum muto fata querar cinere.
> non feret usque suum te propter flere clientem.

> I'll fly for refuge to her grave and I shall sit there her
>   supplicant
> and complain of my fate to her dumb ashes.
> She will not suffer me her protégé to weep on your
>   [Nemesis'] account for ever.

'Belief is Tibullus' most endearing characteristic'.[18]

Nemesis in Greek is the goddess of Retribution, and
Nemesis is Tibullus' 'Retribution': it is presumably a pseudo-
nym, aptly chosen. He does not say what she is retribution
for, and I do not think this is a question to be asked.[19] Not
infrequently, people (perhaps especially lovers) have the feel-
ing that fate or god somehow has it in for them and that they
are paying for an unknown sin or folly. Not infrequently
they enter such punishment 'willingly' (cf. 2. 4. 1-2). Cockneys
willingly embrace their 'trouble and strife'.

So Nemesis appears a different character from Delia. And
the romanticism of Tibullus' poetry now has a different
complexion. Tibullus never imagines *Nemesis* taking her place
in the country, completing the ideal life. But the theme of
rural life occurs, emotively, in his Nemesis poetry. It is a
yardstick of change. We remember the supreme value which
Tibullus attached to rural life in Book 1—and he reminds us
forcefully of his delight in the country (other things being
equal) in 2. 1. But then we find a startling mutation of
attitude. What appeared to be a constant in Tibullus' life is
not a constant. Love and a lover can change it. The nature
and power of love is illuminated.

In 2. 3 a rival has taken Nemesis off to a rural estate, a
uilla; we infer from 65-71 (see below) that they have gone
for harvest festivities. That is the situation of the poem. The
country is involved (although it cannot help it!) in a way
which Tibullus cannot like. How will he react?

'Venus herself', he says 'has moved into the country' and

'Love is learning ploughman's dialect.' (3-4). Nothing surprising yet. Then (5 ff.):

> o ego, dum aspicerem dominam, quam fortiter illic
> uersarem ualido pingue bidente solum
> agricolaeque modo curuum sectarer aratrum,
> dum subigunt steriles arua serenda boues.
> nec quererer quod sol graciles exureret artus,
> laederet et teneras pussula rupta manus.

> Oh, provided that I could see my mistress, how boldly then
> would I turn the rich soil with powerful mattock,
> and in the manner of a farmer follow the curved plough,
> while gelded oxen tamed the fields for sowing.
> Nor would I complain because the sun burnt my thin limbs,
> and broken blisters hurt my soft hands.

That is, Tibullus is willing to move to the country to do rough, rural work, if in that way he may be within sight of his beloved. The attitude to rural life and work here is a transformation. For his point is that he is prepared to do *humiliating, demeaning* work, if only he can be near Nemesis. He emphasizes this in his elaborate account of Apollo's agricultural slavery to Admetus, which he cites as a precedent for his plan. Compare, for example, 21-30:

> o quotiens illo uitulum gestante per agros
> dicitur occurrens erubuisse soror!
> o quotiens ausae, caneret dum ualle sub alta,
> rumpere mugitu carmina docta boues!
> saepe duces trepidis petiere oracula rebus,
> uenit et a templis irrita turba domum.
> saepe horrere sacros doluit Latona capillos
> quos admirata est ipsa nouerca prius.
> quisquis inornatumque caput crinesque solutos
> aspiceret, Phoebi quaereret ille comam.

> O how many times his sister blushed to meet him
> carrying a bull-calf home through the fields,
> or while he sang in some deep valley, cows presumed
> to interrupt his music with their moos!
> Leaders in time of crisis sought his oracles
> & trooped home disappointed from the shrine.
> The sacred locks that even Juno used to envy
> in disarray dismayed his mother Leto.

> Anyone who saw the shaggy head & tousled tresses
> must have looked in vain for Apollo's hair-style.
>
> (Lee)

Work 'in the manner of a farmer' is humiliating and servile.
Compare too the end of the poem:

> ducite, ad imperium dominae sulcabimus agros.
> non ego me uinclis uerberibusque nego.

> Lead on. I'll plough the furrows at the bidding of a mistress
> & cheerfully accept the leg-irons & the lash.
>
> (Lee)

So Tibullus now views the country as something harsh and
hostile. Agricultural work is unpleasant and humiliating. This
is a far cry from Book 1: Tibullus aspiring to *be* a farmer and
in consequence *happy* is replaced by Tibullus prepared in the
manner of a farmer to *suffer*.

He is even more startling at 65–71:

> at tibi, dura Ceres, Nemesim quae abducis ab urbe,
>   persoluat nulla semina terra fide.
> et tu, Bacche tener, iucundae consitor uuae,
>   tu quoque deuotos, Bacche, relinque lacus.
> haud impune licet formosas tristibus agris
>   abdere: non tanti sunt tua musta, Pater.
> o ualeant fruges, ne sint modo rure puellae . . .

> But for you, harsh Ceres, who seduce Nemesis from the city,
> may the earth not keep faith and repay the seed.
> And you, tender Bacchus, planter of the pleasant vine,
> quit the accursed wine-vats.
> Not without punishment is it possible to hide lovely girls in
>   gloomy fields:
> your new wine, Father Bacchus, is not worth so much.
> Oh farewell fruits of the earth, if only that prevents girls being
>   in the country.

From the standpoint of the town he pronounces curses on
the fruitfulness of the land; the fields are to him 'gloomy'; he
is prepared to see the back of agriculture if it will stop girls
leaving the city—we can return to feeding on acorns: *glans
alat* . . . (72). That is his reaction. It is indeed a metamor-
phosis. Nemesis' offence, which involved the country only
incidentally, induces him to abjure the country. Nemesis'

power over him is such that he will not blame her but curse an innocent party; more than that, curse and repudiate what he has hitherto most valued. So great is the change that she can effect in him. (Not, however, in his sense of humour. The picture of the servile Apollo had obvious witty touches. And Tibullus develops the idea of feeding on acorns into a witty and unexpected reference to the Golden Age (72 ff.):

> glans alat et prisco more bibantur aquae.
> glans aluit ueteres, et passim semper amarunt.
>   quid nocuit sulcos non habuisse satos?
> tum, quibus aspirabat Amor, praebebat aperte
>   mitis in umbrosa gaudia ualle Venus.
> nullus erat custos, nulla exclusura dolentes
>   ianua. si fas est, mos, precor, ille redi.

> Let us live on acorns & drink old-fashioned water.
> The men of old made love on acorns any time or place,
> lost nothing by not having furrows for the seed.
> In their day gentle Venus in every shady valley
> provided Love's enthusiasts with public joy.
> No guard was there or door to bar the broken-hearted.
> May God reintroduce that ancient custom.
>
> (Lee)

Pleasantly incongruous levity.)

It is in fact Nemesis' achievement that she causes the poet to abandon or reverse several cherished values; and it is obviously part of the intention of Book 2 to demonstrate this destructive potential in romantic love. One can sacrifice more than a career or wealth for love. At 2. 3. 39 ff. Tibullus makes characteristic noises about mercenariness (cf. e.g. 1. 2. 67 ff., 1. 10):

> ferrea non Venerem sed praedam saecula laudant;
>   praeda tamen multis est operata malis.
> praeda feras acies cinxit discordibus armis:
>   hinc cruor, hinc caedes mors propiorque uenit.
> praeda uago iussit geminare pericula ponto,
>   bellica cum dubiis rostra dedit ratibus.
> praedator cupit inmensos obsidere campos
>   ut multa innumera iugera pascat oue . . . (etc.)

> Not Love but Loot our iron age applauds:
> but Loot works many evils.

Loot equips fierce battle-lines with jarring arms;
hence bloodshed, slaughter, sudden death.
Loot has doubled danger on the fickle deep
by giving unsafe galleys beaks of war.
The Looter longs to own measureless plains & pasture
wide acres with innumerable sheep. . . . (etc.)

(Lee)

But then at line 53 the poem performs an about-turn—because
of Nemesis:

heu heu diuitibus uideo gaudere puellas:
    iam ueniant praedae si Venus optat opes,
ut mea luxuria Nemesis fluat utque per urbem
    incedat donis conspicienda meis.
illa gerat uestes tenues quas femina Coa
    texuit, auratas disposuitque uias.
illi sint comites fusci quos India torret,
    Solis et admotis inficit ignis equis.
illi selectos certent praebere colores
    Africa puniceum purpureumque Tyros.

Alas I see that girls rejoice in the rich.
Now welcome Loot if Venus desires wealth,
so that my Nemesis may float in luxury and, through the
        city,
parade conspicuous in gifts of mine.
Let her wear fine clothes woven by women of Cos
and bordered with threads of gold.
Let her have dusky attendants whom India has scorched
and the fiery Sun-god coloured by steering his team of
        horses near.
For her let Africa and Tyre vie to offer choice dyes,
Africa scarlet and Tyre purple.

Compare too 2. 4. 21–6

at mihi per caedem et facinus sunt dona paranda,
    ne iaceam clausam flebilis ante domum.
aut rapiam suspensa sacris insignia fanis:
    sed Venus ante alios est uiolanda mihi.
illa malum facinus suadet dominamque rapacem
    dat mihi: sacrilegas sentiat illa manus.

I must take to crime & bloodshed to provide her with the
        gifts
that save me from those weeping vigils at her door;

or steal the sacred offerings hung up on temple walls:
& Venus shall be first to be profaned.
She tempts me to do evil & devotes me to a grasping
mistress; she deserves to suffer sacrilege.

(Lee)

This not only reverses Tibullus' attitude to the place of
money in love; it flouts his previous respect for religion in
general (e.g. 1. 1. above, pp. 156 f.) and Venus in particu-
lar (e.g. 1. 2. 16 ff., 81 ff.)[20] (but there is something of a
recantation in lines 27 ff.). Then at 2. 4. 51-4 comes the
most painful and touching reversal; and it concerns the
country again as well as the gods. After extolling the class of
'kind and generous girl' and sketching the happiness in life
(and death) that awaits such a type Tibullus says:

uera quidem moneo, sed prosunt quid mihi uera?
  illius est nobis lege colendus Amor.
quin etiam sedes iubeat si uendere auitas,
  ite sub imperium sub titulumque, Lares.

True prophecy. And yet what help to the true prophet?
Love's worship means obedience to her [Nemesis'] laws.
Why, even if she bade me sell my ancestral home
I'd pack the Lares off under a bill of sale.

(Lee)

The worship of the God of love must be conducted according
to Nemesis' law. And if she should bid him sell even his ances-
tral farm, then it and the revered Lares will go under the
hammer. So much for the beloved estate, so much for the
beloved country life. So much therefore for Tibullus' great
dream.

It had been Delia's privilege to be the crown of that dream
but by being that crown to render the dream impossible.
Nemesis had the power to make Tibullus simply and com-
pletely renounce it. Delia, the object of fond aspiration, in
fact (in details) degraded her lover (cf. pp. 81, 154). Under
Nemesis Tibullus accepts degradation as his condition of life
(2. 4) and even aspires to it (2. 3). Such is romantic love, in
some of its diversity. So Tibullus demonstrates.

3. Tibullan Romanticism 3: Marathus

Three of Tibullus' poems concern a boy Marathus: 1. 4, 8, and 9. His name is plausible enough for a homosexual love object.[21] He has little individuality beyond the expected characteristics (greed, fickleness)—except in his circumstances. He exists in a triangular relationship with Tibullus: Tibullus loves him, while he, Marathus, has a girl-friend, Pholoe.[22] On this more anon. I consider here 1. 9, the poem most exclusively devoted to Marathus.

> quid mihi, si fueras miseros laesurus amores
>   foedera per diuos clam uiolanda dabas?
> a miser, etsi quis primo periuria celat,
>   sera tamen tacitis Poena uenit pedibus.
> parcite, caelestes: aequum est impune licere
>   numina formosis laedere uestra semel.
> lucra petens habili tauros adiungit aratro
>   et durum terrae rusticus urget opus.
> lucra petituras freta per parentia uentis
>   ducunt instabiles sidera certa rates.
> muneribus meus est captus puer: at deus illa
>   in cinerem et liquidas munera uertat aquas.
> iam mihi persoluet poenas, puluisque decorem
>   detrahet et uentis horrida facta coma.
> uretur facies, urentur sole capilli,
>   deteret inualidos et uia longa pedes.
> admonui quotiens 'auro ne pollue formam:
>   saepe solent auro multa subesse mala.
> diuitiis captus si quis uiolauit amorem,
>   asperaque est illi difficilisque Venus.
> ure meum potius flamma caput et pete ferro
>   corpus et intorto uerbere terga seca . . .'   (22)
>
> haec ego dicebam: nunc me fleuisse loquentem,   (29)
>   nunc pudet ad teneros procubuisse pedes.
> tunc mihi iurabas nullo te diuitis auri
>   pondere, non gemmis uendere uelle fidem,
> non tibi si pretium Campania terra daretur,
>   non tibi si Bacchi cura Falernus ager.
> illis eriperes uerbis mihi sidera caeli
>   lucere et pronas fluminis esse uias.
> quin etiam flebas, at non ego fallere doctus
>   tergebam umentes credulus usque genas.

quid faciam, nisi et ipse fores in amore puellae?
  sic precor: exemplo sit leuis illa tuo.
o quotiens, uerbis ne quisquam conscius esset,
  ipse comes multa lumina nocte tuli!
saepe insperanti uenit tibi munere nostro
  et latuit clausas post adoperta fores.
tum miser interii, stulte confisus amari;
  nam poteram ad laqueos cautior esse tuos.
quin etiam attonita laudes tibi mente canebam!
  ei mihi, nunc nostri Pieridumque pudet.
illa uelim rapida Vulcanus carmina flamma
  torreat et liquida deleat amnis aqua.
tu procul hinc absis, cui formam uendere cura est
  et pretium plena grande referre manu:
at te, qui puerum donis corrumpere es ausus,
  rideat assiduis uxor inulta dolis . . .   (54)

huic tamen accubuit noster puer! illum ego credam   (75)
  cum trucibus Venerem iungere posse feris.
blanditiasne meas aliis tu uendere es ausus?
  tune aliis, demens, oscula ferre mea?
tunc flebis cum me uinctum puer alter habebit
  et geret in regno regna superba tuo.
at tua tum me poena iuuet, Venerique merenti
  fixa notet casus aurea palma meos:
HANC TIBI FALLACI RESOLUTUS AMORE TIBULLUS
DEDICAT ET GRATA SIS DEA MENTE ROGAT.
              (1. 9. 1–22, 29–54, 75–end)

Why give me solemn promises if you intended wronging
my wretched love by breaking them in secret?
Unhappy boy! Though perjury can be hidden for a time,
punishment is bound to catch you in the end.
Forgive him, Heavenly Powers. Beauty has a right
to wrong your godheads once & go unpunished.
For profit peasants yoke their bulls to the wieldy plough
& press their hard work forward on the land.
For profit, over waters obedient to the winds,
unstable ships are drawn by fixed stars.
My boy was caught by bribery. May God convert those
      bribes
to ash & running water.
Later he will pay me the punishment in full:
dust & wind-blown hair will slight his charm;
the sun will burn his beauty, bleach his locks;

the long road chafe those vulnerable feet.
'Don't' I often warned him 'don't pollute your bloom with
    gold.
Behind the gold are sufferings in plenty.
If anyone for money does violence to love,
Venus is hard on him, & difficult.
I'd sooner have my hair burnt off, my body stabbed,
my shoulders lashed with knotted thongs.   (22)

Such my advice, but now it shames me to remember   (29)
that as I spoke I wept & fell down at your feet.
Then you'd swear to me once more that you'd never sell your
    promise,
not for pearls & not for pounds of gold,
not for an estate in rich Campania,
not for the Falernian acres Bacchus loves.
Those words could well have robbed me of my certainty
that rivers run downhill & stars shine in the sky.
Yes, you even wept, and I, unschooled in guile,
trusted you & wiped away the tears.
What *should* I do if you were not in love yourself?
May Pholoe be faithless—in your fashion.
How many times I carried the torch as your attendant
lest any overhear you both conversing,
& paid her money to appear when you despaired of her
or hide outside the door as a surprise!
That was my undoing. Poor fool, I thought you loved me.
I should have been more wary of your snares.
I even versified your praises, moonstruck as I was.
Alas, we & the Muses—how embarrassing!
Let Vulcan roast those eulogies in roaring flame
and the running river liquidate them.
Out of my sight! You only love to sell your looks
& carry home, full-fisted, a fat fee.
But as for you who dared corrupt my boy with bribes,
may your own wife gull you with her cuckoldry . . .   (54)

To think my boy has bedded with this creature!   (75)
He's capable of coupling with wild beasts.
How could you sell my tendernesses to another man?
How export my kisses? You must be out of your mind.
Just wait till your replacement takes me prisoner
and proudly rules your kingdom—you'll weep then.

And I'll enjoy your grief and dedicate to Venus
my rescuer a golden leaf of palm inscribed:
TIBULLUS FREED FROM LOVE DECEITFUL, GODDESS,
OFFERS THIS AND ASKS FOR GRATITUDE.
(Lee; the translation is debatable in places.)[23]

What is very remarkable is the close thematic correspondence between this poem and Tibullus' love poems to Delia and Nemesis, and the love poems of the other romantic love-poets to their mistresses. First I briefly and selectively document this. The making and breaking of a *foedus* between the lovers (1-2) recalls Catullan love (above, pp. 33 ff.)—and Tibullus' appeal to Delia at 1. 5. 7. Tibullus' implied slavery to Marathus (21-2) is characteristic of his relationship with Delia and Nemesis (e.g. 1. 5. 5 f. and 2. 4; cf. above, p. 81). The sentimental pleas (5 ff.) to the gods *not* to pursue punishment deserved by the beloved echoes a similar plea concerning Delia (1. 6. 55 ff.). A rival's interference (11 ff.) of course hardly needs paralleling (1. 2. 89, 1. 5. 47, 2. 3.). But this rival is (incidentally) interesting; and Tibullus' attitude is significant. The rival intends taking Marathus on military campaign or provincial service (*militia*): with *uia longa* in 16 compare 1. 3. 36. It is not implausible that a provincial administrator or officer should take a *puer delicatus* abroad with him—far from it: Scipio Aemilianus found the Roman camp at Numantia full of such boys.[24] And what is Tibullus' reaction? He dwells on the discomforts that the boy will suffer, with some sympathy (note *inualidos*). That recalls very closely Propertius in a similar situation as regards Cynthia (1. 8), and Gallus and Lycoris (Vergil, *Ecl.* 10, drawing on a Gallan Elegy). Tibullus' passionate curse on the rival (53 ff.) also recalls (although it is more robust) Propertius (2. 9. 48) and the Delia-Tibullus (1. 2. 89 ff.).

Now these parallels are very significant. They show that Tibullus is professing the same sort of combination of tenderness, profundity, abjectness, and intensity in his love for Marathus as that professed by the romantic love poets, including himself, in their love for their mistresses. This is unexpected. The situation suggested is after all man and *puer delicatus*, fancy boy, *eromenos*; not a mature relationship between coevals—and this is not Greece.[25] The attitude is certainly untypical of the Latin romantic poets. Catullus writes physically enthusiastic poems to Juventius; but there is no question of *foedus*, *amicitia*, or spiritual tenderness in this affair. For Propertius love of boys is something to be recommended bitterly, when he is tortured by romantic love of woman: recommended because boy-love is emotionally uncomplicated and undemanding (2. 4. 17–22); we may conjecture that that was part of its attraction to Horace. Ovid, incidentally, from a non-romantic point of view, still does not favour love of boys: because of the lack of physical reciprocity, because the boy does not share the pleasure (*Ars Amatoria* 2. 683–4). There is therefore (it seems) another side to Tibullan romanticism: he sacrifices dignity and freedom for love of *a boy*.

Now let us pick up the poem again at lines 29–30. Tibullus reports how he grovelled to Marathus—grovelled to a remarkable and (significantly) Ovidian extent.[26] At 37–8 he reports sentimental, gullible *obsequium*, 'compliant service' (another romantic Elegiac theme). And then, at 39–40, a surprise—a surprise, I think, even after 1. 8 where the topic was prominent: Marathus has a girl-friend.[27] 'What *should* I do if you were not in love yourself?/May Pholoe be faithless—in your fashion.'

I think our expectation now is that the poem will swing: from reproach to a certain amount of *Schadenfreude*, if not jubilation, at Marathus' trials. Not so. Tibullus proceeds to sketch a piquant and perverse triangular relationship between himself, Marathus, and the girl which reveals *yet greater* humiliating devotion to Marathus on his part. He accepted the servile job of lamp-carrier for Marathus in his assignations with Pholoe; part of his *obsequium* was to organize such meetings; and he even used his poetry to praise Marathus to her (41–8). Intense and humiliating devotion indeed! Even the spirited and very amusing imprecations launched at the rival (53 ff.), describing among other things how physically disgusting he is, end up with yet another realization of humiliation: 'but my boy went to bed with *him*.' (75).

We discover thus that this new side to Tibullan romanticism is more striking than we thought. Not only does he profess a tenderness and intensity of love for Marathus comparable with that for Delia, and make sacrifices of dignity and freedom accordingly; the sacrifices seem even greater than those made for Delia. Now if we ask the (rather crude) question, *why* did Tibullus write this poem, several answers offer themselves. First, there is no reason why the basis of the poem should not be real and the source therefore (ultimately or partly) life. But I think it is clear that Tibullus plays up his role; he relishes describing his humiliation. And a second and main aim of the poem is, I think, to be provocative, to trump his shocking predecessors. Propertius had displayed his abjectness (trumping Catullus) before his *domina*. Tibullus reveals himself grovelling before a boy—an *eromenos*, a passive. Thirdly, Tibullus clearly likes the slightly perverse piquancy of the triangular relationship; and we should not underestimate the element of humour, as well as provocativeness in the whole. Tibullus makes his own abjectness amusing. It is in fact in the dramatic interests of the poem to do so. At the time of writing Tibullus is conscious of and regretting his past excesses of abjectness: he is in the mood therefore to exaggerate them and mock himself. But he goes farther than that. The situations he contrives for himself—or the way he describes them—smack virtually of mime or comedy (and note the Ovidian colour mentioned above). Finally, I doubt that Tibullus was unaware of the incongruousness of professing humiliated love for two beloveds in one book.

4. Tibullan structure and technique

Tibullus liked flexibility of organization and structure; and he experimented in variety and surprise.[28] For example, 1. 4 unexpectedly introduces a Priapus obliging with urbane advice on how to love boys successfully. 1. 8 contrives the impression of a three-character mime without breaking the Elegiac convention that excludes parts and dialogue.[29] 2. 5 starts by celebrating the election of Messalinus to a religious office but manages to include *inter alia* the Sibyl's prophecy to Aeneas (which is quoted) and a vivid description of country festivals. But I shall concentrate on Tibullus' more typical love poems and more typical technique. Poem 1. 5:

> asper eram et bene discidium me ferre loquebar,
>   at mihi nunc longe gloria fortis abest;
> namque agor ut per plana citus sola uerbere turben
>   quem celer adsueta uersat ab arte puer.
> ure ferum et torque, libeat ne dicere quicquam
>   magnificum post haec: horrida uerba doma.
> parce tamen, per te furtiui foedera lecti,
>   per Venerem quaeso compositumque caput.
>
> I was angry and said that I could bear separation,
> but now such glorious bravery is far away. ·
> I am driven like a whirling top over a flat surface,
> whipped by an agile boy who knows his art.
> Brand and rack me for my wildness, lest I should want to speak
> grandiloquently again. Tame my rough speech.
> But forgive me, I beseech you, by the pact of stolen love,
> by Venus, and our nights together.

Lines 1–8: Tibullus addresses Delia. He regrets bold words of his in which he had said he could tolerate a severance. He cannot. He invites Delia to punish him; then, changing his mind, begs her for mercy.

At line 9 he adopts a different mood and different approach:

> ille ego cum tristi morbo defessa iaceres
>   te dicor uotis eripuisse meis . . .
>
> When you lay exhausted on the bed of fever,
> mine, I am assured, were the prayers that saved you . . .
>   (Lee)

Winsomely he recalls his past devotion. At 19 there is another clear break: Tibullus recollects his former dreams of happiness, and recites them (19–36, quoted above, p. 162). He still seems to be addressing Delia (*fuisses* 19); perhaps he hopes his forlorn tale will have pathetic appeal. With 37, yet another shift. Tibullus recounts his attempts to blunt and diversify his love, and explains their failure:

> saepe ego temptaui curas depellere uino:
>   at dolor in lacrimas uerterat omne merum.
> saepe aliam tenui: sed iam cum gaudia adirem,
>   admonuit dominae deseruitque Venus.

tunc me, discedens, deuotum femina dixit—
a pudet!—et narrat scire nefanda meam.
non facit hoc uerbis, facie tenerisque lacertis
deuouet et flauis nostra puella comis.
talis ad Haemonium Nereis Pelea quondam
uecta est frenato caerula pisce Thetis.   (37–46)

Often have I tried to drive away my troubles with wine:
but sorrow turned every wine to tears;
often I embraced another girl: but when I was on the brink
of joy
Venus reminded me of my mistress and deserted me.
Then, leaving me, the woman called me bewitched
and—the shame of it!—tells tales that my girl knows black
arts.
But she doesn't do this with spells: she bewitches me with
her fair face
soft arms and yellow hair.
Even such was the Nereid who once
was carried on a bridled dolphin to Peleus, blue-eyed Thetis.

And the shift of standpoint here is more profound. Tibullus
can (surely) no longer be directly addressing Delia; he is
soliloquizing.

In 47, he sums up the previous few lines, the ones telling
of his sexual failure. 'These things (i.e. Delia's beautiful
features) brought my downfall', *haec nocuere mihi*. There
then follows another very abrupt shift—abrupt, but the
psychological connection or stimulus is fairly clear. Tibullus
has in the last lines been becoming increasingly sentimental,
inclined to be easy on Delia. How in these circumstances is he
going to deal with the ugly fact, disclosed in line 17, that she
has gone off with another man? He must face it some time.
He jumps swiftly to deal with it now. He tells himself:

quod adest huic diues amator
uenit in exitium callida lena meum.   (47 f.)

As for the fact that a rich lover is with her,
it's a crafty bawd who has turned up to my ruin.

That is, it is the *lena*'s fault; and that leads him into a conven-
tional, though colourful, section of curses upon the bawd.
After this he turns, quite logically, to appeal to Delia to reject

her; to eschew the bawd's despicable but ruinously effective advice (59 f.):

> at tu quam primum sagae praecepta rapacis
>   desere: num donis uincitur omnis amor?

> O Delia reject forthwith that grasping witch's guidance.
> Must every love surrender to a bribe?
>
> (Lee)

And the implied criticism of money playing a role in love leads neatly into yet another distinct section, a compensatory recital of the advantageous service that the poor lover can provide (61-6). Finally, the last section of the poem is engineered by another and profound shift of standpoint, involving another addressee. Tibullus rounds on and warns his rival (69 ff.)—and includes a brilliant little cameo scene.

> at tu, qui potior nunc es, mea fata timeto:
>   uersatur celeri Fors leuis orbe rotae.
> non frustra quidam iam nunc in limine perstat
>   sedulus, ac crebro prospicit, ac refugit,
> et simulat transire domum, mox deinde recurrit
>   solus, et ante ipsas exscreat usque fores.
> nescioquid furtiuus Amor parat. utere, quaeso,
>   dum licet: in liquida nam tibi linter aqua.

> But you, her darling of today, take warning from my fate.
> Fortune's fickle wheel quickly turns.
> Not for nothing even now someone stands upon her
>   threshold—
> first he looks about him, then he backs away,
> and pretends to pass the house, then returns without his
>   slave
> and coughs persistently right by the door.
> Love the thief has plans. Take your pleasure while you may.
> Water is unstable and your ship is still at sea.
>
> (Lee)

There are points which we can notice immediately. First and obviously: Tibullus shifts his standpoint. He not only changes mood and theme, but switches addressees and varies his apostrophes with soliloquy. He allows his poem to develop in a way quite *unlike* a poem of Propertius' *monobiblos*. We have the impression of a sequence of thought evolving; the poem's unity (if that is the word) is 'psychological', deriving solely from the personality of the poet (I come back to this: p. 183).

Secondly, however, we must notice that Tibullus does in fact offer a dramatic setting and occasion for the poem (*like* Propertius in the *monobiblos*), in lines that I omitted from my analysis just now:

> heu, canimus frustra, nec uerbis uicta patescit
> ianua, sed plena est percutienda manu. (67–8)

> Alas I sing in vain. Her door unmoved by words
> is waiting for the knock of a money-laden hand.
> (Lee)

These lines seem suddenly to imply that the poem *is* a drama, unified and happening: Tibullus stands (or lies) in the traditional position of the excluded lover at the mistress's door,[30] and the poem is his song. He has, it seems, attempted to make his poem dramatic–situational, in the manner of the Propertian *monobiblos*. But it is not a rigorous attempt. Much of the poem is hardly plausible as an excluded lover's song and in practice one is (even must be) oblivious of the supposed setting during much of the poem. It is difficult (for example) to imagine Tibullus uttering 39–47 (his attempt to diversify) as part of a serenade; and 69 ff., the address to the successful rival, seem flatly inconsistent with the suggested situation. So Tibullus pays lip-service to dramatic unity but is obviously interested in other things, in another way of composing, and in other effects.

1. 2

The same rather half-hearted evocation of dramatic situation is observable in 1. 2. Again what Tibullus actually does is to shift his standpoint, and let his thoughts and themes evolve; he is uninterested in a single or specific setting. I comment briefly on the composition of the poem; there is another Tibullan characteristic to be observed.

Tibullus bids a slave pour him strong wine to drown his sorrows; no one is to rouse him; he tells us that his girl (Delia) is locked indoors and unapproachable. There seems to be our 'dramatic situation': Delia is shut away and Tibullus is at home (or in a tavern) getting drunk.

He doesn't fall asleep, as he had hoped. Lines 7–14 switch abruptly, comprising an address to the door: threats which he hastily (and amusingly) converts to humble pleas:

> ianua difficilis domini[31] te uerberet imber,
>   te Iouis imperio fulmina missa petant.
> ianua, iam pateas uni mihi, uicta querellis,
>   neu furtim uerso cardine aperta sones.
> et mala siqua tibi dixit dementia nostra,
>   ignoscas: capiti sint precor illa meo.
> te meminisse decet quae plurima uoce peregi
>   supplice cum posti florida serta darem.

> O door, stubborn as your master,[31] may the rainstorm lash
>   you
> and launched at Jove's command may flash of lightning blast
>   you!
> Please, door—open just for me, moved by my complaining.
> But silence, as you swing on slowly turning hinge!
> Forgive me if I cursed you in my infatuation.
> Let the curses light on my own head.
> It's right you should remember all my prayers and promises
> when I hung those garlands of flowers on your post.
>
> (Lee)

These lines of course closely resemble the conventional excluded lover's song (more than any part of 1. 5 does in fact). But Tibullus is presumably only addressing Delia's door in his thoughts. The same applies to the rest of the poem: all the apostrophes, speeches, and reflections must I think be imaginings. When (and if) we want to picture him, he must presumably be still at his table getting smashed.

In 15 ff. he apostrophizes Delia, urging her to slip stealthily but boldly to the door; Venus aids the vigorous, he says (15–24). He then adduces his own experience of Venus' aid to the bold—which allows him to shift into different thematic material, into conventional remarks about the inviolability of the lover (25 ff.). At 35 ff. he is bidding passers-by be discreet if they meet him outside Delia's house. The drunken Tibullus seems to have transported himself in his thoughts quite remarkably; another abrupt shift. And so the poem progresses. Tibullus allows a sequence of thoughts and themes to develop out of his basic topic, exclusion. He *likes* this evolving structure; he likes to allow the poem to reflect the process of thought.

It is a consequence of this liking that he not only allows his poems to *shift* distinctly but to *drift* more subtly. I consider lines 43 ff. of the same poem.

> nec tamen huic credet coniunx tuus, ut mihi uerax
> pollicita est magico saga ministerio.
> hanc ego de caelo ducentem sidera uidi;
> fluminis haec rapidi carmine uertit iter:
> haec cantu finditque solum manesque sepulcris
> elicit . . .

> haec mihi composuit cantus quis fallere posses;   (55)
> ter cane, ter dictis despue carminibus:
> ille nihil poterit de nobis credere cuiquam,
> non sibi, si in molli uiderit ipse toro.
> tu tamen abstineas aliis, nam cetera cernet
> omnia, de me uno sentiet ille nihil.
> quid credam? nempe haec eadem se dixit amores
> cantibus aut herbis soluere posse meos,
> et me lustrauit taedis, et nocte serena
> concidit ad magicos hostia pulla deos.
> non ego totus abesset amor sed mutuus esset
> orabam, nec te posse carere uelim.

> In any case your husband won't believe him, Delia;
> for so an honest witch assured me by her magic.
> I have seen her drawing down the stars from heaven.
> Her chanting can reverse the river's flow.
> Her spells can split the ground, lure ghosts from graves . . . (47)

> She has written me a spell to enable you to trick him.   (55)
> Speak it thrice and spit thrice when you have spoken.
> He'll then believe no story anyone may tell of us—
> not even his own eyes if he catches us in bed.
> But keep away from other men. He'll see everything else.
> I'm the only one he will never notice.
> The same witch even promised, though it passes my belief,
> by her spells or herbs to free me of my love.

> She fumigated me with pitch-pine on a moonlit night
> and slaughtered a black victim to the gods below.
> I prayed that love be mutual, not absent altogether.
> How could I ever wish to live without you?
>
> (Lee)

In the previous section he has told possible tell-tales that Venus takes her vengeance on the likes of them. In our passage he turns to reassure Delia: her husband would not believe any stories anyway, since he (Tibullus) has the assistance of a witch's magic (43-4). We are, I think, to imagine this magic as something in Tibullus' power to offer (he has indeed consulted a witch). But his own underlying attitude to it is sceptical and blatantly utilitarian (so the text suggests): he reinterprets its significance according to need and clearly regards it as a bait to persuade Delia (if only she could hear!) rather than a resource genuinely to be believed in.

A section now develops (45 ff.) built round the stock figure of Roman love life and literature, the bawd-*cum*-witch.[32] After a cheering, hyperbolic list of the witch's supposed powers, Tibullus reaches her relevance to himself and Delia. She has, he says, supplied a ritual that will ensure the husband's total gullibility (55-8). But then Tibullus thinks of something. No, it's not *total* gullibility, it's total gullibility *in his case* (59-60). He sees the flaw in his splendid persuasion and hastily and wittily corrects himself. At line 61 he suggests more evidence of her power; or rather he cites evidence of her own confidence in her power. Is it believable? (*quid credam?* is a formula to introduce something barely credible) she has even said she could cure him of his love—and has put the ritual into effect (61-4). Now to cure love like Tibullus' would indeed be a convincing demonstration of magical power, one that would surely convince Tibullus (and one that, despite incredulity, he might well think worth trying). But it is hardly a tactful case to cite to Delia. Tibullus perceives his tactical error and again—and again with humorous effect— hastily corrects himself (65-6).

The humour here I shall return to. My immediate point concerns composition. Tibullus not only allows his text to follow the shifts that characterize the processes of thought; he also allows it to drift as thought does: in this case in humorously unfortunate directions. A drifting sequence within distinct sections is characteristic of his method.

It is now possible to draw some conclusions on Tibullan structure and technique. In the manner of Propertius' *monobiblos* Tibullus' love poems may start from a specific event or setting: they are to an extent 'dramatic–situational'. But only to an extent. Propertius in the *monobiblos* created poems that seemed to be distinct parts of single and tangible dramas, to be utterances provoked by and responding directly to the external stimuli of a specific situation. In consequence they had *dramaturgical* immediacy and unity; and via these utterances we learned about feelings, personality, and love (Chapter V). It was a wonderfully suggestive and vivid method. But it was, we should note, limiting in its way. Each poem was restricted to communicating the thoughts and feelings of one time and occasion. Tibullus is interested in variety, in the successions of thoughts, feelings, and themes that may evolve out of an original event or situation; he is interested in letting the poem reflect the psychological process, the shifts and drifts of thought, *his* thought. So we cannot expect the type of immediacy or unity that we find in a *monobiblos* poem. The most important type of unity we shall find in Tibullus' reflective sequences is that provided by our sense of a single person thinking: '*psychological* unity' (cf. above, p. 179). Though the terms are overworked and I hate them, we could say that Propertius gives his *monobiblos* poems an *objective* unity, Tibullus a *subjective* one.

Tibullus' practice of giving some of his poems an apparent dramatic situation may reflect the influence of the Propertian *monobiblos*. But he then evolved his own idiosyncratic method. And it seems that Propertius was in turn influenced by him. Propertius' temperament was naturally attracted to the flexibility of the Tibullan method, its ability easily, indeed facilely, to accommodate different aspects of the lover's experience; his later work shows the signs. But his better examples show more distinct and rhetorical structuring than Tibullus'; and in some cases he frees himself further from dramatic situation than Tibullus does (see above, pp. 124-133).

5. The Tibullan Experience: concluding thoughts

There seems to be a certain credulousness and facility in Tibullus' feelings. The ethos of his poetry seems very different from Propertius'.

For example, sentimentality comes readily (the appeal by the bones of Nemesis' dead sister, 2. 6. 29-40; the lines on Delia's mother, 1. 6. 57 ff.). He responds, too, to thoughts of death and the Underworld with a comfortable plangency which contrasts sharply with the stark visions of Propertius. Note 1. 1. 59-68:

> te spectem suprema mihi cum uenerit hora;
> te teneam moriens deficiente manu.
> flebis et arsuro positum me, Delia, lecto,
> tristibus et lacrimis oscula mixta dabis.
> flebis: non tua sunt duro praecordia ferro
> uincta, nec in tenero stat tibi corde silex.
> illo non iuuenis poterit de funere quisquam,
> lumina non uirgo sicca referre domum.
> tu manes ne laede meos, sed parce solutis
> crinibus et teneris, Delia, parce genis.

> O let me gaze at you, when my last hour comes—
> hold you, as I die, in my failing grasp!
> Delia, you will weep for me laid on the bed of burning
> and you will give me kisses mixed with bitter tears.
> Yes, you will weep: your heart is not encased in iron
> nor is there flint in your tender breast.
> There will be no young man and no unmarried girl
> going home dry-eyed from my funeral.
> But do no violence, Delia, to my departed spirit:
> spare your flowing tresses and spare your tender cheeks.
>
> (Lee)

Note too the picture of the Underworld at 1. 3. 57 ff.:

> sed me, quod facilis tenero sum semper amori,
> ipsa Venus campos ducet in Elysios.
> hic choreae cantusque uigent . . .

My spirit, though, as I have always welcomed tender love,
Venus herself will lead to the Elysian fields.
There songs and dances flourish . . .

(Lee)

Now re-read Propertius 1. 19: the contrast is startling. And
while Propertius is particularly fond of talking of his rela-
tionship with Cynthia in terms of marriage, Tibullus talks
tenderly and romantically of a regular marriage in society
(2. 2). Propertius only approaches that when a political point
is to be scored (3. 12, 4. 3). 'Belief is Tibullus' most endear-
ing characteristic.'[33]

Tibullus' happy, aspiring thoughts can flow for a long
period before any complication even surfaces (1. 1). He
seems to have to be pushed into confronting the clash between
vision and reality (Propertius' constant exercise): 1. 5.

And passivity seems to characterize our loving equestrian—
although he can give vent to vigorous plaint at times (e.g.
2. 4. 7–10). We noticed passivity of attitude in a detail above
(p. 157). And we noticed it more widely in the phenomenon
of *seruitium*. In their respective 'real' worlds (outside 'myth'
and mythology) Propertius and Tibullus found themselves
the slaves of their *dominae*. But whereas Propertius (at first)
accepts this unwillingly and despairingly, Tibullus submits to
servile punishments with a complaisance and gratuitousness
approaching masochism—and not only from Delia and
Nemesis, but from the boy, the *eromenos*, Marathus (1. 5. 5,
2. 3. 84, 1. 9. 17–22, 41–4); and with Nemesis he even
aspires to servility (2.3): see above, pp. 81, 165–9, 173. And
how about this for masochism in love (2.5. 108–10)?

> heu heu quam multis ars dedit ista malum.
> et mihi praecipue, iaceo cum saucius annum
> et faueo morbo—quin iuuat ipse dolor.

> Alas, how much misfortune your archer's art [Cupid] has
>   brought!
> On me especially, for I have lain a year now stricken,
> clinging to my sickness, finding pleasure in the pain.

(Lee)

But our credulous, facile, and masochistic love poet is

continually capable of humour—as we have noticed above. This introduces a complication, which we shall have to assess. But first I shall illustrate Tibullan humour a little more.

The main effect of 1. 4, Priapus' guidebook to loving boys, is to be (shockingly) amusing. As well as insistence on humorous humiliation we find witty cynicism. The cynicism is an unexpected turn in this romantic book: Tibullus contrives it by introducing his comic spokesman, Priapus. The cynical counsel is a foretaste of Ovid's *Ars Amatoria*; the device that gets it into this book is like Ovid's use of the *lena* in *Amores* 1. 8 (below, p. 276). A couple of points to notice. First, in the subject matter. Counselling *obsequium* to a boy is, in the Roman context, rather more delightfully incongruous than counselling *obsequium* to a woman (lines 39-56): cf. above, pp. 173 f. Second, in the language. Tibullus makes pleasant use of elevated phrasing (befitting a didactic!)—as Ovid will do. For example line 9.[34]

> o fuge te tenerae puerorum credere turbae

> o flee and never trust thee to the troop of tender boys.
>
> (Lee)

Note too the unexpected come-down for Tibullus at the end, where he speaks *in propria persona*:

> heu heu, quam Marathus lento me torquet amore.
>   deficiunt artes deficiuntque doli.
> parce, puer, quaeso—ne turpis fabula fiam
>   cum mea ridebunt uana magisteria.

> Alas, how Marathus torments me with protracted love!
> Skill profits nothing, deceptions profit nothing.
> Have pity, boy, I beg you, lest I become a byword, disgraced,
> and all ridicule my useless teachings.

1. 6 offers an argument whose contrived implausibility is hard to believe—and hard not to find amusing; the humour of this poem is of course particularly important because it is one of the Delia cycle. Tibullus finds Delia's husband not watchful enough—for Delia is having affairs not just with Tibullus. 'Look out for me as well', Tibullus helpfully suggests to the

husband, 'if that will stop her' (15–16). Even better, 'Make *me* her watchdog.' 37–42:

> at mihi seruandam credas: non saeua recuso
> uerbera, detrecto non ego uincla pedum.
> tunc procul absitis, quisquis colit arte capillos,
>   et fluit effuso cui toga laxa sinu;
> quisquis et occurret, ne possit crimen habere
>   stet procul aut alia transeat ille uia.[35]

> But let *me* be her keeper. You could flog me when you liked
> or fling me into fetters & I'd take my punishment.
> Then they'd have to clear off, all those fops with curly hair
> and expansive togas falling in loose folds.
> Anyone who met us would be halted at a distance
> or pass us by another road to prove his innocence.
>
> (Lee)

Tibullus gives his delightfully ludicrous offer to be Delia's watchdog (a slave's job) additional humour by expressing his willingness to accept the punishments that might go with such a position: once again he offers to be painfully and absurdly servile. We are not far from the amusing situational piquancy of the Marathus poem, 1. 9. More importantly, in the incongruous contrivance of the plot we again have an advance taste of Ovid[36] —just as, incidentally, the discomfiture of Apollo which Tibullus sketched in 2. 3 (above, pp. 165 and 167) anticipated Ovidian practice and indeed strategy in much of the *Metamorphoses*.

What we should particularly notice about the end of 1. 4, about 1. 6, and the examples of humour mentioned above (pp. 157 etc.), is that they involve an ability to be humorous *at expense of self*. When therefore Tibullus sketches his plight in terms that tempt us to smile (as I think he quite often does) we should probably suspect Tibullan policy and not resist that temptation. For example, in 2. 3. 9 f. quoted above (p. 165). And if he includes a humorous punning allusion to his degraded self when we do not expect it, it is not to be regarded as a figment of our imagination. 2. 6. 25–6:

> Spes etiam ualida solatur compede uinctum.
> crura sonant ferro, sed canit inter opus

> Hope comforts even him who is bound with a strong fetter.
> The iron clanks on his leg, but he sings while he works.

This *exemplum* of the power of Hope cites a slave in a chain-gang—and alludes to the slave of Nemesis (cf. 2. 4. 3–4; and *canit* is pointed).

And there is one further, very important factor to take into account before we can deliver a final judgement on our credulous, facile, and masochistic love poet: style. Again the name of Ovid intrudes. Guy Lee[37] directs our attention to the fact that much of what we regard as Ovidian style in fact originates with Tibullus: 'the grace, the easy and natural flow, the subdivision of the elegiac couplet into smaller self-contained units . . . the predominance of the dissyllabic ending to the pentameter—all these Ovidian features are present in the elegiacs of Tibullus.' Lee also observes an 'Ovidian' trick of word-patterning at 1. 4. 61–2 (making a couplet end as it began). Word-patterning needs slightly more attention. It is Tibullus who, perhaps more than any other Augustan poet apart from Ovid, picks up the Neoteric penchant for the artful and symmetrical disposition of words in a line: the abAB or abBA patterns of epithets and nouns (1. 9. 4 sera tamen tacitis *poena* uenit *pedibus*, 1. 5. 4 quem celer adsueta uersat ab *arte puer*) and the many other shapes that the Neoterics fostered as a device of art largely for art's sake.[38] It was features such as these, together with a careful purity of diction (avoidance of overt poeticisms, and of colloquialisms such as Catullus had liked and Propertius still admitted),[39] that earned Tibullus homogeneous labels of approval from various quarters. Quintilian (10. 1. 93) called him *tersus atque elegans*, 'spruce' (referring, I think, to his diction) and 'elegant' or 'tasteful'; Velleius (2. 36. 3) couples him, significantly, with Ovid: *Tibullus et Naso perfectissimi in forma operis sui*, 'Tibullus and Naso (Ovid) are most finished in the form of their work'; and Ovid himself (*Am.* 1. 15. 28) apostrophizes *culte Tibulle*, cultivated, civilized Tibullus. The style of Tibullus displays careful, controlled artistry; it is supremely tasteful. We could say urbane: it is exclusively the function of the *urbanus* to be *cultus* and *elegans*.

Now style projects a mood. Tasteful, urbane style projects a tasteful, urbane mood. More than that, it is an ancient commonplace—and the most natural of thoughts—that the 'style is the man'.[40] We note that Quintilian and Ovid instinctively, as we ourselves might, refer their stylistic terms to the poet—and not his work. Style projects a *personality* as well as a mood. We must recognize therefore that there is often a tension between the man of Tibullus' style and the man of Tibullus' content. The former is self-possessed, urbane, *cultus*, the latter often grovelling, passionate, and bent on being a farmer. This tension suggests a certain Tibullan distance from the Tibullan story.

Our final judgement is not easy. The Tibullan effect is subtle and chameleon-like. It is important, I think, not to try to 'resolve' the various factors: we do not want an 'average' for that is not how a text affects us. It affects us in all its parts. Tibullus does strike us as credulous, sentimental, facile, masochistic; he does strike us as a provocatively romantic lover. And yet we detect Tibullan amusement at Tibullus: not only in the patent touches of humorous self-mockery, but in the *elegant* picture he offers of his own woeful, provocative, and grovelling self. And we detect inconsistency: Tibullus who does so endearingly believe can delight in cynicism; Tibullus the romantic can smile at the romantic's discomfiture. All this in fact seems to me very plausible: people *are* inconsistent and (especially at a distance) can find their own earnestness amusing. I am sure that those who listened to Tibullus recite in the circle of Messalla experienced a delightfully evasive but *plausible* personality (or *persona* if you prefer); tender and moving, provocative, amusing, cynical —all in a pleasing and sometimes inextricable *mélange*; wittily a step ahead or naïvely a step behind.

And I like to believe that he *was* snappily dressed, especially when he recited 1. 1.

VII

Horace: Preliminaries

Horace was born in Venusia, Apulia in 65 BC and was fourteen years or so older than Propertius and Tibullus. But his love odes—I concentrate on the *Odes*—tend to react to the Elegists rather than the other way round (Propertius does not start responding to Horace until his third book). Hence I treat these poets in the order that I do.

Horace was an enthusiastic autobiographer (Horace's readers should swiftly absorb—for example—*Satires* 1. 6), but given to irony and evasion. It would therefore be silly as well as superfluous to attempt a thumbnail biographical sketch. I mention here only one or two salient points.[1] It is the poems that will reveal the man—in all his irony. And the poems I consider will reveal some of the man.

The equestrian-born Elegists were quite grand, compared with Horace. Horace's father was a freedman, who devoted himself to the elevation of his son. In 42 BC Horace was impulsive or idealistic enough to fight for the republican side at Philippi and lose. It is a fact we should never forget. Horace never did (cf. *Odes* 3. 14. 28 and below, p. 236). After Philippi he was sensible and astute enough to get a job as a secretary to the quaestors under the victors; and then he was talented enough to become patronized by Maecenas (in about 38 BC).

Patronage meant more to Horace than to the Elegists. There was a strong and genuine affection between himself and Maecenas. He needed financial support. Horace had firm grounds for gratitude to the new regime. He was sensible enough to show it.

Sense is always visible in Horace; in the *Satires*, in the *Odes*, in the *Epistles*. Sense, scorned by the grander Elegists, led Horace to profess a cheerful sexual catholicity, the reality of which we have no reason to doubt. He allows a reference to his 'thousand passions for girls, and thousand for boys' (*Satires*, 2. 3. 325); and if our knowledge of Horace's humour compels us to recognize hyperbole, the substance is confirmed by other references: *Satires*, 1. 2. 117, *Epodes*, 11. 4, *Odes*, 2. 5. 17 ff.

But Horatian sense is nearly always blended with Horatian sensibility; and always with art.

VIII

The Social Background to Horace's Odes

Horace's erotic odes suggest a society liberally supplied with charming but essentially temporary erotic company; a world rather different from the Elegists'. Instead of the single dominating courtesan, amateur or professional, we find (typically) attractive and fundamentally unexacting figures who change as the poems change: girls with Greek names who entertain in pleasant settings with lyre and love; and the occasional boy. The extent and significance of the contrast with the Elegists I shall consider in the next chapter. It is my purpose here simply to assess this social background—to see what kind of reality there is behind Horace's enticing parade. This is not just a matter of circumstantial interest. It is an important literary question too. How did Horace's readers react to these poems? Did the poems seem to them fancies spun out of patently fictional names, places, and situations? Or did they seem to reflect, albeit discreetly, an actual society? Or what? The background supposed affects response and we must recover that background.

We must identify the society suggested by Horace's *Odes* more exactly and then proceed to assess its relation to reality. The poems which provide most circumstantial detail are clearly most useful.

The common, indeed characteristic, setting of an erotic ode is a drinking-party. The party may be happening or envisaged, sketched with some detail (garlands for the drinkers, scattered roses, perfumes, rules for drinking) or just adumbrated; and the participants may be two or several; but the constant idea is of a drinking-party: cf. 1. 4, 11, 17, 27, 36; 2. 11; 3. 19, 21, 28; 4. 1, 11, 13.

On several occasions it is made clear that the girls present are musical entertainers as well as lovers; indeed on occasions that seems their primary, or prima-facie, function. In 1. 17 Tyndaris is a singer and lyre-player (18–20: *et fide Teia/dices laborantis in uno/Penelopen uitreamque Circen*, 'accompanying yourself on Tean lyre you will sing of Penelope and glittering Circe who both toiled in love for one man'); Lyde of 2. 11 is to bring her lyre; and a Lyde will sing to the lyre in 3. 28. Phyllis in 4. 11 is a singer: in 4. 13 Lyce is an ageing singer and Chia a harp-player, a *psaltria* (she is *docta psallere*). There is musical entertainment mentioned in passing in 3. 19 and 4. 1: a *tibia* (an oboe-like instrument) and a lyre.

Wine, garlands, perfumes, music, girls. Horace writes with a tasteful selectivity and a strong tendency to stylize, particularly his locale; but one is directly and constantly reminded in all this of *symposia*, the institutionalized drinking-parties of Hellenized cultures habitual in Classical and Hellenistic times and documented for us by innumerable literary references and depictions in visual art.[1] At these parties men gathered to converse and carouse late into the night, indoors, or sometimes in the open.[2] Girls, and boys, were made available or made themselves available as entertainment for a fee. They might be slaves in the power of (effectively) a pimp,[3] foreigners or freedwomen or even free citizens reduced to earning their living by their accomplishments.[4] And these accomplishments were things like dancing, lyre- and harp-playing, and, of course, sex.[5] These symposiac professionals were, we should note, much less grand than contemporary 'courtesans'. Even if they controlled their own destiny, their typical hire would be for one night—while the courtesan sought and found arrangements much more lasting, comfortable, and profitable (some were sensationally successful: Thargelia, Phryne, Thais, Lamia).[6]

Among innumerable relevant documents the *Symposion* dialogues of Plato and Xenophon are probably the most famous and obviously interesting; but in both cases the party is necessarily to an extent untypical. The calibre of guest and most particularly the presence of Socrates ensure that the tone becomes ever more highbrow—the reverse we may assume of normal practice. Xenophon in fact marks points of departure quite clearly and rather interestingly. A luxurious perfume, offered quite casually to the guests, is turned down by Socrates with a little philosophical speech (2. 3-4). More interesting is the attitude to the entertainers (the troupe, led by a Syracusan, offers the usual musical attractions with some elaboration: there is a girl trick-dancer, as well as a flute-girl and a boy cithara-player and dancer; and they can do pantomime). When they have performed Charmides' response is (in essence) the expected one. He remarks (3. 1): 'It seems to me that . . . this mingling of youthful beauty with music while lulling cares arouses desire (*aphrodite*).' He has, clearly, his thoughts on the other pleasures that the troupe might offer. As Horace says to the lyre-player Lyde (3. 28. 9 ff.):

> nos cantabimus inuicem
> Neptunum et uiridis Nereidum comas;
>   tu curua recines lyra
> Latonam . . .
>   summo carmine, quae Cnidon
> fulgentisque tenet Cycladas . . .   (14)
> dicetur merita Nox quoque nenia   (16)

We shall both sing turn about of Neptune and the green locks of the Nereids; you shall sing, to the curved lyre, of Latona . . . in your last song, of her who dwells in Cnidos and the gleaming Cyclades [i.e. Venus] . . . Night too shall be praised in a well-merited coda.

(translation, G. Williams)

In other words, 'after the musical entertainment, love-making'. Xenophon's Socrates, however, heads Charmides off: 'My friends, these people indeed appear capable of delighting us. But we are of the opinion, I am sure, that we are much better than they. Is it not base if we shall not even try—assembled together as we are—to aid and gladden one another?'[7] And the party proceeds up the path of intellectual pleasure.

This was not, we may assume, all that usual. The explicit sexual scenes on red-figure cups and wine-bowls tell their story.[8] At Aristophanes, *Clouds*, 996 f. *orchestris* (dancer) is synonymous with *pornidion* ('little whore')—and other references in Aristophanes' plays imply that *fellatio* was as

much a part of a flute-girl's symposiac duties as flute-playing.[9]
In the popular comedy of Hellenistic times, the *citharistria* or
psaltria is in theory and in practice also a *hetaera* ('companion',
the gentle Greek word for the pleasanter class of prostitute):
cf. Habrotonon in Menander's *Epitrepontes* or Phaedria's
lover in Terence's *Phormio*; and *hetaerae* might anyway be
present at *symposia* unequivocally as *hetaerae*. And the
following passage of Persaeus, pupil of Zeno the Stoic, seems
(in effect) like a fair retort to the Xenophontic Socrates—and
it offers fascinating insight into life *c.*200 BC (quoted by
Athenaeus at 13. 607 b–d):

If men skilled in dialectic should converse on the subject of syllogisms
when they have gathered for a drinking-party, one might protest that
they were acting in a way alien to the occasion, when even a true
gentleman might get drunk. Moreover, people who desire very earnestly
to be sober maintain that ideal up to a certain point in their drinking-
parties; later, when the spirit of the wine slips by their guard, then
they reveal the whole gamut of impropriety. This actually happened the
other day when the delegation from Arcadia visited Antigonus [King of
Macedonia]. They ate very solemnly and properly (as they thought),
not only not glancing at any of us, but even casting no looks at one
another. But when the drinking was going on apace and there entered,
among other entertaining shows, those Thessalian dancing-girls who
danced, as their custom is, naked except for loin-cloths, they could no
longer restrain themselves but started up from their couches and
shouted aloud at the wonderful sight they were seeing; and they hailed
the king as a blessed man because he was privileged to enjoy these
things; and they proceeded to commit very many other vulgarities
similar to that. And there was a philosopher drinking with us; and when
a flute-girl entered and desired to sit beside him, although there was
plenty of room for the girl at his side, he refused to permit it, and acted
the ascetic. But later, when the flute-girl was put up for the highest
bidder, as is the custom in drinking-bouts, he became very frisky during
the bargaining, and when the auctioneer too quickly assigned the girl
to some one else, he expostulated with him, denying that he had com-
pleted the sale, and finally that ascetic philosopher came to blows,
although at the beginning he would not permit the flute-girl even to sit
beside him.

Athenaeus' follow-up to this quotation is also illuminating.

Possibly it was Persaeus himself who got into the fist-fight; for Anti-
gonus of Carystus mentions him in his work *On Zeno*, writing as

follows: 'Zeno of Citium, when Persaeus bought a little flute-player at a drinking-party but hesitated to take her home because he lived in the same house with Zeno, no sooner perceived this than he hauled the girl into the house and shut her up with Persaeus.'

(Translations, C. B. Gulick with adaptations.)

Thus the Greek *symposion*. But to what extent was it current in *Horace's* time? Does Horace, alluding to the institution of the *symposion* with its attendant girls and pretty-boys and consequent opportunities for casual erotic encounter, allude to an institution of his own society?

The basic answer to that is 'Yes, clearly.' In Chapter I we saw that Livy and Polybius bore witness to an invasion of Italy by a Greek-style life of pleasure in the earlier part of the second century BC. It is worth recalling those passages. Polybius writes about the increasing dissoluteness in the 160s (31. 25. 4 Büttner–Wobst): 'Some young men had given themselves up to fancy-boys, some to *hetaerae*; many to musical displays (*acroamata*), drinking-parties (*potoi*) and extravagance in these things; in the war with Perseus they had swiftly caught the Greek proclivity for these pursuits.' Livy is even more interesting for us, commenting on the earlier morally disastrous episode, the triumph in 187 BC of Manlius Volso (39. 6. 7 f.): 'Then female harpists (*psaltriae*), female *sambuca* (a kind of harp) players, and the convivial pleasures of games [*ludi*: presumably dancers, pantomimists, etc.] became part of the [Roman] banqueting scene.' As we might expect the great *demi-mondaines* were actually preceded by a '*quart-monde*' of less grand pleasuremongers, the world of *symposia* and one-night standers.

It was a world that of course continued to exist. To Livy *psaltriae* and *sambucistriae* are an old phenomenon; but his wording also implies they are a continuing and contemporary phenomenon.[10] The Augustan historian starts to confirm the reality behind the *conuiuia*, *citharistriae*, and *psaltriae* of Horace. So does much other evidence. Perhaps the most attractive comes from the visual and plastic arts. Wall-paintings at Pompeii depict drinking-parties indoors and outdoors, complete with glamorous *hetaerae*, amorous scenes, flute-girls, and vomiting.[11] And this was not purely nostalgic reproduction of vanished Greek life. At Arezzo for example, around the turn of the millennium, elegant craters (wine-bowls) were turned out from factories in large quantities overlaid with explicit scenes of versatile love-making.[12] Sexually-atmosphered *symposia* were clearly at this time neither fictional nor rare—this sort of ware was aimed at a middle-class market.

Roman symposiac society in the first century is further illuminated by (among other things)[13] the many references of hostile witnesses. I quote one *exempli gratia* and refer to others in a note.[14] Cicero, *Against Catiline* 2. 10:

Their means have long failed them; lately their loyalty begins to as well. Only their lust remains as copious as it was. But if revels (*comissationes*) and whores (*scorta*), with wine and dicing, were their only pursuit they would be hopeless types but tolerable. However who can bear this, that layabouts plot against the valiant, fools against the circumspect, drunks against sober folk, somnolent against wakeful? See, they recline at their banquets (*conuiuia*) embracing immoral women, flaccid with wine, stuffed with food, bound with garlands, smeared with perfumes, enfeebled with debauch, and in their conversation belching out—the slaughter of the good classes and the firing of the city.

Again wine, women, garlands, perfumes, games: the customary ingredients. *Conuiuium* is the term the Romans used to cover the Greek *symposion*, as we know from elsewhere;[15] and the Romans often pragmatically combined their drinking-parties with dinner. So Cicero depicts Catiline's constituents at a lurid Roman version of a *symposion* where the conversation turns not the highbrow way of Socrates and his friends but towards revolution. The scene must of course have been in its essentials convincing or Cicero's rhetoric would have fallen flat.

By *scorta* ('tarts', perhaps, rather than 'whores') Cicero means the entertainers customarily present at *symposia*, the harpists-cum-*hetaerae*, etc. *Scortum* in fact in the first century BC is the typical, indeed virtually technical, derogatory term for symposiac entertainers: its characteristic use is in conjunction with *conuiuium* (= *symposion*);[16] and if it was

at *conuiuia* that *scorta* were typically to be found, that
rather defines their function. The term is normally used by
hostile witnesses; but its bluntness could serve other purposes
—casually humorous realism for example. Cf. Catullus' use of
the diminutive in poem 10:

> Varus me meus ad suos amores
> uisum duxerat e foro otiosum,
> scortillum, ut mihi tum repente uisum est,
> non sane illepidum neque inuenustum.

> My friend Varus had led me off from the forum to see his
> lover (I had nothing to do at the time), quite a smart and
> attractive little tart, at first glance.

And note the conclusion to Horace's invitation to Quinctius
to a *symposion* (2.11):

> quis deuium scortum eliciet domo
> Lyden? eburna dic age cum lyra
>   maturet incomptum Lacaenae
>   more comae religata nodum.

> Which (slave) will coax out the sequestered tart Lyde
> from her house? Quick, tell her make haste, with her ivory
> lyre, her hair bound back in a simple bun in the Spartan
> fashion.

Here Horace momentarily opens the door a little wider onto
the world behind his poems.

The Greek names of Horace's girls should now be noted. Far
from suggesting poems set in an alien or literary setting, they
can reinforce our impression of a poetry that is adumbrating
a recognizable background. They are just the sort of names
which flute-girls and the other kinds of entertainers at late
first-century Roman *symposia* might possess. Some are iden-
tifiably the names of freedwomen or slaves, the classes of
women who would typically be such entertainers; some
indeed are identifiably the names of *hetaerae*. All are plausible
in the circumstances: the Greek East was commonly the

provenance of such women;[17] and Greek anyway provided much of the language of love.[18]

Some selective facts. The name Glycera (1. 19 and 30) was, as Nisbet and Hubbard say (on 1. 19. 5), 'frequently affected by *hetaerae*, presumably by way of advertisement' (*glukeros* = 'sweet'), and they cite some literary references. But it is also a name attested innumerable times on the tombstones of freedwomen and others in Rome and Italy.[19] Inscriptions give important background to other names in Horace. Lalage (1. 22 and 2. 5) is a comparatively rare name but known on inscriptions in Rome.[20] Damalis (1. 36) occurs fairly frequently as a name on the tombs of slaves and freedwomen.[21] So does Chloe (1. 23, etc.)—the occurrences of this name are not only frequent but interesting. For example, one Chloe was the dresser of Tiberius' slave-boys.[22] Asterie (3. 7) is rare but attested;[23] Galatea (3. 27) seems to have been a common name for freedwomen (and one Galatea we know was again a slave in the household of Tiberius).[24] The name Myrtale (1. 33) was not only often borne by freedwomen but is also explicitly associated in literary sources with *hetaerae* (the name was well suited to them, given the myrtle's association with Aphrodite).[25] Horace, we may note, specifies that his Myrtale was a *libertina*, a freedwoman (1. 33. 15). He also specifies that Lyde (who again figures commonly on inscriptions)[26] was a 'tart', a *scortum* (2. 11. 21; see above; Lyde occurs also in 3. 11 and 28). Just occasionally, then, he himself confirms the picture that the literary and epigraphical evidence suggests. As for Tyndaris (1. 17), *Satires* 1. 1. 100 seems to me to imply that it was a common professional name; and it too is well enough attested in Roman inscriptions.[27]

None of this is supposed to prove that Horace's love poems are every one about individually identifiable people. It is supposed to confirm our impression of a plausible poetry about possible people. We saw that Horace's typical setting of an erotic-atmosphered *symposion* reflected, in a stylized fashion, a contemporary social institution; we now see that the girls he mentions bear names that contemporary 'entertainers' in that society might plausibly have borne. As for the *pueri delicati*, the pretty-boys with Greek names— Lycidas, Gyges, Nearchus:[28] these too are plausible. Homosexual love which was regular in Greece is regular enough at Rome;[29] and boy charmers of symposiastic society will have sported such names for the same reasons as girls: because their origin actually was Greek–Eastern and/or because Greek was the language of *erotica* (cf. above, p. 199). A more complex matter is Horace's attribution of Greek names to males in heterosexual affairs: Sybaris in 1. 8, Telephus in 1. 13, and so on. To be brief, Horace may mean (sometimes) to suggest freedmen; or they are meant to sound fictional, and it is a measure further to stylize the poems, to blur their relation to reality; or (and here is an important and interesting point) the names may be intended as pseudonyms for Romans, not necessarily identifiable Romans—for reasons of discretion or romance. There is in fact good evidence that Augustan Romans liked to affect Greek names.[30] Telephus in *Odes* 3. 19 and 4. 11 (for example) gives me the clear impression of being pseudonymous rather than fictional.

To sum up: in Horace's time, we may infer, the *symposion* was a standard and current institution, maintaining the traditional ingredients of garlands, perfumes, conversation, wine, and musical and sexual entertainers (both girls and boys). Such parties will have ranged from the genial to the debauched. Genial but erotic *symposia* are the background that Horace's love odes so often obviously presuppose; when specific details do not sketch in the setting, the names of the girls point to that society. Of course Horace writes discreetly —stylizes, romanticizes: the locale becomes the *locus amoenus*, the men often have Greek names and the girls tend to be the better class of entertainer, lyre-players.[31] But the background to his poems is recognizable and has substance.

IX

The Love Odes of Horace

The society alluded to in Horace's love odes is thus rather
different from the world of the Elegists. It will suggest its
own set of priorities and values. The casual symposiac enter-
tainer should elicit a very different sort of love from that
demanded by the domineering courtesan, amateur or profes-
sional; the total, tortured devotion of the Elegists has no
obvious place. Now in fact (and this is an important point to
grasp) many of Horace's ideas about love, his presuppositions
and his attitudes in the *Odes*, are essentially conventional
(cf. Ch. I). The spectacle of men confessing themselves bound,
indeed enslaved, to courtesans, and flaunting a belief that
love is life, shocked society. But if youth amused itself
erotically with professional entertainers in times of relaxation
it would shock no one—provided that those entertainers
remained in their place (psychologically as well as socially),[1]
and provided too that love remained in its place, as the delight
of the youthful idle hour. So it is—or should be—in Horace.
Horatian love has its sadnesses, as we shall see; but in the
Odes the proper place of love and lovers is on the amusing
margins of youthful life. We shall expect a very different love
poetry from Elegy.

'Now the distinction between Horace and the Elegists is not
just implicit; it is effectively asserted by Horace. Horace the
contemporary of Propertius and Tibullus is (among other
things) a poet of what I call the anti-romantic reaction. I shall
not here probe Horace's enigmatic sally against Propertius in
Epist. 2. 2. 91 ff. Rather I would draw attention to a most
important poem, *Odes* 1. 32.

Most of this ode is occupied with giving an image of
Alcaeus. I quote lines 3–12:

> age dic Latinum,
> barbite, carmen,
> Lesbio primum modulate ciui,
> qui ferox bello tamen inter arma,

> siue iactatam religarat udo
> litore nauim,
> Liberum et Musas Veneremque et illi
> semper haerentem puerum canebat
> et Lycum nigris oculis nigroque
> crine decorum.

> Come, o lyre, sing a Latin song, lyre played by the Lesbian
> citizen, who fierce in war nevertheless between battles, or if
> he had moored his storm-tossed ship on the wet shore, used
> to sing of Bacchus and the Muses and Venus and the boy
> (Cupid) always clinging to her side, and of Lycus handsome
> with his black eyes and black hair.

This is an image rather than a true picture: the label 'Lesbian
citizen' carries flattering and indeed anachronistic implica-
tions[2] for an aristocrat engaged in the ebb and flow of a
factional, aristocratic civil war. But *qua* image it is most
interesting. For having Horace's image of Alcaeus, we probably
also have Horace's image of Horace—since Horace suggested
that he was the Roman Alcaeus.[3]

Alcaeus, says Horace, was the *engagé* citizen, intensely
active in the battles of his time. Yet Alcaeus knew there was
a place for *otium*; and he could write a literature of *otium*:
symposiac drinking and love songs. Horace therefore paints a
picture of Alcaeus and by implication of himself as a man
and poet of love and wine, *who had such things in perspective*.
Love and wine were the occupations of the idle hour: *inter
arma*; for *otium*. They did not interfere with duty, *negotium*.
Nor did the poetry of love and wine interfere with a proper
poetry of *negotium*; Alcaeus had written famous poetry to
accompany his deeds in arms. Horace who is here primarily
concerned with symposiac poetry and its place and function
(that is already suggested by the introduction, lines 1–3; see
too p. 203 below) chooses not to draw attention to it. But he
means us to recall it (cf. *Odes* 2. 13). And he means us to
appreciate that the Roman Alcaeus too, if not an *engagé ciuis*,
was an *engagé* poet, who wrote poetry to parallel his model's
political and battle poetry: the political and public odes.

Here then is invaluable insight not only into Horace's idea
of himself as a symposiac poet but as the whole artist. We see

how he squared his delicate little love poems with his role as *sacerdos Musarum* ('priest of the Muses') and *uates* ('prophet') of Rome:[4] within his Alcaean image. He saw himself, like Alcaeus, as the committed public poet—*utilis urbi*, 'useful to the state', to quote a phrase from his own account of the function of the poet[5] —who nevertheless knew when and how to relax and could write a literature for the occasion. There was a time and place for symposiac pleasure and literature, for love and love poetry. And just so long as the love and love poetry did not involve disproportionate or untimely attention, and its energies were directed in appropriate ways and towards the appropriate classes, conventional opinion would have agreed that there was no inconsistency in his moral or artistic standpoint.

We can see straight away how repugnant to Horace the moral and literary stance of Propertius must have been—who elevates love and *otium* to a way of life (to *negotium*) triumphantly contrasting it with more conventional notions of *engagé negotium* (note especially 2. 15; above, p. 130); and who puts love poetry on a par with or superior to national, edifying epic (e.g. 2. 1). And we should note what ode follows 1. 32. It has been carefully positioned. Horace follows his poem on Alcaeus, his image of the *responsible* poet of love, with an ode addressed to Albius Tibullus. This was the Elegist whom Horace found more congenial than Propertius; but he now pointedly chides him for his unnatural preoccupation with love's sorrows and the repetitive and unbalanced preoccupation of his literature. 1. 32 and 33 are a pair, suggesting opposite poles of propriety in love and love poetry. Now we see why the emphasis of 1. 32 was what it was.

It is useful to see Horace as a love poet of the anti-romantic, more particularly anti-Elegiac, reaction, and I shall continue to draw the contrast. But such categorization must not obscure the subtleties of Horace's manner and message. I shall now consider some of the special aspects of Horace's philosophy of love and examine some of the wealth of poems that result.

For Horace love is mortal: love begins and ends. That, I suppose, is an unavoidable fact when love resides on the margins of youthful life. For Horace it is an important truth of large and small aspect, and many tones. It informs most of his poems. Many of his poems, we might say, are designed to illustrate it.

Let us look first at the larger implications of the dictum as Horace sees them. There is a time in life when love is appropriate and there is a time in life when it is not. Love is the province of youth. It ends (or it should end) with age. This is Horace's belief, a belief which he shares with a wide range of thinkers, including conventional Roman thinkers (e.g. Cicero), but which is usually anathema to the Elegists.[6] We can detect it fuelling (in a crude form) two early poems, the two invectives *Epodes* 8 and 12; and it surfaces time and time again in one form or another in the *Odes*.[7] On three occasions (at least) it preoccupies a poem: 3.15, 1.25, and 4.13. To illustrate the truth of the belief, Horace demonstrates the folly of challenging it. Love beyond its season presents an absurd spectacle. But—and here the flexibility of Horace as man and poet starts to be revealed—he makes the point now with humour, now with savagery, now with sympathy.

First 3.15. To illustrate his dictum, to demonstrate the folly of challenging it, Horace adapts what is in fact a traditional topic: sneers and insults at a woman who has become old.[8] (In a cruder and more basic version he had adapted the *topos* in *Epodes* 8 and 12; cf. too the next two poems discussed).

> uxor pauperis Ibyci,
> tandem nequitiae fige modum tuae
> famosisque laboribus:
> maturo propior desine funeri
>
> inter ludere uirgines   5
> et stellis nebulam spargere candidis.

non, si quid Pholoen satis,
et te, Chlori, decet: filia rectius

expugnat iuuenum domos,
pulso Thyias uti concita tympano.   10
    illam cogit amor Nothi
lasciuae similem ludere capreae:

te lanae prope nobilem
tonsae Luceriam, non citharae decent
    nec flos purpureus rosae   15
nec poti uetulam faece tenus cadi.

Wife of poor Ibycus, do at last set a limit to your wanton-
ness and your scandalous efforts: nearer to a death at the
normal age, cease to play [remember the erotic sense to
'play', *ludus* above pp. 1 2] among the girls (5) and cast a
cloud over shining-white stars. Just because something is
right for Pholoe, it is not also right for you, Chloris: your
daughter, with more propriety, tries to take young men's
homes by storm, like a Bacchante intoxicated by the beating
of the tambourine (10). Love for Nothus compels her to
play like a frisky doe: for you wool shorn near famous
Luceria is suitable, not lyres nor the crimson flower of the
rose (15) nor wine-casks drunk right down to the dregs—you
old woman.
    (translation, G. Williams with slight adaptations.)

Note first that unexpected details give the poem unexpected
realism and verisimilitude; in consequence its message gains in
immediacy and relevance. I refer to the poor milieu, the
woman's married status, and the appearance of her daughter.

It may seem rather a savage poem. Certainly 1-4 are blunt
enough. But by previous standards in the topic the insult
element is played down (cf. e.g. *Epodes* 8 and 12): this is not
insult for insult's sake. And the presence of the daughter
helps to make the poem positive rather than negative. There
is a time for love. Lines 13-14 work similarly: there *is* a
proper occupation for Chloris. But the daughter's presence
and the contrast drawn is nevertheless a pointed and concrete
reminder of the negative message, the inappropriateness of
Chloris' conduct. Love ends, or should end.

Line 6 is, I think, particularly interesting. Chloris' actions scatter a cloud on the *shining-white* stars. The stars of course symbolize the young girls, the beauty of the young girls in the sympotic scene. But *bright* stars (note the specification: contrast *sidere pulchrior* in 3. 9. 21 below) grow less bright: they *set* (*dum rediens fugat astra Phoebus, Odes* 3. 21. 24, 'until the Sun returning puts to flight the stars'; cf. too 2. 11. 10 *neque uno Luna rubens nitet/uultu*, 'nor is the blushing moon radiant with one face alone'). The picture starts to suggest something else besides the young girls and their beauty. And another thought must be prompted by the use of such imagery. Compare Catullus 5. 4 ff.

> soles occidere et redire possunt:
>   nobis cum semel occidit breuis lux,
>   nox est perpetua una dormienda

> The sun can fall and come back again. We, when once our
> brief light has fallen, have one everlasting night to sleep

and Horace, *Odes* 4. 7. 13 ff.

> damna tamen celeres reparant caelestia lunae:
>   nos ubi decidimus
> quo . . .
>   puluis et umbra sumus.   (16)

> Yet swift moons repair all that is lost in heaven [i.e. the
> waning of the moon itself and the damage done by its suc-
> cessive changes; by, that is, the seasons]. But when we have
> sunk [to the Underworld] we are dust and shadow.

The girls will set like stars, becoming no longer *candidae*; and they *won't* like stars rise again.

The imagery is complex, suggesting not only the girls and their beauty, but also (quite emphatically I think) the *impermanence* of them and their beauty. And the ultimate distinction between the girls and their apparent equivalent must be felt to be a sad one. We and the poet can only presumably regret the ways in which the girls are *not* like stars. So the fact of life that these girls will grow old is implicitly there in the poem; and, for all that it is a fact of life, it is implicitly regretted. Hence, partly, Horace's anger against Chloris. It is not just that she cuts an absurd figure: she is clouding the spectacle of youth and love which is already clouded without her. Behind the anger is sorrow, sorrow at the scheme of things. The poem is certainly more humane as well as subtler than we may have first imagined.

The names in the poem rate comment (cf. above, pp. 198 ff.). The poem's message clearly has a sharp relevance to contemporary Rome. But Horace, by nature disinclined to commit himself, chooses names which blur its immediate reality—though they do not blur it as much as most scholars have suggested. Pholoe and Chloris are plausible enough freedwoman names (but one suspects that Horace has picked 'Chloris' largely because the name may suggest, ironically, youth, LSJ Χλωρός III. 2). Nothus is a paralleled slave or freedman name;[9] but Ibycus, the name of the famous Greek lyric poet, is so far as I can tell not the sort of name anybody in contemporary Rome would have borne. So Horace seems (according to his common *Odes* manner) to be slightly distancing his poem, stylizing a message of ultimately keen relevance. I think, however, that he may well be teasing us (in the men's names) with the possibility of pseudonyms (perhaps indeed Horace's contemporaries will have known an 'Ibycus' and a 'Nothus'). We should note that both have humorous potential: *nothos* is the Greek for 'bastard' and Ibycus was proverbial for old-fashionedness and stupidity.[10] Anyway, however far the names do distance the poem, mention of wool produced near Luceria in 13-14 brings the poem abruptly back into Roman experience.

The same belief that love ought to end emerges (more ferociously, I think) in 1. 25, though the poem does not appear in the first place to be making this specific point. At the beginning it recalls a slightly different and traditional motif, in which a rejected lover tells his beloved that her beauty and power will fade.[11] In this case they already are fading, lines 1-8:

> parcius iunctas quatiunt fenestras
> iactibus crebris iuuenes proterui,
> nec tibi somnos adimunt, amatque
> ianua limen,

quae prius multum facilis mouebat
cardines; audis minus et minus iam:
'me tuo longas pereunte noctes,
    Lydia, dormis?'

More sparingly do impudent young men shake your closed
windows with frequent blows; they do not take away your
sleep and the door cleaves to the threshold, the door which
before moved its hinges very easily. Less and less you hear:
'Lydia, do you sleep while I your lover perish during long
nights?'

The scorned Horace represents himself as jubilant—and cut-
tingly anti-romantic. We should note his delighted use of the
Elegists' 'excluded lover' topic. For the Elegists, the lover
romantically immobilized outside the mistress's door is
pretty much a law of life;[12] for Horace the law of life is that
such states of affairs pass (with the passing of life) and roles
may be unexpectedly reversed. (Amused, sardonic or cynical
manipulation of Elegiac themes or devices is a tactic Horace
favours.)[13]

Horace reveals why he is so confidently jubilant. Not only
are Lydia's charms already patently fading. He is convinced
that her erotic desires will not suitably diminish with the
passing of her season. She will therefore become an absurd,
even repellent spectacle. Lines 9–15:

inuicem moechos anus arrogantes
flebis in solo leuis angiportu,
Thracio bacchante magis sub inter-
    lunia uento,
cum tibi flagrans amor et libido,
quae solet matres furiare equorum,
saeuiet circa iecur ulcerosum.

In your turn you a despised old woman in a lonely alley will
bewail the insolence of philanderers, the Thracian wind rev-
elling more wildly as the moonless nights draw near, when
burning love and lust which is wont to madden mares shall
rage around your ulcered liver [often regarded as the seat
of erotic feelings in antiquity].

The poem therefore registers a specific triumph (Lydia's
pride falling); but it also reads a general lesson, for the

mortification of Lydia and the reader's edification: the remorseless lesson of life. There is a time for loving and a time for ceasing to love. Flout that and you do not make a pretty picture. In the demonstration of the lesson and Horace's patent conviction lies the heart of the poem.

In the symposiac imagery of the concluding lines, implacable but no longer crude, some sympathy for Lydia is evident, diluting the earlier ferocity. Lines 16 ff.:

> non sine questu
> laeta quod pubes hedera uirenti
> gaudeat pulla magis atque myrto,
> aridas frondis hiemis sodali
> dedicet Euro.[14]

> and you will complain because happy youth takes more joy in flourishing ivy and dark myrtle, but withered leaves it commits to the East wind, the companion of winter.

4. 13 offers a most interesting comparison with both 3. 15 and 1. 25. Apparently Horace prayed that one Lyce would suffer the fate that Lydia is already suffering in 1. 25, namely the painful fading of her charms. Finally of course she did; yet she still tries to keep up with the young girls, very much in the manner of Chloe in 3. 15. The poem is set at this time. Horace comments thus:

> audiuere, Lyce, di mea uota, di
> audiuere, Lyce: fis anus, et tamen
> .uis formosa uideri
> ludisque et bibis impudens
> et cantu tremulo pota Cupidinem   5
> lentum sollicitas. ille uirentis et
> doctae psallere Chiae
> pulchris excubat in genis.
> importunus enim transuolat aridas
> quercus et refugit te, quia luridi   10
> dentes, te quia rugae
> turpant et capitis niues.
> nec Coae referunt iam tibi purpurae
> nec cari lapides tempora, quae semel
> notis condita fastis   15
> inclusit uolucris dies.

quo fugit uenus, heu, quoue color? decens
quo motus? quid habes illius, illius,
   quae spirabat amores,
      quae me surpuerat mihi,   20
felix post Cinaram, notaque et artium
gratarum facies? sed Cinarae breues
   annos fata dederunt,
      seruatura diu parem
cornicis uetulae temporibus Lycen,   25
possent ut iuuenes uisere feruidi
   multo non sine risu
      dilapsam in cineres facem.

Lyce the gods have heard my prayer, the gods have heard it,
Lyce. You grow old, and yet you still want to seem attrac-
tive, and you play (*ludis*) and drink shamelessly and, drunk,
you solicit lagging Cupid with quavering song (5). He keeps
vigil on the beautiful cheeks of blooming Chia, the skilled
harpist. Unaccommodating, he flies past withered oaks and
shuns you because yellow teeth (10) disfigure you, because
wrinkles and your head's snow disfigure you. Neither purple
Coan dresses nor costly jewels bring back to you the time
which fleeting days have shut in the calendars known to all
(15). Whither has fled your charm, alas, whither your com-
plexion? Whither your graceful movement? What do you
have of her, of *her* whose breath was love, who stole me from
myself (20): Cinara's favoured successor, renowned and a
spectacle of graceful arts? But the fates gave brief years to
Cinara—to keep Lyce to the age of an old crow (25), so that
glowing young men might be able to see, with great mirth,
a torch collapsed into ashes.

First a word on addressee and setting. In many of Horace's
odes we must allow the dramatic implications of an addressee
their fullest scope (see e.g., 1. 5 and 1. 23 below): we must
imagine the addressee hearing and responding.[15] In others it
matters less if we imagine the poem as Horace's unheard
comment (e.g. 3. 15). In some others the dramatic scene is
vital, and to realize Horace is present is vital; but it is equally
vital to realize that Horace is soliloquizing: a 'soliloquy in a
scene'.

    4. 13 is a 'soliloquy in a scene' (Kenneth Quinn's phrase;
he discusses this poem admirably).[16] The shift into third
person in 22 ff. confirms that this is a soliloquy and not a

direct address, and the poem hardly makes poetic sense as the latter. Horace meditates on the spectacle of a girl grown old (as he had prayed) and unwilling to face the fact; a woman who tries to be part of love's scene out of season. His reaction is not what he or we would have expected when he uttered his original prayer.

For he is sorry. When he sees Lyce's performance he finds it as appalling as expected. But he is *sorry* for her; he is even sympathetic. The spectacle she offers is drawn with stark realism (e.g. 10 ff.) and cruelly relevant imagery (28: the torch is a weapon of Cupid and a symbol of love). The law of life and love is therefore still insisted upon as implacably as ever, and demonstrated devastatingly. But Horace can find in himself no jubilation. The law is now presented as a cruel one. The repetitions in the first two lines suggest that Horace's horrific evocation comes not with the expected sense of triumph but in sorrow—repetition tends in Horace to be a pathetic device. This is confirmed by the openly lamenting fifth stanza (also displaying a pathetic repetition). Note too the way the contrast is drawn (6 ff.) between Lyce and the harpist Chia, who demonstrates, as Pholoe and the *uirgines* had done in 3. 15, the right time for love. It is a detailed and harsh contrast: their respective 'freshness' (*uirentis, aridas*), musical talent, and ability to arouse erotically, are pointedly opposed; but Horace does not, as in 3. 15, use the contrast to criticize and moralize. It is simply a fact. And notice too the youths, rightly (we should suppose) mirthful at Lyce's spectacle (25-8). There is an insinuation of their comeuppance. *feruidi*, things that glow, *also* become ashes—though *feruidi* tend to forget it.

There is a time of life in which love ought to end. Horace now, in 4. 13, makes this point in a quite different mood from that of 3. 15 or 1. 25. If one looks for a reason for the change of mood there is a simple one to hand. When Horace came to write the fourth book of the *Odes* he was himself considerably older (around fifty).[17] His sense of his own age has affected him for some time and colours other poems in this book;[18] even in the present poem the passing of his own

life intrudes into his references to Lyce (18 ff.): Cinara we
should note is the name Horace has come to associate with
his youthful love.[19] And most significantly, he confessed an
untimely love of his own, with honesty, delicacy, and bril-
liance, in the opening poem of the book.

This is a fine piece, worthy of attention. Here are the first
twelve lines:

> intermissa, Venus, diu
> rursus bella moues? parce, precor, precor.
> non sum qualis eram bonae
> sub regno Cinarae. desine, dulcium
> mater saeua Cupidinum,   (5)
> circa lustra decem flectere mollibus
> iam durum imperiis: abi,
> quo blandae iuuenum te reuocant preces.
> tempestiuius in domum
> Paulli, purpureis ales oloribus,   (10)
> comissabere Maximi,
> si torrere iecur quaeris idoneum.

Venus do you start war again after so long an interruption?
Spare me, I pray, I pray. I am not the man I was under
Cinara's rule [on Cinara see above]. Cease, savage mother
of the sweet Loves (5), to bend [to your reins; a metaphor
from guiding a horse] one close on ten *lustra* [i.e. nearly
50], now hard in the face of your soft commands. Away
back to where the beguiling prayers of young men call you.
More seasonably will you go in revel to the house of Paullus
Maximus winged by shining swans (10), if you seek to scorch
a suitable liver [for 'liver' see above, p. 208].

Line 5 recalls *Odes* 1. 19. 1, *mater saeua Cupidinum*. The
poems are interesting to compare. In 1. 19 the 'savage mother
of the Loves' orders Horace to turn his attention again to
finitis amoribus, 'love that was finished'. Horace describes the
love in question, and then orders his slaves to arrange a
propitiatory sacrifice for the goddess; but his purpose is not
to win release but simply to ensure that she comes 'more
gently', *lenior*. Horace was younger then. By contrast, when
Venus afflicts him in 4. 1, he is considerably older—pushing
fifty; and Horatian sense, obedience to the law of life about
the propriety of love in age, seems duly to assert itself. Love

suits the young. Love suits (for example) the young, talented, and fortunate Paullus Maximus.[20] That is where Venus should fly; and Paullus who will be grateful for love will honour her (all this is elaborated in 13-28). The poem seems to be taking up the theme of 3. 15 (above, pp. 204 ff.) with the exception that Horace is now in the elderly role—and soberly applying his advice to himself.[21] Note how we have, as in 3. 15 (and 4. 13), picture and counter-picture: Chloris and Pholoe, Lyce and Chia, Horace and Paullus. The inappropriate and the appropriate.

Actually, one thing Horace is not doing is applying his advice *soberly*. The abrupt, short sentences, the swift shifts from question to prayer, to statement, to command, and the striking enjambement, all bespeak intensity. Notice too his use of military imagery of love (*bella*): that is Elegiac; so too is the idea of *regnum*.[22] Generally Horace uses such intense, earnest imagery for humorous or parodic effect, since it is excessive for his type of love.[23] But now it seems to suit. Finally we should observe the striking (striking even for Horace) oxymora, *dulcium . . . saeua* and *mollibus . . . durum*, which suggest a serious ambivalence (contrast the cheerful ambivalence of 3. 26).[24] In short this new love is a love that Horace feels intensely; his attitude to its nature is strongly ambivalent; and his prayer to be rid of it is (in the circumstances) understandably impassioned.

After the picture of seasonable love and pleasure (Paullus), back comes Horace insistently contrasting himself again: for him love and *symposia* are no longer pleasures (29-32):

> me nec femina nec puer
>   iam nec spes animi credula mutui,
> nec certare iuuat mero,
>   nec uincire nouis tempora floribus.

> *I* find pleasure in neither woman nor boy, nor now in the fond hope of mutual affection; nor in wine contests or binding my temples with fresh flowers.

Notice the insistence: the emphatic *me*, then anaphora of *nec*. Horace protests too much, perhaps. Passion, intensity, insistence. Horace is having difficulty in applying Horatian sense.

The poem then switches abruptly (*sed*) to reveal what we by now probably expect—but with a pathos we couldn't expect. This is no ordinary love. 33 ff.:

> sed cur heu, Ligurine, cur
>   manat rara meas lacrima per genas?
> cur facunda parum decoro
>   inter uerba cadit lingua silentio?
> nocturnis ego somniis
>   iam captum teneo, iam uolucrem sequor
> te per gramina Martii
>   Campi, te per aquas, dure, uolubiles.

> But why, alas, Ligurinus, does a tear from time to time flow over my cheeks? Why does my fluent tongue fall in unseemly silence in the middle of a sentence? In my dreams at night, now I hold you clasped, now I follow you, fleet as you are, over the grassy Campus Martius, I follow you, hard one, through the rolling water.

The tears and faltering speech are obvious enough signs of love—but again surprisingly Elegiac.[25] Then, in his description of his dreams (a striking example incidentally of dreams as wish-fulfilment) Horace vividly and poignantly evokes a yearning, hopeless love.[26] In his dreams—but only in his dreams—he holds Ligurinus. In his dreams, too, he is young again: the reference is to the typical sports that a youth (and his youthful lover) would in reality pursue[27]—but which come less easily at forty-nine.

durus Horace (line 7) has met his match (*dure* line 40). Horace has learnt something of Elegiac love[28] (as his imagery reveals) and something of Elegiac weakness: the progress of his poem from relative decisiveness to wistful yearning reflects Catullan and Propertian patterns.[29] To apply the laws of life can be easier in theory than in practice and in this poem Horace shows himself—with great delicacy—confronting one of the dilemmas of practice. This is a new Horace. No wonder 4. 13 has the tone it does. (Another very significant love poem in this book is 4. 11; but this is well discussed not only by Syndikus but by Commager.)[30]

A final note. For once the love-object in a homosexual

love poem does not have a Greek name (cf. above, p. 200). Ligurinus ('Ligurian') is a perfectly plausible Roman *cognomen*, paralleled for example in Martial.[31] Horace begins his last book of *Odes*, which we are told he produced under imperial pressure and which contains some of his most frigid court poetry,[32] with what is from some points of view his most personal poem of all.

Love begins and love ends: love has its season. There is another, more attractive side to this grand law. Love should begin as well as end appropriately. Chloe, we are told, resists this fact, and Horace points it out to her with charm and discretion: *Odes* 1. 23:

> uitas hinnuleo me similis, Chloë,
> quaerenti pauidam montibus auiis
>   matrem non sine uano
>   aurarum et siluae metu.
> nam seu mobilibus ueris inhorruit
> aduentus foliis seu uirides rubum
>   dimouere lacertae,
>   et corde et genibus tremit.
> atqui non ego te tigris ut aspera
> Gaetulusue leo frangere persequor:
>   tandem desine matrem
>   tempestiua sequi uiro.

You avoid me, Chloe, like a fawn seeking its frightened mother on pathless mountains, with many an empty fear of breezes and wood. For whether the arrival of spring has begun to shiver in restless leaves or green lizards have parted a bramble bush, it trembles in heart and knees. However I do not press to crunch you like a fierce tiger or Gaetulian lion. Cease finally to follow your mother now that you are seasonable for a man.

Here we must imagine a real and direct address (cf. above, p. 210). The words have a wit and life that only emerges if the poem is so considered. Horace is in fact using dramatic technique in the manner of Catullus or Propertius to convey his Horatian message. The message is a general one, but this is a delightfully particular and therefore more interesting instance.

The key word is *tempestiua* (12), the key idea in which is 'season': 'seasonable', 'timely', 'ripe' (cf. of course 4. 1. 9, *tempestiuius in domum/Paulli* ...). Chloe, Horace says, is now at the right season for love (youthful maturity) and therefore she should not shun his advances. He packages the message gracefully. He gives a humorously exaggerated picture of her timidity in the image of the fawn (which he has borrowed from Anacreon)[33] and balances that with the images of the lion and tiger—a humorous exaggeration of his own supposed ferocity. Deft hyperbole thus gives a light and witty dress to a message that is essentially complimentary—but needs sensitive handling. Horace delivers his message with an eye to his recipient (Chloe); he has a case to make and he chooses humour as his tactic. The message, made particular, comes alive.

We should look closely at the second and middle stanza.[34] There, at the heart of the poem in the image of the fawn, is Horace's message insinuated in symbolic form. The fawn is irrationally frightened at the arrival of spring. Chloe *tempestiua uiro* is afraid of the arrival of her youthful season, her spring. She too is being irrational. Horace also chooses subtlety to make his message persuasive. (Contrast the imagery involving *winter* applied to Lydia in 1. 25 above, p. 209.)

Horace makes the same sort of point as he makes in 1. 23 in 2. 5, though with rather more twist and a little less delicacy. There is an excellent discussion of it in Nisbet and Hubbard. I should like simply to quote Horace's unexpected way of saying how time is bringing a girl into the season for love (13-15; he is addressing himself):

> currit enim ferox
> aetas et illi quos tibi dempserit
> apponet annos; . . .

> For time runs fiercely on, and will add to her the years
> it takes from you.

That introduces of course *another* preoccupation of Horace's (his own ageing) and suggests a nice dilemma.

Horace also makes the same sort of point in 4. 10 to

Ligurinus—but in such a different mood, from such a different perspective.[35]

Love begins and love ends. That law applies not only to the grand seasons of life, but to the everyday progress of life. Love is whimsical, changeable; Love we might say has an odd sense of humour. It pleases Venus

> imparis
> formas atque animos sub iuga aenea
> saeuo mittere cum ioco

> to put under brazen yokes forms and minds ill-matched,
> in a savage joke

as Horace said when remonstrating with Tibullus (1. 33. 10-12; cf. above, p. 203). And if A loves B, then A will not love B for long. Meantime B may well not love A; but may love C; so soon may A: again compare what Horace said to Tibullus in 1. 33 (lines 5 ff.). Love is like a species of musical chairs. In the sequence of days as well as seasons, love begins and ends. And since love in conventional eyes belongs to the amusing margins of youthful life, that in conventional eyes would probably be deemed right, proper—or at least inevitable. It is a truth which permeates the *Odes*. But again of course it is one that is normally anathema to the Elegists, to Tibullus as well as Propertius.[36]

It is the sort of truth that young romantic youths do not know. The youth in the Pyrrha *Ode* (1. 5) for example: he believes his present happiness will be eternal.

> quis multa gracilis te puer in rosa
> perfusus liquidis urget odoribus,
>   grato, Pyrrha, sub antro?
>   cui flauam religas comam,
> simplex munditiis? heu quotiens fidem
> mutatosque deos flebit et aspera
>   nigris aequora uentis
>   emirabitur insolens,
> qui nunc te fruitur credulus aurea;

qui semper uacuam semper amabilem
sperat nescius aurae
fallacis. miseri, quibus
intemptata nites! me tabula sacer
uotiua paries indicat uuida
suspendisse potenti
uestimenta maris deae.[37]

What slim boy, Pyrrha, drenched in liquid scents presses
you in an abundance of roses under some pleasing grotto?
For whom are you binding back your blonde hair in simple
elegance? [*simplex munditiis*, a particularly untranslatable
phrase: more literally, 'simple in <your> elegance'.] Alas
how often will he bewail fidelity and the gods changed and
wonder amazed at the sea made harsh by dark winds, he
who now trustfully enjoys golden you; he who expects
you always available, always lovable—ignorant of the
deceiving breeze. Wretched are they for whom you shine
untried! [Both these last two words are ambiguous in the
Latin, applicable to the sea of the preceding image (for
which see below) and to a person.] The temple wall with
its votive plaque declares that *I* have hung up in offering
my dripping clothes to the goddess [Venus] with power
over the sea.

In the long central section (5-12) Horace laments that the
boy will find out his error, that he will find out the truth of
love. 'Lament' is of course not quite the right word: Horace
finds the boy's infatuated gullibility somewhat amusing.
Horace knows the law. Behind the emotive exclamation
heu quotiens . . . flebit . . . and Horace's very striking version
of the conventional erotic sea image (*aspera nigris . . .*)[38] we
detect the poet's irony. Horace is unlikely to offer such
elaborately emotional sympathy straight. This is confirmed.
Horace gently mocks the boy's coming discomfiture: the
phrase in the sea image which foreshadows that discomfiture
(*nescius aurae/fallacis*) plays on and thus rather exposes the
word which empathetically expressed his rapture (*aurea*).[39]
The plural *miseri* (12) also throws ironic light on the boy's
gullibility, on his sense of being eternally chosen, uniquely
happy. There are queues of people waiting to be in that un-
fortunate position.

The gist of the poem seems clear. The boy is unaware of Pyrrha's fickleness. It is more general than that: he is unaware of love's fickleness, that love is musical chairs, that love begins and ends: *nescius aurae fallacis*, 'ignorant of the deceiving breeze'. That is a general comment. Pyrrha is highly individual but nevertheless symptomatic. The boy will learn the truth of love in time; meanwhile the spectacle is not unamusing.

However, though simple in essence, this poem is one of Horace's most famous, if not finest. It epitomizes the flexibility of Horace the man and the subtlety of Horace the poet. It has been well discussed,[40] so I can be brief and selective in my comments.

First, by way of introduction, The *quis* and *cui* sentences of the first six lines do not refer to simultaneous actions in one scene. Pyrrha is not doing her hair in the *antrum*. They are two ways of asking the same general question, 'Who is your new lover?' First, *quis . . .?* Horace has inferred that Pyrrha has another lover and asks who it is; but he asks the question vividly, setting it in a specific scene (which I shall come back to): 'Who makes love to you in a pleasing grotto?' He has also noticed that Pyrrha has of late been adopting a special if simple coiffure and a careful, tasteful *toilette*. That can mean only one thing. 'Who is it for?' he asks. Two questions therefore are getting at the same point.

Now a word on the scene imagined in the *quis . . .?* clause. I am in agreement with West that this setting (the 'grotto' (*antrum*), etc.) is meant to be essentially realistic: lavish but realistic. Profusely scattered roses and liberally applied scents are desirable features of real Roman sympotic–erotic scenes; and there is good evidence that (artificial) grottoes were popular constructions in private and public gardens and places of entertainment: the equivalent of summerhouses or gazebos.[41] One can make quite a good case for supposing that the grecism *antrum* was a fashionable term for them.[42] Horace is picturing Pyrrha being made love to in an elaborately seductive but plausible setting; and it is, I think, of the *boy*'s making or choosing (quite an important point: I return to it).

Now Horace's amusement at the boy's gullibility is countered by touches of fun at his own expense, and thus robbed of malice. Suggestions of self-mockery run a teasing course through the poem. In the first place, mention of a 'slim boy' making love to Pyrrha brings to mind Horace neither very young nor slim;[43] and the fact that Horace asks Pyrrha who the boy is who is now having her might suggest that he is jealous. The desirability of Pyrrha and love with Pyrrha as Horace seems to draw it strengthens this impression.[44]

Then comes the first surprise. Instead of jealous, Horace is pitying. The significance of the boy's youth is not his greater attractiveness but his ignorance: *heu quotiens . . .?* But rather than pitying, Horace is superior. We remember the irony in the central section and the irony and loftiness of *miseri quibus intemptata nites*, 'wretched are they for whom you shine untried!'

But then comes a further surprise—by this time probably not such a surprise. It is certainly prepared for by *intemptata*, 'untried'. Horace is superior only because he himself has learned the hard way. For him Pyrrha is not *intemptata*. He too has loved her and just as credulously. He has been shipwrecked on the same erotic sea. Horace suggests a certain sympathy with the boy, linking their fates in the same imagery (13–16).

But the sympathy is equivocal, amused, and qualified. Horace's emphasis in the last stanza is on the fact that he has come through. To be sure he was Pyrrha's lover; he has experienced that 'shining sea', and the storms that await the boy. But he has been saved. His rescue, the rescue for which he seems warmly thankful, is the point of focus for the stanza, imaged in the rescue of the sailor. The stanza suggests therefore not so much sympathy as superiority in experience—if not a sense of superiority.

The imagery of this last stanza is to be carefully noted. It is highly witty, and (since an ability to be funny about a thing implies distance from that thing) the wit increases our impression of Horace's detachment from love and the lover's (the boy's) plight.

He is extending the conventional area of erotic imagery (love as—dangerous—seafaring, etc.) into *another topos*. We know that 'it was a common practice to commemorate an escape from danger by affixing a tablet to a temple wall . . . the plaque often told its story by means of a picture.' And 'rescued sailors sometimes dedicated their clothes *ex voto* to the gods.' Both these practices had their reflection in literary forms and motifs.[45] Horace has combined the two into one with the latter predominating. And he has given it erotic metaphorical significance.

Now it was, as I say, conventional to picture love in terms of sea-faring, even troubled lovers as shipwrecked sailors. It was *not* usual, however, to extend the erotic sea metaphor into the *other* sea *topos*, the *topos* of shipwrecked sailors dedicating their clothes to the god of the sea if they were saved. It introduces an oddly incongruous, prosaic, and irrelevantly detailed notion (the clothes) which Horace unerringly highlights by choosing a very prosaic word for them (*uestimenta*).[46] It is a witty conceit. Horace therefore not only concentrates in this stanza on his lucky rescue, but recounts it, and alludes to his entanglement with Pyrrha, in a witty and therefore detached way. He adds another touch of pure wit by substituting at the last moment (in a way which cannot be reproduced in translation) another and brilliantly relevant deity of the sea for the expected Neptune: Venus.

Our sense of Horace's sense of superiority is corroborated. Sympathy for the boy is far from unequivocal. Horace speaks as the amused 'old salt' (to use West's apt phrase). The address to Pyrrha which seemed initially the querulous complaint of a jealous lover is actually the knowing, amused question of a seasoned campaigner. Horace is amused by Pyrrha. He can spare a thought for what the new victim will go through and admit to his own past folly; but his own past involvement *was* folly and the present spectacle is unmistakably amusing. Horace perceives the work of an expert as well as an imminent *exemplum* of a law of love. Horace addresses Pyrrha in a kind of complicity.

It will be evident from the above that in my view the address in this poem is again to be taken literally: that is to say, we are to imagine Horace addressing Pyrrha directly and throughout (cf. p. 210). The poem makes better sense this way and all sorts of details come alive. Let me mention a few things not already mentioned. For example, Horace clearly knows without asking that Pyrrha is occupied with a 'slim' and gullible boy. That is pointed and plausible in a speech from one old hand to another. The mock-serious sympathy towards the boy in 5 ff., the ironic loftiness of *miseri quibus intemptata nites*, 'wretched are they for whom you shine untried', and the witty detachment of the last stanza are all more amusing, more *alive*, if we imagine Pyrrha actually listening. In stressing the boy's elaborate seductive preparations (1-3), Horace has his eye on the boy's coming disappointment—but he is also sharing what must be Pyrrha's amusement. Rather different in effect but just as lively is the emphasis on the simplicity of Pyrrha's own make-up (4-5). As Nisbet and Hubbard say (ad loc.), some people might foolishly expect her innocent appearance to be matched by ingenuous behaviour. This no doubt was exactly Pyrrha's motive—as Horace would know only too well. And Pyrrha would know that Horace would know only too well; the allusion becomes an amusingly barbed jibe—in a direct address. All these details come alive if we grant the address its full reality. It seems perverse not to. Nothing is impaired when we do.

In short Horace is again using a technique similar to the dramatic technique of Catullus and Propertius, but to imply a message they would have to reject. The poem also offers wit, insight into human relations, and a delightful impression of personality—particularly Horace's own: teasing, witty, ironic, and sympathetic. Simple messages may lead to rich poems, and of course I am only beginning (as I end) to spell it all out.

Odes 3. 9 is, I think, one of the pleasantest illustrations of the musical chairs of love—and one of Horace's pleasantest odes.

donec gratus eram tibi
nec quisquam potior bracchia candidae
 ceruici iuuenis dabat,
Persarum uigui rege beatior.   (4)

 'donec non alia magis
arsisti neque erat Lydia post Chloen,
 multi Lydia nominis
Romana uigui clarior Ilia.'   (8)

 me nunc Thressa Chloe regit,
dulcis docta modos et citharae sciens,
 pro qua non metuam mori
si parcent animae fata superstiti.   (12)

 'me torret face mutua
Thurini Calais filius Ornyti,
 pro quo bis patiar mori
si parcent puero fata superstiti.'   (16)

 quid si prisca redit Venus
diductosque iugo cogit aeneo,
 si flaua excutitur Chloe
reicctacque patet ianua Lydiae?   (20)

 'quamquam sidere pulchrior
ille est, tu leuior cortice et improbo
 iracundior Hadria,
tecum uiuere amem, tecum obeam libens.'

As long as I found favour with you and no young man, preferred to me, put his arms round your white neck, I flourished richer than the king of the Persians. (4)

'As long as you were not more deeply on fire for another girl and Lydia did not take second place to Chloe, I, Lydia of great fame, flourished more distinguished than Ilia of Rome.' (8)

Now Thracian Chloe rules over me, she who is knowledgeable in sweet songs and skilled with the lyre, for whom I shall not fear to die if the fates shall spare my darling to survive me. (12)

'Calais, son of Ornytus of Thurium, burns me with a fire he feels too, for whom I shall suffer death twice over, if the fates shall spare the boy to survive me.' (16)

What if our former love returns and forces us, now separated, together under a brazen yoke, if blonde Chloe is thrown out and the door opened to Lydia who was rejected? (20)

'Although he is more beautiful than a star, while you are more lightweight than a cork and more quick-tempered than the violent Adriatic, yet with you should I love to live, with you should I willingly die.'

          (translated by G. Williams.)

There are some immediate points to be made. First something simple. We should take the 'I' of the poem in its most natural way: as Horace; we should tie the poem to him, to the poet we know, and not to some putative *persona*. The intrinsic likeliness of this is confirmed. The speaker is a poet: that is in Lydia's mind when she says *multi Lydia nominis/ Romana uigui clarior Ilia*, 'I, Lydia of great fame, flourished more distinguished than Ilia of Rome' (Ilia had been made *clara* by Ennius: Ovid, *Trist*. 2. 259 ff.); and the characterization of 22 f. fits Horace.[47] Secondly, although the form of the poem follows a sophisticated amoebean pattern (in the first 16 lines in particular 'antistrophe' closely responds to 'strophe' in both form and content), in other respects the poem is very close to ordinary speech, much closer than Horace normally is: the word-order, sentence-construction, imagery, and use of proverbial expressions all suggest conversation.[48] Thirdly, the speakers are to an extent characterized —on top of the explicit characterization of Horace offered by Lydia. Horace we find is preoccupied with externals; he talks concretely, physically: 2, 10, 18–20. Lydia on the other hand talks more of feelings, of states of mind and emotion. One senses at the very least an attempt to differentiate a male and female mode of sensibility.

These last two points suggest that, in spite of the complex amoebean form, Horace is trying to create the impression of a plausible, dramatic *dialogue*. This is the case (though it is denied or ignored by most interpreters). What we find, if we give the poem its chance, is a drama, a delightful interplay of sophisticated personalities—in which the amoebean sophistication has an integral part. (Again, therefore, as in 1. 5 Horace is exploiting 'dramatic situation', but this time it is the drama of mime or epigram,[49] staged drama (as it were) such as we barely find in the Elegists.)[50]

It is clear from the start that Horace is interested in reviving his affair with Lydia. His words in 1–4 are a perspicuous overture; no one is likely to tell an ex-lover that he was incomparably happy during their affair without having a resumption in mind, and without wanting the lover to get that message. But Horace does not, it seems, want to commit himself to the embarrassing exposure of a direct proposal— perhaps we sense that the man wants the woman to make the first open move.

Lydia must know that, but she chooses not to respond, not in an immediate way. She does not want to make the first open move either (we shall learn why in a moment). She counters simply but ingeniously with a similar comment on the past affair (5–8). It too is of course an overture; but only an overture. It must be disconcerting for Horace (as it is amusing for us) to find his overture countered, even mimicked in this way rather than more directly responded to, as he had wished. The formal amoebean structure has a dramatic function.

Horace tries again to get a more positive response (9–12). He tries the time-honoured tactic of expressing enthusiasm for another girl to arouse jealousy and therefore reaction. Most people's experience provides parallels for the tactic; but it is entertainingly documented by Terence at *Eunuchus*, 434 ff.:

THRASO: By the way, what about this girl Pamphila: should I rid Thais of her suspicions that I'm attracted to her?

GNATHO: Certainly not. You'd do better to increase them.

THRASO: Why?

GNATHO: Why? You know how it galls you if ever she praises Phaedria [Thraso's rival] or even mentions his name?

THRASO: Yes, yes, I know.

GNATHO: There's only one way of stopping it. When she names Phaedria, you retaliate with Pamphila; if ever she suggests asking Phaedria in to supper, we'll invite Pamphila to sing, and if she praises his good looks, you praise hers. We can give her tit for tat and cut her to the quick.

(translated by Betty Radice)

Compare too, Ovid, *Ars*, 2. 435–66.

Lydia refuses to rise to the bait. She knows what he is up to. She also knows that two can play at that game, and she proceeds to do so. Instead of reacting, *she* expresses her

enthusiasm for another lover, once more virtually mimicking
Horace. And in fact she trumps him: she pointedly caps him:
pro quo bis patiar mori, 'for whom I shall suffer death twice
over'. Again the amoebean form has a dramatic function.

Balked in his efforts to manœuvre Lydia into making the
open proposal, Horace gives in. He makes the suggestion as
off-handedly as possible (*quid si . . .?*, 17), saving face; but he
is now forced to be explicit (17–20). And at last we learn
why Lydia was disinclined to be the first to declare. Although
Horace rather implied at the beginning (*donec gratus eram*)
that she had thrown him over, it was in fact (as he now
admits) the other way round. Lydia had been 'rejected'.
Therefore, Lydia thought, Horace ought to be the one to
humble himself to the extent of making an explicit proposal.
Therefore she forced him into doing just that.

But her object achieved and Horace forced into the open,
Lydia herself then openly responds—graciously, humorously,
sweetly—and soberly. A few words on her last line are neces-
sary. It rather sounds as if the seal is being set on a romantic,
Elegiac love. But it isn't.

Lydia's words in fact contrast with the romantic (and
phoney) asseverations of 11 and 15, and contrast too with
Elegiac statements about *Liebestod* and the identity of life
and love. To express a wish to live with someone is not to
equate love and life; to be willing to die with someone is not
to dwell upon or look forward to that event.[51] Besides (and
most importantly) Lydia speaks *hypothetically*. No doubt
she would like to stay Horace's lover (in the Horatian not the
Elegiac sense of that word): such a thought suits her more
feeling nature. But she also knows the score; she knows the
law of life, love, and Horace. Horace is 'more lightweight
than a cork'; Lydia knows and says he is 'more lightweight
than a cork'. With this knowledge, and given that she is, as
well as a woman of feeling, a woman of deft and witty
sophistication (this the poem has also admirably demon-
strated), she must know that another rift and no doubt another
reconciliation will soon occur. Love begins, love ends, love
begins. She does know. That is why she speaks hypothetically.

The poem is a drama, an interplay of two personalities, the careful sparring of two urbane people who have a common end in view but different ideas of how to get there. It reflects —we could say it demonstrates—the truth that love begins and love ends; it mirrors a moment in the cycle. But (again) it does a great deal more. And the demonstration of the truth is perhaps more interesting than the truth demonstrated. That thought can lead to another way of looking at Horace's love odes.

So far I have shown how Horace's love poems exemplify or presuppose a basic belief: love begins, love ends. There is another way of looking at them. Most, perhaps all, share a characteristic emphasis, a characteristic interest. This characteristic interest is natural enough in view of the belief, and intimately connected with it; but it is important to identify it and consider it for its own sake. Horace tends to be interested not in the emotion of love but in the behaviour of lovers. Love is the context: the attention of the poem is on the people in that context and the games they play.

It is most natural that Horace should choose this emphasis; and it is illuminating at this point to contrast Catullus and the Elegists. Catullus, Propertius, and Tibullus are profoundly concerned with the emotion of love, and with the expression of it. They (in particular Propertius) do stage dramas of love; they describe the behaviour of lovers. But their attention is egocentric and generally we interpret their dramas as means to an end, as devices to communicate their feelings in love or insight into their own or their mistresses' psychology. But Horace can have no profound interest in the emotion, for the emotion he is concerned with is not profound. Love to him is not all-important; but people occupying themselves in this margin are most interesting. Horace describes the behaviour of lovers because he is interested in the behaviour of lovers. From a detached point of view he observes the games of the species *homo amator*, its ritualized and engaging behaviour in the leisurely margins of life, and he stages that behaviour for our amusement in his verses. A truth, a law of life, is always inherent. But the illustration of the truth is generally far more striking than the truth illustrated.

This description fits the poems I have discussed above, even the ones in which Horace talks in the first person. In these Horace is the representative of the species described. Horace the poet chronicles the behaviour of Horace the lover, observing him with much the same detachment as he would another member of the species. It is a situation in which the supreme ironist finds himself very happy. The description obviously suits the numerous poems that introduce lovers in the third person. The focus of Horace's interest in love explains in fact why so many of his love poems are about other people, as for example *uxor pauperis Ibyci* (3. 15) above.

Or let us consider *quid fles Asterie?* (3. 7):

quid fles, Asterie, quem tibi candidi
primo restituent uere Fauonii
    Thyna merce beatum,
        constantis iuuenem fide

Gygen? ille Notis actus ad Oricum   (5)
post insana Caprae sidera frigidas
    noctes non sine multis
        insomnis lacrimis agit.   (8)

atqui sollicitae nuntius hospitae,
suspirare Chloen et miseram tuis
    dicens ignibus uri,
        temptat mille uafer modis.   (12)

ut Proetum mulier perfida credulum
falsis impulerit criminibus nimis
    casto Bellerophontae
        maturare necem refert;   (16)

narrat paene datum Pelea Tartaro,
Magnessam Hippolyten dum fugit abstinens;
    et peccare docentis
        fallax historias monet.   (20)

frustra: nam scopulis surdior Icari
uoces audit adhuc integer. at tibi   (22)
    ne uicinus Enipeus
        plus iusto placeat caue,   (24)

quamuis non alius flectere equum sciens
aeque conspicitur gramine Martio,
   nec quisquam citus aeque
    Tusco denatat alueo. (28)

prima nocte domum claude neque in uias
sub cantu querulae despice tibiae,
   et te saepe uocanti
    duram difficilis mane.

Why weep for Gyges, Asterie, a young man of steadfast
fidelity whom cloudless west winds will restore to you at
the beginning of spring rich with merchandise of Bithynia
(5)? He, driven in to Oricus by storms from the South after
(the rising of) Capra's wild star, spends chill nights, sleep-
less, with many a tear (8).

And yet a messenger from his excited hostess, telling
him that Chloe sighs and is desperately in love with your
lover, tempts him cunningly in a thousand ways (12). He
recalls how a faithless woman with false accusations drove
the credulous Proetus to bring an early death on Bellerophon
who was too chaste (16); he tells of Peleus almost sent
down to Tartarus through saying 'No' and refusing Hippolyte
of Magnesia; and, in an underhand way, he warns him of
stories that teach him to sin (20).

In vain: for, deafer than the rocks of Icarus, he hears
the voices and is untouched (22).

But take care that your neighbour Enipeus does not find
more favour with you than is right (24)—though no other is
seen on the field of Mars so skilful to control a horse nor
does any so speedily swim down the Tuscan stream (28). At
nightfall lock your house and, at the quavering note of a
flute, do not look down into the street below, and, though
he often calls you hard-hearted, stay stubborn.

                    (translated by G. Williams.)

Note first of all how Horace stylizes, slightly distances reality
in much the same way as he did in *uxor pauperis Ibyci*. All
that Gyges and Enipeus do is plausibly Roman. Enipeus
exercises as a young Roman would do and where a young
Roman would do. Many a businessman must have faced
Gyges' travelling problems, if not his erotic problems: he has
been engaged on business in the Eastern provinces, he has
delayed his departure back to Italy for too long, and has been

driven to seek refuge *en route* in the Illyrian port of Oricus where he is now trapped until the new navigation season.[52] However, Gyges' and Enipeus' names (although not Asterie's or Chloe's) must be fictional—or pseudonyms.

The poem presupposes the truth that love begins and love ends—the truth that love is musical chairs. But the attention of the poem is on the amusing illustration, the behaviour of the lovers.

Asterie is weeping for her lover across the sea, fearing for his fidelity under the onslaught of his unscrupulous hostess. Solicitously Horace reassures her, taking the opportunity to fill his readers in on circumstantial details. Now thematically and linguistically the lamenting Asterie recalls Elegiac lovers.[53] That is how Horace makes her sound when he addresses her. Knowing what we do about Horace's views on Elegiac love, we should be on the alert for some Horatian sally; we may suspect that his solicitous tone is disingenuous.

The truth is revealed in 22 ff. Horace's earnest speech of reassurance was uttered in amusement and irony; Asterie's tears and anxiety are consciously or unconsciously an act or cant. For from reassurance Horace switches to warning, and in a cameo that neatly corresponds to Gyges' trial by Chloe, he reveals that Asterie is being tempted by Enipeus (the male Enipeus parades and serenades where the female Chloe cajoles and threatens; the sexes behave in character). And Asterie, it seems, is in much more danger of succumbing than Gyges. Behind the lamenting devotion of the romantic lover Horace perceives and demonstrates the truth of love. Love is slight and mortal—and romance is bogus. Here love is beginning and love is ending, though the protagonists themselves are perhaps not fully aware of the fact. An imminent change of chairs here affords pleasant irony, a cut at Elegy, an amusing drama.

Another, most pleasant poem, 3. 20:

> non uides quanto moueas periclo,
> Pyrrhe, Gaetulae catulos leaenae?
> dura post paulo fugies inaudax
>   proelia raptor,

cum per obstantis iuuenum cateruas   (5)
ibit insignem repetens Nearchum,
grande certamen, tibi praeda cedat
    maior an illa.

interim, dum tu celeris sagittas
promis, haec dentis acuit timendos,   (10)
arbiter pugnae posuisse nudo
    sub pede palmam

fertur et leni recreare uento
sparsum odoratis umerum capillis,   (14)
qualis aut Nireus fuit aut aquosa
    raptus ab Ida.

Do you not see at what peril, Pyrrhus, you stir the cubs of a Gaetulian lioness? In a short while you will run away from the stern contest, a cowardly plunderer, when, through the crowds of young men in her path (5), she will come looking for her splendid Nearchus, a mighty contest (to settle) whether the booty falls to you or she is the stronger.

Meanwhile, as you are bringing out swift arrows and she is sharpening her terrifying teeth (10), the umpire of the contest is said to have put the palm under his bare foot and, in the gentle breeze, to be refreshing his shoulders covered with his scented hair (14), as beautiful as either Nireus was or he who was carried off from watery Ida.

(translated by G. Williams, with slight adaptations).

Again we have a poem that amusingly illustrates love's proneness to end as well as begin—and it makes another related point. The poem dramatically illustrates how much energy can be unnecessarily wasted in the process. However, as in 3. 7, the illustration of the poem's truth strikes one more than the truth illustrated. Horace stages the behaviour of lovers for our amusement. (Again, we should consider the stylizing effect of an unexpected Greek name, Pyrrhus.)

Horace addresses Pyrrhus in epic imagery. Pyrrhus is stirring up someone or something who deserves, it seems, Homerically heroic imagery: in the *Iliad* we find heroes compared not only to a lion but to a lion or even (it might be argued) a lioness robbed of his/her young.[54] Two details, we should note, maintain and confirm a Homeric ambience—while they delay and obscure the revelation of what is actually behind the image: the plural of *catulos* and the crowd of young men belong to Homer's similes, but they not only give no hint of, they actually conceal what Horace is coming to: nothing corresponds to them on the literal plane.

Lines 6–7 finally reveal what is behind the image. No hero, no heroic world, but a woman who will react passionately to an attempt to steal her lover. Now such a person in such a state does not, in Horace's book, deserve heroic imagery. And the contrived delay increases the bathos and incongruity of the revelation. So the grand imagery was ironic. Horace finds so much potential emotional reaction amusing. Nor does Pyrrhus who is also prepared to expend passionate energy for the boy escape Horace's amusing mockery. Especially in 3–4: he is all bravery now but soon he will turn tail: the neologism *inaudax*, 'soon *un*bold', emphasizes the jibe.

Having revealed the point of reference of the image, Horace (perhaps rather unexpectedly) does not let it go. He continues for another two lines to talk metaphorically in its terms (9–10). However, his hand declared, he heightens its incongruousness; and thus more blatantly mocks Pyrrhus' and the woman's passionate expenditure of energy. Immediately after revealing that he is talking merely of an erotic feud, he talks in details which would scarcely suit a heroic simile in a heroic context but which are wildly inappropriate for Pyrrhus and his rival: sharpening of teeth and preparation of arrows. The idea of whetting, we should note, is excessive even for an Homeric lioness: it belongs to boar imagery; boars have tusks which they can and do sharpen. The imagery is therefore extraordinarily extravagant, patently incongruous. Humour at the rivals' expense is clear and increasing. But the main jibe is yet to come.

While Pyrrhus and the woman are thus preparing to do battle, something else is happening: *interim, dum* . . .; presumably, since the rivals are confined to a subordinate clause, something more important. And we expect it to be at least comparably vigorous. Instead Horace switches imagery, and delivers a superb ironic surprise. He introduces, at last, the love-object himself, Nearchus. And the important action is inaction; Nearchus is ineffably indifferent to the whole business. Bored. Horace, now using the imagery of a sporting contest at palaestra or gymnasium, gives this indifference superb concrete expression (11–14). Nearchus, who should be the one to decide the contest and award the palm, rests his foot on the palm and concentrates on the wind blowing pleasantly through his hair. He couldn't care two hoots who wins. Such indifference mutely but devastatingly exposes the folly of the rivals' fury, the waste of their energy; more devastatingly than the irony of Horace's heroic imagery.

But it is still of course Horace who is delivering the message to us—and to Pyrrhus. The direct address of the poem should again be accepted for what it is. The mockery is more pointed if we suppose the poem uttered to Pyrrhus himself. Consider a detail: the studied casualness with which Horace objectively reports on Nearchus, reflecting Nearchus' own lack of interest (*posuisse . . . fertur . . .*, 'he is said to have put . . .'; note how casualness is reproduced in rhythm (enjambement)), is cruelly pointed in an address to Pyrrhus, less relevant if we imagine that address to be a convention, a peg.

The poem suggests a superb play. That is its interest; that is what strikes us. But it offers a message as well as action. The theme is classifiable as musical chairs; and it associates another theme. The poem demonstrates the folly of expending much energy and passion in the game. It is the lesson that Horace read to Albius Tibullus in the pair of poems 1. 32 and 33 (above, p. 203); it is one of the crucial provisos introduced by Cicero (above, pp. 1–2). Love belongs to the amusing margins of life; it is part of *otium*. When this principle is observed, love is fine. Look at Nearchus. The concluding sketch of him is beautiful. To fight for him is folly, but he is patently worth having. The poem ends focused on him.

Love should be confined to the amusing margins of life. That is to put it negatively. There is a positive side—as there was to the insistence that love is the province of youth (above, pp. 215 ff.). Horace has nothing against one enjoying a Nearchus appropriately. Elsewhere he phrases himself directly. There *should* be love in the *otium* margin of life. That is for example the clear implication of 3. 19. The point is clearly and delicately made in 3. 28:

> festo quid potius die
> Neptuni faciam? prome reconditum,
>   Lyde, strenua Caecubum
> munitaeque adhibe uim sapientiae.   (4)
>
>   inclinare meridiem
> sentis ac, ueluti stet uolucris dies,
>   parcis deripere horreo
> cessantem Bibuli consulis amphoram?
>
>   nos cantabimus inuicem
> Neptunum et uiridis Nereidum comas;   (10)
>   tu curua recines lyra
> Latonam et celeris spicula Cynthiae,
>
>   summo carmine, quae Cnidon
> fulgentisque tenet Cycladas et Paphum
>   iunctis uisit oloribus: (15)
> dicetur merita Nox quoque nenia.

What better can I do on the feast-day of Neptune? Stir yourself Lyde, and bring out the Caecuban that is stored away, and make an assault on entrenched wisdom (4). Do you notice that the midday is declining and, as if the swift day were standing still, are you hesitating to snatch from the wine-store the bottle that is slacking there (from the time) of the consul Bibulus? We shall both sing turn about of Neptune and the green locks of the Nereids (10): you shall sing, to the curved lyre, of Latona and the darts of swift Cynthia, in your last song, of her [Venus] who dwells in Cnidos and the gleaming Cyclades and visits Paphos with her team of swans (15): Night too shall be praised in a well-merited coda.

(translated by G. Williams.)

It is a holiday, the *Neptunalia* (and therefore *otium*). What shall I do on this holiday? Horace asks. The poem shows the answer. Drink good wine, make music—and love (see above, p. 194). It is true that love and other symposiac pleasure should not displace *negotium*; but it is equally true that *otium* is not *otium* without it. And this is a point fairly urgently to be made. Horace is already anxious about the day passing at midday.

The point is made more robustly in 2. 11. The poem is an invitation to Quinctius to come to a party; there is no special occasion, but one gathers that Quinctius is, in Horace's view, excessively concerned with troubles that are unnecessary—or out of his hands. He needs encouragement to *otium*. I pick the poem up at line 13:

> cur non sub alta uel platano uel hac
> pinu iacentes sic temere et rosa
>   canos odorati capillos,
>   dum licet, Assyriaque nardo
> potamus uncti? dissipat Euhius
> curas edaces. quis puer ocius
>   restinguet ardentis Falerni
>   pocula praetereunte lympha?
> quis deuium scortum eliciet domo
> Lyden? eburna, dic age, cum lyra
>   maturet incomptum Lacaenae
>   more comae religata nodum.

Why do we not without more ado lie under the tall plane-tree or this pine and, while it is possible, tope with our hoary hair scented with rose-garlands and anointed with Syrian nard? (17)

Euhius [Bacchus] scatters gnawing cares. Which slave-boy will quench the fiery cups of Falernian with water (from the stream) flowing by, and be sharp about it? (20)

Which one will coax out the sequestered tart Lyde from her house? Quick tell her make haste, with her ivory lyre, her hair bound back in a simple bun in the Spartan fashion.

Quinctius is invited to pleasure, to *otium*, and for part of that pleasure Lyde seems urgently indispensable: she is to come post-haste not even bothering to do her hair elegantly. This is an interesting poem, not just for the use of the uncompromising word *scortum* (cf. above, pp. 197 f.). Other terms are grosser than is usual in Horatian sympotic diction (*potamus*, *uncti*); and colloquialisms confirm the robust realism (*ocius*, *dic age*, intransitive *maturet*).[55] In fact it is all quite a refreshing change—but it needs explanation. Perhaps that lies in the personality of Quinctius. Or perhaps rather it lies in the hoary hair. For someone of Horace's belief greying hair focuses *dum licet* rather sharply, encouraging him to be urgent and brusque, and to dispense with delicacy of diction. (But Horace was prematurely grey[56] and his reference to it here and the consequences that then follow in the way the poem is expressed I take to be humorously intended.)

A rather different attitude, incidentally, (a few crucial years on?) and an amusing comparison is offered by 3. 14. Horace determines to celebrate Augustus' return from Spain in 24 BC: that is, it is pleasure time again (lines 17 ff.):

> i pete unguentum, puer, et coronas
> et cadum Marsi memorem duelli,
> Spartacum si qua potuit uagantem
>   fallere testa.
>
> dic et argutae properet Neaerae
> murreum nodo cohibere crinem;
> si per inuisum mora ianitorem
>   fiet, abito.
>
> lenit albescens animos capillus
> litium et rixae cupidos proteruae:
> non ego hoc ferrem calidus iuuenta
>   consule Planco.

> Go, find ointment, slave, and garlands of flowers and a cask of wine that remembers the Marsian war —if any bottle was able to escape the notice of the ravaging Spartacus (20). And bid sweet-voiced Neaera hurry to put up her light-brown hair in a knot; if interference shall be made by the hateful janitor, come way. Greying hair soothes a spirit once eager for disputes and heated quarrelling (26): I would not have put up with this, hot with youth when Plancus was consul [i.e. in 42 BC, the year of Philippi] .
>
>   (translated by G. Williams.)

This time the tart is dispensable. It is a long time since Plancus was consul: 42 BC, a splendid allusion.[57]

To revert to Horace in more youthful or at least spirited mood. I quote one final example of the belief positively stated: there *should* be love in *otium*. *Odes* 1. 11 makes the point with the discretion of 3. 28, but more generally and more emphatically:

> tu ne quaesieris, scire nefas, quem mihi, quem tibi
> finem di dederint, Leuconoe, nec Babylonios
> temptaris numeros. ut melius, quidquid erit pati,
> seu pluris hiemes seu tribuit Iuppiter ultimam,
> quae nunc oppositis debilitat pumicibus mare
> Tyrrhenum. sapias, uina liques, et spatio breui
> spem longam reseces. dum loquimur, fugerit inuida
> aetas: carpe diem quam minimum credula postero.

> Don't play with horoscopes, Leuconoe, don't ask what end
> the gods have in store for me or for yourself. They don't
> want us to know. Far better to endure whatever comes,
> whether Jupiter gives us more winters or whether this is our
> last now exhausting the Mediterranean on the pumice rocks
> that block its waves. Be sensible, strain the wine, and cut
> back your long hopes to a short term. As we speak, miserly
> time has flashed past. Harvest the day and leave as little as
> you can for tomorrow.
>
> (translated by David West.)

The ode is excellently discussed by Nisbet and Hubbard, West, and Syndikus.[58] I draw attention simply to two points. First, the message is in the final count quite general; but it is not one of blanket hedonism. Horace is addressing a girl, a certain type of girl (a girl with a Greek name, some sort of *libertina*) and this narrows the scope of the poem. He is speaking within a certain context, the context in which such girls belong: *otium* (note the presence of wine). Within this context he tells Leuconoe to disregard misplaced superstitious fears ('feminine nonsense' as David West aptly remarks) and to enjoy the day. Secondly, when he tells her to enjoy the day, Horace uses an image (*carpe* suggests gathering *flowers*) that has clear erotic implications.[59] (Syndikus acutely remarks that Leuconoe's concern for him as well as herself (line 1) suggests a tender relationship.)[60] So Horace urges Leuconoe to (among other things) love. The message has immediate relevance: Horace wants it now—and not prattle about horoscopes. And it is general: pleasure including the pleasure of love should—at the appropriate time—never be neglected.

Horace does not limit his injunction to Leuconoe to this present occasion; and quite clearly it has implications for us the eavesdroppers too. Pleasure in *otium*, including love, is a vital part of this all-too-fleeting life.

dum loquimur . . .

X

The *Amores* of Ovid

Ovid was kind enough to leave us a potted poetical biography of himself (*Tristia* 4. 10), which can be supplemented from other sources.[1]

He was born at Sulmo in central Italy in 43 BC, of an old equestrian family. Prominent rhetoricians at Rome provided his education. He then held various minor judicial posts, but in the end withdrew to devote himself to poetry (see further below, pp. 284 ff.). He knew Horace, was a friend of Propertius, and wrote an eloquent Elegy on the death of Tibullus (*Am.* 3. 9). He was encouraged in his poetry by the great Messalla, Tibullus' patron, but does not seem to have been as fixed a member of Messalla's circle as Tibullus was.

The chronology and dating of Ovid's works is a very vexed question.[2] I limit myself to the briefest of comments. The *Amores* were Ovid's first essay in poetry. He began to recite his poems in public around 25 BC. The *Amores* will have appeared in the succeeding years: exactly when is a matter of conjecture. Perhaps the first edition was complete by 15 BC. We know that this first edition consisted of five books, and we can infer that they were published separately. The second edition in three books, which is what we possess—Ovid cut poems, no doubt revised others, and very possibly added one or two—appeared around the turn of the millennium. One point (an important point) we can be sure of: Ovid had access to Propertius Books 1-3 and probably 4, and (at least) Tibullus 1, during the period of composition of the first edition.[3] The whole of Propertius and the whole of Tibullus were certainly available for his second edition.

A word on the personality of Corinna (Ovid's mistress in many poems). No tradition concerning an identity behind the pseudonym (if it was a pseudonym) reached Apuleius (*Apologia*, 10); contrast the situation with Cynthia and Delia. It is plausible to suppose that Ovid put more invention into the character of his enthralling beloved than those Elegists who were more convincingly enthralled. Nevertheless, a reasonable picture does emerge from the poems,[4] and striking episodes like Corinna's abortion (2. 13 and 14) might be thought to confirm her individuality. Nor does Ovid invite us to consider her fictional. On the contrary (it might be argued) some passages depend for their point on the assumption of an elusive but existing Corinna: *Am.* 2.17.29 ff., *Ars*, 3. 538, also *Am.* 3. 12.[5]

What class and status for Corinna do the poems imply, what sort of society are we in in the *Amores*? The inventive and sportive Ovid should not be expected to give us a factual or even consistent picture. But one or two questions, answers, and remarks are in order.

In spite of the fun, frivolity, and caricature of the books, one does in general have the sense of a real society behind it all: the *demi-monde* once again.[6] *ingenuas* in 1. 7. 50 may imply that Corinna was freeborn (but in that rhetorically emotional poem hyperbole may be at play); cf. 3. 4. 33 (below, p. 279), of another woman. If Corinna is to be taken as freeborn we may conclude that, for one of many possible reasons, she was unable or unwilling to live in 'respectable' society.[7]

She seems to be married (1. 4); so, more explicitly, do other girls whom Ovid pursues in the *Amores* (e.g. 2. 19, 3. 4). Now it may be that these would have been understood as *de facto* 'marriages':[8] for example, a girl might live as the *concubina* of a man of superior class (see p. 159) and the terminology of official marriage (*uxor*, *maritus*, *uir*, which Ovid uses) would often be applied to such a liaison.[9] But it seems to me that legal marriage is the most natural or at least immediate inference (in spite of the *demi-monde* ambience), especially in 2. 19 and 3. 4; and what is certain, and important, is that Ovid writes in explicitly adulterous terms (which Propertius and Tibullus do not—not unequivocally), and he does so *after* Augustus' laws against adultery (above, p. 65 with n.). The desire to be provocative if nothing else is clear.

> iusta precor. quae me nuper praedata puella est
> aut amet aut faciat cur ego semper amem.

a nimium uolui. tantum patiatur amari—
   audierit nostras tot Cytherea preces.
accipe per longos tibi qui deseruiat annos,
   accipe qui pura norit amare fide.
si me non ueterum commendant magna parentum
   nomina, si nostri sanguinis auctor eques,
nec meus innumeris renouatur campus aratris,
   temperat et sumptus parcus uterque parens,
at Phoebus comitesque nouem uitisque repertor
   hac faciunt, et me qui tibi donat Amor,
et nulli cessura fides, sine crimine mores,
   nudaque simplicitas purpureusque pudor.
non mihi mille placent, non sum desultor amoris.
   tu mihi, siqua fides, cura perennis eris.
tecum quos dederint annos mihi fila Sororum
   uiuere contingat, teque dolente mori.
te mihi materiem felicem in carmina praebe—
   prouenient causa carmina digna sua.
carmine nomen habent exterrita cornibus Io
   et quam fluminea lusit adulter aue
quaeque super pontum simulato uecta iuuenco
   uirginea tenuit cornua uara manu.
nos quoque per totum pariter cantabimur orbem
   iunctaque semper erunt nomina nostra tuis.

My prayer is just. May the girl who lately made me her prey
either love me or give me reason why I should always love.
Ah I have wished too much. May she only allow herself to be
      loved,
and Venus will have heard my many prayers.
Accept one who would be your slave through long years,
accept one who knows how to love with sure fidelity.
Though renowned names in my ancestry do not commend me,
though the source of my being is but a knight,
though my acres are not renewed by uncountable ploughs,
and both my parents frugally restrain their spending,
yet Apollo and his nine companions (the Muses) and the
      discoverer of the vine
are with me, and Love also who gives me to you.
And I have fidelity that will yield to none, ways without
      reproach,
naked simplicity and blushing modesty.
I am not attracted to thousands, I am not a switchback-rider
      in love.
If there be any fidelity, you will be my everlasting love.

With you may it be my lot to live the years which the Fates'
    threads have granted me;
and with you grieving to die.
Offer yourself as happy matter for my songs—
songs shall issue forth worthy of their cause.
Through song came renown to Io terrified by her horns,
and to her (Leda), whom an adulterer deluded in the guise of
    a river bird,
and to her (Europa), who, carried over the ocean on a
    pretended bull,
held curling horns in her maiden hand.
We too in like manner shall be sung throughout the world
and my name will always be joined to yours.

Amores 1. 3: Ovid confesses himself the booty of a girl. He
prays for her to love him or at least sleep with him (give him
reason why he should love her).[10] But no: it is enough if she
simply allows herself to be the object of love (1-4). Then he
declares his devotion; he will be her lasting slave (5 ff.). And
he states his credentials: though he has neither wealth nor
grand aristocratic background, he can boast qualities like
faithfulness and modesty; and he has on his side the deities of
poetry; his poems will bestow fame on her. It seems to be a
profession of love in the Elegiac mould: the profession of a
romantic lover, Roman-style. The tones and themes of
Catullus, Propertius, and Tibullus echo through it.[11]

    From poem 1 onwards, indeed, we might have got the
impression of an Elegiac love beginning. 1: Cupid strikes.
2: the victim's insomnia, bewilderment, realization, and
submission. 3: the declaration. And then with 4, the decep-
tion of the husband, the affair begins to gather substance.
In 5 the girl is named: Corinna (I think we can assume that
Corinna is the subject of all the love poems in Book 1—and
indeed of the love poems in the other books which do not
give us reason to believe otherwise). The adulterous tone of 4
may be unusually explicit. But the scenes and topics that
then follow are more or less typical of Elegiac love and Elegiac
love poetry. It seems clear that, in the first book, Ovid wants
us to think of him as the successor of Catullus, Propertius,
and Tibullus—in particular (as will emerge) Propertius—a poet

and a lover in their mould. It is also quite clear that his tongue is in his cheek: adopting this character and genre he is effectively parodying both.

Am. 1. 6

ianitor—indignum! —dura religate catena,
  difficilem moto cardine pande forem.
quod precor exiguum est. aditu fac ianua paruo
  obliquum capiat semiadaperta latus.
longus amor tales corpus tenuauit in usus   5
  aptaque subducto corpore membra dedit.
ille per excubias custodum leniter ire
  monstrat, inoffensos derigit ille pedes.
at quondam noctem simulacraque uana timebam.
  mirabar tenebris quisquis iturus erat.   10
risit ut audirem tenera cum matre Cupido
  et leuiter 'fies tu quoque fortis' ait,
nec mora, uenit amor. non umbras nocte uolantis,
  non timeo strictas in mea fata manus.
te nimium lentum timeo, tibi blandior uni.   15
  tu me quo possis perdere fulmen habes.
aspice—uti uideas immitia claustra relaxa—
  uda sit ut lacrimis ianua facta meis.
certe ego, cum posita stares ad uerbera ueste,
  ad dominam pro te uerba tremente tuli.   20
ergo quae ualuit pro te quoque gratia quondam—
  heu facinus!—pro me nunc ualet illa parum?
redde uicem meritis. grato licet esse, quod optas.[12]
  tempora noctis eunt. excute poste seram.
excute, sic umquam longa releuere catena   25
  nec tibi perpetuo serua bibatur aqua.
ferreus orantem nequiquam, ianitor, audis;
  roboribus duris ianua fulta riget.
urbibus obsessis clausae munimina portae
  prosunt: in media pace quid arma times?   30
quid facies hosti, qui sic excludis amantem?
  tempora noctis eunt. excute poste seram.
non ego militibus uenio comitatus et armis.
  solus eram si non saeuus adesset Amor.
hunc ego, si cupiam, nusquam dimittere possum;   35
  ante uel a membris diuidar ipse meis.
ergo Amor et modicum circa mea tempora uinum
  mecum est et madidis lapsa corona comis.
arma quis haec timeat? quis non eat obuius illis?
  tempora noctis eunt. excute poste seram.   40

lentus es? an somnus—qui te male perdat!—amantis
    uerba dat in uentos aure repulsa tua?
at memini primo, cum te celare uolebam,
    peruigil in mediae sidera noctis eras.
forsitan et tecum tua nunc requiescit amica.   45
    heu melior quanto sors tua sorte mea!
dummodo sic, in me durae transite catenae.
    tempora noctis eunt. excute poste seram.
fallimur an uerso sonuerunt cardine postes,
    raucaque concussae signa dedere fores?   50
fallimur. impulsa est animoso ianua uento.
    ei mihi quam longe spem tulit aura meam!
si satis es raptae, Borea, memor Orithyiae,
    huc ades et surdas flamine tunde foris.
urbe silent tota uitreoque madentia rore   55
    tempora noctis eunt. excute poste seram.
aut ego iam ferroque ignique paratior ipse
    quem face sustineo tecta superba petam.
nox et Amor uinumque nihil moderabile suadent.
    illa pudore uacat, Liber Amorque metu.   60
omnia consumpsi, nec te precibusque minisque
    mouimus, o foribus durior ipse tuis!
non te formosae decuit seruare puellae
    limina. sollicito carcere dignus eras.
iamque pruinosos molitur Lucifer axes,   65
    inque suum miseros excitat ales opus.
at tu, non laetis detracta corona capillis,
    dura super tota limina nocte iace.
tu dominae, cum te proiectam mane uidebit,
    temporis absumpti tam male testis eris.   70
qualiscumque uale sentique abeuntis honorem,
    lente nec admisso turpis amante—uale.
uos quoque, crudeles rigido cum limine postes
    duraque conseruae ligna, ualete, fores.

Porter!—poor wretch, chained like a dog—
please open up.
I don't ask much—a mere crack
so there's room to squeeze through sideways.
Love has made me slim enough,
halved my weight and alerted my limbs.
He can teach you to slip past sentries—
never lets you put a foot wrong.
I used to be scared of the dark—
admired people who went out at night.

But Cupid and his mother, laughing in my ear,
whispered 'You too can be brave'
and brought me love. I'm not afraid of ghosts now
or hands raised to strike me down.
It's only you I'm frightened of. You're so slow.
It's only you who make me crawl. Your bolt can destroy me.
Just look at this door. Unbar it so you can see.
It's all wet with my tears.
That day you were stripped for a whipping—remember?—
I got your mistress to let you off.
I helped you then and now you won't help me.
Do you call that fair?
One good turn deserves another. Now's your chance to thank
    me.[12]
The night is slipping by. Unbar the door.
And soon you'll be rid of your long chain,
drinking the wine of freedom at last . . .
Porter, you're hard. You can hear me pleading
but this heavy door hasn't moved an inch.
Beleaguered cities bar their gates.
But why be afraid of weapons in peacetime?
Lock out lovers and what have you left for enemies?
The night is slipping by. Unbar the door.
I'm not here with an armed guard—
I'd be alone if cruel Love weren't with me.
I could never dismiss *him* —
I'd have to be dismembered first.
So there's me, and Love, and a little wine (gone to my head),
and a garland askew on my damp hair.
Who's afraid of an outfit like that? Who wouldn't welcome it?
The night is slipping by. Unbar the door.
Perhaps you're asleep, damn you,
and my words aren't sinking in.
But you stayed awake till starry midnight
in the old days when I tried to slip out.
Or have you a girl-friend in your cell?
If so you're better off than me.
To be with mine I'd gladly wear your chain.
The night is slipping by. Unbar the door.
Listen! Did those hinges creak?
Was that something hitting the door? . . .
Only a gust of wind against it
blowing my poor hopes out of reach.
Ah Boreas, if you still remember the bride you ravished
blow this way and bang on these deaf panels . . .

Silence in Rome, and bright dew falling,
and *night slipping by. Unbar the door.*
Or I'll use my torch's fire and steel
to teach this lordly house a lesson.
Night and wine and love can't abide half measures.
Love and wine are fearless. Night has no shame . . .
I've tried everything. Threats and entreaties are useless.
This oak has a softer heart than yours.
Guarding the door of a pretty girl?
You ought to be a prison warder.
And now the morning star looms in a frosty sky.
Cocks are crowing to wake the world's workers.
I'm out of luck. I'll pull this garland off my head
and throw it down on the doorstep.
My love will see it lying there
in token of a wasted night.
Meanwhile, you oafish locker-out of lovers,
I do you the honour of saying goodbye.
You too, stone steps, deaf posts, and wooden door,
goodbye—and thanks for your servility.

(Lee)

The piece has the structure of a Propertian *monobiblos* poem.
Ovid excluded pleads with the doorkeeper to let him in to his
beloved. That is the poem: the plaint of the 'excluded lover'
(*paraclausithyron*), the event itself, dramatized. The subject
is Elegiac; or rather it is an elaborate working-up of a subject
that Propertius and Tibullus treat (significantly) with some
discretion.[13] The poem also includes or alludes to a number
of other erotic *topoi*: among these are the lover's proverbial
thinness, and *seruitium amoris*. Let us watch how Ovid treats
these topics; in particular how Ovid treats himself, the
exclusus amator.

   Throughout most of the poem he is pleading, even wheedling
(15) in the doorway damp with his tears (18). Interestingly,
he uses the device of a refrain (24, 32, 40, 48, 56) to strengthen
the suggestion that this is a lengthily intoned, even sung,
monologue; the refrain also gives us a dramatic sense of time
passing. He has come from a party and wears sympotic garlands
and scents, feels the effects of sympotic wine (37–8). After
time has passed, he loses patience, changes tactics, and
threatens to force an entry (57–8). But threats are no more

effective than his pleadings (61–2); and when dawn approaches (66) he gives up; he leaves his garlands on the doorstep as a sign of his devoted vigil and bids farewell to the door.

Except for the (very pleasant) idea of a refrain, the details here can be paralleled in other accounts of the excluded lover, though not all in Elegy: see below. There is excellent reason to believe, too, that a nocturnal witness in contemporary Rome would have descried the occasional *exclusus amator* garlanded and singing songs outside his mistress's door.[14] And yet not many people can read Ovid's poem without finding it implausible and humorous. He seems to be *guying* the role of the excluded lover while casting himself in it. Can we put our finger on what he does?

In the hands of Propertius and Tibullus the topic of the lover's exclusion and plaint had been used with care: they made of it an effective vehicle of romantic expression. Exclusion reveals the lover in an inglorious, humiliated, lonely role: that suited their purpose and in consequence they exploited the scene. Some traditional details (crowbars and torches) suggested comedy (as Roman Comedy confirms),[15] and that suited them less; so they left them out. The plaint itself (if they introduced it) they handled with care. They had it uttered to the unfeeling door and/or the unheeding mistress: in this way the passion of the lover and the lack of response, the lack even of possible response, by the beloved was stressed; the lover's anguished, miserable frustration was acutely, *dramatically* demonstrated. Thus the Elegiac 'excluded lover' *topos*. To all intents and purposes the institution was the same as the later Serenade, and the earlier Elegists observed its romance.

Ovid of course revels in the dangerously comic details. More important is this question: does one serenade a *janitor*? We at once discern Ovid's basic parodic tactic. Instead of the unfeeling door or the heedless mistress's ear and a monologue consequently pregnant with yearning frustration, we have an unresponsive janitor and a monologue pregnant with incongruities. Ovid is of course being logical. Why plead with what will not or cannot listen? The janitor might actually be able to do something for the lover. But such logic ruins the romantic potential of the *topos*. Against a tradition of lovers pouring out their souls to a pitiless, heedless mistress, or a pitiless mistress symbolized in a heedless door, Ovid pours out his amorous problems to a slave doorman. He is parodying the romantic *exclusus amator* and his plaint. (Note the sly allusion to a conventional form of *paraclausithyron* in 61-2, and Ovid's eventual adoption of it in 73-4.)

At times Ovid does literally *serenade* the janitor; the refrain of course enhances this humorous incongruity. He addresses items of pathos, persuasion, and circumstantial detail borrowed from the tradition and suiting the beloved—to the janitor: lines 15, 18, 38. The incongruity is clear. Otherwise he adapts his song (we remember it does give some impression of *song*) to its new idiosyncratic circumstances; and humour is derived from the fact that we find devious argumentation with a slave where tradition suggests we should find romantic moaning.[16] For example in 19 ff.: Ovid attempts to trade on past *gratia*: one good turn deserves another.

Another devious argument brings into play one of the other erotic *topoi*, and demolishes it: the lover's thinness (3-6).

The topic of the lover's thinness, with its basis in truth and more importantly its role in lovers' mythology, could be useful in love poetry.[17] Propertius for example could claim (1. 5) that he was pale and thin and expect people to deduce therefrom that he was suffering from love, indeed suffering physically. But he did not mean that he was approaching the two-dimensional. It would be far from his mind that in consequence of his thinness he might now squeeze through narrow spaces. That was not the point. His and claims like it are the flamboyant claims of lovers, the graphic descriptions of lover-poets, not the scientific observations of a doctor or budding escapologist. They depend for their effect on a realization in the reader that the poet is speaking rhetorically and romantically; not wholly literally. Ovid knew this as well as any other lover-poet—and *therefore* treats his own lover's thinness with remorseless literalism. The janitor need only open the door a crack—since Ovid *qua* anguished lover can slip through the tiniest of gaps. This encourages precisely the sort of thought that would be ruinous in a genuinely romantic context. And Ovid has of course combined *two* Elegiac motifs here (exclusion, thinness), using the combination to dispel the romantic potential of both. Both are viewed in a logical, literal light and then made to work together in a way which enhances the incongruous effect of that literalism. The motifs now contribute to a scene evocative of comedy, rather than being (as they might have been) expansively suggestive of feeling. Here in a specific instance is fairly straightforward and delightful parody.

Now let us look at lines 45-7. The 'slavery of love' was the earlier Elegists' eloquent mode of communicating degradation (pp. 78 ff.). These lines of Ovid's must bring the idea to mind. Ovid writes indeed in the grand tradition: he offers to be a slave for love. But again his version is comically destructive. Again he treats the motif on too literal a level. The suggestion that he change places with the slave doorkeeper suggests a complete change of roles, a literal servitude which is so implausible that it is comic. Contrast Propertius' use of selective servile terms to suggest a real but partial, plausible servility: servility of mind and feeling. Ovid's allusion is something of a mockery. It is meant to be. The whole poem is clearly parodic.

What Ovid does in 1. 6 is (among other things)[18] take over scenes and themes of the previous Elegists but then treat them with a literalness that dispels their romantic potential and leaves them incongruous; he pursues them relentlessly to their logical, unromantic, and eventually funny ends. The anguished excluded lover wants to get into a house, so he asks the janitor; and because he is anguished he is of course thin, so the janitor only needs to open the door a fraction. Propertius and Tibullus had been at times aware of the comic side of their doleful plight and had indulged in humour at their own expense. But never with the implacable zest of the parodist.

Another example: 1. 7. The question of hitting one's beloved was something that occupied the earlier Elegists.[19] It could be a cue for remarks on the nature of love. Romantic poets had other habits: stating or implying the beloved to be like family to them, like a mistress (to their slave: *seruitium*), like a goddess.[20] Ovid puts these together, accepts the implications of what he says with a literalness that the earlier poets did not mean, and pursues the consequences remorselessly. He has laid hands on his girl. Therefore (considering what the girl was to him: family, mistress, goddess) he is guilty of impiety, heinous illegality, and sacrilege. The poem's vast emotional rhetoric then squares with his own logic but is clearly out of all proportion to the original act. For example:

> adde manus in uincla meas (meruere catenas),
>   dum furor omnis abit, si quis amicus ades:
> nam furor in dominam temeraria bracchia mouit;
>   flet mea uesana laesa puella manu.
> tunc ego uel caros potui uiolare parentes
>   saeua uel in sanctos uerbera ferre deos.   (1–6)

Put my hands in bonds, any friend of mine here
(they deserved chains), till my madness wholly parts.
For madness roused my reckless arms against my mistress;
my girl weeps injured by my raving hand.
In that moment I could have outraged my beloved parents,
or dealt cruel blows to the holy gods.

> quid mihi uobiscum, caedis scelerumque ministrae?
>   debita sacrilegae uincla subite manus.
> an si pulsassem minimum de plebe Quiritem,
>   plecterer, in dominam ius mihi maius erit?
> pessima Tydides scelerum monimenta reliquit:
>   ille deam primus perculit; alter ego.   (27–32)

What have I with you, you servants of slaughter and crime?
Sacrilegious hands submit to the bonds you deserve!
Had I struck the meanest among the citizenry
I should be punished: shall I have greater rights over my
  mistress?
Diomedes left an iniquitous example of crime:
he first smote a goddess; I was the second.

> i nunc, magnificos uictor molire triumphos,
>   cinge comam lauro uotaque redde Ioui ...   (35 f.)

Go now, victor! Make ready splendid triumphs,
circle your hair with laurel and pay your vows to Jupiter . . .

sanguis erat lacrimae, quas dabat illa, meus.   (60)

The tears which she shed were my blood.

The emotionalism is amusing and incongruous. Ovid virtually
admits this at the end of the poem, unexpectedly revealing
his hand in a neat bathos.

neue mei sceleris tam tristia signa supersint,
    pone recompositas in statione comas.

Or at least, lest the sad signs of my crime remain,
put your hair back into order again.

After all the prostrate, grovelling laments of this long poem
it suddenly seems rather easy to make things all right. We see
clearly how incongruous the previous emotionalism has been.
The poem is based impeccably on Ovid's predecessors' practice
and attitudes but conclusions are drawn and implications
pursued in a way which is alien to them. We could again say
that it is essentially parodic.

Another example, 1. 9. Propertius and Tibullus had
developed the figure of *militia amoris* to declare concretely
and provocatively their public philosophy: their dissociation
from a conventional equestrian career and their dissociation
from war, a virtual pacifism (above, pp. 71 ff.). As with
seruitium their use of the figure had to be suggestive. If they
had taken it too literally or too far, humorous incongruity
not striking paradox would have been the result. Propertius
and Tibullus did not pursue it too literally or too far—though
there was wit as well as provocativeness in their paradoxical
statements. But Ovid—*hanc me militiam fata subire uolunt*,
Propertius had said, and Tibullus *hic ego dux milesque bonus*.
Ovid pursues possible implications to the comic extremities.
So the lover is a soldier is he? How? In what *detailed* ways
can a lover be represented as a soldier? *Amores* 1. 9 tells us. It
tells us all the conceivable and inconceivable ways the lover

can be so represented. It is a brilliant parade of wit and *inuentio*. For example:

> peruigilant ambo, terra requiescit uterque;
>   ille fores dominae seruat, at ille ducis.
> militis officium longa est uia: mitte puellam,
>   strenuus exempto fine sequetur amans.   (7–10)

> Lovers too keep watch, bivouac, mount guard—
> at the mistress' door instead of H.Q.
> They have their forced marches,
> tramping miles for love.
>
> (Lee)

> saepe soporatos inuadere profuit hostes
>   caedere et armata uulgus inerme manu . . .
> nempe maritorum somnis utuntur amantes
>   et sua sopitis hostibus arma mouent.   (21 f., 25 f.)

> Tacticians recommend the night attack,
> use of the spearhead, catching the foe asleep . . .
> Lovers use them too—to exploit a sleeping husband,
> thrusting hard while the enemy snores.
>
> (Lee)

A suggestive and ultimately serious motif has become. a conceit. An intention seriously if wittily to provoke is replaced by a desire almost entirely for wit, albeit irreverent. Again parody is at work. Perhaps at this point we might qualify that word. A sentence of Du Quesnay's is helpful (p. 7): 'it is . . . the kind of parody in which the laughter is directed at the parody itself rather than at what is being parodied.' I suppose my point is that the poem is not as directly and consistently tied to previous poetry, as parasitical, as the label parody might suggest. It—like 6 and 7—is rather a light-hearted, irreverent, ingenious *development* of a theme that Ovid's predecessors use for different and more earnest purposes.

Ovid's use of myth suggests his romantic, Propertian schooling. But again we detect the parodist. His weapons are those we are becoming accustomed to: logic, literalism, a delight in the inappropriate. 1. 10. 1 ff. is a good passage to look

at first, since the parodic intentions are most plain. The poem
opens:

> qualis ab Eurota Phrygiis auecta carinis
>   coniugibus belli causa duobus erat,
> qualis erat Lede, quam plumis abditus albis
>   callidus in falsa lusit adulter aue,
> qualis Amymone siccis errauit in Argis,
>   cum premeret summi uerticis urna comas,
> talis eras . . .

> Just as Helen, who, carried away from Sparta in a
>   Phrygian bark
> was cause of war to two husbands,
> just as Leda, who was deluded by a cunning adulterer
> concealing himself in white feathers, feigning the shape
>   of a bird,
> just as Amymone, wandering in parched Argos
> carrying a pitcher on the locks of her head,
> even so were you . . .

Ovid is clearly echoing the splendid opening of Prop. 1. 3
(above, p. 98):

> qualis Thesea iacuit cedente carina
>   languida desertis Cnosia litoribus;
> qualis et accubuit primo Cepheia somno
>   libera iam duris cotibus Andromede;
> nec minus assiduis Edonis fessa choreis
>   qualis in herboso concidit Apidano:
> talis uisa . . .

> Just as Ariadne lay, swooning on the deserted beach
> as Theseus' bark departed; just as Andromeda reclined
> in her first sleep free now from the harsh rocks; just as
> the Bacchante, no less wearied <than Andromeda>
> by her continuous dances, fell in sleep by the grassy
> Apidanus; so she seemed . . ,

Propertius demonstrably echoed by a purportedly Propertian
poet: the myths should presumably be performing their
Propertian function. This they seem to do: the lines depict
romantic heroines from the world of myth and imply belief
in heightened, romantic qualities (beauty; a fatal power
to attract)[21] in the girl under comparison. However (*talis*

eras . . .): such belief is now a thing of the past. That too has a Propertian ring: Propertius' belief in myth tends to be precarious and myth in a poem is often, as here, a foil for an enforced realism (it is in Prop. 1. 3). All therefore seems to be in order—nearly anyway.[22] But before Ovid explains why he no longer feels as he used to, he adds an unexpected elaboration of the myths:

> aquilamque in te taurumque timebam
> et quicquid magno de Ioue fecit amor.

> for your sake I was afraid of the eagle and the bull
> and whatever form love has made out of great Jupiter.

—and here the Propertian illusion collapses. He continues the myths into a conclusion that is incompatible with their Propertian function. Of course it is *logical*. But it is ruinously logical. To suggest an equivalence between one's girl and Helen, Leda, or Amymone is one thing; to infer from that equivalence the danger of Jupiter turning up as a raping eagle or swan is another.[23] That is of course the sort of thing that Jupiter did in myth; but equally it is the sort of story that was potentially *funny* to the Roman mind (Ovid will exploit such stories for amusement's sake in the *Metamorphoses*) and therefore inappropriate in myths introduced for *romantic* suggestiveness. Ovid puts together two incompatible moods of myth, and the accumulated romance collapses in a designed bathos. The 'Propertian' poet mocks Propertian mythological comparison.[24]

Parodic but less specifically so is 1. 7. 11 ff.:

> ergo ego digestos potui laniare capillos?

> So! I could ravel that ordered hair?

exclaims Ovid. At which he remarks:

> nec dominam motae dedecuere comae,
> sic formosa fuit.

> But her disordered hair did not ill-suit her.
> She was beautiful thus.

It is, we should note, untimely to interject admiration for

dishevelled hair when one is otherwise grovellingly apologizing for having caused that dishevelment. It rather undermines the whole-hearted sincerity of the apology—and is of course meant to. Nor is it a momentary lapse. Ovid maintains his untimely admiration in a triad of myths, splendid and Propertian. Here are the first two:

> talem Schoeneida dicam
> Maenalias arcu sollicitasse feras.
> talis periuri promissaque uelaque Thesei
> fleuit praecipites Cressa tulisse Notos.

> Such I should say was Atalanta
> when she harried the beasts of Maenalus with her bow.
> Such was Ariadne, bewailing that both sails and
> promises of perjured Theseus
> were carried off by the headlong south winds.

Everything about the myths seems (apart from the fact of untimeliness) fine. The romantic poet wants to communicate something of his wonderment at his mistress's beauty. Therefore he invokes the world of myth and the figures of mythical heroines; he even enhances their mystique in the Propertian way by using recherché antonomasia.[25] But something is wrong. Ovid is tying the myths to a too limited point of comparison. The myths deploy all their suggestive power to expound belief not in the mistress's beauty (that would be Propertian) but in the beauty of her displaced hair. The glamour of the world of Atalanta and Ariadne is tied to an illumination of this trivial point and the one is simply too much for the other. The comparison is ludicrously unbalanced. Incongruity again; a playful, parodic use of Propertian myth.

Similar to this, indeed a clearer illustration of the same technique (it is frequent in the *Amores*)[26], is 3. 2. 29-32:

> talia Milanion Atalantes crura fugacis
> optauit manibus sustinuisse suis;
> talia pinguntur succinctae crura Dianae,
> cum sequitur fortes fortior ipsa feras.

> Such were the legs of fleet-footed Atalanta
> that Milanion longed to hold up with his hands;[27]

> such in pictures are the legs of high-girded Diana,
> when she pursues the brave wild beasts, she braver than they.

The poem reports Ovid's words to a female neighbour at the circus. After offering to lift up her dress which is brushing the ground, and calling the dress 'mean' because it concealed her legs, Ovid cites these myths. Here once more is the traditional Elegiac figure of Atalanta; Diana too, superb goddess of the chase. Their romantic world is deployed to expound belief in—the beauty of legs. Again the one is much too much for the other; romance is scattered by the inappropriate, trivial use. Again Ovid uses the achievement of his predecessors (the nurturing of myth's romantic resonance) to contrive an essentially parodic humour of incongruity.

In 1. 7 there is still a myth to come. Lines 17-18:

> sic, nisi uittatis quod erat, Cassandra, capillis,
> procubuit templo, casta Minerua, tuo.

> Such, except for the fact that fillets bound her hair, was
>   Cassandra,
> when she prostrated herself, chaste Minerva, at your temple.

In one respect this is even more a mockery of the Elegiac material. The emotive scene of Cassandra is deployed further to illumine dishevelled hair—and simultaneously Ovid cheerfully admits a flaw in the comparison: *nisi uittatis quod erat . . . capillis*. She wore sacred fillets and so she was *not* so dishevelled. On the other hand, the use of myth is arguably more in keeping with Propertian practice. We recall the sacrilege of Cassandra's rape, and that bears upon the sacrilege of Ovid's assault on Corinna. It expounds his belief in the romantic horror of his action—and in so doing enhances the basic incongruity and eventual bathos of the poem.

It should now be clear that, when he adopts the role and genre of the romantic Elegist, Ovid is effectively parodying both (see p. 252 for a qualification of 'parody', also below, p. 264). His essays in the genre display a wit which undermines their ostensibly earnest purpose. Further very good illustration

of Ovid's methods is offered by Du Quesnay's discussion of
1. 11 and 12, the Nape poems.[28]

Already in fact in the romantic declaration of 1. 3, the
poem with which I started, signs of lack of seriousness were
evident. For example note the profession of fidelity in lines
13-14 (above, p. 241). Ovid has not got wealth on his side
but he has unrivalled fidelity, morality, simplicity, and
modesty. Knowing the later Ovid we may be allowed to
snigger. But is there anything suspicious in the text? Should
simplicitas and *pudor* actually have small or capital initial
letters? *nuda* and *purpureus* suggest personification.[29] That is
a point. Personified figures of *Naked Simplicity* and *Blushing
Modesty* are hard seriously to countenance; and they certainly
ill cohere with the deep, unobscured, abstract Roman earnest-
ness of *fides*. The lines contain an identifiable incongruity, an
identifiable suggestion of wit even as Ovid utters his earnest
protestation of moral devotion.

Then let us consider the myths (21 ff.). They illustrate the
fabulous power of Ovid's poetry to bestow renown on the
beloved (a Propertian-Tibullan view of the function of love
poetry)[30]—and incidentally on himself, a neatly egoistic
touch. They also show in action *one* lover, the most powerful
philanderer of them all (Jupiter), and *three* of his duped
victims. That is hardly a tactful choice in a poem professing
faithful, exclusive devotion. It is not meant to be. Ovid
disclaims in shocked moral tones the role of 'switchback rider
in love', but hints at the possibility of his being exactly that.[31]
The hint is later vindicated.

Poems 1 and 2 which seemed to introduce Ovid's Elegiac
love are also similarly undermined. In poem 2 insomniac Ovid
debates what can be wrong with him. He decides (after a
witty red herring: 5)[32] that it is love. He then debates whether
he should submit or not. He surrenders immediately on
logical grounds, adducing a series of reasonable *exempla*
(9 ff.):

cedimus, an subitum luctando accendimus ignem?
cedamus: leue fit, quod bene fertur, onus.

uidi ego iactatas mota face crescere flammas
    et uidi nullo concutiente mori.   (9-12)

en ego, confiteor, tua sum noua praeda, Cupido;
    porrigimus uictas ad tua iura manus.   (19-20)

Shall I give in? Or fan the flame by fighting it?
Better give in. Balance makes a burden light.
Shake a torch and it flares up—
leave it alone and it dies.   (9-12)

Then I submit, Cupid. I'm your latest victim
standing here with my hands up.   (19-20)
                        (Lee)

And then there follows an elaborate, ingenious description of
the triumph of *Amor*, with Ovid himself in the train. For
example 29 ff.

ipse ego, praeda recens, factum modo uulnus habebo
    et noua captiua uincula mente feram.
Mens Bona ducetur manibus post terga retortis
    et Pudor et castris quidquid Amoris obest.

I'll be among them, your fresh prey, with my recently inflicted
    wound.
I shall bear my new chains; my mind will be your prisoner.
Good Sense will be led along, her hands tied behind her back:
likewise Modesty and every foe of Love's camp.

I confine myself to two or three salient points (Barsby
Amores Book I and E. Reitzenstein discuss the poem well).
Ovid describes his surrender to *passionate* love as a *reasoned*
process (9 ff.). Again he introduces logical thinking at an in-
appropriate moment; again we have incongruity and we scent
the parodist. We scent parody too when Ovid offers himself to
slavery in an uncomplicated, unagonized way (19 f.). Contrast
(on both these points) the plausibly despairing, uncomprehend-
ing attitude of Propertius (e.g. 1.1, 1.5, 1.6); and with line 9
compare and contrast Gallus in Verg. *Ecl.* 10.69.

The description of *Amor*'s coming triumph is exuberant
and witty—not plausibly uttered by a man submitting to
servile love. It exploits paradoxes ingeniously. The paradoxes
are essentially two: love celebrating *military* triumph (a fanci-
ful development of *militia amoris*); and love the *child* receiving

military *man*'s supreme accolade. One thing to note. Prominent in the triumphal train (which probably recalls Propertius 3. 1) is *Mens Bona. Mens Bona* had been prominent in Propertius' expression of his final *cure* from love, 3. 24. 19:

> Mens Bona, si qua dea es, tua me in sacraria dono.
>
> Good Sense, if goddess you be, I devote myself to your shrine.

Ovid cheerfully foresees the loss of Propertius' hard-won health of mind. The Propertian story is, it seems, being re-played. We see the particular tradition with which Ovid wants us to associate him.

And we see his difference. Propertius exited reasoning from love. That was natural: it was the assertion of rationality that allowed him to exit. Ovid enters reasoning; he starts potentially superior to the emotion that purportedly enthralls him —a paradoxical Elegist. Ovid also enters exuberantly. Such exuberance is typical, and it has its implications. Finding room for exuberance in Propertian situations is the work of a parodist. But it also suggests (a suggestion which is confirmed) a positive attitude to love—and love poetry. It is *fun.* Not perhaps a profound view, but a valid one; and, interestingly, it recalls Horace rather than Ovid's ostensible predecessors Propertius and Tibullus.

We can now look briefly at poem 1, the programmatic poem of our apparently romantic poet. Ovid was, he says, preparing to write on epic themes. But Cupid intervened and showed his wish for an Ovidian elegy in no uncertain terms, 1–4:

> arma graui numero uiolentaque bella parabam
>   edere, materia conueniente modis.
> par erat inferior uersus; risisse Cupido
>   dicitur atque unum surripuisse pedem.
>
> My epic was under construction—wars and armed violence
> in the grand manner, with metre matching theme.
> I had written the second hexameter when Cupid grinned
> and calmly removed one of its feet.
>
> (Lee)

The poem is set in the mould of the *recusatio* (above, p. 147

with n.) with Cupid playing the role of Apollo. But Ovid un-
expectedly resists his divine authority. He objects to Cupid's
interruption and argues the case with him spiritedly: literature
is not Cupid's sphere of power and besides Ovid is not even in
love (5-20). Cupid responds by making him fall in love (21-6).

   This is a witty, amusing variation on *recusatio* (the poem is
fun); it is, incidentally, well discussed by E. Reitzenstein.
Considered as the introductory poem of an Elegist, a romantic,
it is most revealing—and again the contrast with Propertius is
remarkable. *Amor* cruelly changed Propertius' whole mode of
life (1. 1); the boy Cupid steals one of Ovid's metrical feet:
a question of life, a question of metre. Propertius writes love
Elegy because (so he says) of the demands and inspiration of
love.[33] Ovid writes Elegy because Cupid trespassing into
aesthetics wants a certain type of literature. His decision to
write about love actually precedes the acquisition of a lover.
How different from Propertius' picture! We expect something
artificial, playful, fun, to follow. Our expectations are not
defeated.

Before I leave Book 1 I should like to give poem 5 brief con-
sideration. It is a splendid poem. It is for one thing genuinely
but tastefully sensuous. And it illuminates Ovidian thought
and art.

> aestus erat, mediamque dies exegerat horam.
>   adposui medio membra leuanda toro.
> pars adaperta fuit, pars altera clausa fenestrae,
>   quale fere siluae lumen habere solent,
> qualia sublucent fugiente crepuscula Phoebo   5
>   aut ubi nox abiit nec tamen orta dies.
> illa uerecundis lux est praebenda puellis,
>   qua timidus latebras speret habere pudor.
> ecce, Corinna uenit, tunica uelata recincta,
>   candida diuidua colla tegente coma,   10
> qualiter in thalamos formosa Semiramis isse
>   dicitur et multis Lais amata uiris.
> deripui tunicam—nec multum rara nocebat,
>   pugnabat tunica sed tamen illa tegi.
> quae cum ita pugnaret tamquam quae uincere nollet   15
>   uicta est non aegre proditione sua.

ut stetit ante oculos posito uelamine nostros,
    in toto nusquam corpore menda fuit.
quos umeros, quales uidi tetigique lacertos!
    forma papillarum quam fuit apta premi!   20
quam castigato planus sub pectore uenter!
    quantum et quale latus! quam iuuenale femur!
singula quid referam? nil non laudabile uidi,
    et nudam pressi corpus ad usque meum.
cetera quis nescit? lassi requieuimus ambo.   25
    proueniant medii sic mihi saepe dies.

Siesta time in sultry summer.
I lay relaxed on the divan.
One shutter closed, the other ajar,
made sylvan semi-darkness,
a glimmering dusk, as after sunset,   5
or between night's end and day's beginning—
the half light shy girls need
to hide their hesitation.
At last[34] —Corinna. On the loose in a short dress,
long hair parted and tumbling past the pale neck—   10
lovely as Lais of the many lovers,
Queen Semiramis gliding in.
I grabbed the dress; it didn't hide much,
but she fought to keep it,
only half-heartedly though.   15
Victory was easy, a self-betrayal.
There she stood, faultless beauty
in front of me, naked.
Shoulders and arms challenging eyes and fingers.
Nipples firmly demanding attention.   20
Breasts in high relief above the smooth belly.
Long and slender waist. Thighs of a girl.
Why list perfection?
I hugged her tight.
The rest can be imagined—we fell asleep.   25
Such afternoons are rare.

                                              (Lee)

Ovid describes how he was taking his siesta. Apparently he
did not expect Corinna. That is the clear point of *medio*
. . . *toro* in line 2. Those who sleep in the 'middle of their
beds' are sleeping alone: cf. 2. 10. 18. What *is* implied how-
ever is that Ovid was very much in the mood for her. He
was randy. He manages to communicate this in the siesta

description. He evokes that occasion with the feelings of the time.

He evokes an *erotic* atmosphere. That is how he felt it to be at the time (projecting his feelings). *Aestus* can and indeed in a book of love poems virtually must bring to mind erotic heat as well as the heat of the day (cf. 'sultry'; Ovid in fact puns on these two senses at *Am.* 3. 2. 39 and *Met.* 7. 815). By a play on words the poet indicates how the atmosphere seemed. And the half-light, which might have encouraged others to sleep, was to Ovid a stimulus to thoughts of sex. Corinna may not have been expected but she was certainly needed. Somewhat in the manner of Propertius 1. 3 or Catullus 68 Ovid is using dramatic evocation ('reportorial technique') to suggest the feelings of the time. And he suggests more or more tastefully than he ever could explicitly tell.

Now we should consider the description of Corinna that follows, and the allusion to love-making. If we compare relevant Greek epigrams we shall focus the vividness as well as the taste of Ovid.[35] But the contrast I want to draw is with Catullus, Propertius, and Tibullus. How and how often do they describe the physical attributes of their mistresses? How and how often do they refer to sex?

We must realize that both presented problems. As romantics they must regard the mistress as unique. To describe her would inevitably run the risk of limiting her, of making her sound like *other* girls. Many girls after all have or can be said to have black eyes and a milk-and-roses complexion. Similarly with sex. The greatest mystery, the final ecstasy, risks sounding most familiar. After all the romantic lover doesn't actually *do* very different things from Mr Average.

And the answer to my questions is that they describe the mistress (that is to say the *important*, the *romantic* mistress)[36] rarely, carefully qualifying themselves; and they refer to sex with her even more rarely and with equal care. Propertius for example will sometimes tell us about Cynthia's looks; but he manages to suggest that *that* is not *it*. There is something *else*, something less definite and definable that is her *real* attraction.[37] Tibullus, manœuvred by his sequence of thought

into listing Delia's beautiful features—and *defining* them as
her *magic* (an awkward moment for a romantic!)—hastily
leaps off into myth, an uncharacteristic tactic forced upon
him by the special circumstances. In this way he too adum-
brates that 'something else', the indefinable *romantic* beauty.[38]
Tib. 1. 5. 39 ff.:

> sed iam cum gaudia adirem
> admonuit dominae deseruitque Venus.
> tunc me, discedens, deuotum femina dixit—
> a pudet—et narrat scire nefanda meam.
> non facit hoc uerbis; facie tenerisque lacertis
> deuouet et flauis nostra puella comis.
> talis ad Haemonium Nereis Pelea quondam
> uecta est frenato caerula pisce Thetis.

> But when I approached pleasure's end
> Venus reminded me of my mistress and deserted me.
> Then the woman left, calling me bewitched—
> the shame of it!—and spreading stories that my girl
>   knows the black arts.
> She doesn't do this by spells. With her face,
> her soft arms and yellow hair my girl bewitches me—
> like the Nereid blue-eyed Thetis who once upon a time
> rode a bridled dolphin to Haemonian Peleus.

Catullus leaps off into myth to expound a night of love
(and much else) with his *candida diua* (68: above, pp. 52 ff.).
Propertius communicates the splendour of a night with
Cynthia in paradoxical imagery (2. 15. 1) and amusing
hyperbole, 2. 15. 37–40:

> quod mihi si interdum talis concedere noctes
>   illa uelit, uitae longus et annus erit.
> si dabit et multas, fiam immortalis in illis:
>   nocte una quiuis uel deus esse potest.

> But if she should sometimes be willing to grant me nights
>   such as this,
> a year of life will be long.
> If further she gives me many, they will make me immortal:
> in one such night anyone can be a god.

Instead of describing sex and making it sound only too natural,

Propertius suggests its supernatural nature by composing these witty conceits (cf. too 2. 14).

Ovid stands revealed. He revels in the attractive but *definable* beauty of Corinna. He describes her delightedly, without qualms. As for sex, he does not describe it: what he does is in romantic terms even more shocking. The words *cetera quis nescit?* cut at the roots of romance. It must be one of the romantic lover's articles of faith that other people do *not* know the rest—the inconceivable, unknowable union with the unique beloved. Who could know Propertius' joys? That was Propertius' point. Ovid may not be deliberately parodying Elegy here, nor (I think) is this poem primarily humorous in its impact. But Ovid blandly *lassus* and *requiescens* is an incongruous Elegist and he probably knows it; in its own way *Am.* 1. 5 undermines his romantic status as surely as, say, poem 6 does. Ovid writes a poem in the guise of a Propertian lover which with its satisfied, explicit, unmysterious, and splendid sensuality is something that Propertius would never have written.

Ovid's 'romantic' role and poetry continues in Books 2 and 3 —in some poems. For example 1. 4 rebounds in 2. 5. In the former Ovid had instructed Corinna how to contact him at a banquet in her husband's, or what may be her husband's, presence. In 2. 5 she has put that sort of advice into action, with another lover in Ovid's presence. The two are linked by verbal and thematic echoes, e.g. 1. 4. 39–40

> oscula si dederis, fiam manifestus amator
>   et dicam 'mea sunt' iniciamque manum.

> If you kiss him, I'll become the Open Lover
>   and grab you and declare 'I claim what is mine.'

and 2. 5. 29–30

> 'quid facis?' exclamo 'quo nunc mea gaudia defers?
>   iniciam dominas in mea iura manus.'

> 'What are you up to?' I shouted. 'Where are you
>   taking *my* pleasure?
> I shall forcibly claim my rights.'

Note too how jealous frustration anticipated (1. 4. 61-70) becomes jealous frustration painfully actual (2. 5. *passim*, especially 9-12). Ovid casts himself in the role of jealous, discomfited lover, victim of a fateful irony; but he is quite clearly amused by the part and plays it to amuse us.

2. 6 is a dirge for the death of Corinna's parrot—in the tradition of Catullus' dirge for Lesbia's sparrow (poem 3). Catullus uses mock-solemnity for a tactical purpose in a drama. Ovid simply enjoys and expects us to enjoy mock-solemnity—and a parade of other conceits. For example 46-52:

> et stabat uacuo iam tibi Parca colo;
> nec tamen ignauo stupuerunt uerba palato:
>   clamauit moriens lingua 'Corinna, uale.'
> colle sub Elysio nigra nemus ilice frondet
>   udaque perpetuo gramine terra uiret.
> si qua fides dubiis, uolucrum locus ille piarum
>   dicitur, obscenae quo prohibentur aues . . .

> Destiny stood with empty distaff.
> But weak as he was he could still speak,
> and his last words were *Goodbye, Corinna.* –
> Under a hill in Elysium, a grove of black ilex grows,
> and the ground is ever moist and green.
> There, to the eye of faith, is the good birds' heaven,
> barred to all birds of prey.
>
> (Lee)

Compare that with Tibull. 1. 3. 58 ff. To appreciate the high, splendid absurdity of *Corinna, uale* one has to remember that this poignant valediction, whose phrasing recalls epitaphs (cf. Catull. 101. 10), is uttered in parrot tones.

Ovid's propempticon for Corinna in 2. 11 is amusingly sentimental and decorative compared with Propertius 1. 8A. His poems on Corinna's abortion in 2. 13 and 14 are largely devoted to making inventive play of the subject (not altogether to everyone's taste). Poem 17 starts in apparently serious Elegiac vein, recalling Propertius[39] as well as Ovid's own 1. 3. Lines 1-6:

> si quis erit, qui turpe putet seruire puellae,
>   illo conuincar iudice turpis ego.

sim licet infamis, dum me moderatius urat
    quae Paphon et fluctu pulsa Cythera tenet.
atque utinam dominae miti quoque praeda fuissem,
    formosae quoniam praeda futurus eram.

If anyone thinks it base to be the slave of a girl,
in his judgement I shall be proved base.
But let me be disgraced, provided that Venus burns me
        more mildly,
she who inhabits Paphos and wave-beaten Cythera.
And oh that I had fallen prey to a gentle mistress, too,
since I was to become the prey of a beautiful one.

But its capacity to appear serious is neatly undermined by
such frivolous strokes as this:

carminis hoc ipsum genus impar, sed tamen apte
    iungitur herous cum breuiore modo   (21-2)

This kind of verse is unequal; nevertheless
the heroic line is fitly joined to the shorter.

the last in a list of *exempla* illustrating that superior may lie
with inferior; or this

tu quoque me, mea lux, in quaslibet accipe leges;
    te deceat medio iura dedisse foro.   (23-4)

Receive me, light of my life—and make the laws.
You would suitably legislate in the forum.

which pursues to an over-logical, over-literal conclusion an
inherited romantic idea (the mistress as the one who makes
the rules, *leges*).[40]

In Book 3 there are also 'romantic' poems of this type:
ostensibly romantic poems that are actually parodic, witty,
entertainingly artificial, and thus other than romantic in
effect: 3, 6, 8, 10, 11, 11B, 12. (But the penultimate poem
in Book 3, the 'romantic' poem 14, I find unexpectedly and
disconcertingly serious.)[41]

In all these (except perhaps 3. 14) we can still loosely call
Ovid *parodic* (cf. above p. 252). He adopts the role of Proper-
tian lover but makes fun or art of it. However, it is only in
Book 1 that he does this *consistently* (a fact which gets
curiously obscured in accounts of the *Amores*). In many of

the poems of Books 2 and 3 the mask is off. (It would be interesting to know how 'romantic' and non-romantic poems were distributed in the original five books.) The message is cheerfully even cynically promiscuous; love is explicitly (usually) fun. The wit that is contrived now supports the role Ovid adopts instead of undermining it. The character that we detected behind the mask of the parodic poems declares himself: ·a less discreet, more provocative and (in some but not all ways) more cynical version of Horace. Ovid is many things: and one thing we could say he is is a member of the anti-romantic reaction.

Book 2 opens, after another amusing *recusatio*, with two poems addressed to a eunuch slave Bagoas. Ovid here exploits an idea he is fond of, derived from Propertius:[42] having two dramatic poems enact successive stages in a drama. Verisimilitude is kept in view: for example, no play is made with Bagoas' castrated state until the second poem, after Ovid's elaborate instructions have fallen on deaf ears.

The instructions of the first (poem 2) are offered as a manual on 'how to guard a mistress'. They are written from Ovid the prospective lover's point of view. They are in fact a manual on how to allow a girl to cuckold her 'man'. The poem is amusingly cynical and quite realistic. In the second poem (3) Ovid reproaches Bagoas for not following his advice, and exhorts him again.

Here Ovid is scouting an affair with a woman who is *not* Corinna: she is quite clearly a new interest and still only a potential lover. 2. 2. 3-6:

> hesterna uidi spatiantem luce puellam
>   illa quae Danai porticus agmen habet.
> protinus, ut placuit, misi scriptoque rogaui;
>   rescripsit trepida 'non licet' illa manu . . .

> Yesterday I saw the girl strolling
> in the portico which has the Danaid statues.
> I fancied her straight away. I sent her a note asking
>   for a meeting.
> Back came the timorously written reply 'I can't.'

What price now *et nulli cessura fides* (1. 3. 13)? Ovidian romantic devotion gives place to what we always sensed: cheerful, worldly promiscuity. Nor is it unambiguously a promiscuity of an innocuous, Horatian sort. Ovid at least flirts with the suggestion (more explicitly in other poems: below, pp. 274 ff.) that his promiscuity, like his 'romantic' love, involves adultery (cf. above, p. 240).[43]

2. 4 is the manifesto of Ovid the promiscuous lover. The sort of thing that Propertius had uttered in desperation and then retracted (above, p. 63), Ovid now broadcasts without retraction or qualification, and (as far as we can tell) he lives up to it. Parts of 2. 4 should be quoted.

> non ego mendosos ausim defendere mores
>   falsaque pro uitiis arma mouere meis.
> confiteor, si quid prodest delicta fateri;
>   in mea nunc demens crimina fassus eo.
> odi, nec possum, cupiens, non esse quod odi:
>   heu quam, quae studeas ponere, ferre graue est.
> nam desunt uires ad me mihi iusque regendum;
>   auferor, ut rapida concita puppis aqua.
> non est certa meos quae forma inuitet amores:
>   centum sunt causae cur ego semper amem.
> siue aliqua est oculos in se deiecta modestos,
>   uror, et insidiae sunt pudor ille meae;
> siue procax aliqua est, capior quia rustica non est ...   (1–13)

> I would not venture to defend my ways,
> or take up false arms in defence of my faults.
> I confess—if there is any benefit in confessing sins.
> Madly I proceed to my own prosecution.
> I hate what I am but cannot, in spite of my desire, not be
>   what I hate.
> Alas how grievous it is to bear what you long to lay aside.
> For I lack the strength and authority to rule myself;
> I am carried away like a ship tossed on rushing water.
> There's no one type of beauty that invites my love.
> There are a hundred reasons why I always love.
> If a girl casts her eyes primly down,
> I'm on fire, and that very modesty is my snare.
> If she's forward, I'm taken because she not provincial ...

> me noua sollicitat, me tangit serior aetas:
>   haec melior specie, moribus illa placet.
> denique quas tota quisquam probat urbe puellas,
>   noster in has omnis ambitiosus amor.   (45–8)

I fall for the young and feel for the not so young—
one has the looks, the other the experience.
Put it like this—there's beauty in Rome to please all tastes
and mine are all-embracing.

(Lee)

Ovid defeats expectations maliciously in the opening lines.
They recall romantic passion. In particular line 5 recalls
Catullus 85 and line 6 Catullus 76. But the burden that is
hard to bear, the ambivalence that oppresses, concerns not an
enthralling lover, as the Catullan reminiscences would lead us
to believe, but love: *any* lover, as the poem then elaborately
declares. Cheerful Ovidian promiscuity replaces expected
Catullan devotion (Horace's *Epode* 11 is interesting to com-
pare here).[44] Ovid is enjoying putting aside his mask.

Poems 7 and 8 are another dramatic diptych. *et nulli
cessura fides* . . . The drama plays against that memory. The
first poem is addressed to Corinna. Ovid protests vehemently,
unanswerably it seems, that he has not, as she alleges, slept
with her slave-girl Cypassis. Propertius similarly had to deny
an affair with the slave-girl Licynna in 3. 15. In poem 8 Ovid
addresses Cypassis herself. How have they been rumbled? He
concludes, after canvassing the options, that it must have
been her fault—and requests that she oblige him again as a
penalty. Ovid's actual attitude to love and romance could
not be more acutely demonstrated. *et nulli cessura fides.*

The diptych drama technique is skilfully handled. Note
how the second poem adds unexpected colour to the first.
We learn that Cypassis was present on the former occasion,
witnessing Ovid's barefaced lie. Our respect for Ovid's men-
dacity increases: he wasn't a bit put out by the fact that his
indignant denial of an affair with Cypassis had to be made in
front of Cypassis herself. Note 8. 15–16:

> ut tamen iratos in te defixit ocellos,
> uidi te totis erubuisse genis.

> Corinna looked daggers at *you* though.
> And how you blushed! I saw you.
>
> (Lee)

And 8. 9–10

> quid quod, in ancilla si quis delinquere possit,
>   illum ego contendi mente carere bona?

> Having an affair with a maid, a slave-girl!
> I argued that a man like that was out of his mind.

recalls 7. 21–6

> quis Veneris famulae conubia liber inire
>   tergaque conplecti uerbere secta uelit?
> adde quod ornandis illa est operosa capillis
>   et tibi per doctas grata ministra manus.
> scilicet ancillam, quod erat tibi fida, rogarem?
>   quid, nisi ut indicio iuncta repulsa foret?

> What man of breeding would sleep with a slave
> or embrace a body scarred by the lash?
> Besides, she's your coiffeuse—her skill
> makes her a favourite of yours.
> I'd be mad to ask a maid so devoted to you.
> She'd only turn me down and tell.
>
> > (Lee)

—the cheek of that!—and 8. 17–18

> at quanto, si forte refers, praesentior ipse
>   per Veneris feci numina magna fidem.

> But I saved the day, you must admit,
> by swearing my Venus oath.
>
> > (Lee)

recalls 7. 27–8

> per Venerem iuro puerique uolatilis arcus
>   me non admissi criminis esse reum.

> By Venus and Cupid's bow,
> I'm innocent—I swear it!
>
> > (Lee)

This is Catullan and Propertian dramatic technique developed and adapted. By juxtaposing his passionate, convincing protestation of innocence to Corinna with his address to Cypassis Ovid enacts the outrageous mendacity of a cynical, promiscuous lover; and the drama implies more or more vivid things than a description or analysis would ever tell.

In 2. 10 Ovid is in love with two girls simultaneously. The poem develops wittily from this basic *datum* (there are Greek epigrams on comparable themes).[45] We might note the structure: it opens as an address to a friend of the poet's and then proceeds through a sequence of rhetorical apostrophe, assertion, and exclamation in the manner of Tibullus or later Propertius (Ovid in fact uses all the structures).[46] Here are the first eight lines:

> tu mihi, tu certe, memini, Graecine, negabas
>   uno posse aliquem tempore amare duas.
> per te ego decipior, per te deprensus inermis
>   ecce duas uno tempore turpis amo.
> utraque formosa est, operosae cultibus ambae,
>   artibus in dubio est haec sit an illa prior;
> pulchrior hac illa est, haec est quoque pulchrior illa,
>   et magis haec nobis et magis illa placet.

> It was you, definitely you, Graecinus, who denied
> that anyone can love two girls at once.
> You deceived me: because of you I've been caught defenceless.
> Look! I love two girls at one time, disgrace that I am.
> Each is attractive, both tasteful in dress;
> as for accomplishments, it's disputable who pips whom.
> The one is more beautiful than the other—and vice versa.
> This one pleases me more—and so does that one.

His love life is in a pleasing, piquant state of balance; and it has its amusing side. This Ovid conveys not only by what he says but by the way he says it. Form supports content superbly. For example: *uno* and *duas* poised at opposite poles of the line (2), *per te* repeated in anaphora after the caesura (3), *duas* and *uno* juxtaposed in the first half of the line balanced by a *t* alliteration in the second (4), and rime at mid-point and end of the line (*uno . . . amo*) (4), pronouns and adjectives disposed in an A1b1b2A2 pattern round the caesura (5): these and similar formal devices make the lines appear like elegantly balanced see-saws, and consequently emphasize the amusing symmetry of Ovid's life. Form and content are beautifully consonant.

Here is a neat illustration of a general truth of Ovid's witty, promiscuous poems. Ovid is the greatest devotee of Neoteric word-patterning and formal artistry among the Augustan poets.[47] His content (in these poems) is urbane and sophisticated to a degree unmatched by the others. His form supports content. Urbanity of style partners urbanity of subject-matter. The man of Ovid's style and the man of his content are harmonious, both are *cultus*. Contrast the technique of Tibullus who contrived a discrepancy between the man of his style and the man of his content (above, p. 189). Contrast too Ovid in his 'Propertian' poems. The form is there equally *cultus*, the content at times grovelling. Tibullan discrepancy between form and content is yet another method that Ovid uses to undermine his 'romantic' role.[48] For example in 2. 11: Ovid laments Corinna's impending departure overseas, but includes such elegantly, playfully artistic lines as these:

> quid tibi, me miserum, Zephyros Eurosque timebo
>   et gelidum Borean egelidumque Notum?   (9–10)

> Darling, why make me afraid of winds from east and west,
> from icy north and spicy south?[49]

>   (Lee)

> uestrum crimen erit talis iactura puellae,
>   Nereidesque deae Nereidumque pater.   (35–6)

> If such a girl is lost, the crime will be yours
> Nereid goddesses and father of the Nereids.

Significantly they recall elegant and happy subject-matter in the Neoteric Catullus (4. 27, 46. 1).

The end of 2. 10 (to return to that poem) makes a splendidly witty point:

> sufficiam: graciles, non sunt sine uiribus artus.
>   pondere, non neruis, corpora nostra carent.
> et lateri dabit in uires alimenta uoluptas.
>   decepta est opera nulla puella mea.
> saepe ego lasciue consumpsi tempora noctis,
>   utilis et forti corpore mane fui.
> felix quem Veneris certamina mutua perdunt!
>   di faciant leti causa sit ista mei!

induat aduersis contraria pectora telis
  miles et aeternum sanguine nomen emat.
quaerat auarus opes et quae lassarit arando
  aequora periuro naufragus ore bibat.
at mihi contingat Veneris languescere motu
  cum moriar, medium soluar et inter opus.
atque aliquis nostro lacrimans in funere dicat
  'conueniens uitae mors fuit ista tuae.'   (23–38)

I can take it. I may be thin and under weight
but I've muscle and stamina.
Pleasure's a food that builds me up.
I've never disappointed a girl.
Many's the night I've spent in love
and been fighting fit the morning after.
To die in love's duel—what final bliss!
It's the death I should choose.
Let soldiers impale their hearts on a pike
and pay down blood for glory.
Let seafaring merchants make their millions
till they and their lies are shipwrecked at last.
But when *I* die let me faint in the to and fro of love
and fade out at its climax.
I can just imagine the mourners' comment:
'Death was the consummation of his life.'

                                                    (Lee)

Ovid maintains that he is physically capable of his demanding
sex life. Anyway, what a way to die! It is a consummation
devoutly to be wished. The obvious fun of this is put in yet
more pleasant focus if it is compared, as it is meant to be
compared, with romantic statements about love and death.
For example[50] Propertius had expressed the romantic belief
that he and Cynthia would die together, still in love:

ambos una fides auferet, una dies
              (2. 20. 18)

one selfsame day shall bear us both away in one selfsame love.

Tibullus had uttered the sentimental wish to die in his beloved's
loving presence:

te spectem, suprema mihi cum uenerit hora,
  te teneam moriens deficiente manu.
              (1. 1. 59 f.)

> Oh let me gaze at you, when my last hour comes—
> hold you, as I die, in my failing grasp!
>
> (Lee)

Ovid's wish to die on the job, heard against these comparable but less lusty utterances, has an amusingly blunt even cynical ring.

The same process operates when we read the conclusion to Ovid's poem (37 f.), his imagined epitaph succinctly uttered by someone at his funeral. We must recollect that Propertius had a penchant for romantically evoking his tomb and epitaph. Cf. especially Prop. 2. 1. 77-8:

> taliaque illacrimans mutae iace uerba fauillae:
>   'huic misero fatum dura puella fuit.'

> And weeping utter these words to my silent ashes:
>   'A harsh girl was this pitiable man's doom.'

Ovid's cheerfully incongruous mixture of levity and death is given added point by the fact that it brings to mind the characteristic gloom of his predecessor. Ovid in fact is again indulging in parody, but from an undisguised standpoint.

Cynicism, wit, fun, and splendid power of *inuentio* are all very evident in 2. 19 and 3. 4. In 2. 19 Ovid lectures a husband on the need to guard his wife—or else Ovid will not fancy her; the husband is spoiling his fun. The basis of his argument is the proverbial idea of 'forbidden fruits',[51] but Ovid pushes it to paradoxical extremes. For example 45-60:

> ille potest uacuo furari litore harenas,
>   *uxorem* stulti si quis amare potest.
> iamque ego praemoneo: nisi tu seruare puellam
>   incipis, incipiet desinere esse mea.
> multa diuque tuli; speraui saepe futurum
>   cum bene seruasses, ut bene uerba darem.
> lentus es et pateris nulli patienda *marito*;
>   at mihi concessi finis amoris erit.
> scilicet infelix numquam prohibebor adire?
>   nox mihi sub nullo uindice semper erit?
> nil metuam? per nulla traham suspiria somnos?
>   nil facies, cur te iure perisse uelim?
> quid mihi cum facili, quid cum lenone *marito*?
>   corrumpit uitio gaudia nostra suo.

quin alium, quem tanta iuuet patientia, quaeris?
    me tibi riualem si iuuat esse, ueta.

An affair with the wife of a fool
is stealing sand from the beach.
I'm warning you: start guarding your girl
or I'll stop wanting her.
I've suffered long enough—in the vain hope
you'd take precautions so I could take advantage.
But you won't react like a normal husband
and I can't make love on sufferance.
Shall I never be locked out
or face reprisals one fine night?
Never be scared? Never insomniac or sad?
Can't you give me some excuse for wishing you dead?
I don't approve of uncomplaining, pimping husbands—
their immorality ruins my pleasure.
Find someone who can appreciate your perversion,
or, if you value *me* as a rival, use your veto.

                                        (Lee)

Style supports splendid paradoxes: for instance, a neatly
balanced chiasmus in 47–8 underlines the strange, dependent
relationship that Ovid is in with the husband. And again Ovid
sports with the romantics. Line 49 recalls the long-suffering
patience and hope of the lover awaiting his mistress's favour;[52]
Ovid endures in patient hope that her husband will try to
prevent it. But the neatest and most provocative paradox
here is that Ovid contrives to arraign the erring husband
under the terms of the *Lex Iulia de adulteriis* (lines 51 and
57):[53] pimping by a husband was specifically covered in the
law. It should be stressed that in 2. 19 and 3. 4 Ovid's language
(see the underlined words above and in the following quota-
tions) explicitly evokes legal marriage and adultery—what-
ever *de facto* institution he might have hoped, or not hoped,
that we should actually infer.

Ovid also includes a lecture based on the principle of
'forbidden fruits' to the mistress herself (this poem too
proceeds through a sequence of rhetorical addresses and
apostrophes). 9–20:

        uiderat hoc in me uitium uersuta Corinna
            quaque capi possem callida norat opem.

a quotiens sani capitis mentita dolores
    cunctantem tardo iussit abire pede!
a quotiens finxit culpam, quantumque licebat
    insonti, speciem praebuit esse nocens!
sic ubi uexarat tepidosque refouerat ignis,
    rursus erat uotis comis et apta meis.
quas mihi blanditias, quam dulcia uerba parabat!
    oscula, di magni, qualia quotque dabat!
tu quoque quae nostros rapuisti nuper ocellos
    saepe time insidias, saepe rogata nega . . .

Corinna, clever girl, noticed this weakness of mine
and knew the best way to exploit it.
Sometimes she'd invent a head-ache
and tell me to clear off,
sometimes she'd say she'd been unfaithful
and look as if she really had.
Then, having fanned my fading passion to a blaze,
she'd be sweet again and exquisitely obliging.
What irresistible temptation she could offer,
and oh my God the artistry of her kisses!
You too, latest and dearest, must learn to look alarmed
and master the art of saying No.

(Lee)

It is, incidentally, pleasant to recall 1. 3 again. The splendid
unreality of this is notable. Ovid might plausibly lecture a
woman on how to keep other men thus (and the advice is
quite sound), but it is hardly plausible to deliver the lecture
with his own self in view. He might just see through her
stratagems. It is nearly as unreal as the lecture to the husband.
But here of course is one of the strengths of the poem, one of
its sources of wit. Ovid translates sound logical thinking into
beautifully implausible action.

The passage also demonstrates another fact about Ovid:
simply that he likes to lecture, he likes teaching the sophisti-
cated and cynical arts of urbane love. He contrives to do it in
unexpected places. He managed to get cynical advice into his
'romantic' book without compromising his own 'romantic'
character: by borrowing Propertius' *lena* (procuress) and
effectively leaving her the stage (1. 8).[54] In 1. 8, 2. 19 and
elsewhere we have a clear foretaste of the poem that will

indulge this liking openly and extensively, the *Ars Amatoria.*[55]

Here are some more lines from the lecture to the wife (25–30):

> pinguis amor nimiumque patens in taedia nobis
>   uertitur et stomacho dulcis ut esca nocet.
> si numquam Danaen habuisset aenea turris,
>   non esset Danae de Ioue facta parens.
> dum seruat Iuno mutatam cornibus Io,
>   facta est quam fuerat gratior illa Ioui.

> Love on a plate soon palls—
> like eating too much cake.
> Danae unconfined
> would have missed her famous confinement.
> Io as a heifer ⟨and under guard⟩
> doubled her human charm.
>   (Lee, except for the indicated addition)

This demonstrates another Ovidian way with myth. The individual, cynical construction that he here puts on resonant Elegiac myths reveals without camouflage his anti-romanticism, his cynical character and wit. For something similar see 3. 2. 15 f. (Pelops), 3. 8. 29 ff. (Danae), and again we can see a parallel in Horace.[56]

3. 4 exploits the same proverbial idea of 'forbidden fruits' and Ovid again lectures his mistress's 'husband' (this time throughout, in a 'dramatic' poem). And at times the arguments are exactly the same. Cf. 25–32:

> quidquid seruatur, cupimus magis, ipsaque furem
>   cura uocat; pauci, quod sinit alter, amant.
> nec facie placet illa sua, sed amore *mariti*:
>   nescioquid, quod te ceperit, esse putant.
> non proba fit, quam uir seruat, sed *adultera* cara:
>   ipse timor pretium corpore maius habet.
> indignere licet, iuuat inconcessa uoluptas:
>   sola placet, 'timeo' dicere si qua potest.

> Locked up means more desirable. Security
> is a challenge to thieves. Few can love by another
>   man's leave.
> Your wife's beauty is less of a draw than your passion
>   for her—

she's got something special, we think, to hold you.
By being possessive you make her more worthwhile as a
mistress;
in fact her fear counts for more than her figure.
Storm as you please, forbidden fruit is sweet.
The woman who says 'I daren't' is the one for me.

(Lee)

But now the burden of the lecture is that the husband should
not guard his wife ('It's no good guarding a young girl'). Ovid
deploys the arguments of 2. 19 *speciously*—presumably—so
that his path to the mistress may be smoothed. The poet's
inuentio, his delight in sheer intellectual ingenuity, is neatly
shown.

He deploys other arguments. 1–10:

dure uir, imposito tenerae custode puellae
    nil agis: ingenio est quaeque tuenda suo.
si qua metu dempto casta est, ea denique casta est;
    quae, quia non liceat, non facit, illa facit.
ut iam seruaris bene corpus, *adultera* mens est
    nec custodiri, ne uelit, ulla potest;
nec corpus seruare potes, licet omnia claudas:
    omnibus occlusis intus *adulter* erit.
cui peccare licet, peccat minus: ipsa potestas
    semina nequitiae languidiora facit.

It's no good guarding a young girl, insensitive fellow.
Her own nature must be each woman's protection.
Take away fear, and if she's chaste then, she's really chaste.
If she doesn't do it because she can't, in effect she does it.
Though you guard her body well, her mind is adulterous,
and you cannot imprison a woman's will.
And you can't even guard her body, though you lock every
door.
With all locked out, there'll be an adulterer within.
She who can sin sins less. The very ability to do it
makes the spur to sleep around less sharp.

Adultery is a matter of intention; there is no secure defence
against clandestine lovers except the wife's will. It is ingeni-
ously argued and, as always, pointedly expressed. It is also
flatly against the spirit of the *Lex Iulia de adulteriis* which

sought precisely to *enforce* married chastity. Propertius had made the same point as Ovid but more discreetly.[57]
Even more openly provocative is 33 ff.:

> nec tamen ingenuam ius est seruare puellam;
>   hic metus externae corpora gentis agat.
> scilicet ut possit custos 'ego' dicere 'feci',
>   in laudem serui casta sit illa tui?
> rusticus est nimium, quem laedit *adultera* coniunx,
>   et notos mores non satis urbis habet,
> in qua Martigenae non sunt sine crimine nati
>   Romulus Iliades Iliadesque Remus.
> quo tibi formosam, si non nisi casta placebat?
>   non possunt ullis ista coire modis.
> si sapis, indulge dominae uultusque seueros
>   exue nec rigidi iura tuere uiri
> et cole quos dederit (multos dabit) *uxor* amicos:
>   gratia sic minimo magna labore uenit;
> sic poteris iuuenum conuiuia semper inire
>   et quae non dederis, multa uidere domi.

> However you've no right to imprison a free-born girl.
> Such sanctions are for foreigners only.
> And her warder will say it's thanks to him. Do you want
>   a slave
> to take the credit for her chastity?
> To fret about adultery is too provincial
> and shows ignorance of Roman manners—
> after all, the Martian twins were born out of wedlock,
> Ilia's children, Romulus and Remus.
> Why marry good looks if all you wanted was good behaviour?
> The two things never mix.
> Be sensible and give in to her. Stop being a prig.
> Don't press your rights as a husband,
> but cultivate the many friends she'll bring you.
> You'll reap a rich reward for doing nothing,
> go out when you like to all the gay parties,
> or stay at home and enjoy the presents you never gave her.

Ovid argues that guarding girls is un-Roman; objecting to adultery is unsophisticated and simply not the way of the metropolis, whose lax morals are sanctioned by the history of her origins; beauty and chastity do not mix; there are benefits for a complaisant husband. All this is not only outrageously against the spirit of Augustus' law, it even suggests its particular infringement: the concluding lines advocate what the *Lex Iulia* would have regarded as the husband's pimping (*lenocinium*), the very crime for which Ovid, with characteristic ingenuity and cheek, had blamed the husband in 2. 19. Ovid here wittily, strikingly, and very provocatively defends sophisticated promiscuity; and (I repeat) his language suggests married adultery. *puella* and *custodes* may suggest a *demi-monde* or even the conventions of the Comic stage, but *ingenuam, adultera coniunx,* and *uxor* suggest the class of people and type of marriage that Augustus and his law was only too concerned with.

3. 2 illustrates the fun of Ovidian love (in a particular aspect) and another facet of Ovidian technique. The poem lengthily stages Ovid's successful attempt to chat up a woman neighbour at the circus races. In most of it Ovid is addressing the woman, but he includes—without excessively straining dramatic plausibility—an aside to her dress (27 f.), sundry apostrophes and exclamations (45 ff.), and instructions to the charioteer (71 f.). Ovid shows his predecessors' interest in 'Elegiac mime' (cf. most immediately Prop. 3. 6):[58] he quotes only one line by the woman, but manages to suggest her presence throughout. Not only that, he manages to suggest in detail the action that is going on around them. Here is a sample:

> non ego nobilium sedeo studiosus equorum;
>   cui tamen ipsa faues, uincat ut ille, precor.
> ut loquerer tecum, ueni, tecumque sederem . . .
> dum loquor, alba leui sparsa est tibi puluere uestis:
>   sordide de niueo corpore puluis abi.
> sed iam pompa uenit: linguis animisque fauete;
>   tempus adest plausus: aurea pompa uenit.
> prima loco fertur passis Victoria pinnis:
>   huc ades et meus hic fac, dea, uincat, amor . . .
> sed pendent tibi crura: potes, si forte iuuabit,
>   cancellis primos inseruisse pedes.
> maxima iam uacuo praetor spectacula Circo
>   quadriiugos aequo carcere misit equos.
> cui studeas, uideo; uincet, cuicumque fauebis:
>   quid cupias, ipsi scire uidentur equi.

me miserum, metam spatioso circuit orbe;
　quid facis? admoto proximus axe subit.
quid facis, infelix? perdis bona uota puellae;
　tende, precor, ualida lora sinistra manu.
fauimus ignauo. sed enim reuocate, Quirites,
　et date iactatis undique signa togis.
en reuocant; at ne turbet toga mota capillos,
　in nostros abdas te licet usque sinus.
(1-3, 41-6, 63-76)

It's not the horses that bring me here
though I hope your favourite wins.
To sit with you and talk with you is why I've come— . . .
Just then a speck of dust fell on your white dress.
Forgive me—out, damned spot!
But here's the procession. Everybody hush.
Give them a hand. The golden procession's here.
First comes Victory, wings outstretched.
Goddess, grant me victory in love! . . .
But the seat's a bit too high for you.
Why not rest your feet on the railing in front?
Now, they've cleared the course. The Praetor's starting
　　the first race.
Four-horse chariots. Look—they're off.
There's your driver. Anyone *you* back is bound to win.
Even the horses seem to know what you want.
My God, he's taking the corner too wide.
What are you doing? The man behind is drawing level.
What are you doing, wretch? Breaking a poor girl's heart.
For pity's sake pull on your left rein!
We've backed a loser. Come on everyone, all together,
flap your togas and signal a fresh start.
Look, they're calling them back. Lean your head against me
so the waving togas don't disarrange your hair . . .
(Lee)

The poem is, we should note, entirely devoted to the process
of chatting up. It ends before the real action begins. Ovid
delights in the game preparatory to love, just as elsewhere he
manifestly delights in the games peripheral to love. The fun
of pursuit, the fun of thwarting obstacles (1. 4, 2. 19, 3. 4)—
these are part of the fun of love for Ovid. In his interest in
the game we are reminded, significantly, of Horace. But Ovid,
with his irrepressible ingenuity and tendentious irreverence

more often prefers to teach the rules than simply stage the game (as Horace does, for the delight of the spectacle or for subtler didactic implication); and his games are more *risqué*. In 1. 4 (when he is still preserving his romantic character) Ovid displays his zest for the game, a liking for teaching, his provocativeness—and his ability to bring the details of action before our eyes. For example 15-28:

> cum premet ille torum, uultu comes ipsa modesto
>   ibis ut accumbas, clam mihi tange pedem;
> me specta nutusque meos uultumque loquacem:
>   excipe furtiuas et refer ipsa notas.
> uerba superciliis sine uoce loquentia dicam;
>   uerba leges digitis, uerba notata mero.
> cum tibi succurret Veneris lasciuia nostrae,
>   purpureas tenero pollice tange genas;
> si quid erit, de me tacita quod mente queraris,
>   pendeat extrema mollis ab aure manus;
> cum tibi, quae faciam, mea lux, dicamue, placebunt,
>   uersetur digitis anulus usque tuis;
> tange manu mensam, tangunt quo more precantes,
>   optabis merito cum mala multa uiro.

> When he takes his place on the couch and you go to join him
> looking angelic, secretly touch my foot.
> Watch me for nods and looks that talk
> and unobserved return my signals
> in the language of eyebrows and fingers
> with annotations in wine.
> Whenever you think of our love-making
> stroke that rosy cheek with your thumb.
> If you're cross with me, darling,
> press the lobe of your ear
> but turn your ring round if you're pleased
> with anything I say or do.
> When you feel like cursing your fool of a husband
> touch the table as if you were praying.

(Lee)

Many of the *Amores* (as I have said before, pp. 276 f.) are close in theme and purpose to the *Ars Amatoria.*

The spirit of Ovid is irreverent. His poems shoot malicious shafts at Augustus' laws against adultery (especially 2. 19 and

3. 4). His celebration of promiscuous love (which in Horatian form offends no one) is perhaps tactlessly enthusiastic and exclusive, given that the Emperor has recently introduced a law to encourage marriage in the free classes (cf. Prop. 2. 7).[59] He mocks the life of action and war as much as or more than Propertius or Tibullus—so it might be argued: as well as 1. 9, cf. 2. 12. More openly than Propertius (3. 13. 25 ff.) he mocks the politically fashionable cult of old simplicity (1. 8. 39 ff.). All these irreverent tendencies are strengthened in the *Ars Amatoria*: for example 2. 151 ff., 685 f., 3. 483 ff.,[60] 585 f., 3. 113-28.

Ovid's targets are often the same as the earlier Elegists'. But Ovid's targets are also those Elegists themselves. 1. 9 may exploit military life for humour, but it is also a *reductio ad absurdum* of the Propertian-Tibullan paradox. In *Am.* 1. 6 we observed what Ovid did to Elegiac *seruitium amoris* and other themes. And both his guyed romanticism and his professed promiscuity are often directed explicitly against Propertius (or Tibullus). As well as the examples above, note Ovid's malicious use of the language of Elegiac devotion to make his casual pick-up at the circus.[61] 3. 2. 61 f.:

> per tibi tot iuro testes pompamque deorum
> te dominam nobis tempus in omne peti.

> I swear to you by all these witnesses, by the procession
>   of gods,
> that I seek you as my mistress for ever.

Such cynical use of romantic language is, again, a foretaste of the *Ars Amatoria*.[62]

Ovid stands out against the moral earnestness of Augustan Rome; he also stands out against the romantic earnestness of his poetic predecessors. And he stands out against the discretion of his closest erotic confrère, Horace.[63] One gets the impression that Ovid would have stood out against anything earnestly uttered or authoritatively imposed. He stands out against the constraints of his own subject-matter, shooting in humorous asides and parentheses, piling up *exempla* or comparisons gratuitously, extending a myth because the fancy takes him.[64] He is irreverent by nature, without prejudice. Certainly any topic is fair game for his wit, even abortion. In that we have a taste of the *Metamorphoses*.

But I do talk of irreverence not of defiance. There is nothing (anyway at this stage) of the political tone of, say, Prop. 1. 21, 2. 1, or 2. 7. Ovid sees postures, pretensions, and beliefs as butts for his ingenuity. The achievement of humour, point, or wit was an end in itself. His butt (not that he needed a butt) could be virtually anything. Such catholic irreverence clearly precludes any interpretation of Ovid as a moral protester. But others might take offence where no offence was *seriously* intended.

Did he have any positive beliefs? Belief is a strong word and perhaps Ovid only believed in one thing. What it is is probably already evident.

Note *Am.* 1. 15 (the concluding poem to book 1). 1–8:

> quid mihi, Liuor edax, ignauos obicis annos
>   ingeniique uocas carmen inertis opus,
> non me more patrum, dum strenua sustinet aetas,
>   praemia militiae puluerulenta sequi
> nec me uerbosas leges ediscere nec me
>   ingrato uocem prostituisse foro?
> mortale est, quod quaeris, opus; mihi fama perennis
>   quaeritur, in toto semper ut orbe canar.

> Devouring Envy why lay lazy years to my charge,
> and call poetry the work of an idle talent?
> Why <complain> that I do not, after the manner of our
>   fathers, while vigorous youth sustains,
> pursue the dusty prizes of soldiering
> or learn garrulous law,
> and tout rhetoric in the ungrateful forum?
> The work you ask for is but mortal; undying fame
> is what I want, to be sung throughout the world.

Compare too Ovid's own autobiography, *Trist.* 4. 10. 15–26, 33–40:

> protinus excolimur teneri curaque parentis
>   imus ad insignes urbis ab arte uiros.
> frater ad eloquium uiridi tendebat ab aeuo,
>   fortia uerbosi natus ad arma fori;

at mihi iam puero caelestia sacra placebant,
   inque suum furtim Musa trahebat opus.
saepe pater dixit 'studium quid inutile temptas?
   Maeonides nullas ipse reliquit opes.'
motus eram dictis, totoque Helicone relicto
   scribere temptabam uerba soluta modis.
sponte sua carmen numeros ueniebat ad aptos,
   et quod temptabam dicere uersus erat . . .   (26)
cepimus et tenerae primos aetatis honores,   (33)
   eque uiris quondam pars tribus una fui.
curia restabat: claui mensura coacta est;
   maius erat nostris uiribus illud onus.
nec patiens corpus, nec mens fuit apta labori,
   sollicitaeque fugax ambitionis eram,
et petere Aoniae suadebant tuta sorores
   otia, iudicio semper amata meo.

While still in our youth we gained education and, thanks
     to my father,
went to teachers famous for their skill in Rome.
My brother aimed for eloquence from early years;
he was born for the bold battles of the wordy forum.
But already as a boy I was attracted to heavenly mysteries,
and the Muse drew me covertly to her work.
Often my father said 'why try a useless pursuit?
Homer himself left no money.'
I was influenced by his words, and abandoning Helicon in
     its entirety
I tried to write in prose.
But poetry fell into appropriate metre spontaneously,
and whatever I tried to say was verse . . .   (26)
I attained youth's first honours   (33)
and was a member of the Board of Three.
It remained to enter the Senate;
that burden was too great for my strength.
My body was not enduring, nor was my mind suited to toil.
I was timid in the face of the anxieties of ambition,
and the Muses urged me to seek the safety of leisure—
which I had always judged amiable.

In both passages Ovid refers to his rejection of a conventional career. In both he recalls Propertian and Tibullan declarations, their rejection of *militia* and wealth, and he uses language reminiscent of them.[65] Comparison focuses a vital difference.

Whereas Propertius and Tibullus rejected wealth and *militia* for *militia amoris*, the life of love, Ovid makes his renunciation in favour of poetry. The love poets who lived for *otium*, peace, and love are replaced by the love poet who lives for poetry (and writes a love song to his Muse).[66] There are implications here for all three poets. Proclamations like these cannot of course be taken with complete literalness. But art was, I think, what Ovid most valued, most believed in, for its own sake—all his life. The achievement of art (to rephrase a sentence above) was for him an end in itself.

But if 'belief' is a strong word, let us try 'liking' or 'favour'. What do we infer Ovid liked, what view of life and love (besides irreverence) do the *Amores* suggest?

Ovid favoured love that was fun. Naturally therefore he favoured promiscuity. He favoured love poetry that was amusing. Love and love poetry were to be *pleasurable*. That of course put him in a different camp from the earlier Elegists, and, because he possessed a tendentious taste for the *risqué* and lacked the discretion of Horace, it put him in a different camp from Horace too—and from Augustus.

Ovid liked the sophistication of life and manners which modernity and empire brought. In the *Amores* we can sense the poet who will shortly write the great praise of *cultus* (*Ars.* 3. 113-28). In a way, in fact, Ovid was a true voice of his imperial age. Moral reforms and sumptuary legislation are introduced to fight a prevailing tendency, the spirit of the age. It has been correctly argued that politically Ovid was un-Augustan rather than anti-Augustan[67] (cf. my comments above). There is a sense in which Ovid was truly *Augustan*—the Augustan poet *par excellence*. The Augustan Romans thought so. They praised him to the skies.[68]

Why does Latin Love Poetry as we understand it finish with Ovid?[69] Scholars look for a cause, not unreasonably. We may find one in the spirit of the age, in the fact that Ovid reflected his age. It was not anything that Ovid did to the genre. The significant factor was independent of him, preceded him.

The impulse for the genre had been romantic and personal.

That too had been its continuity. Catullus, Propertius, Tibullus, all showed the individual in love, considered what the individual might do for love, explored the nature of love; they investigated ways of putting this into poetry. Horace participated. He took issue precisely on the question of romanticism. Is this the way an individual should love? He produced an elegant, satisfying alternative. He conducted a dialogue; romanticism mattered.

Sooner or later sophistication (and other factors) may create a climate in which romanticism is simply irrelevant. Abject devotion becomes too absurd for words. Horatian promiscuity—discreet, courtly, often philosophical—is likewise hardly interesting. *Of course* promiscuity is the way. Love is a game, an institution. Concern with the individual in love (even the amount of concern we find in Horace) is also therefore dated. Since the lover is a player in a universally shared game he lacks individuality. Let the erotic writer recount the game amusingly, suggest variations inventively, provide facts.

Literature responds naturally to the spirit of the age, or is forced to follow suit. Otherwise it doesn't get read. Ovid spoke for his society. It amused him for a time to write in the tradition of his predecessors, or at least to play against it. It amused his readers too. But it was his *Ars Amatoria*, that witty informative guidebook of love, that more clearly caught the erotic mood of the New Order. The New Order of course then stamped on its natural but too revealing poem. Latin Love Poetry ceases or rather changes direction because of history. Its continuation in the *Amores* was really posthumous, artificial (significantly that work often covertly anticipates the *Ars*). We must be glad that there was a poet ingenious and irreverent enough to construct such an artifice—and conclude a period of literary history with such neatness.

Notes

Preface

1. Oscar Wilde, *The Critic as Artist*, Part II. See particularly the paragraph beginning 'The difference between objective and subjective work is one of external form merely.'
2. I would not have changed this sentence even if Cairns's work had been available to me. But his chapter 9, 'The origins of Latin love-elegy', does have a constructively positive attitude towards the Greek background. I would draw particular attention to my word 'comparable'.
3. Cf. C. S. Lewis, *The Four Loves* (London, 1960).

Chapter I

1. Plaut. *Curc.* 33–8.
2. Porphyrio and Pseudo-Acron on Hor. *Satires*, 1. 2. 31–2.
3. Kroll, 53–5, *RE* IV. A. 423, Pomeroy, 160.
4. Cic. *Cael.* 28.
5. Cic. *Cael.* 42.
6. Cic. *Cael.* 38 and 49.
7. See G. E. Duckworth, *The Nature of Roman Comedy* (Princeton, 1952), 280–2. To engineer a state of love between social equals the dramatist may also resort to rape: Duckworth 281.
8. Plut. *Mor.* 279F.
9. Plut. *Cato Maior*, 17. 7. The anecdote ends with saving humour: 'Cato expelled another senator from the senate . . . because he embraced his wife in open day before the eyes of his daughter. For his own part, he said, he never embraced his wife unless it thundered loudly; and he used to joke that he was a happy man when it thundered.'
10. Lucr. 4. 1274–7.
11. Liv. *Per.* 59. Interestingly, Augustus read out Metellus' speech to the senate when introducing his own legislation to encourage marriage: cf. Liv. loc. cit., Suet. *Aug.* 89. 2. The issues did not change much. The passage I quote is preserved by Aul. Gell. 1. 6. 1 who, however, attributes the speech to Metellus Numidicus, censor in 102 BC. Cf. further Grimal, 98 ff.
12. Val. Max. 6. 7. 1.
13. For whole love in comedy cf. Duckworth, op. cit., 280.
14. Cf. J. A. Crook, *Law and Life of Rome* (London, 1967), 99–101, Balsdon, 173 ff., Grimal, ch. 3 esp. pp. 70–3, *Oxford Classical Dictionary*, 'Marriage, Law of' and 'Marriage Ceremonies'; and see next note.
15. Note the definitions of marriage in Justinian's *Digest*, 23. 2. 1–2 *nuptiae sunt coniunctio maris et feminae et consortium omnis uitae, diuini et humani iuris communicatio . . . nuptiae consistere non possunt nisi consentiunt omnes, id est qui coeunt quorumque in potestate sunt.*
16. Cic. *Att.* 1. 3. 3. Tullia was in this year (67 BC) about twelve years old.
17. Plut. *Cicero*, 41. 3.
18. *Cambridge Ancient History*, x. 44.

19. *CAH*, x, 30.
20. See e.g. Plut. *Pompey*, 4. 1–4, 9. 2, 47. 6, *Antony*, 19 and 31; Pomeroy, 156 ff., 186.
21. Plut. *Tiberius Gracchus*, 4. 1.
22. See the index to *CIL*, vol. vi (city of Rome) s.v. *obsequium*; also *CIL*, viii, 3290, 4426, 5646, 7665, etc.
23. *Carm. Epigr.* 52. 8.
24. Suet. *Aug.* 64 and 73.
25. See the *Laudatio Turiae*, edited and translated into English by E. Wistrand (Göteborg, 1976), esp. sect. 30.
26. Val. Max. 6. 3. 10.
27. Cf. Hor. *Satires*, 1. 2. 98.
28. Cf., as well as the passage from the *Verres* quoted, the words of Cato at Liv. 34. 2. 9–10.
29. Cic. *Verr.* 1. 94.
30. Aul. Gell. 10. 23. 4.
31. Val. Max. 6. 3. 9; cf. too Plin. *Nat. Hist.* 14. 89 f. and Plut. *Mor.* 265 on the same topic.
32. Aul. Gell. 10. 23. 5.
33. See the very useful account of H. Herter, 'Die Soziologie der antiken Prostitution im Lichte des heidnischen und christlichen Schriftums', *JbAC* 3 (1960), 70–111.
34. See E. Fraenkel, *Elementi Plautini in Plauto* (Florence, 1960), 140–1, 143–5.
35. Liv. 39. 6. 8. On the erotic function of *psaltriae*, etc. see below, pp. 193 ff.
36. Polyb. 31. 25. 4 Büttner-Wobst.
37. Terence's plays are traditionally dated from 166–160 BC. This dating has been doubted, but is still generally accepted: for discussion and bibliography see W. G. Arnott, *Menander, Plautus, Terence* (*Greece and Rome*, New Surveys in the Classics, No. 9 (1975)), 47 and 60 n. 78.
38. Ter. *Phorm.* 80–90.
39. It is courtesans or their equivalent whom Horace has in mind in the phrase *secunda classis* (*Sat.* 1. 2. 48–53); and his synonym for them is *libertinae*. (In this passage Horace distinguishes *libertinae* and *meretrices*, the latter of which he seems to be using in its traditional sense of 'prostitute'. If one does not spend ruinously on a *libertina*, *nec sibi damno/dedecorique foret*; but if *est cum meretricibus*, then *fama malum grauius quam res trahit*. See further Kiessling-Heinze ad loc.). On the status (and nationality) of courtesans see further Herter, 71, 77–8, 83, S. Treggiari, *CW* 64 (1971), 197. On the word *scortum* see further below, pp. 197 f.
40. Aul. Gell. 4. 14.
41. Hymnis: frs. 888–9 Marx (= 887–8 Warmington), 894 (= 889), 940–1 (= 896), 1115–16 (= 1166–7), 1193 (= 1168), also possibly 818–19 (= 890–1), and 810 (= 964), and others (cf. C. Cichorius, *Untersuchungen zu Lucilius* (Zürich/Berlin, 1964), 167–71, 176 f.). Collyra: fr. 517 Marx (see after 622 Warmington), Cichorius, 93 f.
42. Plut. *Sulla*, 1. 2, 2. 3, 36. 1.
43. Plut. *Sulla*, 2. 4.
44. Cic. *Verr.* 1. 104, 135 ff., 5. 34, 38.
45. Cic. *Verr.* 3. 78, 5. 31.
46. Plut. *Pompey*, 2. 3–4.

47. Plut. *Antony*, 9. 3–5, Cic. *Att.* 10. 10. 5, 15. 22.
48. *Fam.* 9. 26.
49. Verg. *Ecl.* 10, Serv. on *Ecl.* 10. 1 and 10. 46, Kroll 45, *RE*, 'Kytheris' (xii, 218).
50. Above, p. 1. Horace seems to suggest at *Sat.* 1. 2. 58 that a prostitute, though not a courtesan, was hazardous for one's reputation (cf. above, n. 39). Later in the satire he supports the claims of the prostitute (*togata*): line 82.
51. Cf. Ter. *Adelph.* 32–3, 61–2, 102.
52. Cic. *Cael.* 28.
53. Cf. e.g. Cic. *Tusc.* 4. 72 ff. and Hor. *Sat.* 1. 2. 48 (next note); above, p. 71.
54. Lucr. 4. 1121 ff. Hor. *Sat.* 1. 2. 47–9 cuts at Sallustius, romantic (insane) lover of *libertinae*; and the main body of the satire, on adulterers, is directed more particularly at their insane romanticism.
55. Cic. *Att.* 10. 10. 5, *hic* (sc. *Antonius*) *tamen Cytherida secum lectica aperta portat, alteram uxorem.*
56. Suet. *Div. Iul.* 50.
57. Sall. *Cat.* 25. It was respectable for a lady to have accomplishments of certain types and in moderation: note the interesting description of Cornelia, wife of Pompey, at Plut. *Pomp.* 55, and cf. Pomeroy, 171.
58. Hor. *Sat.* 1. 2. 95 and Porphyrio ad loc.
59. Cic. *Att.* 1. 16. 5, 1. 18. 3, Val. Max. 9. 1. 7.
60. Val. Max. 9. 1. 8.
61. See e.g. Cic. *Fam.* 5. 2. 6.
62. Cic. *Cael.* 35–6, 38, etc.
63. Schol. Bob. Cic. *Sest.* 116.
64. Cael. *ap.* Quint. 8. 6. 53, *in triclinio coam, in cubiculo nolam* (*Coam, Nolanam?*).
65. Cael. loc. cit., *quadrantariam Clytemestram.*
66. Plut. *Cic.* 29. 4.
67. Cic. *Cael.* 62. See Austin ad loc.
68. Cic. *Cael.* 32. In context the insult is masked in an ambiguity hard to reproduce in English: *ea quam omnes semper amicam omnium potius quam cuiusquam inimicam putauerunt.*
69. Cic. *Cael.* 38.
70. Cic. *Har. Resp.* 38, *Cael.* 49. Clodia's eyes and/or her alleged incestuous relationship with her brother are what inspire Cicero's nickname for her, 'ox-eyed', *boopis* (the Homeric epithet of Zeus' wife and sister Hera): Cic. *Att.* 2. 9. 1, 12. 2, 14. 1, 22. 5, 23. 3.
71. For these identifications see conveniently K. Quinn, *Catullus, The Poems* (2nd edn, London, 1973), xv–xx. T. P. Wiseman, *Catullan Questions* (Leicester, 1969), 50–60 puts the case against too facile an identification of Lesbia with Clodia Metelli (as opposed to one of her sisters), but the exercise is salutary rather than finally convincing. On p. 56 he points out that the Caelius of Catullus, poem 100 is hardly likely to be M. Caelius Rufus; but this does not determine the fate of the Caelius of 58, nor of the Rufus of 69 and 77.
72. Line 4 of the *domum seruauit lanam fecit* epitaph (probably from the Gracchan period; for a Claudia) reads *suom mareitum corde dilexit suo*; cf. too R. Lattimore, *Themes in Greek and Latin Epitaphs* (Urbana, 1942), 277–8. Interesting, but perhaps not too significant for our question, are the

elegiac notes struck by Cicero in letters to his wife when he was agonizing in exile: *ego uero te quam primum, mea uita, cupio uidere et in tuo complexu emori (Fam.* 14. 4. 1), *mea lux, meum desiderium (Fam.* 14. 2. 2); cf. too *Fam.* 14. 3. 5. A notable example of an apparently passionate, indeed 'whole love' marriage, is Pompey's to Julia; cf. Plut. *Pompey* 48. 5 and 53; but significantly it was regarded as something extraordinary: 'the girl's love of her husband *(to philandron)* was notorious *(periboeton)*.'

73. For the marriage's extraordinary felicity, see e.g. 27-9 (Wistrand). Turia's *fides* and *pietas* to her husband are celebrated (26, II. 2, 43) and her passing arouses *dolor, maeror, luctus, metus,* and *desiderium*(II. 54, 63, 66); but nothing nearer love or passion is mentioned. Incidentally, the childless Turia's selfless offer (II. 31 ff.) to divorce her husband so that he could have children by another wife—she herself would find a suitable wife for him and henceforth be as a sister and mother-in-law—though it was declined, shows us that we are in a different world.

Chapter II

1. On the biography of Catullus see further Fordyce, ix ff.
2. Catull. 68. 70, 160.
3. Otto Weinreich, *Die Distichen des Catull* (Tübingen, 1926), 49 ff. investigates the precedents both for what Catullus says in poem 85 and the way he says it.
4. Important modern works concerned with the aristocratic social code and its terminology are: P. A. Brunt, *'Amicitia* in the Roman Republic', *PCPhS* n.s. 11 (1965), 1-20, esp. 1-8; M. Gelzer, *Die Nobilität der römischen Republik* (Leipzig/Berlin, 1912), which is usefully indexed; K. Meister, 'Die Freundschaft bei den Griechen und Römern', *Gymnasium* 57 (1950), 3-8 = *Römische Wertbegriffe,* ed. H. Oppermann (Darmstadt, 1967), 323-9. Cicero's letters to P. Lentulus Spinther *(Fam.* 1. 1-9) and his letter to Curio *(Fam.* 2. 6) all offer convenient illustrations. Note too, very interestingly, Catullus' poems 30 and 73 (cf. too 77 and 91) which discuss the faithfulness of a friend in the terminology, and confirm and illustrate the provenance of the Lesbia epigrams' diction. R. Reitzenstein, 15-35 is the best account to date of the *amicitia* terminology in Catullus' Lesbia epigrams.

   Further refs. on some of the terminology: *amicitia:* F. Schulz, *Principles of Roman Law* (Oxford, 1936), 233 ff., Cic. *Amic.* 19-20, 26-7 and *passim, Inv.* 2. 166-7, *Fam.* 3. 10, esp. sect. 9, etc. Both [Q.Cic.] *Commentariolum Petitionis* 16-25 and Cic. *Att.* 1. 18 usefully distinguish genuine from cynical-political *amicitia* (on which see below). *pietas:* defined well by Fordyce on Catull. 76. 2; Cic. *Fam.* 1. 9. 1, *Inv.* 2. 161, Planc. ap. Cic. *Fam.* 10. 24. 1, etc; J. Liegle, 'Pietas', *Zeitschrift für Numismatik* 42 (1932), 59-100 = *Röm. Wertbegriffe* (above), 229-73. *beneuolentia, bene uelle:* Cic. *Fam.* 7. 14. 2, 13. 60. 1-2, *Amic.* 19, 26, etc. *gratia:* Gelzer, 61 f.; Cic. *Inv.* 2. 161, *Quinct.* 1, *Mur.* 10, *Brut.* 97, *Scaur.* 31, *Quint. Fratr.* 2. 3. 6, 2. 14. 2, *Fam.* 3. 10. 9, *Att.* 1. 1. 4, etc. *fides:* Schulz, 223 ff., E. Fraenkel, 'Zur Geschichte des Wortes *fides', RhM* 71 (1916), 187-99 = *Kleine Beiträge* i, 15-26; R. Heinze, *'fides', Hermes* 64 (1929), 140-66. *officium:* Gelzer,

53 f.; Cic. *Fam.* 6. 6. 1, 7. 31. 1, Serv. Sulp. *ap.* Cic. *Fam.* 4. 12. 3, Cic. *de Orat.* 3. 7, etc.

5. Cf. Owen Barfield, *Poetic Diction* (2nd ed London, 1952), 136.
6. Ross, *Style and Tradition*, 80-95.
7. Cf. J. Hellegouarc'h, *Le Vocabulaire latin des relations et des partis politiques sous la République* (Paris, 1963), and the bibliography in note 4 above.
8. Stressed by Gelzer, op. cit., 53 f.
9. Cf. Catull. 73. 3 and n. 4 above.
10. P. A. Brunt, op. cit., 6.
11. *Fam.* 5. 8. 5.
12. *Trist.* 1. 8. 15 f. and 27.
13. Ov. *Her.* 5. 101, Verg. *Aen.* 4. 520, Hor. *Odes* 3. 24. 23, etc.
14. See Ross, *Style and Tradition*, 76 ff.
15. It is noticeable and interesting that passion, which Catullus mentions in his bitter analyses of ambivalence (72, 75), is missing from this description. One can sense several reasons for this; but we may note that Catullus is generally (and naturally) reticent on physical matters *when he is in romantic mood*: pp. 262-3.
16. On the question of passion see the previous note.
17. Cf. too the simile at 68. 119 ff. illustrating Laodamia's love—and, ultimately, Catullus'. Cf. n. 30 below.
18. Cic. *Fam.* 1. 9. 20, *Att.* 10. 8B. 1, Sen. *Ben.* 6. 8. 3, Hellegouarc'h, op. cit., 166.
19. This traditional attitude is neatly reflected in Ov. *Met.* 1. 481: *saepe pater dixit: 'generum mihi, filia, debes'*, 659.
20. In connection with Catullus' 'family' simile, we should note the line of imagery going back to Andromache's words in the *Iliad* (6. 429-30):

> Hektor, thus you are father to me, and my honoured mother,
> You are my brother, and you it is who are my young husband.
> (trans. R. Lattimore)

See Leaf ad. loc. for the relevant references. But Andromache herself speaks practically rather than spiritually ('since I have no father, no honoured mother'), and this kind of utterance obviously comes quite naturally to defenceless women.

21. Cf. my *Catullus, Handbook* (Cambridge, 1975), 18-19.
22. op. cit., 19-20.
23. Contrast what happens in poem 109 (above, p. 35). In 72 and 75 Lesbia is addressed throughout, but without any real sense of drama (we recall the conventional interlocutor of epigram). The unexpectedness of the apostrophe in 87 gives it its effect.
24. This is not to say Catullus was incapable of achieving antithetical effect in hendecasyllables: cf. poem 49.
25. See the commentaries of (e.g.) Fordyce and Quinn on these points. *Iouis aestuosi* is simultaneously learned and funny. Catullus is referring to an originally Egyptian god (Ammon) who had a famous temple and oracle in the Libyan desert, and was identified with the Graeco-Roman Jupiter. *aestuosi* places him as the Libyan god—it can be understood as transferred from the locality to him (enallage); but it also raises the thought that, as an Olympian god stuck in the African desert, he must be very hot: literally 'sweltering'.

26. Cf. Tibull. 1. 6. 6: *nescio quem tacita callida nocte fouet.*
27. On the interpretation of *desiderio meo nitenti* see R. G. M. Nisbet, *PCPhS* n.s. 24 (1978), 92 f.
28. See my *Catullus, Handbook* (Cambridge, 1975), 30-3.
29. Fordyce aptly refers to Catull. 61. 31 but comes to a different conclusion on the sense of *dominae*. (The MS tradition actually offers *dominam*; for further discussion of this problematic line and, again, a different conclusion from mine see L. P. Wilkinson, *CR* n.s. 20 (1970), 290.)
30. Cf. C. W. Macleod's paper, *CQ* n.s. 24 (1974), 82-93. My only criticism of this helpful discussion is that the effect of the myth *as it unfolds* is neglected. Thus 'The passion of Laodamia corresponds not with Lesbia's but with Catullus'.' (Macleod.) True, but this must not obscure the fact that Catullus *says* that the correspondence is with Lesbia—and we must interpret accordingly.
31. The *Assyrius odor* typifies the festive preparations that would greet a bride.
32. Cicero's indulgent talk of men's *ludus* radiates such an attitude (above, pp. 1-2). So does the very frequent animal imagery used by the poets (Nisbet and Hubbard, ii, 78). Note the implications of the images used by boys *and* girls in Catullus' wedding poem, 62. 39-58—in spite of conventional talk of *par conubium* (cf. Kroll's commentary on 62. 56); note too lines 59 ff., though there the implications are perhaps more social than psychological.

Chapter III

1. For Propertius' biography see Prop. 1. 22, 4. 1. 120 ff., Camps, *Propertius Book I*, 5, Hubbard, vii.
2. Contrast recent views on Cynthia: Williams, *Tradition and Originality*, 529-35 (a summary at 535); L. Richardson, *Propertius, Elegies I-IV* (Univ. of Oklahoma Press, 1977), 5.
3. Some passages which illuminate Cynthia: 1. 2. 27 ff., 3. 41 f., 2. 1. 9 f., 3. 17 ff. (accomplishments); 2. 33B, 3, 10. 24 (lower sympotic pleasures); 2. 20 reveals in a favourable light the plaintiveness which 1. 3 reveals unfavourably; 1. 4. 17 f., 5. 8, etc. (temper); 2. 29. 27, 32. 3 ff., 33A, 4. 8 (superstition). Among many other interesting poems 2. 6 offers oddly specific circumstantial details.
4. Prop. 2. 7 is capable of various interpretations: see the commentaries, also Williams, *Tradition and Originality*, 531-4. I find Boucher very sensible (452). Griffin's comments on the status of Cynthia are exemplary (103); and see Syme, 201-3.
5. Cf. Cic. *Tusc.* 4. 75, Ov. *Rem.* 441 ff. Tibullus tried the cure but found it wanting: 1. 5. 39.
6. Cf. Shackleton Bailey ad loc.
7. The anonymous *Life* and the epigram on Tibullus' death which suggests the date of his demise are printed at the end of Lee's text (*Tibullus: Elegies*), and at the end of Postgate's Oxford Classical Text (2nd edn, 1915). Further biographical information may be seen in Lee's introduction, or. Smith, 30 ff. The suggestion that Tibullus was something of a dandy may be an inference from Tibull. 2. 3. 82.
8. On Messalla see the interesting discussion by G. Williams, *Change and Decline*

(University of California Press, 1978), 65–70; Syme, 116, 132–3. Note too Hor. *Odes* 3. 21, an illuminating piece. Messalla held the consulship with Augustus (then Octavian) in the year of the battle of Actium, 31 BC.

9. For the date of Propertius' first and second books and Tibullus' first book see Camps, *Propertius Book II*, 1, Enk, *Properti Liber Secundus. pars prior*, 34–46, Hubbard, 44, above pp. 120, 132.

10. Prop. 2. 5 seems to me clearly critical of Tibullus' idea of a desirable *rixa*: cf. Tibull. 1. 10. 53 ff. and note esp. Propertius' *rusticus haec* . . . (25). I have the impression, too, that Prop. 2. 19 indulges in a little fun at Tibullus' expense.

11. Poem 2. 5; see Smith's introduction (443 f.) and Syme, 118 (Syme dates Messalinus' priesthood to 21 or 20 BC). But some detect Tibullan planning in Book 2, e.g. Bright, 264–8.

Chapter IV

1. For Augustus' moral legislation (his law to curb adultery, the *Lex Iulia de adulteriis*, and his law to encourage marriage, the *Lex Iulia de maritandis ordinibus*, are those that particularly concern us) see *Cambridge Ancient History*, vol. x, 441 ff., P. A. Brunt, *Italian Manpower* (Oxford, 1971), 558 ff.; also Stroh, *Ovids Liebeskunst*.

2. Very helpful on this topic are Boucher's first chapter, Burck, Stroh, *Liebes-elegie*, 222 ff.

3. See 2. 2, above, pp. 96 ff. 2. 18B is an interesting poem. Aurora who loved the (explicitly) aged Tithonus is held up as an *exemplum* for Cynthia. But the *exemplum* encourages her to love (it questions why she does not love) the *youthful* Propertius. Propertius' own old age is merely an hypothesis: *quid mea si canis aetas candesceret aetas?* Here Propertius admits the full impli-cations of love surviving into age but at one remove, in myth (in the *romantic* world: cf. pp. 82 ff.). The admission is uncharacteristic—but not total. The poem is also uncharacteristic at the end. Bitterness makes Propertius advert brutally to Cynthia's coming old age (19) in Horatian fashion (pp. 204–209); he does this again in his bitter concluding poem: 3. 25. 11 ff. (cf. especially Horace, *Odes* 1. 25).

   Cf. too Prop. 2. 25. 9–10:

   > at me ab amore tuo deducet nulla senectus
   > siue ego Tithonus, siue ego Nestor ero.

   > But no old age will lead me from my love of you,
   > whether I shall be Tithonus or whether Nestor.

   Propertius refers to his possible old age but romanticizes it (puts it in myth-ical terms); and of course the main point of *senectus* is not to evoke love accommodating senility but love enduring through life—a fabulously long life. He is in fact making his usual sort of romantic declaration, but choosing an unfortunate or half-honest word to do so.

   3. 10. 17 shows a suppressed appreciation of Time's winged chariot: see *GR* 20 (1973), 43. The tenderness and sensitivity of this partial admission is in eloquent contrast to 3. 25. 11 ff.

4. If it is not *decens* to love in old age and to make 'pretty speeches with white

hair', it is difficult to justify 1. 1. 59 ff. and (even more) 1. 6. 85-6. It is evident in fact that Tibullus had—at least he expresses—quite strong Horatian sympathies on the topic of Age and Love, Time and Love. Horatian beliefs are implicit at 1. 2. 89 ff., 1. 5. 70, 1. 8. 47 f., 2. 1. 73 f. (cf. also Bright, 234-5, Geiger, 11) and explicitly uttered by Priapus at 1. 4. 27 ff. Tibullus' romantic aspiration does seem odd alongside these passages. It is of course not at all impossible that he should be inconsistent; or perhaps he means to distinguish more carefully than his language actually does between *acts* of love and affection-love. Or perhaps we have another and different spot of evidence (cf. pp. 186-189) that Tibullus' romanticism is not quite as earnest as may first appear: it may have its histrionic aspect.

5. Cf. poems 10, 28, 31, and 46.

6. It wasn't even profitable, as Catullus is not too romantic to point out: 10. 5 ff., 28. 7-10. Poems 46 and 31 capture Catullus' sense of relief and happiness at the ending of his provincial duty.

7. Cf. poem 95.

8. Note especially *Pro Sestio*, 136 ff.

9. When Catullus talks positively about a 'life of love' he uses neutral words (poem 5) or his own special positive vocabulary (109; above, pp. 35-7). When love torments him he can use conventional pejorative terms from a conventional point of view; he does not more or less willingly accept and emblazon 'disease' or 'madness' like Propertius or Tibullus (on this aspect of Propertius and Tibullus see further below): see poem 76. In this connection poem 51 is interesting. According to my reading of the poem, Catullus feels uncomfortable about the jealous feelings he describes in the first three stanzas—he feels uncomfortable about the effects of his romantic love—and in consequence reads a moralizing lesson to himself: 'you've got too much *otium* on your hands, Catullus', i.e. too much time to indulge in love (cf. Ov. *Rem. Am.* 139 ff., *otia si tollas, periere Cupidinis arcus* . . .). The choice of the word *otium* here, the assumption it implies that love is properly a marginal, leisure occupation, shows Catullus thinking again in conventionally moral terms. Catullus' attitude to a 'life of love' is natural, fluid, never tendentious.

10. Cf. Allen esp. sect. II, F. Cairns, *CQ* n.s. 24 (1974), 102-7. For condemnations of romantic love from a more or less conventional viewpoint cf. Lucr. 4. 1073 ff. and Cic. *Tusc.* 4. 68-76. Cf. also Plato, *Phaedrus* 231 C-D, *Symposium* 183A, etc. See pp. 93-5, where there is further discussion of Prop. 1. 1.

11. e.g. Prop. 2. 15. 41 ff. (below, p. 130), the delightful 2. 30B; Tibull. 2. 4.

12. Useful references on *militia amoris* in E. Spies, *Militat omnis amans* (Diss. Tübingen, 1930), Burck, *passim* esp. 177, Lilja (but she interprets them very oddly), 64-7. For Plautus' and Terence's use of the figure see G. E. Duckworth, *The Nature of Roman Comedy* (Princeton, 1952), 337 with refs. and bibliography, E. Fantham, *Comparative Studies in Republican Latin Imagery* (Toronto, 1972), 26-33 and 84.

13. It is interesting to observe that Apuleius uses *military* images for sex where the Greek author of *Lucius or the Ass* uses *wrestling* images (*Met.* 2. 17; *L. o. A*, 9, printed in Loeb edn of Lucian, vol. viii): we can gain insight here into the difference between Greek and Roman tastes.

14. Cicero's letters to Trebatius: *Fam.* 7. 6, 17, 18.

15. Cf. Tibull. 1. 3, 7. 9–12, 10. 11–13.
16. It seems likely to me that Cornelius Gallus encouraged the efflorescence of the *militia amoris* figure. He appears to have felt and expressed the rival claims of love and soldiering strongly—this is indicated by Verg. *Ecl.* 10 (note particularly the problematic lines 44 f.) and the famous Servian note on line 46. The *militia* figure could have provided him with some neat ironies and paradoxes.
17. Quoted p. 130. It may be in fact that these lines exploit *militia amoris*: Camps thinks we should read Fontein's *proelia* instead of *pocula* in line 48.
18. Shackleton Bailey, 75 well explains this line. He concludes: 'Translate then "But were I following my mistress' camp—real warfare that—then . . ." . . . The condition, it may be urged, is unwarranted since Propertius *is* already a soldier in this sense. True. He "contaminates" two ideas, one positive, "I follow my mistress' camp, the true camp for me", the other conditional, "If Caesar's camp were the camp of my mistress, then I should be a mighty soldier." The couplet is influenced by both but properly expresses neither.'
19. Cf. Camps, *Propertius Book II*, 92.
20. Cf. too 2. 5. 17, 8. 29, 9. 3 ff. and 17, 15. 27 f., 16. 22; also 1. 3 (p. 119).
21. Prop. 3. 20 which employs much *amicitia* vocabulary is from more than one point of view a special case (I do not think it concerns Cynthia). It is interesting that Cynthia uses *iniuria* (cf. above, p. 118) sarcastically at 1. 3. 35. *fides* is quite common in both poets but is too vague to suggest *amicitia* without supporting words; the same applies to an unqualified use of *amicus* or *amica*: Catullus 72. 3 (for example) shows how casual *amica* can be. In 2. 9 Propertius talks more in *amicitia* terms than in most poems.
22. See above, p. 71. Cf. too Tibull. 2. 5. 110, *et faueo morbo, quin iuuat ipse dolor* (below, p. 185).
23. I have discussed *seruitium amoris* at length in *CQ* n.s. 29 (1979), 117 ff. and I allow myself to be brief in the text—on admittedly contentious topics. I still do not believe that *seruitium amoris* had very significant currency before Propertius, but a couple of qualifications need making (the article in *CQ* omits a few Greek references (see Stroh, *Liebeselegie*, 218 ff.) but my argument easily accommodates them). I omitted to mention that Lucilius (730 M) seems to have called one of his mistresses *domina*; and the new fragment of Cornelius Gallus (see *JRS* 69, 1979) shows that Gallus referred to Lycoris thus. This makes it more likely that part of the efflorescence of the 'figure' is due to Gallus. But Gallus may have had no more developed a system of *seruitium* than Catullus, who refers to Lesbia as *era*; and for the reasons mentioned in my paper I still think that the efflorescence is largely to be put down to Propertius.
24. I explain my reasons for being chary of calling *seruitium amoris* a figure, loc. cit. I also further discuss the difference between Propertius and Tibullus in their use of *seruitium*.
25. On the interpretation of Prop. 1. 1. 27–8 see *CQ* n.s. 29 (1979), 129.
26. Cf. Prop. 2. 13. 36, Tibull. 2. 3. 5 f. and the concluding couplet; also 2. 4. Note how when Propertius 'renounces' romantic love in 2. 23 *seruitium* occurs to him as, clearly, its most significant manifestation.

Chapter V

1. Citing comparisons and *exempla* is one of the constant tactics of ancient rhetoric: see Hubbard, 23, Nisbet and Hubbard, i, 144 and ii, 69. But Propertius' exploitation of myth lifts him out of the rhetorical crowd.
2. Vergil, *Ecl.* 10. 50; see R. G. G. Coleman ad loc.
3. D. Strong, *Roman Art* (Penguin Books, 1976), 32.
4. Texts are conveniently collected in O. Vessberg, *Studien zur Kuntsgeschichte der römischen Republik* (Lund and Leipzig, 1941), 46 ff.
5. C. M. Dawson, *Romano-Campanian Mythological Landscape Painting* (Yale Classical Studies ix, 1944) has a catalogue of subjects in ch. III.
6. See Hubbard, 164 ff. and (very usefully) 173, Boucher, 41 ff., Keyssner, *passim*.
7. Cf. Rothstein ad loc., Hubbard, 164, Boucher, 53 f., Keyssner, 268-76. A *sleeping* Andromeda is not precisely paralleled in the visual arts but is very plausible.
8. Maiuri, 81.
9. Idem, 117.
10. Idem, 86.
11. Allen, 130.
12. Cf. e.g. Cicero's attitude to myth evident at *De Orat.* 2. 194, *Tusc.* 1. 5. 10, 21. 48. (Vergilian myth is an exception to my comments hereabouts; but Vergilian myth is—we could say—the creation of Vergil.)
13. With some hesitation I have adopted Francis Cairns's interpretation of this line (*Further Adventures of a Locked-out Lover: Propertius 2. 17* (Inaugural Lecture Series, Liverpool, 1975), 12-13). The conventional way to translate it would be 'how Sisyphus rolls the intractable weight of his stone up the whole hill'. I ought to say that I do not accept Cairns's account of 2. 17 as a whole as a *paraclausithyron* (or *komos*, as Cairns prefers).
14. Cf. Ov. *Rem.* 247, 533, 632 and my edition of *Ciris* (Cambridge, 1978), 168.
15. See Housman, *JPh* 16 (1888), 19-22 = *The Classical Papers*, 42-4. Housman objected that *modo* cannot mean 'sometimes' without an answering *modo* or equivalent, and working on the basis of the closely analogous Ov. *Ars*, 2. 185-92 supplied *multaque desertis fleuerat arboribus/et modo submissa casses ceruice ferebat*. He also read *fides* for *preces* in 16 (and *comminus ille* for *ille uidere* in 12). Keeping *preces* I assume a slightly different supplement. F. Cairns among many others has argued against Housman's lacuna: *CQ* 24 (1974), 94 ff.
16. It seems to me almost certain that Gallus *compared* not *contrasted* himself with Milanion, and in a prominent or programmatic poem: cf. (though neither comes to this exact conclusion) F. Skutsch, *Aus Vergils Fruhzeit* (Leipzig, 1901), 15-16 and Ross, *Gallus*, 89-91.
17. If the fears are resumed, it is in lines 29-32 which Camps detaches from the poem.
18. Cf. Hyg. *Fab.* 103, 251, Lucian, *Dial. Mort.* 23, *RE* 23. 1. 935.
19. On *dum licet* see very usefully Nisbet and Hubbard, ii, 174 f.
20. Gallus' lines at Verg. *Ecl.* 10. 50-1 must have their implications. Propertius defends his poetry *vis à vis* epic (to Ponticus in 1. 7 and 9) just as he defends his erotic *otium vis à vis* honourable action (to Tullus in 1. 1, 6, and 14).

This suggests a more considered and self-conscious self-assessment than does Catullus' very personal abuse of Volusius—or his personal praise of Cinna. Catullus was a genuine student of Callimachus and he is sometimes genuinely a Callimachean poet (and he is obviously influenced by Callimachean literary polemic); but his literary interests are in fact catholic, and he is not concerned to propound or maintain one literary role. To accept that Propertius possessed a high degree of literary self-awareness does *not* mean we have to take his subsequent protestations of Callimacheanism seriously: see above p. 147.

21.　*pateris* confirms its power here. The parallels for a diminished sense cited by Enk are in any case not persuasive.

22.　Cf. R. I. V. Hodge and R. A. Buttimore, *The 'Monobiblios' (sic) of Propertius* (Cambridge, 1977), 78.

23.　Hodge and Buttimore, op. cit., 77.

24.　*lapillus* commonly means a gem or ornamental stone; *pingo* is used most naturally of artificial decoration; even *color* suggests art, though it is commonly used in poetry of flowers (Fordyce on Catullus, 64. 90). The conceit has philosophical background: cf. K. Deichgräber, 'Natura varie ludens', *Akad. d. Wiss. u. Lit. im Mainz, Abh. der geist.- und s.z. Klasse* (1954), 3 and the *Nachtrag* (1965), 4, 205–7.

25.　*persuadent* is regarded as corrupt by most editors. I think the fact that Propertius has a covert motive behind the ostensible purpose of the *exempla* explains the curious construction (no following dative supplied).

26.　For *colo* thus cf. Ter. *Haut.* 389, *Oxford Latin Dictionary*, s.v. 7.

27.　On the translation of *uerba benigna* I follow Hubbard, 28 n. 2; the commentators do not agree, thinking the words in question are Cynthia's.

28.　Cf. 1. 7. 13 f., 8. 40, 9. 5 ff., 3. 3. 49 f; Stroh, *Liebeselegie, passim*.

29.　The event that provides the basis for 1. 10 also provides the basis for 1. 13.

30.　I have discussed this poem in full at *PC Ph S* n.s. 16 (1970), 60–78.

31.　Cf. above, p. 7 and Tibull. 1. 3. 83 ff.

32.　Cf. above, pp. 34 and pp. 79–80.

33.　Note particularly *languidus* (2 and 38), *desertus* (2 and 43), *fessus* (5 and 42), *qualis . . . talis* (1 ff. and 39 f.). See Lyne, art. cit., 76–7.

34.　Lyne, art cit. 78.

35.　Cf. above, p. 139.

36.　Cf. p. 183.

37.　Cf. O. Skutsch, *HSCP* 79 (1975), 229–33.

38.　Cf. above, p. 62, and note that the striking sentiment of line 26 echoes the statement made to Cynthia in 1. 11. 26. Line 21 suggests, I think, not that they have only known each other for six or seven months but that that is the period since the publication of the *monobiblos*: cf. 2. 24. 1–2.

39.　*grauis* is a word of solemn import to the people who invented *grauitas*. *fleo* is higher diction for 'weep', *ploro* the colloquial word.

40.　See note 38.

41.　i.e. 'very often': one of Propertius' many examples of *meiosis* (*litotes*): 1. 4. 18, 5. 8, 7. 21, 13. 26, 2. 26. 58.

42.　This I take to be the sense (cf. Camps ad loc.). Shackleton Bailey ad loc. defends what the Latin appears to say ('you alone').

43.　*nunc curae* is a (by no means certain) conjecture for the transmitted *naturae*: cf. Shackleton Bailey ad loc.

44. I am dogmatically stating my interpretation of a much disputed poem. This, for example, is another view of 11–30: Propertius 'relives a part of [the night before] dramatically in imagination, as if in the present' (Camps).
45. Hubbard, 47 ff.
46. Hubbard, 44; cf. above, p. 64.
47. See Hubbard, 47–64 for Tibullus' influence on Propertius. In pp. 58–64 she discusses Prop. 2. 16 which she sees as influenced by and challenging Tibullus.
48. The interpretation of line 3 is difficult; see conveniently Camps ad loc.
49. Torches were shaken to keep alight. The line has a pleasant ambiguity. Love and his torches perform the function of a kind of divine link-boy; but Love generally has torches and their fanning has its own function (inflaming love).
50. Cf. Tibullus 1. 2. 25 ff. with Smith ad loc. and Nisbet and Hubbard, i, 263.
51. Cf. Prop. 1. 5. 21, Ov. *Ars* 1. 729 *palleat omnis amans.*
52. Prop. 3. 1. 14; 2. 1. 39 ff. *sed neque . . . intonet* angusto pectore *Callimachus, nec mea conueniunt duro praecordia uersu . . . nos contra* angusto *uersantes proelia* lecto: *qua pote quisque, in ea conterat arte diem.*
53. I have discussed 3. 10 at some length in *GR* 20 (1973), 39–45.
54. Ov. *Am.* 1. 6. 47.
55. Cf. Tibull. 1. 8 and see W. Abel, *Die Anredeformen bei den römischen Elegikern* (Diss. Berlin, 1930), esp. pp. 37, 40–1, 50, 98. For another type of mime technique in Propertius see above, p. 132.
56. See J. Griffin, *JRS* 77 (1977), 17–18.
57. I say this *pace* C. W. Macleod, *CQ* n.s. 24 (1974), 92–3.
58. My text prints some but not all of the emendations supported by G. P. Goold in 'Noctes Propertianae', *HSCP* 71 (1966), 59 ff.
59. Hubbard, 152–3.
60. Cf. 1. 7. 23 f., 1. 17. esp. 11 f. and 19 ff., 2. 1. 47 and 71 ff., 2. 13B, 2. 26. 43 f., 3. 16.
61. 1. 14. 14, 2. 15. 36, 2. 24. 33–52, a most striking passage which assumes first of all (Propertius' usual assumption) that he will die first (33 ff.) but envisages the possibility of her going first and his faithfulness to her; but he hopes it will be the other way round (50–2); cf. too 2. 26. 43 f.
62. Compare Camps's and Rothstein's glosses with my discussion. Hubbard makes my point about Propertius' diction with admirable succinctness. Her index has a heading '"bones" means bones'. Incidental examples of Propertius' meaning what he says are 1. 2. 4 *uendere* (he does in the final count mean 'sell'), and 1. 4. 4 *seruitio*: he indeed means 'slavery'.
63. See Hubbard, 35 f. An important text for Propertian views on death is 2. 13. 25 ff. But the later poem 4. 7 suggests a rather different view: one could indeed see it as something of a recantation.
64. For Propertius' interest in Cynthia's attention to his funeral see 1. 17. 19 ff., 2. 13. 27 ff., 3. 16. 21 ff.
65. See Pound's essay 'How to Read' (logopoeia: 'the dance of the intellect among words') reprinted in *Literary Essays of Ezra Pound*, ed. T. S. Eliot (Faber, London, 1954); M. W. Edwards, *TAPA* 92 (1961), 128–44; M. S. Silk, *Interaction in Poetic Imagery* (Cambridge, 1974), 150 ff.
66. See p. 188 with bibliography.
67. For this pattern cf. Williams, *Tradition and Originality*, 727 f. and Ross, *Gallus*, 69 n. 2 and 156.
68. Cf. Ross, *Gallus*, 54 ff.

69. Cf. Stroh, *Liebeselegie*, 18 ff., also 102 ff.
70. Modern critics refer to this use of Callimachus as *recusatio*: see conveniently Nisbet and Hubbard, i, 82.
71. See p. 202.
72. James Boswell, *The Life of Samuel Johnson*, A.D. 1773, Aetat. 64 (Everyman's Library Edition 1906, vol. ii, 487-8).

Chapter VI

1. As well as those mentioned in the text, note 1. 8. 35-8 with Lee's note (it alludes to the myth of Venus and Adonis).
2. D. P. Fowler suggests to me that the reading should be *hoc* (referring to *exiguum pecus*): we expect Tibullus to purify his flock as well as his shepherd at the *Palilia*. This seems to me very possible. (Fowler now finds that *hoc* was suggested by Wölfflin, *Arch. Lat. Lex.* 14 (1906), 516.)
3. These subjunctive lines (15-18) interrupt the sequence of indicatives which starts in 11 and illustrates Tibullus' rural piety. They are tricky to explain. Either they are virtually parenthetical and Tibullus is slipping rather vaguely into hypothetical subjunctives (which is awkward in the vicinity of jussive or optative subjunctives), to muse about details of his coming retirement ('For you Ceres there would be . . .'); or they are displaced (see the apparatus criticus of the Oxford Classical Text or other full critical editions); or they contain corruptions (Lambinus suggested *fit* for *sit* in 15, and *donatur* for *ponatur* in 17; I should prefer *ornatur*: cf. 2. 1. 54).
4. The quotations are from Elder, 65 ff.; contrast Lee, *Tibullus: Elegies*, 17-18.
5. Smith, 32.
6. Plutarch, *Life of Pompey*, 48. 5; cf. too 30. 6. We may note that it was *in the company of a beloved wife* that Pompey liked to enjoy the country: cf. p. 158 and note 14.
7. Cf. 1. 3. 33 ff.; the same sort of situation obtains as in 1. 10.
8. Cf. too 1. 3. 33-4; consider also 2. 1 and 2. 5. 84 ff. which seem to reflect Tibullan experience.
9. 1. 3 and 7 offer insight into this side of Tibullus' life. The *Vita* also refers to Tibullus' *militia*; and see above, p. 63.
10. Cf. R. O. A. M. Lyne in *Quality and Pleasure in Latin Poetry*, ed. T. Woodman and D. West (Cambridge, 1974), 47-9.
11. See Lee, *Otium*, 107.
12. Vischer, 144.
13. For parallels see Smith ad loc.
14. Tibullus is not therefore likely to be as lucky as Pompey sometimes was: cf. note 6.
15. On the biographical details see conveniently Lee, *Tibullus: Elegies*, 14-15; another thought, Syme, 203.
16. On the rights of *libertinae* to marry citizens before and after Augustus' legislation see *Cambridge Ancient History*, x, 448-9; S. Treggiari, *CW* 64 (1971), 198.
17. Hor. *Satires*, 1. 2. 48 and above, pp. 9 ff.
18. Lee, *Tibullus: Elegies*, 15. With some mischievousness I am quoting this out of context. In fact Lee's comment has validity and can be quoted in certain contexts without irony: see further below.

19. Contrast Bright, 202.
20. Cf. Lee, *Tibullus: Elegies*, 15 ff. and 19–21.
21. The name is servile. One of Augustus' freedmen was called Julius Marathus (Suetonius, *Aug.* 79. 2).
22. On this name (which is not attested outside poetry) see Nisbet and Hubbard, i, 373.
23. In line 21 *ure meum caput* probably refers to branding (a servile punishment). Dissen and Smith give an alternative interpretation of 43–4; and I certainly doubt that Tibullus' *munus* should be understood specifically as payment of money.
24. Kroll, *Kultur*, 43.
25. In 5th-century Athens social and other factors determined that homosexual love between man and *eromenos* should be the usual stage for romantic love; and abjectness and intensity are well paralleled: cf. e.g. Plato, *Symposium* 183A; K. J. Dover, *Greek Homosexuality* (Duckworth, London, 1978). The intensity of homosexual love in Verg. *Ecl.* 2 is an exception in the Roman context, and is capable of more than one explanation.
26. *Am.* 1. 7. 61.
27. This situation (beloved boy, *eromenos*, himself in love with a girl) is *not* an erotic *topos*: cf. Meleager, *Anth. Pal.* 12. 109, Williams, *Tradition*, 557.
28. His experimental poems (in particular) show the influence of Callimachus: see Bright, 229, 230, and 240, with bibliography.
29. Cf. above, p. 137.
30. Cf. Copley; J. C. Yardley, 'The Elegiac Paraclausithyron', *Eranos* 76 (1978), 19–34.
31. The text here is very doubtful. If *domini* is right, then *difficilis* must strictly be genitive. Lee seems to infer an ambiguity between nominative and genitive. It seems to me, however, that *difficilis* should unambiguously go with *ianua*. There is a useful bibliographical note on this problem in the F. W. Lenz and G. C. Galinsky edn of Tibullus (Leiden, 1971).
32. Cf. Smith on Tibull. 1. 2. 42, *RE* XII, 1942.
33. Cf. above, n. 18.
34. The use of *fuge* with an infinitive is highly poetical: see Smith ad loc. The effect cannot be reproduced in English, but Lee makes up for it with 'thee'.
35. This line is corrupt in the MSS and conjecturally restored.
36. With Tibullus 1. 6. 37 cf. e.g. Ov. *Am.* 1. 6. 45 ff., 3. 4.
37. Lee, *Tibullus: Elegies*, 9–10.
38. Cf. Ross, *Style and Tradition*, 132–7 and my edition of *Ciris* (Cambridge, 1978), 24, with bibliography.
39. On Catullus see Quinn, *Catullan Revolution*, Ross, *Style and Tradition*, 22 ff.; on Propertius, H. Tränkle, *Die Sprachkunst des Properz und die Tradition der lateinischen Dichtersprache* (Wiesbaden, 1960), 28–9, Hubbard, 22 f., 163; on Tibullus, Tränkle, 10, 28, 30, 58–9, 96 ff., 145 n.1, 150, 160.
40. Cf. e.g. Cic. *Cael.* 45–6, Longinus *On the Sublime*, 41 with D. A. Russell ad loc., Sen. *Epist.* 114.

Chapter VII

1. For details see Fraenkel, Ch. I.

Chapter VIII

1. As well as the references in the text see *RE* IV, 610 ff., VIII, 1347 ff., Daremberg–Saglio, iv. 2. 1579-81; also C. G. Starr, 'An Evening with the Flute-Girls', *La Parola del Passato* 183 (1978), 401-10; also A. Baudet, *Musiciens romains de l'Antiquité* (Montreal, 1973), 66-70. For *symposia* depicted on vases see J. Boardman, *Athenian Black Figure Vases* (London, 1974), 210 with the plates referred to there, and (esp.) J. Boardman, *Athenian Red Figure Vases: The Archaic Age* (London, 1975), 218-19 plus plates ('The symposion drinking party receives its classic expression in Archaic red figure.'); more photographs in W. Zschietzschmann, *Hellas und Rom* (Tübingen, 1959), 260-7.

2. For outdoor settings see Boardman, *Athenian Red Figure Vases*, 218, and (in a Roman context) Nisbet and Hubbard, ii, 53; not even the *fête champêtre* settings of *Odes* 1. 17 is wholly implausible: cf. Griffin, 98-9.

3. e.g. a freedwoman of one of Isaeus' clients managed a house in the Peiraeus, keeping 'young girls' (*paidiskai*) i.e. prostitutes in it. More interestingly [Demosthenes] 59. 18-19 refers to a freedwoman Nicarete who had a keen eye for spotting good looks in children and a talent for bringing them up. For a time she had seven in tow and lived off them. In addition to educating them she referred to them as her daughters (i.e. implied they were free) to get a more cultivated market and fatter fees.

   Pimps renting out girls for *symposia* are of course rife in New Comedy.

4. Cf. Herter, 77-8. Lucian *Dial. Mer.* 6 may be typical enough. A coppersmith who had supported his wife and daughter well died. The wife sold the equipment and she and her daughter lived off that for a while. Then she eked out an existence by spinning and weaving. But when her daughter grew up she decided to exploit that asset. Part of her advice to her daughter is how she should conduct herself when she is taken along to a banquet. Interestingly she sets as the daughter's prime target to make her client fall in love with her.

5. Herter, 97, also 102; and see below.

6. Herter, *passim*, esp. 76, 81-2, 97, 102; Athen. *Deipn.* 13. 586.

7. A rather similar comment on *symposia* is uttered at Plat. *Prot.* 347 c-d.

8. Cf. Boardman, *Athenian Red Figure* (above, n. 1), 219-20.

9. Cf. J. Henderson, *The Maculate Muse* (Yale University Press, 1975), 81 and 183.

10. On *sambucistriae* see too Herter, 97.

11. Karl Schefold, *Die Wände Pompejis* (Berlin, 1957), i, 3, 18 = Museo Nazionale Napoli Inv. 9015 = P. Herrmann-F. Bruckmann, *Denkmäler der Malerei der Altertums* (Munich, 1906 ff.), ii, 20 and 25 and plate 210; Schefold, ix, 1. 22z (in the 'House of Epidus Sabinus') described by R. Schöne (in Italian) in *Bulletino dell' Istituto di Correspondenza Archeologica* (1867), 85 and by W. Helbig (in German) in *Wandgemälde . . . Campaniens* (Leipzig, 1868), no. 1447 (no reproduction that I can find); A. Maiuri, *La Villa dei Misteri* (Rome, 1931), 206-7 and plate 89. And see Schefold's index under 'Gelage'.

12. See A. C. Brown, *Catalogue of Italian Terra-Sigillata in the Ashmolean Museum* (Oxford, 1968), nos. 1, 2, 62 (2 and 62 are moulds designed for mass production), plates I, II, III, IV, XV, XVI, XIX. These and other similar pieces can be seen in the Leeds Room of the Ashmolean Museum, Oxford.

13. Some incidental references: (a) Cicero refers to an obviously *risqué* party actually as a συμπόσιον (*Att.* 2. 12. 2); the same occasion is referred to elsewhere as a *conuiuium delicatum* (*Att.* 2. 14. 1). (b) Horace in the 30s BC satirically invokes the 'college of *ambubaiae*' (*Sat.* 1. 2. 1): these are apparently Syrian flute-girls-*cum-hetaerae* (so we infer from Porphyrio and etymology), a type still favoured by Nero (Suet. *Ner.* 27). (c) Suggestive is a story like this: L. Torquatus called the somewhat histrionic orator Hortensius a 'female pantomimist' and addressed him as Dionysia, 'the name of a most notorious little dancing-girl' (*gesticularia, notissima saltatricula*): Aul. Gell. 1. 5. 2–3.

14. Macrobius, *Saturnalia*, 3. 15. 14–7, quoting a 2nd-century BC source on the scandalous behaviour of *iudices* (very amusing); Cic. *Sen.* 42, on the behaviour of L. Quinctius Flamininus at a *conuiuium*, with which cf. Liv. 39. 43. 2–3 (Valerius Antias' version) and Liv. 39. 42. 7–12 (Livy's own version); Cic. *Phil.* 2. 105 on one of Antony's revels.

15. See note 13.

16. As the passages cited in note 14 demonstrate. Cf. too the elder Cato in Gell. 10. 13. 2 (a tantalizing snippet), Sall. *Cat.* 7. 4, [Sall.] *Epist. ad Caes.* 1. 4. 4, Nep. *Dion.* 4. 4, Liv. 23. 18. 12, 45. 2.

    scortum is often misrepresented: it is frequently suggested that the word denotes the lowest of prostitutes (K. F. Smith on [Tibull.] 4. 10. 3, G. Williams, *Tradition and Originality*, 529). Nisbet–Hubbard, ii, 177 are more accurate.

17. Cf. Griffin, 95, M. L. Gordon, 'The Nationality of Slaves under the Early Roman Empire', *JRS* 14 (1924), 93–111 = *Slavery in Classical Antiquity*, ed. M. I. Finley (Cambridge, 1960), 171–89; and cf. n. 39 above, p. 289.

18. Cf. Griffin, 102.

19. Glycera: *CIL*, VI (City of Rome) 948, 3428, 4776, 4806, 4873, 6707, 7085, 7388, etc., etc.

20. Lalage: *CIL*, VI 3940 and others: see *CIL*, VI, index.

21. Damalis: see *TLL*, *onomasticon* s. nom., and index to *CIL*, VI.

22. See TLL, *onomasticon* s. nom., and index to *CIL*, VI. Note esp. the following: *CIL*, VI 21418, a Chloe who is *liberta Liuiae Augustae*, VI, 33099, *Chloe Ti. Caesaris puerorum ornatrix* (cf. Griffin, 105), and the *Chloe delicium* at XI (Placentia) 1228 and 6176 (Suasa).

23. *CIL*, X (Capua) 4022, *hic sita est Asteria infelicissima sponso tradita puella quae uixit annis XXVIIII* . . . The name is not found in Rome (*CIL*, VI) but many others with *aster* as root are.

24. *CIL*, VI 5239, *Galatea Ti. Claudi Caesaris ancilla*, 9776, 13179, 21473a, etc.

25. Myrtale: see Nisbet and Hubbard on Hor. *Odes* 1. 33. 14, *CIL*, VI, index.

26. *CIL*, VI 9039, *Claudia Lyde*, 33453, *Pompeiae Magn. L. Lyde*, etc.

27. Tyndaris: *CIL*, VI 17997, 12082, etc., and see the sensible comment of Wickham on Hor. *Sat.* 1. 1. 100.

28. Nearchus is, Gyges and Lycidas are not, attested in *CIL*, VI (Rome).

29. Griffin, 100–2.

30. Note Panthus in Prop. 2. 21 (with Camps ad loc.), Demophoon in 2. 22 (cf. Ov. *Pont.* 4. 16. 20), Lynceus in 2. 34 (L. Varius Rufus? Cf. J.-P. Boucher, *REA* 60 (1958), 307 ff.) and Lycotas in 4. 3. See further Hubbard, 142, Sullivan, *Propertius*, 79 who brings into consideration Lygdamus and Cerinthus of the Tibullan corpus, J.-P. Boucher, *Latomus* 35 (1976), 504 ff.

31. Cf. A. W. Gomme and F. H. Sandbach, *Menander: A Commentary* (Oxford,

1973), 292 on the distinction between oboe-players and lyrists (the distinction probably migrated to Rome along with the artists): 'there may have been some difference of esteem, since the κιθάρα was, and the αὐλός was not, regarded as a suitable instrument for the free man to play . . . it is noteworthy that girls who are being trained to be *hetairai* but later turn out to be of citizen birth learn the stringed instrument . . . Phaedria in Ter. *Phormio* buys and frees a *citharistria* to make her his mistress.' Cf. too C. G. Starr (above, n. 1), 401-2.

Chapter IX

1. On the psychological place of women in love see above, p. 61.
2. *ciuis* connoted the sort of duty, responsibility, and fellowship that attached or should attach to *Roman* citizenship. (I am *not* implying that Alcaeus did not or might not use *polites* of himself: cf. e.g. 130. L.-P. 22.)
3. Cf., as well as the implications of lines 3-5 of 1. 32, *Odes* 1. 1. 34, 26. 11, 3. 30. 13 f. and esp. *Epist.* 1. 19. 29-33.
4. Cf. *Odes* 1. 1. 35, 1. 31. 2 with Nisbet and Hubbard ad loc., etc., *Odes* 3. 1. 3, Syndikus, ii. 14 f. This recalls the old Greek idea of the poet as *prophetes* of the Muses.
5. *Epist.* 2. 1. 124.
6. For Cicero cf. above, p. 2; see Nisbet and Hubbard, i. 122, also *Anth. Pal.* 5. 20 (Honestus), 5. 112 (Meleager). For the Elegists cf. pp. 65-7.
7. Cf. e.g. 1. 9. 15 ff., 2. 4. 22 ff., 11. 5 ff., 3. 14. 25 ff.
8. See Nisbet and Hubbard, i, 290 and 296 ('Vetula-Skoptik') with references, Syndikus, ii, 154.
9. Cf. *Carmina Epigraphica*, 1014 (*CIL*, VI 6314) a verse epitaph with the heading *Nothi librari a manu*.
10. Cf. C. M. Bowra, *Greek Lyric Poetry* (2nd edn., Oxford, 1961), 245.
11. Nisbet and Hubbard, i, 289.
12. e.g. Tibull. 1. 2 and 5 (see pp. 176-182), etc., Prop. 1. 5. 13-20, 1. 16; cf. note 30, above, p. 301.
13. Cf. his use of the 'excluded lover' and the 'slavery of love' topic at *Epode* 11 (see *CQ* n.s. 29 (1979), 121-2), of the 'inviolability of the lover' at *Odes* 1. 22, of *recusatio* at 2. 12 (cf. Nisbet and Hubbard ad loc. I take Horace here to be virtually parodying a Propertian excuse, in particular Prop. 2. 1; his use of *domina* (of his own mistress, *not* of Terentia) is very revealing); of the 'excluded lover' again at 3. 10, and 'slavery of love' at 2. 8. 17 f.
14. For the reading *Euro* see Nisbet and Hubbard ad loc., who, however, interpret *magis atque* differently ('rather than').
15. This Richard Heinze regarded as the *general* rule. See *Vom Geist der Römertums* (3rd edn., 1960), 172-89, or (conveniently) Quinn [next note], 84-5.
16. Kenneth Quinn, *Latin Explorations* (London, 1963), 90-9. I ought to mention that Quinn's and my reading of the poem is (as Quinn documents) heterodox (but cf. Commager, 300). It adds to my anxiety that Syndikus also believes the poem begins in triumphant abuse, then to exhibit a *Gefühlsumschwung*.
17. In between *Odes* 1-3 (24 or 23 BC) and *Odes* 4 come the *Carmen Saeculare*

(17 BC) and the various *Epistles*. *Odes* 4. 4, 5, and 14 must have been composed around 15 or 14 BC. Horace was born in 65 BC.

18. Cf. *Epist*. 1. 1. 4 ff., 7. 25 ff., 2. 2. 55-7, 141 f., 214-16, *Odes* 4. 11 as well as 1.

19. *Epist*. 1. 7. 28, 14. 33, *Odes* 4. 1. 4.

20. On Paullus Fabius Maximus see Syme, 135-55. It is conjectured that Horace had his eye on Paullus' coming marriage to Marcia, cousin of Augustus: see Syme, 145, Bradshaw, *CQ* n.s. 20 (1970), 142-53. But one should not overemphasize this aspect of the poem (Syme: 'The peculiar Ode may perhaps be interpreted as a frivolous valedictory to a man on the eve of abandoning celibacy—or a kind of disguised epithalamium.') Incidentally, Horace has cleverly adapted a *topos* here. It is quite frequent in epigram to wish away love on to someone else; but (since one doesn't want it oneself) it is not usually a very friendly wish; see Syndikus, ii, 288.

21. Similarly, the Epicurean Philodemus: *Anth. Pal.* 5. 112. This epigram makes a good comparison with *Odes* 4. 1: 'I loved, who hasn't? I revelled. Who is uninitiated in revels? But I was mad. From what? Was it not from a god? Good riddance to it. Already grey hair presses to replace the black, the harbinger of a wise time of life. When it was time to play, I played. Now when it is no longer the time, I shall apply myself to worthier reflection.'

22. Military imagery of love is a rarity in the *Odes* (humorously in 3. 26); for Elegy's use see above, pp. 71 ff.; for *regnum* cf. Tib. 1. 9. 80, 2. 3. 59, Prop. 2. 16. 28, 3. 10. 18.

23. Cf. the use of *seruitium* in *Epode* 11, in *Odes* 2. 8. 16 ff., and in 2. 12. 13 his parody *recusatio*; and cf. his use of *militia* in 1. 6. 17 which is also a humorously phrased *recusatio*. Cf. note 13.

24. Strong, serious ambivalence of course characterizes Catullus (e.g. poem 85, above, pp. 27 ff.) and Propertius (1. 4, 2. 8).

25. Tears: the Elegists, *passim*; faltering speech: cf. Prop. 1. 5. 14. The closest thing in Horace where Horace is serious is 1. 13, on which see Syndikus, i, 159 ff.

26. Cf. and contrast *Anth. Pal.* 12. 125 (Meleager: non-specific wish-fulfilment), Theocritus 30. 22.

27. Cf. *Odes* 1. 8, 3. 7. 25 ff., Nisbet and Hubbard, i, 108 f.

28. *Epodes* 14, 15, and *Odes* 1. 13 also reveal, in their different ways, a less typical Horace. But in the *Epodes* Horace was in another age and another genre.

29. Catull. 8, Prop. 2. 5.

30. Syndikus, ii, 319 ff., Commager, 302-6. *Anth. Pal.* 11. 41 (Philodemus) offers as interesting a comparison with *Odes* 4. 11 as 5. 112 does with 4. 1 (above, note 21).

31. Martial 3. 44, 45, and 50: he is a boring and importunate poet. On Ligurinus see too Syme, 144.

32. *Vita Horati* (printed at the beginning of Klingner's Teubner edn. (1950)): *eumque coegerit* (sc. *Augustus*) . . . *tribus carminum libris ex longo interuallo quartum addere*.

33. *Poetae Melici Graeci*, ed. D. Page (Oxford, 1962), 408, Nisbet and Hubbard, i, 273-4.

34. The text of the middle stanza of this poem has been disputed. For a balanced discussion see Nisbet and Hubbard ad loc. I have printed, interpreted, and, I hope, supported the MS readings.

35. See the excellent comments of Commager, 298.
36. See above, pp. 65-7. Special circumstances and a particular motive lead Tibullus to say something of the Horatian sort at 1. 5. 69 ff. But with this one should compare Hor. *Epod.* 15. 17 ff.: in similar circumstances to Tibullus' Horace makes the point with much more cool conviction. Propertius 2. 9. 1-2 should be noted: Propertius cites the 'Horatian' view in bitter scorn, proceeding indignantly to criticize it.
37. On the reading *deae* see Nisbet and Hubbard ad loc.
38. In its essence the image is well paralleled: see Nisbet and Hubbard, i, 72, A. La Penna, *Maia* 4 (1951), 202-5.
39. On *aureus* see Nisbet and Hubbard ad loc., and on *aureus/aurae* see Syndikus, i, 82.
40. West, 99 ff., Syndikus, i, 79 ff., Nisbet and Hubbard, i, 72 ff.
41. West, 102, with important references to P. Grimal, *Les jardins romains*; but see also Grimal's index s.v. *antrum*. Cf. the 'boxes' at Vauxhall in Thackeray's *Vanity Fair*.
42. Cf. Prop. 3. 2. 14, *Copa* (in the *Appendix Vergiliana*), 9-10.
43. West, 102.
44. To compare Catull. 8. 16 ff. is perhaps apt.
45. See Nisbet and Hubbard, i, 78.
46. Cf. B. Axelson, *Unpoetische Wörter* (Lund, 1945), 100. The prosaic tone to *uestimentum* is hard to reproduce in English. I don't think we feel 'clothes' as particularly unpoetic, but the Romans did feel *uestimentum* (as opposed to *amictus* and for that matter *uestis*) thus.
47. *Satires* 2. 3. 321 ff., *Epist.* 1. 20. 25.
48. Syndikus, ii, 112.
49. Cf. *Anth. Pal.* 5. 46 (Philodemus), 101 (anon.).
50. Cf. Prop. 2. 3, 2. 24A. Note the lengths to which Propertius goes in 3. 6 to give the impression of a mime without obeying the demands of mime viz. changes of speakers; cf. too Tibull. 1. 8: above, pp. 137, 175; cf. W. Abel, *Die Andredeformen bei den römischen Elegikern*, (diss. Berlin, 1930), 37, 40-2, 50.
51. We should note that Lydia uses the very prosaic word *obeo* for 'die' here (Axelson [note 46], 104 f.)—contrast her asseveration in 15. That is interesting and has various implications.
52. Cf. G. Williams, *Odes III*, ad loc.
53. Her weeping, her anxiety for and suspicion over the fidelity of an absent lover, *flere*, *fides*, *ignibus*, etc.; Prop. 1. 11, 12, Tib. 1. 6. 5 ff., etc., Syndikus, ii, 98.
54. Homer, *Iliad*, 18. 318-22 with Leaf ad loc., but see also H. Fränkel, *Die homerischen Gleichnisse* (2nd edn., Göttingen, 1977), 92-3.
55. On these lexical and grammatical points see Nisbet and Hubbard ad loc.
56. *Epode* 17. 23, *Odes* 3. 14. 25, *Epist.* 1. 7. 26, 20. 24.
57. Horace at his best. The allusion to 42 BC fulfils *three* functions. It reminds us that Horace's fighting days are well over, and therefore it is appropriate that he should only be a bystander, a *laudator* of Augustus' Spanish campaign. It tells us why love is not now so necessary in *otium* (the fervency of his youth is past). And it reminds us that he too had his hour (Philippi).
58. Nisbet and Hubbard, i, 134 ff., West, 58 ff., Syndikus, i, 130 ff.

59. See Nisbet and Hubbard, i. 142, West, 64, Syndikus, i. 133.
60. Syndikus, i, 131.

Chapter X

1. See Barsby, *Ovid (GR)*, 4-5, Du Quesnay, 3-4, Morgan, 5, Syme, ch. I.
2. See note 1, also Alan Cameron, *CQ* n.s. 18 (1968), 320-33.
3. On Ovid's knowledge of Propertius see Morgan, 5-6 and *passim*. It should not be forgotten that Ovid had access to Propertius' poetry through recitation as well as publication: *Trist.* 4. 10. 45 f.
4. A thumbnail sketch is drawn by Sullivan, *Two Problems*, 524, n. 5.
5. And against *uita uerecunda est, Musa iocosa mea* (*Trist.* 2. 354, where after all Ovid has a pressing case to make) we may set *Am.* 2. 1. 2, *ille ego nequitiae Naso poeta meae*. Cf. also *Trist.* 4. 10. 60, *nomine non uero dicta Corinna mihi*.
6. Stroh, *Ovids Liebeskunst*, 332-3.
7. Griffin, 103.
8. Stroh, *Ovids Liebeskunst*, 336-7.
9. Ibid., 333-4.
10. So I understand line 2 (the elucidation of which is avoided by Ovidian commentators). Cf. (though the situations are not precisely similar) Ov. *Her.* 7. 33-4.
11. Cf. Prop. 1. 1 (for love in spite of an absence of sexual response), Catull. 76, Prop. 3. 2. 9 ff., Tibull. 1. 4. 61 ff.
12. G. P. Goold, *HSCP* 69 (1965), 21 interprets *Am.* 1. 6. 23 differently: omit the comma after *esse, grato* means *si gratus mihi fueris* and *esse quod optas* means *liber fieri*.
13. For the *exclusus amator* and *paraclausithyron* see Copley and J. C. Yardley, 'The Elegiac Paraclausithyron', *Eranos* 76 (1978), 19-34. Both Propertius and Tibullus put a little distance between themselves and the song. In 1. 16 Propertius makes the door quote an anonymous song: I think we infer it to be his, but he does not tie himself to the situation. In 1. 2 Tibullus utters what resembles a *paraclausithyron* but not *in situ*; in 1. 5 what he utters is apparently *in situ* but does not much resemble a *paraclausithyron*. Besides these poems the two Elegists have frequent allusions or references to exclusion and plaint, but that is all.
14. This is argued by Copley. A splendid, classic *exclusus amator* (though not, it seems, one in the mood for song) was A. Hostilius Mancinus (above, p. 10). To me a most cogent piece of evidence for the existence of serenades and *exclusi amatores* is Lucretius' satire (4. 1177-9). Lucretius was powered by a desire to reform *life*. It is not in his interest to tilt at windmills, at mere literary *topoi*. His description may be in some measure a caricature, but it would need to have basic plausibility for the satire to be effective. Cf. too the implications of Apuleius, *Apol.* 75.
15. Cf. Ter. *Adelph.* 88 ff., 102, and (especially) *Eunuch.* 771 ff.; note too Hor. *Odes* 3. 26. 6-8.
16. Barsby, *Amores Book I*, gives helpful commentary.
17. Prop. 1. 5. 21-2, 2. 22. 21.
18. See Barsby, *Amores Book I*, ad loc.

19. See particularly Tibull. 1. 1. 73 f., 1. 10. 53 ff., etc., Prop. 2. 5. 20 ff. (above, p. 64), Prop. 2. 15. 17 ff. Cf. the thoughts of Lucian, *Dialogues of the Courtesans*, 8. 1 (299). On Tibullus and *rixa* see Geiger, 66, 74-5. Horace, as we might expect, disapproves of such unsophisticated, unpleasant behaviour: *Odes* 1. 13. 9-11, 17. 24 ff.; even a willingness to brawl *for* a girl is a thing of the past in *Odes* 3. 14. 25 ff.

20. Cf. above, pp. 78 ff.; for the beloved as goddess cf. G. Lieberg, *Puella divina, die Gestalt der göttlichen Geliebten bei Catull im Zusammenhang der antiken Dichtung* (Amsterdam, 1962); Catull. 68. 70 (above, p. 55); Shackleton Bailey on Prop. 1. 1. 33 (though he argues against such a sense at this point); Prop. 1. 5. 32, 1. 10. 25 f. with Hubbard, 26 n. 1, 2. 2 (above, p. 97); Tibull. 1. 5. 21 (there is an implication of divinity, I think, in *custos*: cf. *TLL*, 4. 1576. 72 ff.), Lee, *Tibullus: Elegies*, 21, Bright, 193. And Tibull. 1. 10. 59 f. is very interesting to compare.

21. The rarish story of Amymone (as well as Helen and Leda) is actually a Propertian *exemplum*: for the story see Prop. 2. 26. 45 ff. with Camps ad loc.

22. There are potentially humorous details in the myths: the 'two husbands' (2), the adulterer in feathers (3-4).

23. Prop. 2. 3. 30 f. shows the limit to which Propertius is prepared to go in this direction; cf. too Prop. 2. 28. 1 ff. with Hubbard, 47 ff.; and cf. and contrast 2. 26. 13-16.

24. We can also see here (Mrs P. G. Fowler's point) a parody of Propertian morbid fears: cf. Prop. 2. 6. 9-14.

25. The 'daughter of Schoeneus' for Atalanta, the 'Cretan woman' for Ariadne.

26. Cf. *Am.* 1. 9. 33 ff., 2. 6. 41 f., 2. 8. 11 ff. (which can be interestingly compared with Propertius' use of that myth at 2. 8. 29 ff., above, pp. 91 ff.: the contrasting attitudes of the two poets is neatly revealed). In similar vein but more blatantly humorous is 2. 4. 31 f. (on 2. 4, the manifesto of promiscuity, see below, p. 268):

> ut taceam de me, qui causa tangor ab omni,
>   illic Hippolytum pone, Priapus erit.

Forget me; anything stimulates me:
put Hippolytus in that situation, and he will be a Priapus.

Cf. too 2. 4. 41 ff.:

> seu pendent niuea pulli ceruice capilli,
>   Leda fuit nigra conspicienda coma;
> seu flauent, placuit croceis Aurora capillis:
>   omnibus historiis se meus aptat amor.

If dark locks hang on a snowy neck,
well, Leda's black hair was spectacular;
if there's blonde hair, blonde hair was Dawn's charm:
my love can fit itself to all the stories.

Here Ovid ties myths to small details—and (I think) satirizes Propertius' penchant for assimilating Cynthia to heroines. What Propertius could do with his unique beloved, Ovid could do with any girl one cares to name.

27. This probably involves a sexual allusion: cf. *Ars*, 3. 775.

28. Du Quesnay, 30-6.

29. For *nudus* cf. *Am.* 1. 2. 38, etc., *purpureus* 1. 4. 22, etc., and note *Pudor* at 1. 2. 32 (incidentally the position of *Pudor* in 1. 2 is additional reason to suspect the protestations of 1. 3).
30. Prop. 3. 2. 9 ff., Tibull. 1. 4. 61 ff., 9. 47, Stroh, *Liebeselegie*, 64 ff.
31. This is the interpretation of L. P. Curran, *CPh* 61 (1966), 47–9. On *Am.* 1. 3 see too Morgan, 46–8.
32. See Barsby, *Amores Book I*, ad loc. And see Morgan, 11–12 on the whole poem.
33. Cf. 1. 7 and 9, etc., Stroh, *Liebeselegie*, 18 ff. and *passim*; the function of love Elegy is to persuade the mistress (directly or indirectly); that is the view that Propertius initially and emphatically propounds. 1. 8A and 8B demonstrate it in action. (1. 7. 13–14 suggest another practical function: the love poet is *praeceptor amoris* in romantic love—as Ovid will be in sophisticated love.) In 2. 1. 4 ff. Propertius declares, what he has implied before, that Cynthia is his sole inspiration. (I stress that this is what Propertius *says*; it is the literary manifesto of the romantic lover. We are entitled to infer ulterior artistic motives; and of course Propertius says rather different things later on.)
34. If this suggests to the reader that Corinna was expected by Ovid, the suggestion is wrong: see the discussion.
35. *Anth. Pal.* 5. 132 (Philodemus), 5. 56 (Dioscorides), Luck, 161 ff.
36. Significantly, Catullus has few scruples about sexual description in any context *except* Lesbia (cf. 32, 56, etc.). Ipsitilla was no *candida diua*. And when he becomes disillusioned with Lesbia, he will use explicit sexual terms about her—about her promiscuous activity with others: 11, 58. *She* was no *candida diua* then. In Tibullus note 1. 5. 39, his attempt to make love to *another* girl: even that limited amount of detail is unheard of in Delia or Nemesis contexts.
37. Prop. 2. 3. 1–24. See too Catullus, 43, 86, and 51: description of his *reactions* to the beloved's beauty rather than of the beauty itself; that policy is of course operative in Prop. 1. 3 and other poems. And cf. Prop. 2. 1. 1 ff., where Propertius gives us information on Cynthia's aspect and actions, as in 2. 3. 1–24—and a glimpse of sex; but his emphasis is on the enormous *effect* of these: they inspire him to immense feats of poetry; there is the stuff of *historia* in them. By adding his *reactions* Propertius shows that the descriptions do not begin to tell all of it. Again he avoids confining Cynthia to physical description, while giving us a bit of it.
38. Cf. Prop. 2. 2, above, p. 97.
39. Cf. Prop. 2. 16. 35 ff., also 2. 20. 20.
40. Cf. Tibull. 1. 6. 69, 2. 4. 52, Prop. 3. 20. 15.
41. Luck agrees (173 ff.) but, I am troubled to find, Lee does not (*Gnomon* 32 (1960), 518).
42. Cf. Prop. 1. 8A and 8B, 1. 7 and 9; Ov. *Am.* 1. 11 and 12, 2. 7 and 8; cf. too 1. 4 and 2. 5, 2. 19 and 3. 4.
43. Note incidentally that *puella* (2. 2. 3) does not inevitably suggest an unmarried girl; *OLD*, s.v. 2.
44. Cf. my discussion of *Epode* 11 at *CQ* n.s. 29 (1979), 121–2.
45. Cf. *Anth. Pal.* 12. 173 (Philodemus), 12. 91 (Polystratus), 12. 88 (anon.).
46. 'Dramatic' poems (*monobiblos* type), Propertian 'shifting standpoint' poems, 'mime' poems, are all exemplified above. *Am.* 1. 10 amusingly exploits

Tibullan shift: outrage at Corinna because she asks for gifts gives place, as the poem shifts into generalization, to this more cynical remark: 'however, it's not improper to ask the rich for presents.' *Because* the poem has shifted from an address to Corinna to generalization (Ovid addresses 'beautiful girls') he can include this cynical injunction without rendering his romantic character completely implausible.

47. For bibliography on such patterning see p. 188 with n.

48. Cf. Du Quesnay, 9, 13 ff.

49. *egelidus* actually means 'cool', but Lee's rendering represents the word-play *gelidum–egelidum* better than a literal one.

50. Cf. too above, p. 141.

51. Cf. A. Otto, *Die Sprichwörter der Römer* (Leipzig, 1890), 193 (s.v. *licet*, no. 1), *Anth. Pal.* 12. 102 (Callimachus).

52. Cf. Prop. 3. 17. 12 *spesque timorque animum uersat*, Tibull. 2. 6. 20-6, etc., Prop. 1. 18. 25 *omnia consueui timidus perferre superbae/iussa*, 2. 3. 50, etc. Horace is, I think, alluding particularly to *lover's* hopes at *Epist.* 1. 4. 12. As often we find Horace and Ovid hitting at the same romantic foibles.

53. Cf. above p. 65 with n., Stroh, *Ovids Liebeskunst*, 337-8.

54. For Ovid's relation to Propertius in *Am.* 1. 8 see Morgan, 59-68.

55. Poems in the *Amores* which in one way or another strongly anticipate the *Ars* are 1. 4, 1. 8, 2. 2, 2. 4, 2. 19, 3. 2, 3. 4. Cf. p. 283.

56. Cf. Horace's Danae in *Odes* 3. 16.

57. Cf. Prop. 3. 19. The significance of this poem in its historical context has not been appreciated. To declare that women's passion is ungovernable when legislation is in the offing to enforce married women's chastity (the *Lex Iulia de adulteriis* was aimed more particularly at women) seems to me pointed.

58. Cf. above, p. 137.

59. The law was the *Lex Iulia de maritandis ordinibus*: see above, p. 65 with n. The passages in the *Ars* referred to below in the text plainly show. Ovid's scorn for married love, his *exclusive* liking for promiscuous love.

60. See Stroh, *Ovids Liebeskunst*, 346 on this passage.

61. For *domina* see above, pp. 78 ff.; 'forever' of course evokes Elegiac romanticism (above, pp. 65-7); for *per tibi tot iuro testes* cf. Prop. 2. 20. 15 (above, p. 122).

62. Cf. *Ars* 1. 21 f., 35 f., 2. 321 f., etc. Cf. A. S. Hollis, *Ovid, Ars Amatoria Book I* (Oxford, 1977), xviii.

63. Interesting similarity between Ovid and Horace has been frequently remarked: pp. 259 ff. See too notes 52 and 56.

64. Cf. 1. 6. 17, 1. 7. 48, 2. 8. 11-14, 3. 7. 82, and the interesting article of J. T. Davis, '*Amores* 1. 4. 45-48 and the Ovidian Aside', *Hermes* 107 (1979), 189-99; 2. 5. 35 ff., 2. 14. 29 ff.; 3. 6. 45 ff.

65. Cf. Prop. 1. 6, esp. 29-30 and Tibull. 1. 1, esp. 3, 5, 58 with *Am.* 1. 15. 1-4 and *Trist.* 4. 10, esp. 36-7.

66. *Trist.* 4. 10. 115 ff.: *ergo quod uiuo durisque laboribus obsto . . . gratia, Musa, tibi: nam tu solacia praebes,/tu curae requies, tu medicina uenis . . .*, etc. Cf. Prop. 1. 11. 23. ff., 2. 20. 26, ?Tibull.? 3. 19. 11, *tu mihi curarum requies . . .*

67. Cf. Barsby, *Ovid (GR)*, 11.

68. Cf. Ov. *Trist.* 4. 10. 59 f., 121 f., 125 ff.

69. It is well to remember that it may not have ended as neatly and clearly as our sources suggest: cf. Syme, 204-5.

Index

Index Locorum